The Battle of DIENBIENPHU

The Battle of

Jules Roy

DIENBIENPHU

TRANSLATED FROM THE FRENCH BY **Robert Baldick**

INTRODUCTION BY **Neil Sheehan**

HARPER & ROW, PUBLISHERS

NEW YORK AND EVANSTON

94997

Photos by Daniel Camus, except those captioned "French counterattack on Eliane, after it had fallen to the Viets" and "The
fall of Dienbienphu: 10,000 French prisoners," which are by the
Vietnam People's Army and appeared originally in *Street without
Joy* by Bernard B. Fall (Harrisburg, Stackpole Books, rev. ed.,
1964).

LIBRARY OF CONGRESS CATALOG CARD NUMBER: 64-25121

C-T

Contents

A section of photographs follows page 138.

Introduction

In July of 1963, nine years after the debacle at Dienbienphu, Denis Warner, the Australian journalist, told me how astounded he was to find the American generals in South Vietnam deluding themselves with the same false optimism the French generals had professed during the first Indochina war.

Warner, who has spent the last fifteen years covering Southeast Asia, had just returned from a trip through the villages and rice paddies of the Mekong Delta south of the capital. The Delta was the most important area in the country. The majority of the population and the bulk of the economic resources were concentrated there and the outcome of the struggle in the Delta would decide the war. Warner noted sadly that the Saigon government's position was crumbling there just as rapidly under the hammer blows of the Vietcong guerrillas as the French position in the Tonkin Delta in North Vietnam had eroded under pressure from the Vietminh insurgents in 1952.

On his return to Saigon, however, Warner had been shocked to hear the American generals assure him with the same false confidence the French had shown, that they were winning the war in the Delta. They had cited similarly meaningless statistics on the number of guerrillas supposedly killed and on the number of fortified hamlets that had been built. "I'll bet I could dig out my old notebooks and find almost identical statements by the French," Warner said.

Nine years after the disaster at Dienbienphu had ended more than eighty years of French rule in Indochina, much remained unchanged. The French generals and diplomats had departed, leaving their reputations moldering in the rice paddies. But they had been followed by American generals and diplomats who suffered, or were about to suffer, the same fate for similar reasons. The young French officers and foreign legionaries who had soothed their frayed nerves in the cabarets and bars on Catinat Street were gone or resting forever beneath the Tricolor in the military cemetery near the airport. But the slim Vietnamese prostitutes, their long black hair gracing the shoulders of skin-tight tunics, were still swinging their legs from the bar stools and still warming their beds with foreign soldiers.

The decadent emperor, Bao Dai, was living in exile on the Riviera, but he had been replaced by the Ngo Dinhs, a stiff-necked and self-righteous family who ruled with the unbending arrogance of the ancient mandarins. The head of the family, President Ngo Dinh Diem, a plump little man who waddled like a duck when he walked, was sitting in his air-conditioned office in the presidential palace, isolated from the people by his own choice, surrounded by sycophants and security policemen and convinced he ruled by divine right.

In a nearby office sat his younger brother, Ngo Dinh Nhu. Nhu was a French-educated intellectual. He was delicately built. His long and graceful fingers perpetually held a cigarette and he spoke in a low, rasping voice. He had become a victim of his own talent for intrigue, however, and of his contempt for the rest of the human race. Each day he was plunging the regime further into a suicidal struggle with the Buddhist clergy which would end in the overthrow of the family and the assassination of himself and his brother four months later. His beautiful wife, Madame Ngo Dinh Nhu, who fancied herself the rightful empress of Vietnam, goaded Nhu and her brother-in-law deeper in their folly. She had poured all her woman's passion into the pursuit of power and was consumed by rage at those who dared to challenge her. She taunted the priests and dared them to "barbecue" another of their number.

Each time a Buddhist priest spilled gasoline over his body and lit himself afire in protest against the family's arrogance, the restlessness and anger of the population grew until finally the generals moved their battalions into the city and the infantry stormed the presidential palace as the tank guns barked.

The enemy were no longer called the Vietminh. They were now known as the Vietcong (Vietnamese Communists), but they were the same black-clad little men, lean and hardened by years of warfare, determined to finish the revolution they had begun against the French in 1945 and to unite Vietnam under their rule. They were just as cunning and resourceful and just as intensely self-critical as they had been when they stood on the heights and looked down into the valley of Dienbienphu. They were still just as willing as they had been then to pay the price to achieve their ends and, most important of all, they were again winning the war.

At home in the United States, most Americans, just as the French before them, were too preoccupied with their own lives to become interested in a war in a small Asian country thousands of miles away which they felt didn't concern them directly. Many probably didn't even know where Vietnam was.

Malcolm Browne, of the Associated Press, had recently received a letter from an American business firm addressed to him at "Saigon, French Indonesia." Malcolm immediately sat down and wrote a lengthy reply, patiently explaining that Saigon was in a country called Vietnam, in a region called Indochina, that there had been a long war in Indochina in which thousands of Frenchmen and Vietnamese had died and that there was another long war raging there now in which Americans were dying.

A helicopter pilot back from leave in the United States laughed and told how one of his civilian neighbors had asked him where he was stationed. When he said he was stationed in Saigon, the neighbor had replied: "Well, it's a good thing you're not in that Veetnam. They're shooting down a lot of helicopters over there."

The U.S. Information Service theater was showing a documentary film entitled, *The End of An Empire*. Much of the footage had been filmed by Russian cameramen who had accompanied the Vietminh battalions in the war against the French. There were scenes of the Vietminh, thousands of them, singing as they dragged their cannons across the mountains toward Dienbienphu, fading into the jungle when the French planes appeared and then rushing forward in screaming waves to overwhelm the French garrison. Many of us who saw the film were frightened by it. It showed us how formidable was the enemy our country was now facing.

Jules Roy's account of the battle of Dienbienphu is an important book for the American reader, primarily because it will help him to understand his own country's often bewildering role in South Vietnam.

The nine years of war between the French and the Vietminh, which climaxed at Dienbienphu, brought seventeen million people in North Vietnam under Communist rule and left the economy of Indochina in chaos. Most important, the fact that the Communists had led the anti-colonial struggle enabled them to claim it was they who had driven the French from the nation's soil and that they thus constituted the true nationalist elite within the country. This gave them enormous political credit with the Vietnamese peasantry, who have deep nationalist feelings. The President of North Vietnam, Ho Chi Minh, is still the greatest nationalist leader in the country to much of the peasantry, and the Communists drew deeply and successfully on this credit with the peasantry when, in 1957, they launched what might be called the Second Indochina War against the U.S.-backed government of the Ngo family.

Tens of thousands of Vietnamese men and women who might otherwise have shunned the Communists, had also joined the fight against the French because of an overwhelming desire to achieve national independence. Among them were many of the most talented and patriotic individuals in the country. During the war they had either been absorbed into the Communist ranks or cleverly and brutally silenced in the purges which followed the final victory. Other nationalist elements had either atrophied because they refused to take either side or had joined the French in the fight against the Communists, hoping to achieve independence later by political means, but instead compromising themselves in the eyes of the population because of their collaboration with the hated foreigner.

Thus, when the United States assumed responsibility for South Vietnam in 1954, the human resources the Americans could work with to attempt to build a viable nation-state constituted a mere residue. It was a residue shrunken by years of hesitation, compromise and collaboration, riven by factions and intrigue, its moral fiber weakened by the corruption which had flourished under the French in the venal administration of Bao Dai.

Unfortunately, the United States was to worsen an already perilous situation by committing a series of blunders of its own. Under the pressure of a renewed Communist revolution, these blunders were to lead toward the impending defeat which is now threatening us in South Vietnam. And this impending defeat, although it will in all likelihood lack the drama of Dienbienphu, may be just as calamitous in its effects.

I believe that historians who search in years to come for the causes underlying the American defeat in South Vietnam will find themselves discovering reasons somewhat similar to those which Roy believes brought the earlier French defeat at Dienbienphu.

The debacle occurred, Roy explains, not because of a shortage of men, guns or bullets, but for other, more important and intangible reasons. These were the arrogance and the vanity of the French military and political leaders, their self-delusion and moral weakness and their contempt for the Asian enemy.

The most significant aspects of this book, therefore, are not the details of the battle itself, which unfolded with the grim fatalism of a Greek tragedy once the combatants met, but the motives and reasoning which led the French to deliberately risk battle with the Vietminh at Dienbienphu and to commit their best parachute and Foreign Legion battalions to that valley from which so many failed to return.

General Henri Navarre, the French Commander in Chief in Indochina, decided to risk battle at Dienbienphu, Roy writes, because he believed, on the basis of classic Western military axioms, that he could inflict a stunning defeat on the Vietminh there. According to General Navarre, the Vietminh commander, General Vo nguyen Giap, lacked the logistic capacity to concentrate enough troops to overwhelm the garrison. General Navarre believed the French artillery and airpower would pulverize any artillery the Vietminh attempted to emplace on the heights overlooking the valley. He was certain that these weapons, in combination with his tanks and machine guns, would decimate the Vietminh infantry battalions once they descended into the valley itself. He thought he would be able to keep the two airfields in the valley open during the battle to supply and reinforce the garrison. Dienbienphu ended the search for the classic, set-piece battle in which the French hoped to bring the destructive power of modern technology to bear on the elusive Communist enemy and smash him with an iron fist.

General Navarre and his staff grossly underestimated the skill and the resources of their enemy. They did not realize that these Western military axioms would not only fail to succeed against the revolutionary, politico-military strategy of the enemy, but would actually lead to disaster.

Ironically, as I recall from my two years in Vietnam as a reporter, the responsible American diplomatic and military officials there knew very little of the earlier French experience. If they had bothered to study it they might have seen some of the fatal weaknesses of the French reflected in themselves and drawn back before it was too late.

Listening to the Americans one got the impression that the French had fought badly and deserved to lose. In any case, they said, the French had been attempting to maintain an outdated colonial system and thus were doomed to failure. They, the Americans, knew how to fight wars, since they had defeated the Nazis and the Japanese and had bludgeoned the Chinese Communists to a stalemate in Korea. They were also fighting for democratic ideals and deserved victory, since Communism is bad and Democracy is good.

The Americans, however, did not know that the French Expeditionary Corps had usually fought with more bravery and determination than the Vietnamese government troops they were arming and advising. The Americans did not realize that courage alone was not enough to defeat an enemy with the cunning and resourcefulness of the Vietminh, or the Vietcong as they were now called. The Americans also forgot that many Vietnamese peasants saw little difference between the corrupt and brutal administrators of the Ngo family regime the U.S. was trying to preserve and those who had plagued them during the earlier French days.

The basic reason for the steady growth of Communist control and influence over the South Vietnamese peasantry from 1957 to 1961 had been the corruption, the nepotism and the maladministration of the Ngo family government. At the time the U.S. began its massive commitment of men, money and prestige to South Vietnam in the fall of 1961, however, Washington made only a half-hearted attempt to force the Ngo family to carry out critically needed political and administrative reforms. The reforms might have won the regime the support among the peasantry it so desperately needed.

When the attempt failed, Washington and its generals and diplomats in South Vietnam somehow convinced themselves that the Ngo family had been popular anyway. President Ngo Dinh Diem was "widely respected in the countryside," journalists were told, and the regime was rallying its people around it in "a great national movement" to sweep the Vietcong from the country, to quote the former American ambassador in Saigon, Frederick Nolting, Jr.

Like the French before them, the Americans placed their faith in classic Western military axioms and in practice sought a conventional military solution. They paid lip service to the political and psychological aspects of the war, but in their hearts they believed they could safely ignore these and somehow overwhelm the Vietcong with their vast amounts of money and materiel, their thousands of advisers, and the helicopters, fighter-bombers, armored vehicles and artillery batteries they were pouring into the country.

I remember with what confidence Secretary of Defense Robert S. McNamara assured us, in a briefing at the end of his first visit to Vietnam in May of 1962, that the war was being won. Still dressed in the khaki shirt, trousers and hiking shoes he had worn during a tour of the countryside, his notebooks filled with information gathered by hundreds of questions, Mr. McNamara was certain that the massive American aid program, then barely five months old, was already having effect and that the Vietcong would soon begin weakening under the pressure.

When a skeptical reporter said he could not believe Mr. McNamara was this optimistic, the Secretary replied: "Every *quantitative* measurement we have shows we're winning this war."

The American commander in South Vietnam, General Paul D. Harkins, and his staff sat in their air-conditioned offices in Saigon and waxed optimistic on the same kind of supposedly impressive statistics the French had comforted themselves with during the first Indochina war. They pointed to the number of operations the government commanders were launching, to the mobility the American helicopters and armored personnel carriers had given the government infantry and to the thousands of guerrillas they were supposedly killing with their fighter-bombers, artillery and automatic weapons. Like his French predecessor, General Navarre, General Harkins was a polite and urbane man who had built a reputation as a brilliant staff officer. Perhaps they also both shared the limitations of the Western-trained staff officer confronted with the subtleties of an Asian-style Communist revolution.

Just as bad news was not tolerated in the tranquil rooms of General Navarre's headquarters, so it was also not tolerated in General Harkins' headquarters or in the American embassy in Saigon. In this unreal atmosphere, where doctrine and theory were defended as facts, anything which contradicted the official optimism was simply ignored or derided as false or inconsequential.

Roy relates how General Navarre refused to believe intelligence reports from the staff of his subordinate in Hanoï, Major General René Cogny, that the Vietminh were concentrating the bulk of four infantry divisions on Dienbienphu—a formidable force which would seriously threaten the garrison. "Cogny's team was accused of adopting a spurious pessimism in order to exaggerate the importance of Tonkin and to warn Navarre's team not to infringe on its jurisdiction."

The concentration of four Vietminh divisions at Dienbienphu was regarded by the French as a "utopian project." The French had calculated on the basis of Western military doctrine that the enemy simply did not have the logistic capabilities to supply and maintain such a force far from its bases. General Navarre, Roy writes, "believed that he would be faced with only one division, though considerably reinforced; in other words, about a dozen battalions with a few heavy guns. That was nothing to be alarmed about." Unfortunately for General Navarre, the Vietminh did concentrate and maintain the bulk of four divisions at Dienbienphu, by improvising unorthodox but effective means of moving supplies, and overwhelmed his garrison.

With similar dogmatism, General Harkins and his staff ignored or derided reports in the late summer of 1963 from junior officers in the field that the Vietnamese government's position in the Mekong Delta was deteriorating seriously and that the vaunted strategic hamlet program which was to separate the guerrillas from the peasantry was crumbling under Communist attacks. The reports also warned that the Vietcong were creating large but highly mobile infantry battalions armed with captured American-made weapons which would soon pose a grave challenge to the government forces.

Miss Marguerite Higgins, then covering the war for the *Herald Tribune*, whose dispatches from South Vietnam faithfully reflected the official point of view, wrote in August of that year:

"But as of this moment, General Harkins and his staff flatly contradict published reports that South Vietnam's U.S.-backed fight against the Communists—particularly in the rice-rich Delta—is 'deteriorating' and that a Viet Cong build-up is taking place to the point where the Communists will be able to conduct mobile warfare with battalions as well equipped as the government's."

As late as October General Harkins assured another journalist: "I can tell you categorically that we are winning in the Mekong Delta."

That November, taking advantage of the dislocation immediately following the fall of the Ngo family regime, the Vietcong unleashed their battalions in a series of dazzling attacks which inflicted irreparable damage on the government's already fragile position in the Delta.

The junior American officers who realized what was happening and attempted to bring their superiors in Saigon to their senses, just as some of the lower-ranking French officers had tried to warn General Navarre of the debacle he was creating, wasted their energy. Their reports aroused only irritation and Saigon focused its attention on silencing them instead of abandoning its own illusions.

"Nobody believed in the strategic mobility and logistics of the Vietminh," Roy writes. "Nobody or scarcely anybody, in the French Army had enough imagination to guess at the enemy's cunning and wisdom."

He notes that Lieutenant General Raoul Salan, General Navarre's predecessor as Commander in Chief in Indochina, regarded the Vietminh commander, General Giap, "as a non-commissioned officer learning to handle regiments" and that General Navarre himself made only a half-hearted attempt to understand General Giap.

"Navarre should have kept a photograph of Giap before him at all times in his study," Roy comments, "as Montgomery kept a photograph of Rommel before him during the Egyptian campaign. Perhaps he thought that this would have been paying too much honor to a man who had not attended courses in military strategy and to whom the title of general was given only in quotation marks."

Most of the American generals likewise despised the enemy. They were fond of asserting that the Vietcong commanders were unsophisticated Asians who lacked knowledge of modern warfare. The Vietcong were frequently referred to as "those raggedy little bastards in black pajamas."

"The Vietcong aren't ten feet tall, they're only five feet tall," journalists were told, "and we're going to cut them down even further before we're through." I recall how one American general confidently assured me that "the Vietcong are Vietnamese too and they've got the same failings as these government guys we're supporting. You've got to remember that these people are all pretty unsophisticated and they don't have the military tradition we've got."

Many of the Americans also did not believe in the mobility the Vietcong had gained through their control and influence over the peasantry, their clever use of motorized sampans along the thousands of canals which crisscrossed the countryside, their ability to fight at night and the stamina they had drilled into their infantry.

Miss Higgins quotes one of General Harkins' officers as saying:

"What is mobility? Mobility means vehicles and aircraft. You have seen the way our Vietnamese units are armed—50 radios, 30 or 40 vehicles, rockets, mortars and airplanes. The Vietcong have no vehicles and no airplanes. How can they be mobile?"

Finally, there were the governments back home in Washington and Paris. The successive, weak French cabinets did not want to think very much about Indochina and carefully avoided troublesome decisions on the conduct of the war. Nine years later, the Administration in Washington similarly did not want to hear disturbing news about its war in South Vietnam and scrupulously dodged politically sensitive decisions.

"Once in a while Washington remembers that there is a war in South Vietnam," Max Frankel of the *New York Times* reported in July of 1963. "But for long stretches, the war against Communist-led guerrillas in Vietnam fades from memory here, not because no one cares, but because the men who care most decided long ago to discuss it as little as possible."

"It [the Administration] concedes that President Ngo Dinh Diem has often treated his own intellectuals and officers as more dangerous than the guerrillas, that he resists the decentralization of authority and that he has not done nearly enough to win the loyalists of his largely rural population.

"But every reluctant comment here ends on the same note: that there is no alternative, no intention to seek one, no change of policy and no further comment.

"All they want, officials indicate, is to get on quietly with the war."

The Vietminh commander, General Giap, said to Roy in 1963 as he was leaving Hanoï for a visit to the old battleground at Dienbienphu:

"If you were defeated, you were defeated by yourselves." Perhaps General Giap will make a similar remark to an American writer someday.

NEIL SHEEHAN

[Mr. Sheehan was the correspondent for United Press International in Vietnam from April, 1962, until April, 1964, and is currently with the *New York Times*.]

No one can feel for the Army as I do. These people who talk to us have all fed their children on the fat of the land and dressed them in velvet and silk while we have been away. I have had to see my children dressed in a dirty blanket and an old pair of regimental trousers, and to see them fed on raw salt meat, and nine thousand of my children are lying, from causes which might have been prevented, in their forgotten graves.

—FLORENCE NIGHTINGALE
on the Crimean War

It is not that it is forbidden to be unfortunate. We are not in Carthage, but, without going as far as that, it would be useful to know why a defeated general has been defeated.

—PRINCE DE LIGNE

KING HENRY: What is this castle call'd that stands hard by?
MONTJOY: They call it Agincourt.
KING HENRY: Then call we this the field of Agincourt.

—SHAKESPEARE
Henry V, Act IV

The Etheredges

≒1≒ The Birth of a Myth

A commander in chief cannot take as an excuse for his
mistakes in warfare an order given by his sovereign or his
minister, when the person giving the order is absent from
the field of operations and is imperfectly aware or wholly
unaware of the latest state of affairs. It follows that any
commander in chief who undertakes to carry out a plan
which he considers defective is at fault; he must put
forward his reasons, insist on the plan being changed, and
finally tender his resignation rather than be the instrument
of his army's downfall.

—Napoleon
Military Maxims and Thoughts

May 19, 1953

A commander in chief does not arrive like just any government official.
In the stifling heat of noon, all the generals and admirals of South
Vietnam were waiting in white drill uniforms on the terrace of the Than
Son Nut airdrome at Saigon for the landing of the Constellation from
Paris, delayed for three-quarters of an hour to allow the French High
Commissioner's Dakota, which had come south from Hanoï, to land first.

On board the Constellation, General Navarre gazed thoughtfully at
the huge, formidable stretch of marshes, of liquid rings coiled across
the lowlands. The sea thrust its fingers into the vast land whose
defense had been entrusted to him. The waters gleamed in the sunshine
and straw-roofed villages huddled together under the tufts of gigantic
bamboos. The plane turned north again, flew over the port, the city and
its gardens, rolled along the cement runway and came to a stop.

1

When he appeared in the doorway of the Constellation, Navarre was overwhelmed not merely by the burning heat, which resembled the oven-like atmosphere at the Calcuttta stop. Anyone would have found it hard to resist the ceremonial arranged to welcome him. Admittedly he had been familiar with the ritual ever since he had started carrying the briefcases of commanders in chief and marshals, but this time he himself was the prince whose arrival was being celebrated and under whose nose the fanfares were already sounding and the censers swinging. His predecessor, General Salan, who was prolonging his farewell visits at Tonkin, had savored these ceremonies in full. Navarre would gladly forgo them once he knew their price.

What with the chiefs of staff of the three services, the catering officers, doctors, chemists and vets, administration and signals officers, *barbouzes,* Vietnamese or Hoa-Hoas, a good fifty kepis and caps with gold oak leaves glittered behind the thick, limp, civilian silhouette of the High Commissioner. Two battalions did the appropriate honors with music and flags.

Navarre saw all this power at his feet. He could, if he wished, live like a king. He could, with a gesture or a signature, ruin men or make their fortunes. His remarks and his silences would be studied with care, his oracular utterances eagerly awaited. Every effort would be made to spare him the rigors of the climate. That day, he would catch only a glimpse of Saigon through his escort, but he would hear something of the ferocious din of the city's business, the stock exchange, the money flowing like water. Were those bands celebrating the arrival of a new prince of Indochina or the beginning of a ceremonial liquidation? In the evening, Navarre said with a smile to his aide-de-camp, "Do you know how much our slight delay by the High Commissioner's plane cost the Republic? Two hundred thousand francs."

At the end of the dinner which the High Commissioner gave in his honor, news would arrive of the fall, after two months' resistance, of the post of Muong Khoua, perched on a rocky spur at the junction of the Nam Ou and the Nam Pak, thirty-seven miles southwest of Dienbienphu, a name which Navarre had so far never heard. A company of Laotian soldiers and a few auxiliaries had disappeared. For the first time the Viets were reported to have used phosphorus shells, which had either been taken from the Expeditionary Corps's magazines or had come from China.

This incident did not count for much in the game being played at

Saigon, and the devaluation which had unexpectedly overtaken the piastre a week before was having more important consequences. Businesses were being liquidated to buy dollars, shops were closing their doors, exports were being blocked and stocks checked. The Vietnamese Government was impudently threatening to reconsider its position in the French Union if the French Union interfered with business. On the black market, the collapse of the Indochinese currency represented a far greater catastrophe than the loss of a small garrison.

May 21, 1953

Navarre quickly turned away from the smells of Saigon. In his haste to take possession of his fief and to meet General Salan, who was to hand over its keys to him, he set off for Hanoï with M. Letourneau, the High Commissioner.

He was to set to work quickly, for, once the usual courtesies had been hurriedly observed, the whole of the former High Command of Indochina would follow Salan and disappear into the first-class sections of planes and ships bound for France; the commanding officer in Tonkin, the chief of staff of the combined services at Saigon, the commander of the Air Force, the commanding officer in Laos, and three zone commanders out of five in the Tonkin delta packed their bags. M. Jean Letourneau himself got ready to go, declaring that he felt no anxiety about the future. His rotundity, his false joviality, his pious ruses had accomplished nothing; he had not dared to offend anybody and had invariably met his match.

Later on, the Fourth Republic would be blamed for not having staggered the repatriation of the authorities in Indochina. In point of fact, General Salan, under the paternal gaze of the High Commissioner, had contrived to practice the scorched-earth policy before his successor's arrival. Navarre did not protest. With a touch of naïveté, he imagined that this great vacuum would help him.

A single general had been willing to remain with him: Brigadier General Cogny, who was in command of a marching division in Tonkin. Navarre made inquiries about him. Cogny succeeded in everything he attempted and he was the man of the Red River Delta. Cogny was on the high road to success. Navarre got Letourneau to ask the government to promote him to the rank of lieutenant general.

In the huge territory of 275,000 square miles inhabited by thirty million people, Navarre guessed that there would be no lack of traps and that the most dangerous of these would not be the ones the enemy laid for him. But as a drill ground, how exciting it was compared with his previous commands! For the 375,000 men whom Navarre would have at his disposal with the new armies of the so-called Associated States— Vietnam, Laos and Cambodia—against the 125,000 regular troops, 75,-000 regional troops and 150,000 guerrillas on the other side, what a theater of operations this was: these burning plains cut up into rice fields; these jungles infested with tigers and elephants; these huge rivers spreading their tentacles toward the sea; these chaotic mountains, the great limestone chain swept by the monsoons in the vicinity of China and the Tropic of Cancer; and these sixteen hundred miles of coastline oddly suggestive of the shoulder, neck, skull and profile of the hermit of Colombey, de Gaulle, diving into the Pacific, with his nose and arms pointing toward Singapore!

Navarre's meditations took a disillusioned turn; the machine of which he had just been given command was no longer working properly. The Expeditionary Corps moved only in a block, accompanied by the din of tanks and trucks; incapable of living without an overwhelming superiority of material, in the face of a dangerously mobile and ubiquitous adversary who possessed everything, most of the blows it dealt missed their mark. His men were tired, and the system which controlled them was too clumsy. The war killed just as blindly on a café terrace as on the embankment of a rice field; apparently inoffensive villages concealed citadels; a child leading buffaloes out to pasture was a spy; toothless old women laid mines; laborers assassinated important people. To hold twenty miles of road, several battalions were needed, with gun batteries and armored cars, which withdrew at night far behind fortified positions, leaving the open field to the adversary. If it was possible to believe that a front existed here and there, there was no rear anywhere, for everything represented danger. Who suspected this in France? From nearby China, arms and material flowed toward the divisions of General Vo nguyen Giap, Commander in Chief of the Vietminh forces. Seven years had blunted, not sharpened, the tool intended to obtain victory, and the war which was being fought here was a cut-price war waged with American surplus equipment.

A cut-price war? It was costing one or two billion francs a day, and every ship which weighed anchor at Saigon or Haiphong invariably had one hold filled with coffins. From his aide-de-camp, who was also a friend of his and was returning to Indochina for a third stay, Navarre had learned that treason was rampant; there was not a single remark, a single paper or a single gesture that was not immediately noted and reported. What would happen if the enemy possessed tanks and planes? It might be possible to seize them, but they could do a great deal of damage, for the enemy hordes were convinced that sooner or later they were bound to win, and they had no fear of death.

On the French side, why were they fighting? Nobody knew any more. De Lattre, the Commander in Chief in Indochina from 1950 to the end of 1951, had been the first to explain: for the independence of Vietnam. But nobody cared a damn about the independence of Vietnam, least of all Vietnam herself, which already possessed it, or very nearly. The Vietnamese Army was looking for a faith, and its government had decided to dispense with both authority and honesty. With fifty thousand piastres a man could buy exemption from military service. Newly commissioned officers tended to choose the commissariat and the administrative services, in which they could fill their pockets. Only the least capable joined the fighting corps. Why should they have any desire to get themselves killed for M. Tam, the head of the government, for General Hinh, M. Tam's son, or for H. M. Bao Dai, who had realized that the dynasty of the emperors of Annam was to die out miserably with him and that he had nobody to serve but himself? Marshal de Lattre's legacy consisted of a line of concrete blockhouses intended to break any attack on the edge of the Tonkin delta, and to which the stupid and the stubborn were condemned.

Navarre settled himself comfortably in his armchair. Well, since the atmosphere was unhealthy and the tool in poor shape, it would be necessary to use cunning. A long smile appeared on the features of the new Commander in Chief and gave his face the expression of a somewhat bitter Buddha.

The previous seventh of May, M. René Mayer, the Prime Minister, had summoned him to Paris from Germany, where he was carrying out a tour of inspection. Warned at army headquarters in Fontainebleau of what was in the air by Marshal Juin, for whom he was serving as chief of staff, Navarre took refuge behind the reasons for his refusal: he had never served in Indochina and was totally unqualified. When M. René Mayer, in the midst of the drawing rooms and gardens of the Premier's mansion, suggested that he should take the place of General Salan, Navarre had no time to put forward the arguments which militated against him; the

Prime Minister swept them aside with a wave of his hand. M. René Mayer considered him capable of seeing everything with new eyes and of learning fast; he praised his prudence, his cold intelligence and his wisdom. Admittedly, for such a high post, they had gone a long way down the Army List to find General Henri Navarre, but this objection didn't hold when ability was in such short supply and nobody was an obvious choice. General Valluy, the only man familiar with the problem, and the man responsible for the bombardment of Haiphong in 1946, was unsuitable for what M. René Mayer wanted Navarre to find: an honorable way out which would allow the government to negotiate and bring the war to an end. Reinforcements? They were out of the question; General Navarre would receive nothing substantial. National Service men? M. René Mayer read out to him what M. Édouard Daladier had written that very day in an evening paper: "Parliament will oppose such a folly."

When he left the Matignon mansion, General Navarre's opinion of M. René Mayer was: "He's mad." On his return to Fontainebleau, he gave a report of the interview to Marshal Juin.

"It lies in your power to keep me," he added. "I am supposed to spend at least two years in Central Europe with you."

"It is your duty to accept," replied the marshal, much to Navarre's surprise. "Somebody must take on the job."

To encourage him, Juin gave him his report on a recent tour of inspection. In it the marshal was optimistic; a few battalions and a few months would be enough to settle the problem, but precautions would have to be taken against a general attack on the delta. Altogether, it was thought that the Viets were not yet equipped to wage a mobile war with motorized equipment and that they might find themselves in a tight spot if they were hard pressed. And wasn't Navarre a cavalryman?

He accepted.

Who was Navarre? The name had rung out proudly ever since 1915 when two brothers called Navarre had won fame as fighter pilots. There was no family connection, however, between the airmen and the general, who was fifty-five years old and came from a long line of Norman notaries, judges and attorneys. Physically and morally, he was a cat. Though not lacking in height, with his head and shoulders leaning slightly backward, as if he were always in the saddle, he was somewhat inelegant in bearing and seemed more at ease with maps and tanks than at horse shows. He was not a dashing cavalry officer. With him everything took place in the mind; he had spent nearly all his career in Intelligence and on the General Staff.

At once cordial and distant, debonair and icy, he possessed a rare self-control and great powers of persuasion. He seemed to have both knowledge and truth, even when he was in doubt. Dictatorial and determined, he was capable of listening to long arguments in silence without ever allowing himself to be shaken. He was sure of himself, an eloquent speaker when necessary, firm and alert; his gaze, which would settle in a flash on an interlocutor and then slide away, was in contradiction with his voice, which could be warm, kindly or cutting. He gave the impression of getting to the heart of problems studied long enough for the solution he had chosen to meet no obstacles.

That day, at the Maison de France, the residence of the High Commissioner at Hanoï, M. Letourneau had invited the generals of Tonkin to lunch with Navarre. In the drawing room, Salan exchanged only polite commonplaces, but with furtive gray eyes he studied the man who was going to succeed him. He sized him up and said nothing. Gonzalez de Linarès, the commander of the Tonkin forces, who was known familiarly as Uncle Li, had freer manners, a beautiful Chinese half-caste as a mistress and a reputation for plain speaking. A classmate of Navarre's, he sat on the arm of his chair and spoke to him familiarly.

"Henri, old boy, what the hell have you come to this shit hole for? I'm clearing out."

"That's what's worrying me," said Navarre. "Who's going to take your place? I've asked for Cogny."

"Don't take him," said Linarès, touching Navarre's elbow. "He's a b——."

"Can you suggest anybody else?"

But there was nobody else.

"What do you think, General?" Navarre asked Salan.

Salan's eyes flashed. "Cogny has some good qualities."

A piece of paper had just been delivered to M. Letourneau, who passed it to Navarre. Navarre liked taking risks. It seemed, indeed, as if the disapproval of his peers encouraged him to persevere.

"This is the telegram which makes him a lieutenant general," said Navarre. "In a few minutes I shall appoint him General Commanding in Tonkin."

Cogny, as it happened, appeared at that moment.

What immediately struck you about him was his height—six feet two inches—and his build. Far from taking special advantage of his stature, he always seemed to be apologizing for it. His voice was pleasant, sometimes caressing, his manner affable, his gray eyes ready to soften, his handshake friendly. With the troops, he had no need to assert himself; it was enough for him to appear, with his handsome mug and his football player's shoulders. They liked his simplicity, the bush uniform that he nearly always wore, the coarse leather of his army belt, his broad chest devoid of decorations.

You could tell that he was at home in the midst of things military, with the elegance and courtesy of a gentleman on his estate. This grandson of a peasant, tamed by de Lattre, showed that de Lattre remained the great master and model, an awe-inspiring ghost still capable of anything, even of appearing, of punishing, of giving understanding to the leaders and valor to the men. This nostalgic loyalty to the memory of the Chief was rather moving in the long run. Loathed by his superiors on account of his reputation for questioning orders, and liked by his subordinates, Cogny affected a certain luxury in matters of ceremonial, even in his military household, where he treated his humblest guests with special consideration. Irreverently known as "Coco the Siren" because of his excessive taste for motorcycle escorts, he was accused of wanting to carve out an empire for himself in Indochina, of imposing his opinions and his men on it, and of maintaining secret services there.

A powerful creature of formidable stature, Cogny was a bull in both his massiveness and the strength it contained, the resistance it offered to adversity, the pressure it would bring to bear on obstacles, and the anger which would build up inside and burst with the violence of a Tonkin storm. However, in the armor which seemed to cover him from head to foot, there existed a flaw near the heart: a single word could hurt Cogny deeply. Then he would not forgive, but would always feel the steel which had wounded him. Easy to persuade and guide, he would rush, head down, at the man he believed responsible for his wound and try to trample him underfoot.

In shorts, he looked more monumental than ever, intimidated by his height, which he occasionally reduced in order to listen. Navarre drew him to one side and told him of his appointment to Linarès's post with a third star. Cogny's face lit up, and he showed a sudden burst of emotion.

"You won't regret it," he told Navarre.

That same evening after dinner, when liqueurs were being served, Salan said to Navarre, "General, you must take care, for the Vietminh is

organizing its big units and giving them a European character."
"In that case, it's done for," said Navarre.

May 22, 1953

Navarre, who had not yet been able to have a serious conversation with Salan, asked his aide-de-camp to suggest to him a visit to the theater of operations in Tonkin. First of all, he wanted to see the stronghold of Na San, whose maintenance was causing some concern to the High Command and certain members of the government.

In the course of the previous campaign, before Navarre's arrival, Giap, who already held the greater part of North Tonkin, had, with thirty battalions, taken possession of the whole area between the Red River and the Black River. In the face of his new offensive, which was moving in the direction of the Thai country, what tactics should Salan employ? Should he empty the Thai country of its garrisons and pull them back toward the delta? That would open the road, sooner or later, to Laos. Already, since Lang Son and Cao Bang had been evacuated, all control of the communications between the fortified zone of the rebels and China had been lost. A fresh withdrawal toward the delta would be an admission of weakness. Salan wanted to gain time and surprise the enemy by confronting him with a hedgehog of bristling strength. In order to bar the road to the west and to protect Laï Chau, Salan dropped a fortified camp from the sky, at Na San, deep in enemy territory.

The success of an undertaking whose boldness had taken my breath away the first time I visited the stronghold, of which Brigadier Jean Gilles had just been given command, depended on the inadequacy of Giap's means; either he would be unable to bring up and employ artillery or the maintenance of three divisions and heavy guns a long way from their bases would prove logistically impossible. Giap could also ignore the obstacle, but, if he returned to his Tonkin bases to spend the rainy season there, he ran the risk of seeing the hedgehog break out, cut him off and spread disorder along his lines of communication. Logically, Giap would have to advance on the obstacle and remove it. Salan believed that the enemy offensive would come to a stop there, and that Giap, incapable of feeding the fifty thousand troops and coolies necessary to its maintenance, would beat a retreat without having been able to swallow a morsel too big for him. Salan's bold stroke, however, involved an element of risk: Giap might have made progress in the art of warfare. If, careless of his losses, he decided to launch a mass attack, the attempt to break the Vietminh could turn against Salan in the form of a resounding defeat.

The French and Vietminh generals had met in the course of the negotiations opened six years earlier with Ho Chi Minh, at the time when Leclerc of the French High Command had confronted the colonial government with the alternative of mobilizing the National Service contingent in order to crush the Vietminh insurrection or of coming to an agreement with the rebels. As a result it was believed that Salan, who was known as "the Chinaman," had weighed his direct adversary and could always see through his plans. Salan was an enigmatic figure, with extremely mobile gray eyes and a furtive smile occasionally passing over his bronzed face, his chest ablaze with the imposing battery of medal ribbons which made him the most decorated officer in the French Army, and greatly attached to the pomp due to a commander in chief; he was reputed to seek inspiration in opium. Separated from Giap by a whole stretch of impenetrable regions and secrets, he seemed to be playing poker with him. At that time, whenever a dispatch from Na San came in, he was seen to touch with his fingertips a little ivory elephant which he took with him wherever he went.

The originality of the situation had attracted the pack of leading international reporters. For the first time in this conflict, they realized, the two armies risked meeting in open country, far from the towns or from the human ant heap of the rice plains. Commentators recalled the wars of antiquity, Julius Caesar, Scipio Africanus or Jugurtha, or the Battle of Zama at which Hannibal provoked the Romans. Giap had issued a proclamation to his troops in which he told them that the fate of the war depended on their courage, for, after considerable hesitation, he had finally decided, as Salan had foreseen, to take Na San.

Twice he attacked the camp unsuccessfully, left a thousand dead on the barbed-wire defenses and tiptoed away, contenting himself with holding the garrison with a few battalions. Salan was triumphant, but this tactical success had nothing definitive about it. Part of the French Air Force had to be devoted to supplying and supporting the fortified camp, which would be exposed, if it was maintained much longer, to the dangers of a new offensive.

It was because Na San remained the sore point in the theater of operations that Navarre was in a hurry to visit it. On the eve of his departure for Indochina, suspecting that he was about to collect a poisoned legacy, he had said to M. de Chevigné, the Secretary of State for War, "The evacuation of Na San will be one of my first acts, and I don't intend to undertake any more operations of that sort." Moreover, Cogny had just confirmed him in the opinion that Na San no longer served any useful purpose. In order to judge the whole situation with greater freedom, Navarre even insisted that no member of the Tonkin staff should accompany him. When the pilot asked him at what height he wanted to fly, he replied, "A height at which I shall see something." And he took his place in the crew's cockpit in order to get a better view.

In the vicinity of Moc Chau, where antiaircraft batteries were installed, the pilot didn't dare to alter height. A salvo suddenly straddled the Dakota, and another hit it, though without inflicting serious damage. The plane landed at Na San, its wings riddled with bullet holes.

Navarre was greeted by a somewhat sad, dry, suspicious and apparently colorless man, Colonel Berteil. Berteil had received all the military sacraments and commissions; he was now even speaking the dim, metaphysical language of the exalted posts for which he was preparing himself. His appearance did not help him. He was not a fighter but a staff officer. He was a man of reflection who elaborated theories, who seemed to possess weighty secrets, whose self-assurance was untempered by any sense of humor. He believed, for example, that Na San had been useful, possibly because he had been in command there since the departure of General Gilles, who was the guiding spirit of the place, or possibly because he was unwilling to think that he might be playing only a minor role.

He was extremely attentive to Navarre and showed him round the camp with a certain respectful stiffness. Navarre instinctively recognized an ally in him. Berteil was not impressive like Cogny, who was too touchy a personality. Navarre would remember him when the time came and would make him his operational second-in-command to coordinate the activities of his second and third bureaus. In fact, Berteil would rapidly become the most formidable officer in the entourage of the new Commander in Chief. And although he remained determined to have done with Na San, Navarre had been impressed by the appearance of the entrenched camp where Giap's battalions had bitten the dust, with its atmosphere of strength, morale, and serenity.

May 25, 1953

The characters in the drama were slowly taking their positions behind the curtain which concealed them. Rumors were already beginning to circulate about Navarre, who was being studied everywhere with a critical and vaguely uneasy eye. It was said that he had expressed astonishment that the delta, so solidly occupied by the Expeditionary Corps, should be infested with Viets, and that at an investiture he had, by mistake, pinned the medals on the right side of the recipients' chest. He had opened an officers' meeting with the words, "Gentlemen, in order to win this war . . ." And then, seeing somebody smile, he had broken off and asked for an explanation, which had been deliberately bungled. Nobody any longer thought of winning this war, and indeed winning the war was not the mission which Navarre had been given in Paris. Pulling out with as little damage as possible struck everybody as the formula best suited to the situation.

Ever since the danger of a defeat had become apparent, the big mining companies, the cement works, the spinning mills and the rubber plantations had been transferring their equipment and stocks to other parts of the world; what France still possessed in the Associated States of Indochina did not represent the cost of one year of war: six hundred billion francs and a hundred young officers. Every three years one class of Saint-Cyr cadets was sacrificed for the defense of the West. Since it had begun, the Indochinese War had killed 3 generals, 8 colonels, 18 lieutenant colonels, 69 majors, 341 captains, 1,140 lieutenants, 3,683 NCO's and 6,008 soldiers of French nationality; 12,019 Legionnaires and Africans; and 14,093 natives. These figures did not include the missing—over twenty thousand—or the wounded or those repatriated on health grounds—over 100,000. If America gave dollars, that was to pay for the blood which France shed in her place.

On what crusade? De Lattre had been the first to use that word. America, fighting for her life against Soviet Russia, had every reason to believe in it. But if such a crusade did exist, why did so few young men enlist for the Far East, and why, instead of giving her sons, did France prefer to pay mercenaries? The latter set off in shipfuls to defend a cause in which France did not believe. The only Frenchmen who had the courage to defend it did so for professional reasons or out of some strange inclination: the smallness of their numbers excited them, the tepidity of the rest of the nation whipped up their ardor, the paratroop regiments in which they served became seminaries of courage, abnegation or self-sacrifice freely accepted. "Remember that what awaits you is death," Major Bigeard repeated to his men when he drew up the catechism of his faith. A man did not fight because his tour of duty had come round to Indochina, and it did not matter to him that he would be able to buy a car on his return to France; he fought because it was his duty or because he refused to be beaten, in battle any more than in life.

What, then, of Emperor Bao Dai? For these uncompromising idealists who had chosen in battle the best of life and knew that this best led to death, Bao Dai was the nation's business, not theirs. In the paratroop regiments or at the head of the Foreign Legion units, the same men, separated for years from their loved ones and consumed by their faith, were uneasy. The day independence would be given to Vietnam, they would leave; they all knew that as soon as a region was liberated, the tax collectors arrived close on their heels to gather arrears, and the reign of the mandarins would continue to oppress the people. How, then, could they fight against the hope offered by the Communist regime?

The same notion of duty animated the Air Force and the Navy. Officers excused from serving in Indochina volunteered out of a sense of comradeship. They could not go on drinking in the bars of the Champs-Élysées when their pals were getting themselves killed. A military elite, fighting without an inspiring objective, felt that it was redeeming an indifferent nation which understood nothing about this war and suspected its governments of waging it to protect obscure interests.

Who, indeed, knew what was happening in Indochina, and, if he knew it, who said anything about it? No newspaper would venture as yet to state that General Salan had allowed a clique of informing agents to install themselves on every base and in almost every post, who tortured and acted as they wished, subordinate only to services directly responsible to the Prime Minister, who pretended to know nothing about them. No one in France was prepared to say that, apart from those who had an interest in collaborating with the French, while quite ready to turn traitor later on, or who feared the victory of Communism, the men and women of Vietnam did not support the French. On a tour of inspection, Mr. Adlai Stevenson had been struck by the fact that, unlike the Koreans, nobody smiled as he passed, and had wondered how the mercenaries of the Expeditionary Corps could grasp the meaning of a war for Vietnam against the Vietminh. Another American, David Schoenbrun, a journalist who could scarcely be suspected of Francophobia, had denounced the original sin of the colonial era, those absolute rights which France, forgetful of the lessons of her own Revolution, claimed to possess over the freedom of Vietnam, when in fact she possessed only interests. Turning the need for strategic bases into a crusade of good against evil created a major ambiguity.

Navarre knew all this, but it was as if, rather than depressing him, the contact with reality filled him with a certain optimism. On his return to Hanoï, he completed his team and dug up a secretary in Colonel Revol, previously assistant to General Gilles at Na San. Intended for duty in Africa, Revol was ill at ease in Indochina. On the other hand, his subtle nonconformity and his record as a former weapons instructor at Saint-Cyr appealed to Navarre, who was trying to surround himself with men of unconventional character and even contrary ideas.

Navarre's stay in Hanoï had not been marred by the many things Salan should have told him. Why did Salan fail to show his successor the government directive of April 24, 1953, which instructed him to choose territorial losses in preference to operations that endangered the security of the Expeditionary Corps? This was a document of major importance if ever there was one, which the Commander in Chief was supposed to bear constantly in mind. Did Salan not dare to admit that he had been disowned, or did he think that Navarre had been fully briefed by the Prime Minister who had appointed him? M. René Mayer showed a futile discretion in omitting to communicate to General Navarre the government's opinion of certain operations undertaken in the highlands by his predecessor. Such an opinion would have helped Navarre to see the entrenched camp of Na San, already pregnant with Dienbienphu, in a different light. Did Salan, in the course of his brief conversations with Navarre, warn him of the danger of repeating the Na San experiment, or, considering that Navarre was capable of seeing for himself where wisdom lay, did he refuse to put him on guard against the "hedgehog" strategy? Did he stress Giap's faculty for adjustment when he discovered that Navarre intended to cover the northwest by adding Dienbienphu to the two bases of Laï Chau and Na San in a system already known as the Salan Archipelago, since Salan had been dreaming for a year of conquering Dienbienphu? How tempting it must have been to allow, without any danger to oneself, a rival to risk his innocent stars in such a scheme. . . .

June 16, 1953

What was the Navarre Plan? Simply what the Commander in Chief outlined to the regional commanders when he summoned them to Saigon three weeks after his arrival. He had visited them all, one after another, at their headquarters, during the season which turned the sky into a furnace. He had listened to them, taken notes and gone on to the terrain. He had inspected the units of the Expeditionary Corps, the outposts and battalions of the Vietnamese Army. He had heard the guns booming in the night. He had seen enemy corpses on the barbed-wire defenses, peasants plowing the rice fields behind their buffaloes, bent in two over the handles of their plows or trotting along the roads with poles on their shoulders. He had counted his forces, marked them on the maps and turned the problem over and over in his mind. He had tried to forget everything he had learned in Europe. He had never coveted the post which M. René Mayer's inspiration and the fortunes of war had given him, and nobody could even suspect him of working to obtain another star, for Navarre was an honest man. So far in his career, decisions had escaped him. He had had occasion to propose decisions, but never to take any, at this level, and he was not ignorant of the fact that men die to no purpose when generals make mistakes. But now that, without having plotted or schemed, he had been given the task of commanding, he was going to command.

On June 16, therefore, he explained how he, Navarre, was going to try to solve the problem. First of all, in the coming campaign the French would maintain a cautious restraint in order to reconstitute the Expeditionary Corps and restore its life and vigor. It would be a question of avoiding coming to grips with the main body of the enemy forces.

The most serious danger still lay in the north, but that territory was firmly in the hands of experienced troops; they would continue what was tactfully called "pacification," and they would prevent the enemy's offensive operations by smashing them before they were launched. The situation in the south might worsen if the threats looming there increased. Under the shelter of a movement carried out north of the 18th Parallel, a comparatively simple offensive would liquidate the elements of the 5th military region of the Vietminh, separated from Tonkin by a mountain chain which formed a sort of natural frontier. This offensive would be "Operation Atlante."

On the other hand, during the campaign that would follow, the French would look for a fight. They would attack first the rice granaries, the reserves of men, and finally the enemy battle force itself in order to destroy it. This idea, which General Salan had bequeathed to him together with Dienbienphu, became the basis of the plan.

As for the Vietnamese Army, Navarre adopted the old phrase about it which everybody repeated in front of him in order to hide the incompetence of its cadres and the apathy of the men: the Vietnamese Army would progressively relieve the regular occupation forces and thus enable the French to increase their offensive potential. That was the gospel according to King John, otherwise known as Marshal de Lattre de Tassigny. But King John was dead and Navarre was not taken in by the apparent balance of figures. If the Vietnamese Army looked impressive on the parade grounds, it was less than partial to a fight. That was understandable; unlike the Vietminh, it lacked a reason why—for it knew only too well for whom—it was expected to fight.

Those were the main features of Navarre's strategy. They bore the mark of the cavalryman he was; remaining on the defensive in order to restore the physical and moral health of the Expeditionary Corps, he would adopt an offensive attitude, harry the enemy to prevent him from bringing his divisions together in a combined action and destroy him wherever he was outnumbered. "We can conquer only by attacking," was the theme of his first letter to the Expeditionary Corps.

"Gentlemen, have you any objections to make?"

Cogny had. The stalemate in his delta alarmed him. He considered that his static position risked being submerged in the event of a general attack; he was also afraid that the Commander in Chief would take from his territory mobile units for "Operation Atlante," which was going to require considerable forces. In Tonkin, Cogny had outlined the situation to him with the same maps, the same diagrams and the same ideas which had served, four months earlier, to instruct Marshal Juin. In order to enlighten the new Commander in Chief, Cogny even employed a tone of almost sugary moderation, of exaggerated respect whose signs Navarre accepted with a barely ironic good humor. What Cogny wanted was simple and reasonable: in the highlands, to avoid battles whose issue was doubtful and to risk only guerrillas or highly mobile regular forces; in the plain, where the rot was spreading, to maintain a permanent offensive against the enemy forces which had already infiltrated; and finally to launch frequent, devastating raids on the approaches, in order to spread disorder through the supply system or in the territorial positioning of the Vietminh divisions.

Navarre reassured him. Marshal Juin had put him on his guard. He would therefore make every effort to break the enemy's thrusts before they could take effect. He had already asked Cogny to put forward proposals for a series of actions of this sort, so as to give him the green light.

All this seemed the very embodiment of sense, reason and sanity. The only doubts might have been about the suitability and efficacy of the offensive which Navarre wanted to mount to the south of the 18th Parallel, but his audience applauded when he explained his underlying motive: "My principal aim is to break the force of habit. The Expeditionary Corps lacks aggressiveness and mobility. I am going to do my best to give it back these qualities." This operation did not seem to commit him very far and might help him destroy the growing apathy. With sole responsibility, he was the sole judge. What was welcome and clear was that he had decided and proclaimed that in the first stages, in the campaign about to open, he would avoid a general battle.

July 24, 1953

So far, only the Vietminh had been able to make plans and keep to them. Navarre mistrusted the fuss that was made about his. Victory, he said, came if one compelled it, after destroying everything which lay in its path.

Neat, restrained, his face as though illuminated from within by the victory of Lang Son with which the dispatches of the special correspondents were still ringing, General Navarre expounded with easy assurance, in a firm, clear voice, at the Foreign Ministry in Paris, the plan which bore his name but whose paternity, in fact, he shared with Salan. He had an impressive audience. The President of the Republic, the Prime Minister, eight ministers, four secretaries of state, one marshal of France and the four Chiefs of Staff. Had Cogny, thanks to the hit he had just scored at Lang Son, hoisted Navarre onto a pedestal? To think that would be to show little familiarity with the atmosphere of these political meetings, at which each man is on guard against his neighbors, and takes care to defend the interests of his department. Navarre's youthful glory seemed, on the contrary, to militate against him, since it proved that victories could be won with the inadequate means at his disposal.

Weak and ailing, a prey to the pressures of the cold war and the heavy burden of financing rapid industrialization, the country still wanted an end to the Indochinese war. The new Prime Minister, M. Joseph Laniel, made no attempt to conceal the fact that the government intended to open negotiations with the enemy as soon as the Korean armistice had been signed. It does not seem that the question of Chinese aid, which Navarre himself considered at the very beginning of his recital, on the assumption that it would not increase, raised many objections to his plan. It was only in accordance with long-term policy that China would modify plans involving the efforts of hundreds of millions of men.

In reply to his suggestion of establishing an "air-land" base at Dienbienphu in order to retain Laos, the question of the defense of that territory was raised but not settled. Navarre concluded as a consequence that he had been given carte blanche. In actual fact, if the Chiefs of Staff had recommended that the government not impose on Navarre the task of defending Laos, the government still did not dare to relieve him of that task. They could not "say and even less write that we would not defend Laos." The words are those of the Prime Minister. In the event of a leak, wasn't there a risk of compromising France's obligations to defend the Associated States? Above all, could that decision be taken in Paris? In short, the Committee of National Defense disappeared into a cloud of vagueness as soon as there was any question of giving the Commander in Chief a precise directive. Laos? France had to defend it without defending it while still defending it. She would not say that she would not defend it, and she would act as if she were defending it, but without taking the slightest risk in the defense. As for the Minister of Finance, he declared his opposition to anything that would constitute a drain on the Treasury. Not one sou for the Navarre Plan.

General Corniglion-Molinier, the Minister of State, expressed himself in the picturesque, incisive language for which he was known. Corniglion-Molinier's strength lay in his humor and in his profoundly good heart. As a pilot, he had landed at Dienbienphu in 1946 with Leclerc.

"Dienbienphu?" he exclaimed before the amused and then hypnotized committee. "Imagine an airdrome on the Champs-de-Mars, with the enemy occupying Chaillot Hill. What's more, at such a distance from Hanoï and Haiphong, planes will only be able to fly there and back."

General Navarre replied that this was simply an airman's opinion, which did not correspond with his own view of the situation, but the seed of doubt had been sown. Besides, though recognizing that there would be a very tough battle to be fought, General Navarre had the honesty to say that it might involve serious reverses.

In conclusion, the committee heaped praises on him, but asked him to adapt his plan to the means at his disposal, and to put forward fresh proposals of a more economic nature in a reasonably short time.

It would be useless for Navarre to maintain later on that the minutes of this meeting had never been communicated to him, for he was well aware that M. René Mayer had asked him for one thing only—to find an honorable way out—and that, however ambiguous it might appear in his eyes, the position of the next Prime Minister, Laniel, who would find it difficult to break new ground, did not noticeably differ.

Would nobody help the Commander in Chief and the Secretary of State for Relations with the Associated States get things clear? The Minister for National Defense, M. René Pleven, opposed any increase in the military effort until the Vietnamese Government had created a real army, and asked that General Navarre be given a clearly defined mission, something which was not done. These were what M. Laniel would consider the most precise directives that could be given by a government to a commander in chief. Coming from M. Laniel's lips, these words were highly comic. M. Laniel was a worthy weaver from Calvados who had been pushed into politics by his father and who had become a minister through the usual network of friendships and *quid pro quos*. At the age of sixty-four, events had made a Prime Minister of him, as they would soon make a President of the Republic of M. Coty, both of them the smallest common denominators of their parties.

M. Laniel was neither somebody nor something, but utter nothingness. His ministry was manufactured, like his speeches, with scissors and paste. At Matignon, the Prime Ministerial residence, he was called neither "the Prime Minister" nor "the Chief," but merely "poor Joseph."

July 25, 1953

Navarre showed no particular dissatisfaction on July 24; that is undeniable. He might not swear that his plan had been approved without reservations, but he was certain that it had not been rejected. He did not explode; he did not threaten to tender his resignation. He did not cable Saigon to modify the accepted views on the conduct of operations. The next day, Navarre gave instructions, in the event of an enemy attack on the upper reaches of the Mekong, for the consideration of a preventive action aimed at taking the position of Dienbienphu by surprise.

Navarre had seen and corrected this directive before his departure from Saigon, probably in Paris itself. As he was out of Indochina, it was Admiral Auboyneau who signed it, for the admiral was senior to General Bodet, the Deputy Commander in Chief. In any case, this was an unimportant matter of military formalities; the author of the directive was

Navarre, who had interpreted in his own way instructions which he had not received.

How could Navarre be regarded as guilty of hoping to obtain means which were begrudged him? Who would dare to blame him for wanting to win the war or for practically confronting with a *fait accompli* a government which had never compelled him to refer to it before engaging in any action whatever? When it arrived on the desks of the ministers and the Chiefs of Staff, the directive of July 25 evoked no reaction, although it already showed that Navarre had made no alterations in his plans and that he was preparing to occupy Dienbienphu, which Paris, without knowing what it was and as if by instinct, did not want.

Who, then, was running the war? Nobody. How could an operation such as that of Dienbienphu be about to be launched? Only haphazardly. General Navarre, whose sole mission consisted of finding an honorable way out for the nation, acted as he wished, on condition that he ask for no reinforcements. As a good soldier, he had to give an account of his actions. It is easy to understand his reluctance to engage the Expeditionary Corps on the advice of incompetent high commissioners, of ministers entrusted with vague relations with the Associated States, a euphemistic term for the pseudo governments of Vietnam, Laos and Cambodia, and of local war committees. If, by any chance, a minister felt doubts about the merits of a military operation, he would ask the advice of the Prime Minister, who would not dare to give it and who would agree to almost anything. As for the means of waging war, the men and munitions belonged to the three service departments, which were sparing of their blood, and the money to the Treasury, which gave nothing. This had been the position under nineteen successive governments.

For seven years, things had gone on like this. A single commander in chief, de Lattre, had lost his temper and harried the intermediaries, not so as to obtain orders, which he would have refused to accept, but so that his own wishes might be granted; his protests had reached as far as America, where he had gone to preach the Western crusade. At his death, the frogs had resumed their places and their song, and Salan had moved cautiously through the marshes of official channels. Navarre had agreed to take command under these conditions. "Somebody must take on the job," Marshal Juin had said. Later on, Navarre would write a book to justify himself. The analysis he gives in this work of the political situation, the morale of the Expeditionary Corps and the Vietnamese

Army, the general atmosphere and the enemy's faith and will to win, is accurate and precise. He saw things clearly. He was under no illusions. But his book is an account written after the event, and not a day-to-day journal. On the last Sunday in July, 1953, before returning to Indochina, Navarre repeated at lunch with some friends what he had already told M. de Chevigné in order to reassure him: "I shall not make the same mistakes as my predecessors." He had made the same statement on his return to Saigon, and yet he was preparing to launch Dienbienphu just as Salan had launched Na San.

August, 1953

Cogny seemed at first to see the plan in terms of a transfer of the Na San battalions, man for man, to Dienbienphu. He wrote to Navarre: "I have absolutely no confidence in the value of an entrenched camp as a barrier. Luang Prabang is 125 miles from Dienbienphu; we are running the risk of a new Na San under worse conditions." And he proposed several methods, for the circumstances were no longer the same as they were a month earlier, of evacuating the Na San garrison, by land or by air, leaving on the spot a last battalion which would split up and join the guerrilla zones.

The evacuation was, in fact, finally decided on at Hanoï on August 5, in the course of a visit by Navarre, who had arrived the day before to review a parade and present the honors of Lang Son. Navarre attached another palm to the *Croix de guerre* of Cogny; Gilles; the swaggering, effervescent Colonel Ducournau, who had commanded the raid; Lieutenant Colonel Raberin, who, with his mobile unit, had gone to meet the parachutists; and on the flag of the 6th Battalion, Colonial Paratroops, which Bigeard presented to him in combat dress and shirt-sleeve order, a rigid figure with a red beret as aggressive as a coxcomb on his shaven skull and a thin smile on his lips. Navarre, too, smiled occasionally, even when he decorated Cogny's monumental chest, which he seemed to go on tiptoe to reach. At that season in Tonkin, everybody was breathing fire. Sweat poured down bodies, drenching shirts, while trousers, quickly crumpled, hung limply. At moments, Navarre seemed overwhelmed by a feeling of gravity, if not sadness. He was not a man for great military ceremonies. The leather-bound swagger stick which he held in his left hand seemed to embarrass him. Cogny, for his part, was thinking only of Na San. Dienbienphu? He had relegated that project a long way behind a plan for the equipment of Laï Chau, and so, he believed, had Navarre.

With the object of tricking the Viets, fake messages had been sent by the commander of the entrenched camp of Na San, asking for three battalions. In order to deceive observers, parachutists were dropped from the first Dakotas; then civilian aircraft began the evacuation, which military transports took over at the rate of one aircraft every six minutes. About twelve hundred Thai peasants were also evacuated, and three hundred important personages who had collaborated with the French. Men, women and children clambered into the machines with their luggage, their kitchen utensils, their caldrons stuffed with clothing and bottles, while fighters and B-26's flew over the nearby hills, ready to machine-gun anything that moved.

In spite of the storms that broke every night and littered the landing strip, by late afternoon on August 11 there remained only a few dozen men to take off while the fighters were destroying the ammunition dumps and the trucks. Cogny declared at Hanoï, "I am happier than I was on the evening of Lang Son."

Henri Amouroux later asked Lieutenant Makowiak, the last to leave, "What would you have done if your plane had been unable to land?"

"I would have left on foot."

The absence of any reaction on the part of the Vietminh was due to a minor incident which assumed gigantic proportions: the radio transmitter of the enemy observation post broke down. Once repairs had been completed, the radio transmitted the messages as they were piled up, in reversed chronological order. By the time the Vietminh Command had been informed of the big news, it was too late to take action. Cogny was correct in saying that the operation's success exceeded his greatest hopes. Was it the stupidity of an enemy radio operator the French Air Force had to thank for the congratulations which rained upon them the next day? When, ten years later, I put this question to General Giap, he answered with a smile.

"One of our strategic principles consists of trying to retain the initiative at all times. Navarre talked a lot about keeping his. There were not very many troops stationed at Na San, and the time did not coincide with that of our major operations. We considered that if Navarre evacuated the garrison from Na San, well, that suited us fine."

This optimism seemed to me to conceal a certain spite.

The evacuation of Na San added another success to Navarre's credit. On the threshold of his new campaign, Giap had been determined to take the fortified camp even if he had to send his assault forces in over piles of corpses, for he did not count the dead when victory lay at the end of a fight, and his soldiers accepted the prospect of death with an enthusiasm which would send shivers down our spines. It may reasonably be assumed that the success of the evacuation of Na San was a fairly bitter disappointment to the enemy and one which Giap would try his best to wipe out. The French did what they could to help: they prepared a revenge for him.

First fortnight of November, 1953

Dienbienphu did not happen all by itself. It was thought out. It was talked about. Tons of typing paper and pounds of gray matter were used to weigh the pros and cons of the affair. Opinions were not always unanimous. Discussions about it were even violent.

In the meantime, Navarre had sent his deputy, General Bodet, to deliver a new note to the government in which he maintained the need to carry out his plan without modifications and to receive reinforcements. The reply brought back was evasive. The plan was approved without any precise definition being given of the defense of Laos; the means asked for would be provided as far as was possible. However, on September 11, M. Pleven, the Minister for the Armed Forces, had repeated to General Navarre that he would have to be content with the reinforcements granted him on July 24; in other words, nothing. This decision, whose complete text M. Pleven, as if he were clinging to an anchor, has stubbornly refused to give me, therefore clearly laid down for Navarre the forces on which he could count: namely, those he already possessed. And yet, when the Dienbienphu operation was no longer a concept more or less approved or criticized, but a real plan in the process of being carried out, who would worry? A few men, no doubt. Who would protest? Nobody. The Minister of State entrusted with the task of relieving M. Laniel of Indochinese affairs rarely met the responsible Secretary of State because their offices were not in the same building. In fact, the truth is that nobody in the government understood anything about it.

If he refused to grant Dienbienphu the merit of serving as a barrier, Cogny had been the first to see it as a useful berth in the Thai country, a supporting "air-land" base for political-military activity. There is a world of meaning in this expression of Indochinese jargon. Navarre knew all about it. If he installed himself at Dienbienphu, it was first of all on the pretext of barring the door to Laos, as his predecessor, Salan, had been planning to do.

Now, at the end of October, Giap abandoned the idea of launching a mass attack on the delta and moved his 316th Division northwest, in the direction of Laï Chau. The problem of covering Luang Prabang arose again with an urgency all the greater since the French Government had signed an agreement with Laos in Paris on October 22, placing France under the obligation of defending her associate. Navarre reread in the testament Salan had left him this key sentence: "What will enable us to defend Laos is the impossibility of the Vietminh's maintaining more than 20,000 to 25,000 men there."

No secret note had been sent asking the Commander in Chief to regard the Matignon agreement as a scrap of paper. Since he had been left in ignorance, he could therefore not unreasonably assume that the reticence displayed in the summer had been abandoned and that M. Laniel's government had decided to defend Laos. The Commissioner General could not fail to share his opinion. Now the new Commissioner General in Indochina, M. Maurice Dejean, was not the sort of diplomat to build his judgments on hypotheses. Later on he would write, in a note to the government, that for the French Command the covering of Laos was simply a pretext for attempting to kill Viets, and perhaps he would be right. For the time being, he remained silent and did not ask his minister for any instructions, which seems to show that he, too, failed to realize the importance of Dienbienphu until much later. If he had considered the plan dangerous or futile, wouldn't he have taken the precaution of washing his hands of the affair right away, and of hinting, with all the stylistic nuances so appreciated at the Quai d'Orsay, that this formula for the defense of Laos did not have his approval?

On November 2, the Commander in Chief indicated in another special directive his intention of giving his dispositions in the northwest and the cover for North Laos greater strength and a more carefully planned composition. He wanted to deprive the enemy of the Dienbienphu rice fields and prevent him as long as possible from mounting the strong action that would be necessary to drive out the garrison.

Cogny reacted. His desire to keep the whip hand in the midst of his marshes made him afraid that the Commander in Chief's Dienbienphu might rob him of some battalions. Without opposing the enterprise, because Navarre might possess certain insights which he lacked, and in any case possessed one star more than he did, he merely pointed out, as usual rather confusedly, that to the political advantage of keeping a base in the Thai country was added the strategic advantage of giving cover to North Laos—which seemed to amount to telling Navarre that, on the whole, Navarre was right. But he added—for Cogny's reasoning took some devious paths—that the execution of the Dienbienphu plan would cancel the promise he had made to hold only his delta with what forces he possessed.

The position adopted by Cogny was a strange one. At the end of his directive, Navarre repeated that in his view the Hanoï plain remained the principal theater of operations, that he did not wish to feel threatened there, and that if Cogny considered it impossible to contribute any units, then Navarre would entrust the northwest to the guerrillas and would abandon the Dienbienphu plan indefinitely.

This was a major opportunity which Cogny did not take. Was this because of attachment to the Thai country? But what would become of this attachment if Dienbienphu proved a failure? The reason seems to have been simply that there is a military language and a hierarchy, and that, expressed in a certain way, a leader's wishes become orders. Although Cogny considered the proposed levy on his forces so dangerous that he hinted that he would not accept it at any price, he did not refuse it outright, for Navarre thought it was possible; and since Navarre thought it was possible, Cogny could not regard it as impossible without committing an act of insubordination. Cogny would probably have committed this crime of *lèse-majesté* if he, too, had not been tempted by his own pocket-size Dienbienphu—which was a reasonable proposition —and if he had seen all the dangers of the real Dienbienphu. Perhaps he was wrong, after the successes of Lang Son and Na San, to be so pessimistic about the Navarre Plan? Without expressing approval, his reply was not a refusal either; it floated somewhere in between, a sort of sulky agreement. As a subordinate, Cogny therefore embarked on the study of "Operation Castor": the reoccupation of Dienbienphu. It was to arouse violent reactions among his own staff which would make him change his mind again, but if the operation succeeded, Cogny would be able to take credit for it, and if it failed, the reservations he had expressed would protect him.

Logically, this is the way the facts appear to the historian. Considered chronologically, a fit of giddiness comes over him, for Cogny's dilatory reply to Navarre was sent off on November 6. But the memoranda of

Cogny's staff condemning Dienbienphu were dated November 4. On that day, therefore, Cogny was already equipped to say "no" to his Commander in Chief. Yet, though there were objections, this "no" was never uttered.

Was this because the Commander in Chief was not yet thinking of Dienbienphu as an entrenched camp, but of Dienbienphu in the "original version"? Cogny, who had trembled for Na San, and Gilles, who had been in command there and had bowed his boxer's head in the face of the Viet attacks, had no right to avoid warning Navarre of what awaited him at Dienbienphu. What Cogny did not dare to say openly, he attributed to his chief of staff: "I am convinced that Dienbienphu will become, whether we like it or not, a drain on manpower, without any useful influence, as soon as it is pinned down by a single regiment. . . . The consequences of such a decision may be very serious." But Cogny submitted because discipline was still the chief strength of an army, and nobody could blame him for obeying reluctantly. Besides, with his reputation as a troublesome subordinate, how could he disobey a man he did not yet even know?

The generals were already slipping gently down the slope which, as had correctly been foreseen, would drain away their battalions. They clung to the footholds provided by regulations, directives, interpretations and rank. For the Norman Cogny, who pondered his every argument and his every word, the enemy was not so much the Viets as the Commander in Chief. Cogny owed his third star and his command to Navarre, but he was well aware that Navarre was prejudiced against him and was watching for his reactions; and already a subtle game had begun between the two generals. True, on November 6, Cogny had the damning memoranda from his staff before him, but he pretended not to take them into account for the moment, for he had asked his officers to "lay it on thick." Next, he scented a trap in the last paragraph of the special directive of November 2; he told himself that this excessively accommodating Navarre might later blame him for what had not been done; so Cogny did not reply "no" out of fear of being accused of faintheartedness or of muffing a victory. After all, the decision in question came under the heading of strategy, the province of the Commander in Chief, and, moreover, Cogny could contribute his reinforcements since Giap seemed to have abandoned the idea of attacking the delta. Finally, Cogny had been one of the first to want Dienbienphu. It ought to succeed.

Nothing is quite so simple. To discover that, one does not have to work on documents fifty years after the event, but merely to question the actors in the drama. Appearing almost by chance, the name of Dienbienphu gradually grew in importance. From idea to idea, from expedient to expedient, from temptation to temptation, the men involved drifted toward gigantic misunderstandings. Navarre had been given a mission which was not clear. What was clear to him was that he had to stand up to Giap and that he would be blamed for any reverses he suffered; it was clear, too, that he felt, almost in spite of himself, responsible for the military honor of France, in his awareness of all that would follow for his country every time he yielded—and Navarre was not a man to yield.

On November 11 Colonel Nicot, the officer commanding air transport in the Expeditionary Corps, received the order to assemble his fleet. Intelligent, brave and stubborn, Nicot did not like committing blunders. He knew his aircraft and his material; he knew what could be expected of them. A little stubbornness was just the quality required for an undertaking of this sort!

Not only did Nicot declare that his transport aircraft were not in a position to maintain a permanent flow of supplies to Dienbienphu, but he stated this in writing in a report which I have read. Navarre listened without batting an eyelid. Corniglion-Molinier had already said the same thing in different terms; the airmen would have liked situations to adapt themselves to technique, whereas Navarre demanded the opposite.

Was what happened next a strange about-face or a premonition? Was it the bad temper with which Nicot had spoken against Dienbienphu that produced a sudden uneasiness in Cogny, or was it contact with reality through his study of the situation and through the fog and rain which abruptly descended on the Hanoï plain? Cogny suddenly wondered whether, relieved of Na San, he was not walking into a worse trap. When Colonel Berteil, who had come to settle details of the operation, took the plane back to Saigon, he carried in his wallet a personal letter in which Cogny declared himself resolutely opposed to the Commander in Chief's plan, without going quite so far as to refuse to carry it out.

Henceforth everything was clear. Navarre could not risk six parachute battalions against the advice of the men who would have to carry and supply them. Who but he would have insisted? But if he did not hate objections, he refused to pay any attention to them once he had made up his mind. From the logical and hierarchical point of view, the others had no option but to submit or resign. Cogny submitted and did not resign. After all, this young lieutenant general had done all he could to draw the Commander in Chief's attention to the dangers awaiting him; but for the moment these dangers did not exceed those of "Operation Castor" itself. In the absence of any unexpected complications, the battalions which were about to be sent off could be brought back a month later.

In fact, Cogny would go on being afraid of making a mistake, of failing in his mission, which was far from simple, and of leaving his men in the lurch. Thus the same Cogny who, in June, had urged Navarre to seize Dienbienphu would hesitate between military discipline, which commanded him to obey orders, and civic duty, which impelled him to denounce by his resignation a monumental mistake in which he refused to have any part. But how could the man of the delta plains understand that he was blundering, far from his base, with ill-prepared troops, toward a battle which would place him at a disadvantage?

Colonel Nicot's opinions were clearer: you could not tamper with loading figures and operational instructions in the face of meteorological or tactical circumstances for very long without running the risk of disaster. In any case, Colonel Nicot's judgment, based on the experience of Na San, was unequivocal and was supported by the warnings the Air Force had been giving for the past year, to Salan as well as to Navarre, with regard to Dienbienphu. The realities of the situation were soon to become plain.

November 15, 1953

On his own initiative, M. Marc Jacquet, the Secretary of State responsible for relations with the Associated States, and hence for the conduct of the war, landed at Saigon. Had he been impressed by the decisions taken, two days earlier, at the meeting of the new Committee of National Defense which he had attended? The Prime Minister had simply wished him *bon voyage*. In Indochina M. Jacquet represented the government, at least in his capacity as a letter box. If Navarre were still under any misapprehensions, he would be there to dispel them. Now M. Jacquet confirmed Navarre's opinion that if the Vietminh reached Luang Prabang, the capital of Laos, the shock suffered by public opinion in France would make the continuation of the war impossible. If the Commissioner General expressed an opinion contrary to his minister's, he would have expressed it in the diplomatic report I have read. For Navarre, there was therefore no shadow of doubt; he felt morally obliged to defend Laos and nobody contradicted him.

But how? With the means at his disposal. The defense of Luang Prabang was not an easy matter. The town stood in the middle of forests in the peak-lined valley of Mekong; the airfield was short, with poorly paved approaches. The wisest course of action was clearly to bar the way to Luang Prabang, not with a series of obstacles which the enemy would overcome one after another, but over a hundred miles away to the northwest, in the basin of Dienbienphu, whose advantages Salan had been the first to expound to Navarre.

Navarre would later be blamed for not having informed the Committee of National Defense, the body in Paris responsible for the conduct of the war, before taking action, and M. Jacquet had the impression that Navarre, who did not confide his thoughts to him, seemed more preoccupied with the strategic aspect of his plan than with the special case of Laos. Navarre also knew that the Committee of National Defense was not as easy to convene as a bowling club, that it would ask for fresh information and that it would keep him waiting for its decisions. Besides, was Navarre so very eager to receive precise directives? That was a question for M. Jacquet to ask. As for the other reproach that would be leveled at him, of not having adapted his operations to his means, Navarre genuinely believed that he could meet these extra requirements with what he possessed. Dienbienphu would not cost him more than Na San had cost Salan.

At the time when he was about to decide to dispatch his paratroops to Dienbienphu, Giap's intentions were much clearer. The bulk of the enemy battle corps was moving toward Laos. By installing himself at Dienbienphu, Navarre would be provoking his adversary. It would require complete ignorance of Giap's mentality to imagine that he would not throw in all his forces to wipe out the reverse he had suffered at Na San.

Probably Navarre did not see things as simply as that. The clearest ideas, when translated into the language of the Staff College, are complicated and buried in memoranda, notes or metaphysical directives which cover masses of typewritten paper. A spade ceases to be a spade, difficult airstrips are practicable, hilly country opens up before battalions, mobile units and armor, and the Air Force completes all its missions in spite of adverse atmospheric conditions. But on the spot men become men again and mountains mountains. To stop the Vietminh divisions which were moving forward, invisible at night and indistinguishable from the bush by day, Navarre could think of only one action: catching the enemy before his departure or cutting his lines of communication immediately afterward in order to force him to turn back, and then engaging him in a general battle, which, in his plan, Navarre had declared he wanted to avoid, at least at this time. Referring to this solution, Navarre would later write: "It therefore involved a huge risk," and would acknowledge a certain degree of culpability. To M. Jacquet, however, he showed nothing but optimism. There is a Navarre mystery which has still to be solved.

Navarre therefore believed that by investing Dienbienphu he was going to offer direct protection to the threatened regions. Besides, what was he risking? His chief of staff, his operational deputy and the technicians and specialists on his team all repeatedly assured him, after Salan, that at such a distance from its bases the Vietminh was incapable of maintaining itself for long. In assured tones, with their lips curling slightly in disdain, his Intelligence officers would inform him that in order to live Giap's divisions needed rice transported over great distances by coolies. Navarre had found confirmation of this, to within a few pounds and a few miles, in a top-secret study of the enemy's situation made by his predecessor. What nobody realized at the Staff College was that the subsistence of a battle corps could be maintained by fifty thousand coolies, each carrying a few pounds of rice; what a commander in chief who had spent the whole of his career in Intelligence, and even more so a colonel intoxicated by his new oracular functions, did not imagine either was that the load carried by the coolies could be increased more than tenfold by the use of ingenious rudimentary methods. Those bicycles manufactured at Saint-Étienne or in the Peugeot factories which the Vietminh had been using since 1951, without the French* Command deigning to pay much attention to them, were machines capable of moving over two hundred kilos of rice. Worse still, Navarre, who had never gambled in his life, except at bridge in the starchy, respectable atmosphere of Prefecture receptions, and even less laid bets, was unknowingly gambling with the lives of thousands of men, and was betting, in spite of the fact that the Korean armistice had been signed on July 27, that Chinese aid would not increase.

In Paris that day, on the initiative of the Minister of the Armed Forces, M. René Pleven, and of General Ely, the Chief of Staff of the three services, Rear Admiral Cabanier, Secretary General to the Committee of

National Defense, was summoned to see the President of the Republic and the Prime Minister, who asked him to leave immediately for Saigon. The only solution to the war now appeared to lie in negotiation, and the government was thinking of resuming contact with the Vietminh, a course of action which might be compromised by General Navarre's enterprises. General Ely explained the situation at great length to the admiral, who was being entrusted with a mission which the government did not dare to confide to diplomatic couriers.

November 17, 1953

In Hanoï the conference was being held which was to decide about the operation. In gray, close weather, important political personalities had arrived that same morning from Saigon with Navarre: M. Marc Jacquet, the minister responsible for the conduct of the war; M. Maurice Dejean, the Commissioner General; M. Nguyen van Tam, the Prime Minister of the Vietnamese Government. They were gathered together at half-past five in the afternoon in the map room, where they were told a vague story; in the present scheme of things, only the position of one screw was to be slightly changed. Dienbienphu was merely going to be given the role of Laï Chau. Civilians are not let in on the secrets of the gods; they were not called upon to give their agreement to anything. M. Jacquet would have no report to cable to the Prime Minister; he knew nothing. From the pipe he was sucking, he breathed in and exhaled nothing but smoke.

The really important conference had been held an hour earlier in the Commander in Chief's office, and had been limited to the military.

First of all, Navarre and Cogny had met alone. Cogny had some damning documents with him: the opinion of his chief of staff and his staff officers, in the form of the memoranda for which he had asked them on November 4, when he may still have been dreaming of Dienbienphu as an attractive base for political-military actions in the Thai country, or when he had not yet dared to say "no" to Navarre's plan. These memoranda were all against the operation. Colonel Nicot's opinion had only confirmed them as far as air operations were concerned. Roughly speaking, Cogny presented the following objections to Navarre: Dienbienphu would not prevent Laï Chau from falling to the Vietminh 316th Division and would not bar the way to Laos; the enemy was advancing everywhere and European ideas of strategy were valueless in Indochina. The rice of Dienbienphu was not indispensable to Giap; it represented only a fraction of the supplies which he needed and which he would find, if he wished, in the vicinity. The guerrillas would not cause him much trouble, and air attacks could not bar his way for long. Finally, if the 316th Division was reinforced by other divisions, the five battalions with which it was planned to occupy the region would not be sufficient and the number of troops in the delta would have to be dangerously reduced. However, the operation itself could, with luck, succeed. It was its consequences that would be disastrous. Yet the fact remains that on his return to Saigon General Navarre would declare to his aide-de-camp, "I didn't manage to find out exactly what General Cogny thought. . . ."

Navarre asked Generals Masson, Dechaux and Gilles if they had any objections to make. As it had just been learned that three battalions of the 148th Regiment were stationed in the Dienbienphu region, which had been thought to be free, they were unanimous in advising against the operation, putting forward tactical and technical arguments. Gilles thought that Dienbienphu ought not to be occupied in a single swoop, but taken from several different directions. General Dechaux pointed out that the maintenance of this new base would put a serious strain on French air transport, that on account of the distance the fighter aircraft would wear themselves out without being very effective, and that the weather conditions, often very different between Hanoï and the highlands, would present problems that might compromise the supplying of the new base.

The distance of nearly two hundred miles complicated and aggravated all the Air Force's operational conditions. This limitation struck everybody as enormous, except Navarre, his deputy Bodet and his staff. It represented an enormous waste of personnel and material, multiplied the risk of bad weather, extended the delay in the use of information, increased the consumption of fuel, and, on the other hand, reduced to a few minutes the activity of fighter aircraft over the basin. The extra fuel tanks which the fighters would have to carry would also reduce their maneuverability, and the small number of aircraft in service did not justify wearing them out too quickly.

General Navarre listened politely. The little smile which he had on his lips seemed to imply that subordinates always found good reasons for not carrying out orders as soon as those orders involved difficult adjustments. He maintained his decision. His last question was: "Is it possible?" Yes, it was possible. In that case, the Air Force must adapt itself to these difficulties and do its best to overcome them. Technique owed obedience to tactics. At the end of the conference, Gilles stood up spontaneously and stated that everything would be done to make the operation a success. A brief flash of joy lit up Navarre's face.

General Navarre has since explained his position to me in these terms: "There were objections, but the presence of three enemy battalions represented the only possible cause for anxiety. I held to my decision." Colonel Berteil has added to this: "General Navarre overruled all objections for two reasons: he wanted to bar the road to Laï Chau to the 316th Division and to defend Laos, about which France had just entered into a solemn engagement. Moreover, in General Navarre's mind, it was only a question of 'Operation Castor' and not of its consequences."

Four paratroop officers and two Air Force officers shut themselves up in an isolated villa in Hanoï with a secretary and General Cogny's chauffeur, who knew how to work a duplicator, and drew up the orders for "Operation Castor," which was to be launched on November 18, 19 or 20, depending on the weather. They did not know that they were helping to prepare one of the greatest events that was to shake the West. The stage was now set in readiness for the play to begin. The curtain would soon go up, and the Legion band which had done the honors for the minister went back to its billets through the streets of Hanoï. There remained a tiny chance that something might go wrong at the last moment.

November 19, 1953

November is the month of transition between the rainy season, which turns the plain into a huge lake of mud, and the thin drizzle which sets in with the approach of winter. That year, dull, close weather alternated with gusts of cold wind, but in the afternoons light clouds drifted across the sky torn by the vapor trails of the fighter planes. Hanoï looked like a big garrison town in North Africa, with its trams sounding their bells, its cyclists riding along, its pretty girls in purple tunics, its bars along the shores of its lakes where lovers strolled in the moonlight, hand in hand. Under the calm mirror of the waters, near the dragons of the Jade Pagoda, legend has it that a sword is hidden. Every night, brandished above the delta, it lights up the night with its flashes.

General Bodet had summoned the two battalion commanders of the first wave, Majors Bréchignac and Bigeard, who had been chosen to make sure that nothing went wrong. The day before and that very morning, the operation had been called off because a cold monsoon had blotted out the highlands.

"Everything ought to be all right," he told them. "But if it's too tough down below, don't hesitate. Pull out and fall back on Laos. It's up to you to decide. We'll back you up. Anyway, if the weather report isn't good tomorrow, Dienbienphu will never take place. Thank you, gentlemen."

General Bodet was not cut out to play a role in a tragedy. With his drooping mustache, his cap on one side, his small stature and awkward bearing, he would have been better cast in vaudeville or a Marx Brothers film. But he was a brave, goodhearted man, and being close to Navarre, he enjoyed the confidence of the gods. What, then, did he mean by saying, "If the weather report isn't good . . ."? The fate of an operation of this importance surely did not depend on a few clouds one day or another, unless, of course, more shaken than he wished to admit by the arguments against the operation, Navarre was hesitating. Perhaps, not having much faith in his enterprise, he was trusting to omens, just like a Roman general? No. If the weather report was bad, Dienbienphu would not take place because the enemy would find out what was afoot and the three Viet battalions could no longer be taken by surprise. In order to deceive the enemy, a rumor had been spread that the assembled aircraft were going to be used in an operation in the north, similar to that in July on Lang Son.

From Saigon, Navarre had received a wire that Admiral Cabanier, who had just arrived from Paris, intended to come up to Hanoï to see him as soon as possible. Navarre, who was well aware, if only through M. Jacquet, that the Committee of National Defense had met on November 13, may have thought that the admiral was bringing him the directives which he pretended to be calling for so insistently. And yet, far from showing the slightest eagerness to see these directives, and as if he scented a contretemps, Navarre sent a message to the admiral not to put himself out but to await his imminent return. For, sure enough, he returned that same day, in no great hurry.

If the weather report was good, Dienbienphu would take place **next** day.

⊭2⊭ The Trap

You must take care to choose an elevated position, in
order to fall upon the enemy with greater advantage. But
the most important point is not to gather your army on a
plain situated at the foot of a mountain which the enemy
might be able to occupy unimpeded; for with his artillery
he would crush you from the neighboring heights; in vain
would you try to prevent his batteries from hitting you
ceaselessly and without impediment. Embarrassed by your
own troops, you would find it impossible to harm him.

—MACHIAVELLI
The Art of War, Book IV

Solidarity, that foremost and supreme strength of an
army, is governed by severe disciplinary laws supported by
powerful passions; but to govern is not enough. A surveillance which nobody can avoid in battle, by insuring
the enforcement of discipline, must protect solidarity
against lapses in the face of danger, those lapses which
we all know; and in order to be felt, which is the most
important point, in order to exert a strong moral pressure
and *drive everybody along* out of fear or a sense of
honor, this surveillance, the eye of all watching everyone,
requires the presence in every unit of men who know each
other well and who regard it as a right and a duty in the
common interest. . . .

Four brave men who don't know one another will not
go forward boldly to attack a lion. Four men with less
courage, but knowing one another well, sure of their
solidarity and strong in their mutual support, will go
forward resolutely. The whole art of military organization
lies there.

—COLONEL ARDANT DU PICQ
Essays on Warfare

At the far end of the gray plain of the delta which they border on every side, even on the seashore, rocks cut out of limestone bristle along the horizon. Immediately beyond these rocks, to the north and northwest, there begins a mountainous region through which rivers force their way with the help of the hatchet strokes of their rapids. For hundreds of miles, as far as the Chinese frontier and beyond, the ground rises and falls in steep slopes, covered with jungle vegetation and sturdy trees. Wild animals glide through this jungle, but man has to hack his way with a machete. Only the roads are practicable, and even they make their way with difficulty through gorges where the traveler is at the mercy of a landslide or an ambush. A few wooden, straw-roofed houses are crowded together near torrents wherever a valley makes the cultivation of rice a possibility. On a few heights huts can occasionally be seen near where, apart from the rest of the world, families fatten a few pigs and grow corn and poppies on slopes they have burnt.

However, scattered about in this geographical chaos, bordered with cliffs and jagged peaks, and separated from one another by almost impassable regions, a few hollows have retained former invaders who have taken to plowing fields and raising buffaloes in them.

The demon which impelled the leaders of the Expeditionary Corps to yield to the temptation to establish entrenched bases here, each one shut in upon itself like a rolled-up hedgehog, was called Facility; because it was too difficult to hold the crests, the French installed themselves in the hollows, where planes could be landed and trucks driven. At each experiment, at Hoa Binh as at Na San, no lesson was learned from narrowly avoided catastrophe. The biggest of all the basins, situated at a center of communications between China, Vietnam and Laos, remained the principal lure which became an obsession; the French thought that its vastness would protect it this time against surprise attacks, and that the enemy (to whom they had abandoned the heights, as usual, in the conviction that they themselves possessed superior firepower) would never be able to approach it without breaking himself against it. It bore the name of Dienbienphu.

In the mountainous zone of the Thai country, it is known only by the name of Muong Theng. By its shape it suggests a long oak leaf in which the streams represent the ribs of the leaf and a bigger waterway the median line. Farther on, another river, the Nam Noua, flows into a tributary of the Mekong. "Muong" in the Thai language, like "phu" in Vietnamese, means "administrative center." Nowadays the Vietnamese do not say Dienbienphu, but Dienbien. "Dien" means big, "bien" frontier. Dienbienphu can be translated as "big administrative center on the frontier." No name could be more commonplace.

Laid waste in turn by the Chinese, the Siamese, the Meos and the Thais, Dienbienphu was occupied by the French in 1887 and its government handed over by the Siamese General Phya Surisak to Auguste Pavie, a former first-class writer in the marines who had become a postmaster, explorer and diplomat, and who gave his name to the trail which enables riders to reach Laï Chau. A hundred or so villages and hamlets are occupied by about ten thousand inhabitants, who live on the rice from their rice fields, a few vegetables, poultry and pigs. In the valley live the Thais, who according to legend emerged on this very spot from a pumpkin struck by a god's wand; on the crests, protected by a few rocks and near a watercourse, the Meos grow poppies and their women cut the pods after flowering to collect the juice; halfway up the slopes, the Xas, driven away by both Thais and Meos, serve their betters as slaves and look more like wild beasts than men.

The major axis, lying on a north-south line, is eleven miles long, and the minor axis three miles wide. Hills surround the basin, as round and gentle as breasts, or as sharp limestone masses rising in irregular tiers to pointed peaks which form a jagged amphitheater around the basin, darkened by forests. The difference in level between the transversal river, which bears the name of Nam Youm in the Thai language and Nam Rom in Vietnamese, and the peaks which dominate it on all sides is about two thousand feet.

A strategic position, undoubtedly. For it is true that any enemy coming from the east and making toward the Mekong will be tempted to pass through it in order to rest there and take in supplies, and that whoever controls Dienbienphu will control the whole region and part of Southeast Asia provided he holds both the basin and the heights commanding it, and that he builds roads and an airfield equipped with all modern technical aids, spread out over a vast area; for landing in bad weather is dangerous and, before diving through the clouds into the basin, a pilot has to beware of the mountains close around it. A few well-placed guns are enough to guard this Eden, whose population's chief concern is the gathering of the harvest and the sale of opium. Shut in between mango trees, breadfruit trees, areca palm trees, orange trees and lemon trees, the valley resounds with the clucking of poultry and the grunting of little black pigs which sometimes get killed by a tiger if they venture outside the villages.

In this basin to which the pilots would soon give the ignominious name of "the chamber pot," every general had dreamed of installing himself. Giap himself had decided that the position was of capital importance to whoever held it and dangerous to him if he failed to dislodge the enemy from it. The Japanese had left an airfield there, the French a post whose captain could be seen in period photographs, in a pith helmet and carrying a stick, standing with his lieutenant and a dog in front of a background of sisal plants. Like Salan, Navarre wanted to install himself there with the intention of using it as a base.

In front of a large-scale map, this was not unreasonable. Staff officers with big ideas would stick little flags into the place. For anybody who had to land by parachute or travel on foot through the mountains, circumstances counted for rather more and the myth vanished. As for the solemn civilians, ministers, high commissioners, deputies and chairmen of committees who were to follow one another as expensive and sometimes greedy visitors, few of them would retain the tiniest grain of common sense in the face of the megalomania of the staff. None of them, in any case, would dare to show the slightest reservations. Out of ignorance? Alas, you didn't have to be a magician to observe the risks involved, but you had to be blind to deny them or to insist on taking them in spite of everything.

November 20, 1953

At 4:30 in the morning, behind a four-engined Privateer naval aircraft normally used for observation at sea and which was going to evaluate weather conditions, there took off from one of the Hanoï airfields a Dakota fitted with equipment that would enable it to maintain radio contact with the whole command. It carried a load of officers whose responsibility it was to launch or cancel the greatest operation in the Indochinese War.

After circling above the lights of the city, for it was still dark, the pilot set his course, switched off his navigation lights and settled down to cruising speed. When, about 5:45, day broke, the faces pressed against the windows discovered, in the heart of a chaotic chain of mountains whose peaks were tipped with the light of dawn, a long basin filled with a huge mass of snowy vapor. General Bodet and General Dechaux went over to Gilles, who was examining with his one eye the jumble of crests covered with tropical vegetation.

"Is it going to lift?" asked Gilles.

Gray and swollen, foaming against the lower slopes and filtering into the ravines, the mist was blossoming in the first rays of the sun. The generals looked at one another and shook their heads.

The Dakota continued on its course toward the Chinese frontier, then turned, a few minutes later, 65 degrees to the left, due southwest, to join the valley winding gently toward the Mekong. At 6:30, the deciphered text of the message sent to Hanoï by the radio operator was taken to Cogny's residence on the banks of the Little Lake: "At Dienbienphu, mist clearing."

Gilles rested his chin on the palm of his hand and leaned back gloomily against the elbow rest of his seat. A year earlier, he had been shut up in the entrenched camp of Na San and had spent his nights waiting for Viet attacks. At that time I had seen his marble face, which lit up from time to time, and his heavy carcass, which he moved restlessly round his burrow and dropped onto a camp bed during lulls in the fighting—lulls broken by the ringing of the leather-sheathed telephones. Officers and secretaries lifted the blankets which served as door curtains, and placed papers on his table, where a watch shone beside his maps; a murmur of voices and the clatter of typewriters would come in then, half-muffled by the walls covered with matting and the ceilings supported by tree trunks on which hanging electric lamps burnt night and day. Now and then crumbs of red earth rained onto the floor.

Gilles had survived and had won his brigadier's stars on the edge of that huge trap which could have smashed him if it had closed upon him. The enemy had had its teeth broken on its defenses, but the threat of a general attack hung constantly over the besieged camp. Gilles knew perfectly well that, if they had wanted to and if they had made an all-out effort, the Viets would have defeated him. Besides, he didn't like a city of moles from which you couldn't emerge without coming under the enemy's fire. His delight was to hurl battalions through the doors of Dakotas, to swoop down on an enemy who didn't expect him, to carve him up and then return at full speed, on the rails of a well-mounted operation, in broad daylight. When the Viets had withdrawn, he had asked to be relieved.

He had been sent for again to direct "Operation Castor." To repeat Na San, where so many crack troops had found themselves immobilized, where all supplies had to rain down from the sky, and this time at twice the distance from base? At Gilles's level, a man confines himself to carrying out the orders of the High Command. He would drop his group, nail it to the ground and then hand it over to someone else, for his health was beginning to trouble him. He had been assured that his wishes would be respected.

When the Dakota returned from the south, the mist, which had almost cleared, was stretched out in long trails along the backs of the mountains. Here and there the pattern of the yellow and gray rice fields of Dienbienphu could be made out. A few wisps of smoke were rising from the villages, under a sun already high in the sky. A strong gust of wind blowing from China finally swept away the mattress of gray clouds which had accumulated for the past two days over the highlands. The pilot deviated from his course and reduced the speed of his engines.

At 7:20—twenty minutes past midnight in Paris—the brief message which General Cogny had received and passed on created a considerable stir. The unit commanders had been told their destination and the object of the operation only two days before. It was only under the wings of the planes that their men, gathered on the spot since daybreak, learned where they were going and how the operation was to be carried out, before receiving the order to embark.

At 8:15 the armada began to take off. It was cold. About sixty Dakotas collected during the past three days took the air one after another and formed up again in groups of three, their noses painted blue, yellow or red, in a column extending over seven miles, flanked by B-26 Invaders. In each transport aircraft, twenty-four paratroopers, swathed in their equipment and wearing their helmets, smoked, sang or chewed gum to pass the time. The idea of leaving a plane with only a piece of string between a man and his death has never left anybody unmoved except those who don't jump.

In the basin of Dienbienphu the whole sky was smoking. In broad strips alternately breathed in and expelled by the crests, it came apart and filled up again, only to split open more and more under the sword blows of the sun. The peasants, who had come from all the nearby hamlets, where nobody remained but the old people and the women in charge of children, were hurriedly bringing in the only harvest of the year. On stubble cut high up in order to leave pasture for the buffaloes, the women were binding the stalks of rice laid out the day before and already dry; the men were piling the sheaves in cone-shaped ricks, similar to the fern ricks of the Basque peasants. Elsewhere, other groups were threshing the grain on mats where, turning the yellow, scented mass over with their feet, girls were winnowing it with round fans, raised

above their heads and suddenly brought down with a twisting movement
of the body, to the rhythm of a sacred dance.

At nine o'clock in the morning, in Saigon, Rear Admiral Cabanier was
shown into General Navarre's office. Admiral Cabanier was a calm,
courteous man, to whom the work which he performed had given the
habit of treading softly. The atmosphere of the Commander in Chief's
villa was like that of a clinic. Everything about it suggested neatness and
cleanliness. There was no bustling about; no voices were raised. The
swarming life of business and poverty barely touched the borders of this
residential district. In the study, which had been installed in Madame
Salan's former bedroom, the purr of an air-conditioning apparatus
drowned the distant murmur of the damp, sticky town. The huge room
was bare. There were no pictures on the wall, only a map of Indochina
which filled almost a whole panel in front of Navarre; a safe behind him,
within reach; no photographs or papers on his desk; a few chairs around
a small table.

The admiral felt for his pipe in the pocket of his white linen tunic, but
did not dare take it out yet. Navarre smoked cigarettes made with local
tobacco only after midday. The aide-de-camp came in and put some
dispatches on the desk. Navarre glanced at them and put them to one
side. The admiral sat erect in his armchair; he felt almost cold in this air-
conditioned fishbowl. Once the usual courtesies had been exchanged, he
came to the object of his mission: the President of the Republic and the
Prime Minister asked the Commander in Chief whether he did not think
that on account of the signing of the Korean armistice and the repercussions which this event might have on Chinese aid to the Vietminh, and
on account of the favorable situation created by the recent military successes in Tonkin, the time had not come to open negotiations with a view
to a cease-fire in Indochina.

Navarre bitterly noted an identity of view between M. René Mayer's
anxiety to settle the problem by negotiations with China and the intentions of his successor, Laniel, who had also been struck by the remark
made by de Lattre in 1951, in the drawing rooms of the Élysée: "We
shall manage provided the Chinese don't budge." Wasn't the end of the
Korean War going to lead the Chinese to budge? It seemed reasonable
to think so.

Navarre allowed the silence to deepen. Then he smiled and pushed
over to the admiral the tray in which the dispatches were piled up.

"Read that."

The admiral learned that a vast airborne operation was being carried out in the highlands and that three battalions of paratroops were going to rain down on Dienbienphu within a few moments. Navarre's face lit up with radiant confidence, barely touched with irony. As far as he was concerned, his reply to the government was provided by the action which he had just initiated, and it was in the negative. Why? It would take some time for Chinese aid to increase, and when it did, his Intelligence services would be alerted in time; finally, the military situation would be even better in the spring. The French Government would therefore be able to negotiate under better conditions. In short, a categorical "no."

The admiral registered this reply without a tremor.

It is hard to imagine that General Navarre, unexpectedly presented with the enlightenment he had been waiting for, should have failed to question the admiral about the feelings toward him expressed by the Committee of National Defense at its recent meeting. But Admiral Cabanier had also been entrusted by the government with the task of informing General Navarre of the decisions that had just been taken. At the very moment that he was launching Dienbienphu, therefore, Navarre received confirmation that he could expect nothing from France; the Committee of National Defense once again advised him, without a single reference to the defense of Laos, to adapt his plans to his means, asked him to limit his ambitions to containing the enemy and warned him that he would not receive the reinforcements he had asked for. This meant that the action which he had just begun could not be approved under any circumstances. The news might be termed a bitter blow.

Admiral Cabanier was definitely not going to take out his pipe. He was not the man to ask any questions beyond the one he had just put, or to exceed his instructions. Possibly, in order to console Navarre, he repeated the remark which General Corniglion-Molinier, the Minister of State, had made to General Fay, the Chief of Air Staff, when he had refused to send any new formations to Indochina: "You're a stores orderly and not an airman. You keep your planes like a storeman kept his pairs of boots during the War of 1870!" Navarre may then have thought that the government would be able to force the hand of the Committee of National Defense, as he himself was forcing the government's hand by confronting it with the *fait accompli* of Dienbienphu.

Between 10:35 and 10:45, the first Dakotas appeared from behind the crests and released three thousand parachutes over the two chosen zones, one to the northwest of the villages of Dienbienphu and christened Natacha, where a company of engineers dropped with the 6th Paratroop Battalion under the command of the indomitable Bigeard, and the other, Simone, to the south, for the 2nd Battalion, 1st Paratroops, of Bréchignac.

Rooted to the spot for a moment in amazement, the peasants on the plain fled in terror toward villages which seemed outside the action or toward the mountains. The women, whom I questioned nine years later in the hamlets, still trembled as they relived their memories. One of them, who at the time was living to the north of the basin, at Ban Kê Phaï, had gone to Dienbienphu to pick mulberry leaves for her silkworms. When the cloud of Dakotas left its parachutes behind it, like tufts of cotton wool in the sky, she was so frightened that she fled along the streams toward the nearest slopes and returned home only in the middle of the night, to find the hamlet deserted and her house empty; her daughter of eleven had gone off, taking a pot of rice with her.

On Simone, Bréchignac's battalion spread out over a deserted zone, three miles from Natacha, between the river and the lower slopes to the east, in the region of Hong Cum. On account of poor communication between the air formations, the drop took place too far south and not as accurately as was desired, but the troops met with no resistance.

On Natacha, on the other hand, situated a quarter of a mile to the west of the main airstrip, they encountered a swarm of Viets who fought hard. The companies of the 6th Battalion, Colonial Paratroops, under fire before they had even landed, were pinned to the ground. Bigeard called for help but could not make radio contact until noon. One parachute had failed to open, ten men had been killed, two of them in the air, ten seriously wounded, and twenty-one slightly wounded, eleven of them in landing. Communication with the flying command post was difficult and Bigeard himself was directing the supporting B-26's.

The banks of white and khaki jellyfish floated down onto the rice fields, landed and closed up. The men called to one another, joined up, loaded their weapons and advanced toward the clouds of colored smoke which marked the rallying points, hesitating, then leaping forward and cutting across one another's paths. Some of them, in the shelter of a culvert or an embankment, took drinks from their water bottles. There were bursts of fire. It is no easy matter running across rice fields which have not yet been harvested.

Cogny had left his headquarters at Hanoï and jumped into a Dakota, taking Berteil with him. From the plane, he studied for a long time the mountains covered with a thick fleece of trees and tall grasses which bordered the long gray basin; while Berteil dreamed of another, more powerful Na San, a splendid bait thrown to the Viets to lure them en masse and smash them.

At lunch, the generals of the brains of "Operation Castor" met again fifty miles to the north, in the green swell of the mountains stretching toward China, at Laï Chau. From there, a poor track wound its way along the beds of torrents and through twisting passes toward Dienbienphu.

At Hanoï, the Dakotas which had returned to their bases were refueled. Nobody was allowed to move away from the planes, where snacks were taken to the crews. At 1400 hours, the 1st Battalion, Colonial Paratroops, was dropped on Natacha where Bigeard was barely beginning to sort things out. Half his battalion was cut off, and as yet he did not have a zone where helicopters could land to pick up the wounded. Violent fighting was spreading considerable confusion.

About 1600, the Viets made off toward the south along the right bank' of the river, and poor communication with the group and the flying command post prevented any maneuver to bar their way. By 1730, when night fell, Bigeard had established his command post in Dienbienphu and held the approaches with his four companies. Bréchignac's battalion came up along the left bank and installed itself on the first hills to the east. The 1st Battalion, Colonial Paratroops, two batteries of 75-mm. guns, a company of 120-mm. mortars and a surgical unit dropped during the afternoon remained on Natacha. Captain André, a medical officer making his first jump, had been killed. The 910th Battalion and the 226th Company of the Vietminh had left ninety-six dead and four wounded on the field.

At 1615, the official dispatch, in code and marked very urgent, which informed the government of "Operation Castor" was sent off to Paris. As a matter of form, and in spite of the fact that M. Jacquet was making the rounds of the royal tables of Laos and Cambodia, it was addressed to the Secretary of State for Relations with the Associated States, rue de Lille, where the decoding service was installed.

On the outskirts of the village of Dienbienphu, children wearing greasy berets, old people and women with soft round faces and dark eyes, who had not had time to flee, huddled together at the foot of houses of wood and straw; full of fear and curiosity, they watched the soldiers talking into their radio transmitters with the cricket-like antennae. Without being able to understand a word of their language, the women realized that this hailstorm of armed men was not bringing good fortune to the valley.

Everywhere the battalions searched the mainly deserted houses, which were filled with the stench of the buffalo stables installed between the piles. A wide ladder gave access to the balcony in front of each straw hut, whose floor of bamboo laths gave underfoot. The paratroops pushed aside the door curtains of the bedrooms, which were separated by wickerwork partitions. They burnt any rebel banknotes they found in the fireplace, where the embers were still hot, underneath the cooking pot hanging from a tripod. Frightened cats took refuge in the timberwork. Down below, yellow dogs growled, their hair bristling; the pigs tried to return to their huts, and the little Thai horses, with their bushy manes and tails, stirred restlessly in their cagelike stalls, resting their noses on their empty mangers, hollowed out of tree trunks.

At nightfall silence returned, until nervous barking greeted the full moon as it rose above the mountains.

In Paris, it was midday. Decoded in the rue de Lille, the dispatch from Saigon was sent by M. Jacquet's chief private secretary to the Prime Minister, who passed on its contents to the President of the Republic, the Minister of National Defense, the other ministers and the Chiefs of Staff. It caused tremendous surprise. Those who read it looked at their calendars. As Indochina was six hours ahead of Paris, the dispatch seemed to have arrived before it had been sent, that very same day; but then it was true that Paris seemed to be several years behind Indochina.

Anyone who consults the newspapers for that Friday of November 20, 1953, will find that Gaston Dominici was suspected of having had an accomplice and that the American experimental plane "Sky Rocket" flew at over twelve hundred miles an hour. The great political question of the moment was the European Defense Community. Until five o'clock in the morning, air traffic to Orly had been diverted to Le Bourget on account of fog. It was not yet freezing, but winter was approaching; for the past fortnight, the weather had been very hazy throughout France, except in the Alps and Provence. At the Théatre National Populaire *Lorenzaccio* with Gérard Philippe was playing.

At the moment when Paris was wondering why Navarre had launched such a large-scale operation so far from his bases, M. Maurice Dejean, former French Ambassador in Tokyo, who owed his post of Commissioner General in Indochina to M. Paul Reynaud—who, like M. Jacquet, had the task of relieving the Prime Minister of Indochinese affairs—was giving, as he did almost every evening, a dinner at the Norodom Palace to which Admiral Cabanier was invited, or else was attending a dinner in honor of his visiting minister at Phnom Penh—a dinner more or less, at one place or another, what does it matter? It would be a waste of time to record such events; all over Indochina cocktail parties and dinners were being given, once night had fallen, to escape the fear which rose from that hostile land. Who would swear that champagne was not drunk that day, at some official table, to the success of Dienbienphu?

M. Dejean found it hard to assess the military significance of the operation. As for General Navarre, he toyed with those problems of the conflict which he did not dare face. With his secretive nature, he avoided making any reference to the admiral's mission, and the admiral confined himself to noting the optimism which the High Command was displaying on the threshold of a new campaign; in all civilian and military circles the future was being faced with confidence. The occupation of Dienbienphu appeared as fresh proof of the power and strategic mobility of the Expeditionary Corps. Only General Navarre knew that the government could condemn him for having taken a decision of that sort without consulting it. But since he had weighed all the strategic consequences of Dienbienphu, how could he be running into a trap? The danger with men with this sort of mind is that nothing and nobody can ever convince them they have made a mistake. On the very brink of disaster, they will maintain that they have saved the day, and you will end up wondering whether they have not succeeded in convincing themselves, having failed to convince anyone else, that they alone have access to the truth.

November 21, 1953

Gilles dropped on Natacha with the first wave in the morning, at the same time as Lieutenant Colonel Langlais, who had been given command of the group. He landed correctly, rolled up in a ball, remained flat on his belly for a moment and studied the terrain. In one pocket of his jacket he clutched the glass eye which he always took out before a jump. He had fallen not far from a tall rick in the shape of a sugar loaf which was protected from the buffaloes by a bamboo fence. Men were raining down on all sides. Further off, B-26's were circling around, guided by Bigeard over the lower slopes, where some platoons were still in pursuit of fleeing Viets. He slung his knapsack over his shoulder and made for the rallying point. The photographers of the information service, who had jumped with a couple of chaplains, trained their cameras on him. A few tatters of mist were still clinging to the mountainsides, so far away at the end of the glistening plain that they seemed to be floating on the shores of a lake. The tall stubble of the rice field, whose earth was already dry and cracked, scraped against his trousers. Gilles puffed out his chest, on which two silver stars shone. He felt like shouting as he saw a parachutist preparing to land too stiffly, but merely groaned. Well, at forty-nine and in spite of all the pain he was suffering, Old Gilles, who had obtained his parachutist's certificate only five years before, was not finished yet! All the same, he wished luck to whoever took possession of this basin. For he was not going to stay around here for any price in the world.

A small motor bike was waiting for him. Gilles hung his knapsack on it, took the handlebars and opened the throttle. He was impatient to see Bigeard and his hatchet face, and above all his attentive and virtually indispensable chief of staff, Lieutenant Colonel Fourcade. This was what Gilles liked: all this activity in the sky and on the ground; this noise, this hailstorm of men and packages. Langlais, who had fallen clumsily, had broken his ankle. Humiliated and furious, he said nothing. He would have to be evacuated.

In the afternoon, in the midst of the rain of men, crates of provisions and rolls of barbed wire, which bounced as they hit the ground and were known as fakir's pillows, a seven-ton bulldozer suddenly emerged from the yawning belly of a Packet and plunged nine feet into the earth. A start was made in filling the trenches in the old airstrip, where there were twelve hundred holes to stop up.

In the hundred villages in the basin and on the slopes where fear had driven them, ten thousand Thais gazed silently at the sight. In the valley of Dienbienphu, the parachutes which the troops had not had time to pick up looked like a huge wash spread out among the dead buffaloes. A few crops had been laid waste by this tornado. Wearing close-fitting, ankle-length black dresses, the women called their children to them as they moved away, and pressed to them the infants they carried in bags, against one hip. The more prosperous among them wore a piece of braid on the bodice of their dresses, from the high collar to the belt of silk, leather or vine. The old women had their hair bound in a sort of turban; the married women wore theirs in a thick cylindrical chignon on top of the head; the girls let theirs hang down their backs. Uneasiness was written on every face; it did not occur to the Thais that their ancestors had themselves been invaders. In this country without electricity, nobody had a radio and the transistor had not yet arrived. News traveled, however, by chance encounters on mountain trails, by strange processes which distorted it. What new misfortunes were about to befall them this time, and if they had to leave their homes, where would they go and how would they live? Families of Meos had taken refuge with their horses in caves. Standing on a brick hearth with bamboo sticks burning beneath it, a wretched caldron suddenly became an irreplaceable treasure.

That evening, General Cogny in Hanoï gave free reign to his joy as he met the press. Cogny had weaknesses of this sort. He talked a great deal, mentioning guerrillas and the maquis, perhaps, as he was to maintain later, because he wanted to mislead the enemy. But why did he talk at all? One remark in particular would be remembered: "If I had been able to, I would have moved Na San bodily to Dienbienphu as soon as I took up my command, five months ago."

Cogny in Hanoï was 750 miles from Saigon where Navarre was in command. In Paris that same day, 7,500 miles to the west, the Secretary of the Committee of National Defense, which had met on November 13, sent M. Marc Jacquet, as a matter of form, the committee's decision concerning the conduct of the war in Indochina. M. Jacquet, who knew the decision and had not dared to mention it to Navarre, did not receive it. He continued his visits to the neighboring capitals of Laos and Cambodia and supervised the conduct of the war without even knowing that Admiral Cabanier had been entrusted with a mission to the Commander in Chief.

Nobody now was able to oppose Navarre's enterprise. Not even the Minister of Finance, who, after having replied "Not a sou" to the Navarre Plan, had added, "Unless . . ." He and the Prime Minister had then hatched a diabolical plot. To make the most of the opportunity presented by the Navarre Plan, France had to obtain in dollars from America the hundred billion francs it would cost. Without it, well, France would pull out. This was the sort of cynical proposal heads of governments are experienced in putting forward. For President Eisenhower, it was a question of taking it or leaving it; if the Expeditionary Corps pulled out, America would be faced with her own obligations and a fresh war only a short time after the Korean armistice. On the other hand, if America came across, M. Laniel would propose a meeting with the President of the United States which would end up with a declaration of this sort: "France and America are pursuing the same aim in Indochina and it is useless to hope to separate them. In view of this fact, they urge the enemy to a peaceful settlement of the conflict."

The Bermuda Conference would not take place until December, but America had been shelling out since September. With great satisfaction, the Minister of Finance paid into the empty coffers of the state the hundred billion francs needed for the Navarre Plan, to which he was no longer opposed but whose execution was threatened by the Committee of National Defense, which provided the men. Far from costing money, the Indochinese War was proving profitable, and the troops' blood was being paid for in dollars. The biggest profiteer from the traffic in piastres was the French Government, and if Vietnam protested, it was because it was not getting its commission.

In the morning, a ceremony had taken place in the rice field for the burial of the dead of the 6th Battalion, Colonial Paratroops, whose parachutes served as shrouds. Where was this? Nobody knows now. Certainly not very far from the village. The wooden crosses were painted white and wreaths of flowers laid on the graves, which were surrounded by a hand rope. The cemetery, in the midst of which stood a flagpole, could always be enlarged if necessary.

November 22, 1953

The giant Cogny extricated himself laboriously from a Beaver, unfolded himself and straightened up, armed with an alpenstock, his open shirt baring his wrinkled, leathery neck. With a surly expression on his face and bundled up in his jungle kit, Gilles seemed small and stocky beside him. Cogny returned his salute and shook hands affably, blinking his eyes in the strong light. He looked around at the machinery which manufactured victories and deaths, which he could see in full operation, and smiled. Gilles knew what he thought about all that.

Gilles took him to his combat post, gave him an account of the arrangements he had made to protect the camp against attack, pointed out the siting and purpose of his gun batteries, and explained in detail the reconnoitering expeditions he had carried out. Cogny nodded, and once again gave himself up to the self-examination which he had been pursuing unceasingly for the last five months. He could not help thinking about the hornets' nest of Na San from which he had only just succeeded in extricating himself. Only to put his head into a new one? Now and then he bent down and examined the earth, which he scratched with the iron tip of his swagger stick like a bull with its hoof, and his huge carcass seemed to droop.

He did not want a Na San which risked devouring the delta battalions one by one, and yet the day before he had made a remark which would be held against him for a long time: "If the entrenched camp of Na San had been on wheels, I would have moved it to Dienbienphu." At Na San you felt shut in; within rifle range of the Viets, you could not take a single step without being observed. Here at least . . . The lower slopes, where they would certainly not allow the Viets to install themselves, were three or four miles away, to the east as well as to the west. The real crests were five miles away; to the north, six miles; to the south, even farther. You could breathe, you felt at ease. You had room to maneuver. Cogny took a deep breath. Those distant heights where the enemy would establish itself, weren't they out of range of the 105-mm. and 155-mm. guns? In that case, the Air Force with its bombing raids would take the place of the artillery.

About five thousand men were bustling about Dienbienphu, digging holes, putting up barbed wire, stuffing earth into sacks, bathing in the river, setting up bivouacs and field kitchens, piling up parachutes, opening crates. A few shells were fired off into the mountains to get the range. Smoke and dust rose above the camp as cargo rained down from the planes above. Gilles's offices issued notes, telephones rang, the radio crackled. The atmosphere was the joyful one of a successful operation. Soon the dead themselves would be able to travel back to Hanoï by air.

"Just the same," Gilles said to Cogny in an aside, with the Catalan accent which added to his good-natured charm, "I'll feel happier when you've found a successor for me."

"We're thinking about that."

Gilles, however, was the man who was needed. A bull himself, chewing over the same problem for days on end, he was stocky, stubborn, prudent, and abusive and bad-tempered when he didn't get what he wanted. Was all his valuable experience going to be wasted? Gilles no longer felt in condition, and occasionally he was overcome by sudden fatigue. His heart was giving him trouble and obliged him to take things quietly. He had had enough and scented the approach of danger.

"At Na San I spent six months of my life like a rat. Use me in the open air."

"That's a promise," said Cogny. "It will only be a matter of days."

If Cogny had insisted, Gilles would have given in, and the course of events might have been different.

Not far from the road along which the columns of porters and troops of the 316th Division were passing, in a hut whose foliage merged into the outskirts of the forest, a man was silently studying the big map in front of him. From the messages reaching him, he was trying to evaluate the event which Navarre had set in motion, on November 20, at Dien-bienphu. Without taking his eyes off the map, he questioned his staff officers and fell silent again. Nobody around him showed any impatience. They knew that he was capable of remaining for several days in this state of concentration, from which he would suddenly emerge one morning. Then he would call his assistants and dictate orders, circling around the long trestle table and occasionally hammering it with his fist.

This man of medium height who was still only in his early forties, slow in gesture, clumsy in bearing, far from smart in dress, wearing badly cut trousers and a tunic with a closed collar bare of signs of rank or decorations, was Vo nguyen Giap, the Commander in Chief of the People's Army. Like Ho Chi Minh, he was born in the wide, sandy spaces of central Annam, near the sea, on September 1, 1910, at An Xa, in the province of Quang Binh. At a period when he was known as Vo Giap, he had studied philosophy and law at the University of Hanoï. As soon as his mind saw things clearly, the confidence which appeared on his face was prodigious. Confidence? Let us say, rather, intelligence; that shocking intelligence which gave an erstwhile history master the audacity to stand up to a well-equipped European army, provided with everything necessary to wage war anywhere and at any time, when his own units had to move on foot with their arms, ammunition and supplies. Following the example of his master Mao Tse-tung, Giap made use of the means at his disposal and of the terrain which he knew better than his adversary because it was his own. What in the eyes of the classical strategists constituted an insurmountable inferiority was gradually becoming a superiority which held them in check. What was the use, in most cases, of possessing weapons which could crush the enemy if the enemy escaped? How could you pursue him if he was invisible?

Since he had founded the People's Army in the maquis, Vo nguyen Giap had thought about the enemy as much as about his own forces. His staff college was the bush. So far he had not counted supplies in thousands of tons, but in pounds carried by a single man; his battalions had covered thousands of miles, but in infantry marches; and because he knew that the enemy could swoop on him at any moment, he lived in hiding, ready to disappear if he was driven out of cover. Little by little, he had forged his instrument, extended the influence of the Party, imposed its doctrine by lecturing the faithful and liquidating the lukewarm, and turned the People's Army into a host of interlinked cells ready to sacrifice themselves for the triumph of the revolution. A historian, he had learned that nothing was impossible for those who dared, and had laid the foundations of his own tactics and strategy: when you could not fight the enemy with weapons stronger than his, you had to render his weapons ineffective pending the day when you possessed the same, which would be all the more effective for being unexpected. Never laying himself open to attack, keeping out of sight, attacking from a position of obvious superiority and with the certainty of victory, carrying out preparations slowly and carefully, but acting swiftly and energetically, Giap had patiently adapted the military principles of Alexander the Great and Napoleon to his size and drawn every possible lesson from his reverses. One might even wonder whether he had not studied the Prince de Ligne and Colonel Ardant du Picq. As for Mao Tse-tung's experience, he had drawn from it whatever lessons could serve his purpose: a vacuum around fortresses when they are impregnable, the careful avoidance of battles whose issue is in doubt, constant withdrawal in the face of a strong enemy, attack in the face of withdrawal, and the mobilization of men and souls against the enemy for a simple and intelligible cause. His soldiers would fight for their fathers' hills.

As for hatred, Giap had no difficulty finding the necessary source of it in his heart: his wife, arrested and sentenced to hard labor for life by Hanoï court-martial, had died in a French prison because like him she had fought for her country's independence. Did he once say, "Every minute, hundreds of thousands of men die all over the world. The life and death of a hundred, a thousand, tens of thousands of men, even if they are fellow countrymen, really amount to very little"? He denied it indignantly when I asked him. Yet that cruel remark is not out of place in his mouth, and it seems to me that in his place I would have shouted it at the top of my voice to convince my own brothers that victory could be bought only at that price. The debonair and sometimes humorous face which I saw in places still haunted by the ghosts of King John and his marshals, I could comprehend in the light of the events which had shaped it under the influence of suffering and the desire for vengeance.

That broad face consumed by intelligence, that high, powerful brow framed in a stiff, black mane, were stamped with determination. Irony, kindness, cunning and an indomitable strength were revealed in it one after the other. If, in that fight which Comrade President Ho Chi Minh described to David Schoenbrun, at Fontainebleau, on September 11, 1946, Navarre had an imposing mass of forces at his disposal, Giap was the wild beast getting ready to leap upon him. "It will be a war between a tiger and an elephant. If ever the tiger stops, the elephant will pierce him with his tusks. Only the tiger doesn't stop. He lurks in the jungle by day and emerges only at night. He will leap onto the elephant and rip his back to shreds before disappearing again into the shadows, and the elephant will die from exhaustion and loss of blood." Navarre should have kept a photograph of Giap before him at all times in his study, as Montgomery kept a photograph of Rommel before him during the Egyptian campaign. Perhaps he thought that this would have been paying too much honor to a man who had not attended courses in military strategy and to whom the title of general was given only in quotation marks. Mao Tse-tung was not a professional soldier either, but in all the arts there are cases of late development.

At this period, Giap was no longer at the stage of improvisation. Though he was an amateur who had learned from his very reverses, he had succeeded in forging a battle corps which no longer consisted of a few guerrilla bands, but of six infantry divisions, each comprising three regiments, a heavy division of artillery and engineers, and transport and antiaircraft reserves. How could such a machine fail to attract damaging blows if it imitated European armies? Navarre was probably thinking of that risk when, referring to the Vietminh, he told Salan, "Then it's done for." Yes, if Giap put his trucks and gun batteries on the roads in vulnerable convoys, he was done for. But Navarre was mistaken when he imagined that the former history master could fall into that trap. The tiger Giap moved forward only step by step, never taking his eyes off the elephant he wanted to destroy, testing the ground and never putting his full weight on it unless he felt it could bear it.

Giap had learned all the details of "Operation Castor" with a mixture of fear and joy. Far from despising Navarre and Cogny, he did not assume they would act carelessly, and he asked himself whether this enterprise was intended to parry the initial movement of the 316th Division toward the northwest or whether it formed part of a plan to bar his way to Laos.

In fact, he feared neither of these hypotheses. The 316th Division would reach its objective in spite of the six battalions which Navarre had just dropped into the basin, but it would have to double its precautions to avoid discovery and attack by the fighters and bombers that could be based at Dienbienphu, a few minutes' flight from its zone of deployment. On the other hand, if Navarre intended to install himself there . . . Giap's staff officers agreed with their chief's conclusion: Navarre was caught.

November 23, 1953

At Dienbienphu, the great circus was continuing, dropping fakir's pillows, drums of gas, crates of ammunition, food and frozen wine, packets of shells and material of all sorts which fell like huge hailstones on the outskirts of the little town, where the parachutes sometimes lodged in the trees and on the straw roofs. Some Morane 500's were already taking off from the airstrip to fly over the approaches to the basin and keep an eye on the reconnaissance parties which were searching the villages one by one and climbing the lower slopes in search of Viets who had disappeared into the hills and who were often confused with the frightened inhabitants of the valley.

The day before, chaplains had celebrated Mass on improvised altars, for it had been Sunday. The brushwood in front of the first strong points was being burnt, and the smell of the smoke spread by the wind filled the whole camp. Trees were being chopped down and cut up to make beams and supports.

From the gaping rear of a Packet, a huge mass suddenly fell. Twenty-one multicolored parachutes, tied to one another, burst open above it, like a majestic flower. While a cheer rose toward it, the new bulldozer swayed at the end of its stalk and landed gently in the rice field, upright on its tracks. The failure of the first drop had probably been due to an error in the conversion of American measures of weight. This time, the machine rested on a metal platform widened by a guard of planks which struck out like arms and prevented it from tipping over. Lead weights had lowered its center of gravity. Some men went up to it, touched it and shook their heads. "This one," somebody said, "is sure to stay here."

Paratroopers were trotting about on little Thai horses which had been taken out of their stalls. With submachine guns slung in front of their chests like iron handlebars, and sitting astride crude scooters with tiny wheels, messengers sped backward and forward along the runways. Near Gilles's pennant stuck in front of a hut, among the radio aerials, children were gazing enviously at these noisy toys, but the women's faces showed a fear which grew with every day that passed. Many men were still wandering in the mountains, not knowing where to go. Other toys would rain down, more formidable than these, since the troops of the Expeditionary Corps looked as if they were settling down for a long time. Who was going to pay for the fruit trees which were being cut down? Who was going to gather the harvest? Who was going to prevent the crops still standing from being laid waste? Who was going to pay compensation for the buffaloes that had been killed?

Bigeard and Bréchignac were already bored. The battle was over and they would have to wait months for another, if indeed one ever materialized. The women automatically started husking the rice with their pounders again, and their gestures took on a sublime, derisive significance. The houses were still standing on their piles, between which poultry, pigs and buffaloes sheltered; the families lived above, in a big room with a floor of crudely joined branches covered with matting, and with walls made of bamboo and broad plaited leaves. Extending over a balcony on which the inhabitants slept on summer nights, a roof of grass covered each house with its cross-shaped thatch.

At Saigon, in the summary of Paris press reports supplied by his aide-de-camp, Navarre read the huge headline which had appeared in *France-Soir;* "TONKIN PARATROOPS RAIN DOWN ON DIENBIENPHU." We may imagine Navarre's lips tightening, for spread across the first two columns, in heavy type, was Cogny's declaration: "This is not a raid as at Lang Son, but the beginning of an offensive." Why had Cogny made any declaration at all, and who had given him permission?

For his part, Navarre had kept silent, and nobody on his staff had spoken. It was impossible to telephone from Saigon to Tonkin, at least for anybody who was not a soldier, but the journalists knew where to find Cogny. Possibly informed by him, the special correspondent of *France-Soir* must have gone up to Hanoï and cabled from there. With his secretive character, Navarre did not like these comments on an operation which had scarcely begun and which must have surprised the government as much as the enemy. His dispatch to the Secretary of State for Relations with the Associated States had been sufficient, and the government alone was entitled to give the news what importance it thought fit. To Navarre's mind, Cogny had already adroitly taken the credit for Lang Son for himself. What was the meaning of this logrolling, since it was not Cogny who had decided on Dienbienphu, but the Commander in Chief? The expression "the beginning of an offensive" risked alarming public opinion and the government. Why, indeed, was Cogny interfering? Strategic judgments were none of his business. As far as he was concerned, if Navarre had been able to conduct the war without even telling the journalists what he was doing, he would have done just that. Everything that was said enlightened the enemy and helped him, whereas the French were obliged to guess at his reactions to even the most obvious facts.

November 25, 1953

At about 11:30 that day at Dienbienphu, the first Dakota landed on the airstrip. The engineers were a week ahead of schedule, and transport planes would now be able to land material which was too fragile to be dropped by parachute. A radio beam which had been in service since the day before guided the pilots down through the clouds. It would now be possible to take wounded and paratroops back to Hanoï, and above all the battalions of Gilles's group could be relieved by other, less valuable units. Paratroopers searched the surrounding area and brought in, head down under the threat of submachine guns, men who had tried to escape into the mountains.

Being under suspicion, they were locked up. Intelligence officers interrogated them in an attempt to find out where the battalions surprised by the arrival of the paratroops had taken refuge. The Meos had returned to collect the poultry, cattle and few possessions which they had left behind in their hurried flight.

About fifteen miles up on the heights, among a few families harvesting near a pass, I later found a former guerrilla of that time. Sitting at the foot of his rifle, which he held with its barrel in the air and its butt on the ground, he seemed to be guarding the women dressed in cotton tunics with colored lapels who were threshing the rice and chattering away; the less poverty-stricken among them wore crescent-shaped earrings and silver necklaces. His name was Vu doa Dinh. His weapon, which was more a harquebus than a rifle and had no sights, dwarfed his pygmy body. He had been twenty-six in 1953. Now his son, refusing to go down to work in the fields, went hunting too, equipped as he was like an ancient warrior, with a powderhorn at his belt and a haversack stuffed with shot. Each kept his primers in the case of an old ball cartridge hung from the neck. Both hid their hair under a cap with ear flaps, while the women's heads, which were shaven except for a single lock at the top of the skull, were half-concealed under turbans. Cunning lit up his worn Mongolian face, and his tiny black eyes moved incessantly from my face to the countryside, which they scanned for some sign of game—game which could be killed at short range only, the wild bulls at a distance of ten paces, the deer at a distance of twenty-five.

Together we made our way on foot to a nearby hamlet lodged between some rocks near a stream, and a smoke-filled straw hut with a beaten-earth floor. Among the crude tools used to manufacture weapons, an old army mug lay on a table, and I managed to make out, above a date which had been obliterated, an inscription carved into the metal with a knife: "Louise chérie." There was an old frying pan, which had been transformed into a guitar; some strips of parachute material were drying, nine years later, with the wash; and some children from whom I drew back in fright were playing skittles with old 60-mm. mortar shells. Crouching like an animal, an old woman was stuffing tubers into a sack. From the bamboo beams of the roof hung some sides of bacon and a plucked kite a hunter had just shot.

It was here that Vu doa Din had returned to collect his pigs and his brightly feathered poultry when a dozen partisans in the pay of the French had forced him to accompany them to Dienbienphu, where he found three men and three women from the neighboring tribes who had been put to work as he was. He thought that he had lost his family, his mountains and his forest forever, and his heart was filled with hatred and despair. . . .

In the old district of Dienbienphu, the children plucked up their courage, went up to the soldiers who were digging holes near the houses and asked them for chocolate. They did not know that the houses themselves would end up crashing to the ground like the trees, and that they would go off, clinging to their mothers' skirts or carried on their backs, to take refuge miles away in order to make room for the men of war.

The bivouacs were installed, and at night the men slept in scores of little tents. In the daytime this huge camp took on a gay picnic appearance. The men bathed in the green waters of the Nam Youm, the shallow river flowing peacefully between its ocher banks, and washed their clothes in it, spreading them out to dry on the barbed wire. They heated their rations in borrowed pans, on hearths hollowed out of the earth.

The white and khaki corollas of the parachutes floated down from the Dakotas, and, when the load landed, lay on the ground, where the wind suddenly filled them again before blowing them over. Teams of men unfastened the packages from the parachutes and carried them to the growing stocks. Each package had taken the store men ten minutes and fifty feet of rope to tie up.

Guns boomed. The tubes of the heavy mortars rang out like bells for a moment following the firing of the shells, whose destination was checked by the Moranes buzzing above the slopes.

At Hanoï, General Cogny, his forehead furrowed, was listening to his chief Intelligence officer, Major Levain, explaining the enemy's situation. Levain was a smart, meticulous, level-headed officer, who based his predictions on reliable information only. What he had to say struck him as exceptionally grave, and he accordingly refrained from any comment. During the night, his listening posts had intercepted the orders Giap had issued to the command posts of the 308th, 312th and 351st Divisions.

According to his calculations, the 316th Division, which was already on its way, would reach Dienbienphu about December 6, the 308th about the twenty-fourth, the 351st Heavy Division about the twenty-sixth, and finally the 312th about the twenty-eighth. In Levain's opinion, the destination of these big units, which were being followed night and day, was not a certainty but an extremely serious probability. Cogny immediately sent Navarre a dispatch which would be received at Saigon with a certain skepticism. Cogny's team was accused of adopting a spurious pessimism in order to exaggerate the importance of Tonkin and to warn Navarre's team not to infringe upon its jurisdiction. The question of cross-checking the information was raised. A great many listening posts under the direction of a high-ranking Intelligence officer constantly intercepted the orders of the Vietminh battle corps and transmitted them to Saigon and Hanoï, where they were decoded. Now the Vietminh used a political code, an operational code and a supplies code. The French Command possessed the supplies code and could therefore immediately decipher orders concerning enemy personnel and material. But if Cogny's staff deciphered only what its own listening posts picked up, the scope of Navarre's staff extended to all the listening posts in

Indochina. Navarre concluded as a consequence that, however well informed he might be, Cogny was capable of committing certain errors of interpretation and synthesis. Never would Navarre, to whom obtaining and exploiting information were practically second nature, agree to place any reliance on the diagnosis of others. Except when confronted with undeniable evidence, he would never trust anybody but his own services and, in the last resort, himself. He would not even condescend to question the head of Military Intelligence in Tonkin.

A Vietminh officer who came over to the French side much later would report: "The paratroop operation at Dienbienphu was a pleasant surprise for our command. The first movement of the 316th Division was aimed at getting the French Command to reduce its concentration in the delta and to scatter its forces. It was the Dienbienphu action which led to the decision to send fresh divisions toward the northwest."

On his return to Paris, Rear Admiral Cabanier gave a report on his mission to the President of the Republic and the Prime Minister. The name of Dienbienphu had not yet assumed any great importance in the sumptuous rooms of the Élysée and Matignon. The admiral could only describe the optimism displayed by the High Command of the Expeditionary Corps, which M. Vincent Auriol, M. Joseph Laniel and General Ely noted with cautious satisfaction. The admiral had not met M. Jacquet in the course of his journey, and nobody, not even General Navarre, had told M. Jacquet that the admiral had been sent by Paris. M. Jacquet would not discover this until three weeks later, and it was from me that he would learn or pretend to learn, ten years later, the object of the admiral's mission, of which the Chiefs of Staff, except for General Ely, would never be informed.

M. Jacquet's technical adviser, who had left the minister's briefcase in the luggage rack of the cabin of the Constellation when it landed at Karachi, looked for it in vain when the aircraft took off. It had disappeared. At Beirut, M. Jacquet asked the chargé d'affaires to open an inquiry. The briefcase would not be found until three months later, by the French Embassy in London. Empty.

November 28, 1953

Cogny became suddenly aware of the extent of the threat which was building up. From his delta fortress, he could launch raids, spread disorder in the enemy's rear and lines of communication, make contact with part of the battle corps and possibly force it to turn back. From its bases around Hanoï or Haiphong, the Air Force could go into action en masse. Its fighters could carry out two or three bombing and machine-gun attacks every day on the marching columns.

Navarre disagreed with Cogny, who had returned two days earlier to Dienbienphu. He considered, along with Berteil, that it was not divisions which were going upcountry, but simply elements of those divisions, that it might even be a matter of fake orders and that no conclusions could be drawn for the moment. He wanted to keep the whole of his offensive potential intact so as to have it ready when the time came. Some officers in his entourage even rejoiced openly at the situation. They maintained that the Air Force would crush the divisions on the move and that their route would be cut so often as to be rendered impracticable.

Finally, General Navarre declared that the capabilities of movement and subsistence of the Vietminh divisions seemed to him to have been overestimated. Giap, he had been assured by General Salan, did not have the means to maintain four divisions so long and so far away from their natural bases. Nobody contradicted him; this judgment was accepted by everyone as dogma.

Nobody believed in the strategic mobility and logistics of the Vietminh. Nobody, or scarcely anybody, in the French Army had enough imagination to guess at the enemy's cunning and wisdom. Salan, who had just quit the post of Commander in Chief of the Expeditionary Corps, still regarded Giap as a noncommissioned officer learning to handle regiments, and thought him more formidable because of what he had in his hands than because of any effects he could achieve with it. Navarre did not know his adversary and tried to master his strategy and tactics by studying Intelligence reports and listening to his regional commanders. His only worry was Chinese aid, whose strategic consequences he mistakenly exaggerated, just as he was mistaken in attributing his recent minor successes to his own genius.

And yet, four months after the signature of the Korean armistice, it was necessary for the proper execution of the Navarre Plan that Chinese aid should not increase. After all, if Chinese aid thwarted the plans of the French High Command, the traditional military game would be completely spoiled. If Chinese planes and tanks appeared against French planes and tanks, the High Command could claim that it had been betrayed. But as Navarre was not sure of the enemy's good intentions, he wagered—that is the word he used—that Chinese aid would remain what it was. In every general there is a poker player; the stake is paid in blood.

Why did Berteil, who was no fool, fail to draw his Commander in Chief's attention to the rising curve of Chinese aid to the Vietminh? Why should that curve suddenly flatten out when everything was calculated to make it rise? Moreover, the French High Command knew that the Vietminh campaign of the autumn of 1952 comprised a range of one hundred miles, a duration of two months and a fighting force of thirty thousand men; and the campaign of the spring of 1953 a range of two hundred miles, the same duration, and a fighting force of forty thousand men. A mere corporal could have deduced that the coming campaign would go further and bring greater forces into play.

On most of the staffs of the Expeditionary Corps, the concentration of four Vietminh divisions was also regarded as a utopian project. To keep fifty thousand combat troops alive, fifty thousand coolies would have to carry rice incessantly, material and ammunition would have to be brought up along communication lines where the convoys would be surprised and destroyed by the Air Force. Even supposing that such an effort were possible, it could not, by its very size and volume, continue for more than a fairly limited period of time. The base at Dienbienphu would be exposed to the risk of a general attack, but that attack could not last more than a week on account of the strain it would impose on the logistic rhythm, which would increase at a rate the porters could not maintain. As for the Air Force, it would crush any heavy support, which would have to be brought up unprotected.

There seemed to be no flaw in this reasoning. For so far that was indeed how the army of the Vietminh had been engaged. It moved on foot, and if the distance between Hanoï and Dienbienphu was about two hundred miles in a straight line, it was three hundred miles by the mountain roads and at least four hundred from the divisional bases to Dienbienphu. It was also reasonable to suppose that the enemy units would not be in a state of fighting fitness when they arrived.

November 29, 1953

It was the first Sunday in Advent. In the morning the chaplains of the Expeditionary Corps had read the words of the Introit: *"Deus meus, in te confido, non erubescam neque irrideant me inimici mei. Lord, I put* my trust in Thee; may I not be ashamed and may my enemies not mock me." And the words of St. Paul to the Romans in the Epistle: *"Hora est jam nos de somno surgere.* It is time for us to awaken." In the rococo cathedral of Hanoï, a pathetic building with its bright red and gold chancel and its eagerness to look like a miniature plaster Notre-Dame de Paris, the sun beat down on the stained-glass windows and the children's wooden soles clattered across the floor. As usual, the priests had read the Gospel in both French and Vietnamese.

The fine weather was still holding. At Dienbienphu, as at Hanoï, it was hot. At 1345, a Command Dakota landed. Navarre got out with Cogny. Both of them decorated the paratroopers who had distinguished themselves during "Operation Castor" with a *Croix de guerre,* some of them posthumously.

In the plane, Navarre had reminded Cogny that somebody had to be found to take Gilles's place.

"Who is your candidate?" he asked Cogny.

"There's a man I'd like to suggest—"

"Perhaps we've both got the same man in mind," said Navarre. "Let's see."

"Vanuxem isn't inspiring enough. I'm thinking of Castries. A cavalry-man would be ideal at Dienbienphu, where the situation will be mobile. We need somebody who can harry and harass the Viets."

"He's my choice also," said Navarre. "You can appoint him whenever you like."

"I would rather you told him yourself," said Cogny.

Gilles expressed satisfaction at the news. First of all, because it meant he could get away. To tell the truth, Gilles would never have picked Castries, a cavalryman, for a situation such as this, but rather Colonel Vanuxem, another of de Lattre's marshals, who had acquired a consid-erable reputation as the commander of a mobile group but who was thought to be very uneconomical with his troops. Castries, who had just come from the Staff College with Vanuxem, had made good use of his armor in the delta and knew the sort of war to be waged there.

"A cavalryman," said Cogny, indicating with his stick the imposing dimensions of the basin as if asking for approval. "He'll be able to gallop around here." Gilles smiled, thinking that he was joking. Gallop around? With what and how? Castries would have just enough room to slip into the jungle, and the battalions of paratroops were going to fly back with Gilles.

Cogny had another reason to be pleased at seeing Castries shipped off to Dienbienphu. He did not get along well with the colonel, who had just arrived from Amiens to take command of the southern zone of the delta and who had insisted on being received with ten white-gloved motorcyclists and a solemn Mass. Castries never missed a chance of hinting to his new chief that he was in the way. His posting to Dienbienphu would solve everything. In point of fact, it would be Vanuxem who would take Castries's place, for the colonel would not hold out for long before the wild beast.

As for Navarre, he had thought of Castries because he knew him. He had had him under his command as a sergeant when he had been a lieutenant, as a lieutenant when he had been a captain in the 16th Saint-Germain Dragoons, and later as a major in the First Army, when Navarre had been in command of the 3rd Moroccan Spahis, the regiment in which all the officers and men wore the famous red scarf which had aroused de Lattre's bitter sarcasm. In this country where he was surrounded by people he distrusted, Navarre clung to all the men on whom he thought he could rely.

According to Navarre, who knew him well, Castries was a remarkable officer, open to criticism, much criticized, often abused, but an admirable cavalryman with an instinctive feeling for the terrain. Under Napoleon, he would have been Lassalle, the best avant-garde general in the Grand Army. And it was a cavalryman that was needed here—Navarre no longer had any doubt about that, now that he was lurching along the dusty tracks of the valley in a jeep driven by Gilles. These stretches would have to be beaten down by hard riding to keep the approaches clear. A sort of mental intoxication gradually took hold of him. He breathed in the warm air, scarcely blinking his eyes in the light, which he did not shut out with dark glasses except when he was in mufti. In jumping from one end of the basin to the other and sweeping the crests, Castries, who had been the leader of his vanguard in the Karlsruhe affair, would do wonders with the armored cars they would bring here in dismantled parts. As for the high crests which shut in the horizon on all sides, Navarre had his Air Force to pound them. And if the Viets ventured onto this drill ground of Dienbienphu, Castries would sweep it with the fire of his guns and automatic weapons. The trouble with Indochina, perhaps, was that it had never allowed the cavalry to show what they were capable of; now here was he, Navarre, and Castries, the man of his choice.

How could he have failed to be sure of victory? At 1650, the Dakota took off with the generals and their entourage. Navarre withdrew into a happy silence. The chimeras of Dienbienphu carried him off on their backs at a gallop.

November 30, 1953

At Thaï Binh, at the mouth of the Red River, which Navarre had passed through two months earlier, the joy of seeing Castries again transformed the Commander in Chief. At the foot of the Beaver where Castries stood saluting him, Navarre's face lit up at being reunited with a faithful follower; he radiated happiness, confidence, almost humor. Castries's personality had the gift of putting him in a state of grace beneath the fascinated gaze of Cogny, whose shorts, paratrooper's boots and thick mountain stick suddenly gave him an awkward look. This time, it was a great promotion Navarre had brought his former subordinate: command of Dienbienphu. Castries displayed no exorbitant pleasure. Like Vanuxem, he had been promised his brigadier's stars in the spring. Wasn't he about to be landed in a shit hole?

"If you're thinking of establishing an entrenched camp," he told Navarre, "that isn't my line. I'd rather you picked somebody else."

"Gilles would like to have another Na San," replied Navarre. "I don't agree with him. Dienbienphu must become an offensive base. That's why I've picked you."

In order to convince him, Cogny put in, "We need a mountain cavalryman out there. You will be that cavalryman, and roam the wide-open spaces of the highlands."

With a red forage cap on his head, around his neck the scarlet scarf of the 3rd Spahis which reminded Navarre of a lucky period, a glittering swagger stick in his hand, and followed everywhere by his Moroccan batman, Colonel Christian Marie Ferdinand de la Croix de Castries, Commander of the Legion of Honor, with sixteen mentions in dispatches, typified the aristocratic officer whose character, name, war record and legend could lead, despite all obstacles, to the highest posts in the army. The true soldier must be a nobleman and a cavalryman. Castries had an ancestor who was a marshal of France and Minister of the Marine under Louis XV, and another who was a companion of Lafayette, a lieutenant general and a peer of France. Altogether, his ancestors included one marshal, one admiral, four lieutenant governors, five Knights of the Holy Ghost, and eight lieutenant generals, whose portraits are probably to be found in the barony of Castries, purchased in 1495 in the vicinity of Montpellier.

Sharpened by an aquiline nose, the eyelids drooping heavily under bushy black eyebrows, his thoughtful, rather melancholy El Greco face tapered away into a little chin and a pretty mouth. The body was thin, supple, wiry; the voice somewhat thick, and curiously shrill on the telephone. A remarkable horseman, he had been world champion for the high jump in 1933 with Vol-au-Vent, and for the long jump, two years later, with Tenace. His file was stuffed with youthful indiscretions and gambling debts. A horse to ride, an enemy to kill, a woman in his bed—that could have been his motto. An attractive motto, if you didn't look at it too closely. He was a man of another age whom wars, women and horses linked to our own. De Lattre liked him because he had guts, a name and an air, and he took him off to Indochina with his team. Under the red forage cap with the five gold bands, it was impossible to imagine that there was nothing. He was a hero and a leader. He had his own legend. He ate glass, and excited American women kissed him on the lips in night clubs. He was recognized as possessing the simplicity of a great lord. When dealing with serious matters he often assumed a flippant air, whereas he was excessively serious about less important matters. This sort of irony, not to say cynicism, often puzzled those who did not know him. What kind of a man was he, really? His coat of arms, blue with a cross of gold, decorated the huge organ which the Castries family had presented to Albi Cathedral.

His appointment to command of the Dienbienphu base did not take Castries entirely by surprise. It was Navarre who had asked him to return to Indochina just after he had won another cup for riding at Saumur. He raised no further objections, since Cogny's plan was to wage a defensive-offensive battle in the triangle of Dienbienphu–Laï Chau–Tuan Giao, based on Dienbienphu. What opinion could he have of the rest of the directive, of which he was given a copy, without having the terrain before him? He would study all that as soon as he took up his command. But without knowing the region as he knew the delta, he was puzzled at the idea of a mobile battle in the mountainous triangle described by Cogny, which was fifty miles along its base and forty miles high, and crossed only by poor, infrequent tracks, a few mule trails and one road, the paved Route 41, which was known to be held by the enemy along its whole length. It seemed obvious that only very light units would have any real scope for maneuver.

At Na San, where the terrain was no better, the French forces had been able to maneuver. Gilles had elbowed his way around. Twice a group of two paratroop battalions had thrust southeast, near Moc Chau, and west as far as Ta Kho. Another time, a battalion had gone to Son La and had reached the outskirts of Ta Bu. But the High Command forgot that the Expeditionary Corps was far from being composed of nothing but champions.

December 3, 1953

Navarre issued the Personal and Secret Instructions for the Conduct of Operation No. 949, on which he had been working since his return from Saigon and which the Air Command had tried in vain to get annulled. These instructions were to weigh heavily upon the destiny of Indochina and the Expeditionary Corps.

In the very first paragraph, after the usual banalities and an explanation of the situation, Navarre suddenly expressed his decision to accept battle in the northwest, centering his defenses on the base of Dienbienphu, which was to be held at all costs. Accept battle when one of the main pillars of the Navarre Plan was based on the necessity of avoiding it until the Expeditionary Corps had recovered its strength and vigor—in other words, for another year? Admittedly, Navarre had said and written, the previous July, that it was a general battle he wanted to avoid, while here he was referring simply to a battle in the northwest. But if anybody could misinterpret these instructions, it was certainly not Navarre himself, who was preparing to launch an offensive in the south—"Operation Atlante"—and had decided to confront Giap at Dienbienphu when there was no compulsion upon him to do so, and he had known since November 20 that he would not receive the reinforcements he had asked for. Could he imagine for a moment that such a risk was anything but disproportionate? For a man as cold and cautious as Navarre to allow himself to be drawn toward so great a hazard, it was obvious that the idea of waging battle there had come to him the day he had visited Dienbienphu, and that nobody on his staff had warned him against such a decision or even pointed to the consequences. However little he was given to feeling impulses of the heart or the imagination, he had found himself possessed of the conviction, shared if not inspired by his entourage, that the Vietminh divisions would be unable to move freely about in those mountains and that his grip on the base would never be chal-

lenged. At Dienbienphu he had been given a sudden, dazzling illumina-
tion which swept aside all objections. He knew where the truth lay.

It would be naïve to believe even for a moment that Cogny was in any
way responsible for Navarre's decision. The firm dislike which the two
men already instinctively felt for each other would be enough in itself to
exclude the possibility of any intervention by Cogny. If, by any chance,
Cogny claimed responsibility for Dienbienphu, Navarre would quickly
and rightly take it away from him; victories are shared, but nobody ever
claims his share in a defeat, and Navarre knew that in the case of defeat
he alone would be accused. He insisted on assuming full responsibility in
order to be able to impose his will more easily. In fact, Navarre had been
attracted as much by the proportions of a valley in which the French
armor could crush anybody who ventured into it as by the remoteness
of the high crests which would force enemy artillery to take up position
on the slopes. The same would be true of any antiaircraft guns which
tried to close the air space above the landing strip. In the opinion of all
his gunners, the enemy batteries would be exposed to view from observation posts in the basin during their installation or when in action.
They would promptly be muzzled by fire from the French counterbatteries and by the French bombers.

It is clear that all the gunners were convinced of what they told
Navarre. Cogny himself was a gunner. If he raised the slightest objection
to Dienbienphu as an entrenched camp, it could not be based on a threat
from the enemy artillery. Here, with the Vietminh's inability to maintain
its divisions for long far from their bases, we touch upon the very doctrine of the Expeditionary Corps. This was why Navarre was engaging
himself. This was how he came to build his operations simply on hypotheses from which he drew conclusions that assumed the force of dogmas:
the landing strip would always be available, and if an attack on Dienbienphu took place, it would last only long enough for the enemy to
suffer a reverse. For the last three days, however, the valley of Dienbienphu had been buried under a fog which lifted only in the late
morning, and the French had not yet found a means of continuing to
drop supplies when visibility was zero. As for landing planes at Dienbienphu, that was out of the question with no landing aids on the spot.

Yet it was a brilliant success that Navarre was preparing. Nobody has
ever yet seen a general pick a terrain on which to join battle without
thinking, at least for a moment, that he might not defeat the enemy there.
Cogny expected two enemy divisions at Dienbienphu at the end of the

month, but Navarre suspected Cogny of painting too dark a picture of things and he refused to join in what he considered a guessing game. He believed that he would be faced with only one division, though admittedly considerably reinforced; in other words, about a dozen battalions with a few heavy guns. That was nothing to be alarmed about. Five months earlier, when he had taken over his new command, Navarre had declared, "Victory is a woman who gives herself only to those who know how to take her." That day, the protection of Laos was suddenly relegated to the background and served to camouflage the real reason for Dienbienphu: like all the staffs of the Expeditionary Corps, Navarre believed that he had found an ideal opportunity to obtain a cheap victory over the Viets.

Giap's staff officers, on their side, came to the same conclusions as Navarre: it was essential to join battle at Dienbienphu. But how could they persuade the enemy to do so? They all knew the country only too well; they suffered too much themselves from the obstacles represented by the mountains, the jungle and the lack of proper lines of communication to doubt whether the Expeditionary Corps could even feel comfortable there. In that case, the experience of Na San would come in useful; it would be enough to bring the battle corps on to the site and maintain it. When the question was put to him, the director general of supplies replied unhesitatingly that it would be difficult but the task was not beyond him. The whole people would have to be mobilized and an appeal made to the mass will. Thirty, forty and, if necessary, fifty thousand porters, men and women; thousands of horses, each of them equivalent to four porters; hundreds of sampans which would go up or down rivers with tons of food and supplies; trucks to pull the guns; and a huge number of Peugeot bicycles bought years before in the shops of Hanoï, which had only to be converted to be capable of carrying five hundred pounds each, would move the tons of rice and munitions required over their designated routes.

For so grave a decision, a meeting of the Central Committee of the Party would fix the conduct of the war along a few lines which would establish the policy of the country and the revolution. Giap and his aides went to government headquarters, where they were welcomed by Comrade President Ho Chi Minh, with his bright eyes, his body lost in black cotton pajamas, and his mischievous, determined goatee; the slim, smart Comrade Vice President Pham van Dong, whose voice could assume the quality of a cello; and Comrade Political Commissar Truong

Chinh, in his severe reseda-green clothes. Comrade Giap explained the situation and the various possibilities: the movement of the 316th Division had already led to the scattering of the Expeditionary Corps's units; it was now a matter of deciding on future operations. A threat to Dienbienphu would oblige Navarre to reinforce the garrison, which could then be destroyed. After a minute study of all the details, the Comrade Commander in Chief was instructed to take the necessary measures.

December 4, 1953

The writer who is given access, forty years from now, to the secret archives of the state in order to write the history of the Battle of Dienbienphu will be forced to pause at this day on which Navarre pretended to receive the warning the government had sent him.

Yet the letter sent by the Permanent Secretary General of the Committee for National Defense to M. Marc Jacquet, who himself had been instructed to acquaint Saigon with the decisions taken at the committee meeting of November 13, had been locked for the past two weeks in the Commander in Chief's safe. One wonders therefore why Navarre wanted to appear dumfounded by the contents of a document Admiral Cabanier had already brought him and which had now arrived simply through the normal channels.

Didn't he believe Admiral Cabanier, who had prepared him for this shock, on November 20? Didn't he even suspect what the admiral might have to say to him when he seemed to want to spare him the trouble of coming up to Hanoï? Didn't he prefer to remain at liberty to launch the operation he had decided on, by refusing to submit to any pressure? Did he only now realize the extent of the blame he was incurring and the presumption he had shown? He had such control over his emotions that the consternation he reveals on that December 4 in his memoirs seems better fitted to history than to reality; he could not have been surprised since he already knew. But he was the only one who did know. A secretive man, he had concealed from his entourage the real reason for Admiral Cabanier's journey. His reactions must therefore be regarded as purely external.

Besides, no historian could believe that a decision of such importance, expected by Navarre for months, could have been sent through ordinary channels. The price of a first-class return ticket for a messenger was nothing in comparison with the enormous saving it was bound to effect in money, blood and tears. The fact that M. Jacquet knew nothing about it—assuming that this was a fact—makes no difference. M. Jacquet was only theoretically responsible for the conduct of the war. He understood nothing and did nothing about it. But out of respect for the truth it must be stated that certain men of the Fourth Republic understood that Navarre had to be informed as quickly as possible of a decision which should have prevented the Dienbienphu adventure.

Navarre's first reaction seemed a healthy one: he was tempted to resign. One wonders why he did not have that reaction on November 20. Possibly he drew up the text of the dispatch he was going to send to the Prime Minister, crossed it out, then tore it up. Did he communicate it to his chief of staff, the plump, affable little General Gambiez? Did he hear from his lips that if he resigned, he would be replaced by someone docile, and that the problem would be no nearer solution? Did the feeling that he had just seized hold of victory and would soon be able to hurl that beautiful prey contemptuously onto the table of the astounded committee help him to overcome his initial impulse?

Why, then, confronted with such a situation, had he not tendered his resignation on November 20, when Admiral Cabanier had confirmed the government's repudiation? This is the question Navarre asks himself in his book, but under the date of December 4. He replies with a few empty phrases. What is obvious is that men of character like Lyautey or de Lattre would not have troubled with so many worthy scruples and would have said so straight out, whereas Navarre merely compromised. A brilliant chief of staff, he gave way to those whom circumstances placed above him; an excellent quality in a subordinate, but a major weakness in a leader, who must never yield and still less feed on the hopes and illusions of a political game.

Navarre also makes an admission whose importance escaped and condemns him. "However, I would probably have tendered my resignation if the real situation had been clearly revealed to me before the decisive battle had been engaged"—an admission which proves that at the time he had no idea of the dangers to which he was exposing the Expeditionary Corps. It is to be feared that even in that event General Navarre would have found some other good excuse to give history for having accepted the post of Commander in Chief, and would have recalled yet again Marshal Juin's remark: "Somebody must take on the job." Remarks of that sort have far-reaching effects. Somewhere else, Navarre adds that he did not come up against a wall but against an "eiderdown." Other men would have ripped that eiderdown open with their swords and emptied it of its feathers.

In any case, Navarre could still have cabled Paris that he was canceling his instructions, which were dated only the day before, in order to make the government face up to its responsibilities. He merely wired, as if Admiral Cabanier had never been to Saigon: "I shall add this refusal to the already lengthy list of makeshift solutions which have been forced upon me and which reduce my operational potential." In his book he adds that he was sharply criticized for the tone of this cable, and he concludes his disillusioned reflections with this remark: "This correspondence produced no concrete results." But what could a commander in chief who had to make serious and urgent decisions expect from correspondence? How could he fail to understand that the polite, deferential and vain process of official formulas was no longer valid, that he could no longer be a docile subordinate, but a man who carried the responsibility of the blood and honor of a whole army, and that if he was right he must jump into the plane for Paris, burst into the gilded drawing rooms of the Élysée and Matignon and insist on clear instructions! As a matter of fact, he was far too sure of victory.

December 5, 1953

Covering twenty miles by day, or fifty by night, the Vietminh divisions were advancing rapidly toward Dienbienphu, marching along the sides of the roads. Nothing distinguished the officers from the troops. In any case, there were no officers but simply men to whom certain functions had been given: regiment, battalion, company or battery commanders, section or platoon leaders. If they proved inadequate to their task, a warning was given them. There was no second warning. Nobody had any insignia of rank, as in the French Army, since ranks did not exist. In the event of a second offense, the regiment commander would be told that he was relieved of his post, the platoon leader that he was a private. Usually, self-criticism was sufficient to reveal faults and errors. In the People's Army a man admitted his failings even before they appeared.

Each soldier carried his weapon, sometimes a nonrecoil gun or a mortar tripod, a bag, a thirty-pound bundle of rice slung over one shoulder, his individual shovel, water bottle and a little salt in a bamboo tube. He marched from dawn to sunset, or vice versa, with ten minutes' rest every hour. At night the distance covered was exhausting. On arrival, he dug trenches in which to take shelter and sleep, after washing his feet in a bowl of hot salt water. Not all the soldiers had footwear; many of them, like the porters, had only sandals cut out of tires, which sometimes hurt them. To drive away sleep and fatigue, they sang old songs devoid of the slightest suggestion of smuttiness. If it rained, they naturally chose the rain song with its refrain:

> It is raining, our clothes are wet,
> But not our hearts.

If they met or passed a column of women porters, there would be an explosion of gaiety. The two parties would call out to each other, improvise verses and make jokes. Girls would shout, "Is my husband with you?"; point to certain soldiers, exclaiming joyfully, "There he is!"; and then, shamming vexation, go off sadly to the accompaniment of laughter. When two such columns halted together, the river bathing, the bivouacs and the nocturnal encounters were characterized by an astonishing innocence. It was like an outing of seminarists meeting a party of young nuns. Their church was a total devotion, body and soul, to the fatherland, the sole object of love. In the People's Army, the soldiers' language, commonplace by nature and not given to sublimating the reasons for fighting, resembled that of children playing at war; the only sentiments expressed in it were a flawless discipline and a boyish fervor. If every group of porters wanted to deserve the roll of honor, every soldier's ambition was to sacrifice himself. One begins by smiling, but ends up impressed by the results of this indoctrination.

Inside each unit, the men were bound together in inseparable cells of three, in accordance with the formula imported from China, in order to facilitate training and make consciences easier to penetrate. What thoughts could remain concealed under these conditions? How could the last barriers of the soul resist this incessant watch? The grip of the political commissars turned every soldier into an instrument in the hands of the Commander in Chief and the Party. Orders would not simply be carried out; every man took an oath to try always to surpass himself.

What a terrible machine this was with which Navarre, knowing nothing about it, was to come into conflict!

"Our feet are made of iron," the soldiers of the People's Army used to say by way of a joke. Their hearts, too. If they had not been determined to rid their country of the men whom they called by the general, ignominious term for Westerners, the Tays (pronounced "tie"), they could not have agreed to live so hard and face the enemy's guns and planes. Everywhere they had been told that the struggle would be long, difficult and cruel, and that it would be years before they had the weapons required for victory and could learn to use them. But, since November 26, Giap's first order of the day had raised tremendous hopes. It was at Dienbienphu that the decisive battle might take place. If every soldier in the People's Army was determined to shed his blood, and every man and woman to wear out his legs and shoulders for the battle of liberation, then salvation was in sight. What an opportunity this was! The Tays suspected nothing and displayed the utmost contempt for everything concerned with the mobility and subsistence of the Viets. Since the news had reached the regiments and spread through the villages one by one, joy had lightened loads and shortened distances; roads and bivouacs shook with the sound of singing. The army was consumed with eagerness to reach Dienbienphu and fight, and had to be reminded that the preparations would be more difficult than anything it had seen thus far.

It was in the region of Thanh Hoa, one of the country's rice granaries, that the chief of staff of the 57th Regiment, in the 304th Division, was informed of the event. Of the three regiments which made up that division, the first was to take part in the Central Annam campaign, the second was to remain on guard near the delta, and only one was to go to Dienbienphu: his own. It was by a series of deductions, thanks to the indication of its original stationing and the date of its arrival at Dienbienphu, that I succeeded in identifying it. None of the officers of the People's Army whom I questioned would give me the number of his unit. Ten years after the event, it is hard to see how that can still be regarded as a state secret, and these little mysteries annoyed me until I realized that nobody had been released from his oath of secrecy; Giap himself refused to confirm the list of his forces which French Intelligence had drawn up in detail. Probably this was because, in view of the fact that the war for the unification of Vietnam was not over, he did not consider himself free to reveal plans which were still in the course of execution.

The chief of staff of the 57th Regiment accompanied me during my visit to Dienbienphu. Twelve days together helped me to get to know him. Instructed to help me with my traveling arrangements and my relations with the local authorities, he soon showed a friendliness toward me which I reciprocated. My eagerness to know everything astonished him at first. Others found it hard to conceal a certain distrust of a former enemy looking for information on the spot; but once it was realized that my presence was inspired by a desire for objectivity, the welcome became warmer and confidences were gradually imparted.

The former chief of staff of the 57th Regiment holds the rank of captain in the present-day army. His name is Nguyen Hien. The son of peasants and from the region of Phu Li, in the plain, he had gone to school in Hanoï and understood French. Of frail appearance since childhood, he had been wounded in the face as soon as he had joined the army, and a little later he was hit in the spine by a shell splinter which embedded itself near the heart and could not be removed. This latter wound left him with a star-shaped scar between his shoulderblades. Given up for lost by the doctors, he had survived and gone back to an infantry unit. He suffered a great deal; his comrades helped him to march by carrying his load of rice.

When I knew him, he weighed less than one hundred pounds; his arms and legs looked like drumsticks. At the time of Dienbienphu, he was twenty-four years old and even thinner. On his long sensitive face, rather Spanish in complexion, forehead and nose, with eyes which were barely Oriental, his joys and sorrows appeared in furtive gleams in which the simple feelings of his people could be distinguished. His regiment covered over six hundred miles on foot before receiving the final order to go to Dienbienphu.

December 6, 1953

General Giap issued a mobilization order, in accordance with a decision of the Central Committee of the Party. This was a major document, which the listening posts did not intercept because it was probably not broadcast by radio, and which nobody on the staffs of the Expeditionary Corps has ever noted or wanted to note, except in a very vague way, possibly because it was not found on any prisoner or corpse. In it Giap clearly stated the object to be attained and defined the mission of every man in the People's Army: "You must repair the roads, overcome all obstacles, surmount all difficulties, fight unflinchingly, defeat cold and hunger, carry heavy loads across mountains and valleys, and strike right into the enemy's camp to destroy him and free our fellow countrymen. . . . Comrades, forward!"

It may be assumed that extraordinary precautions were taken to prevent the enemy from laying hands on a document which left no doubt whatever about the intentions of the Vietminh command. Two days' march from Giap's headquarters, and leading the same life as he, in straw huts hidden in forests away from the villages, the Central Committee directed the conduct of the war. As for indiscretions about the presence of Uncle Ho or of Giap, the discipline in force proved its worth with men, who, ten years later, still pretended not to know to what regiment they belonged. Moreover, everybody took care never to mention the names of Giap and Dienbienphu, using instead their conventional appellations: "Ngoc" for Giap and "Tran Dinh" for Dienbienphu.

December 7, 1953

It was only the previous evening that the Commander in Chief's decision to accept battle had reached Hanoï. In a long dispatch, Cogny acknowledged its tardy receipt; since Navarre, in his instructions, had asked for a garrison to be maintained at Laï Chau as long as possible, Cogny gave the reasons why he was hurriedly evacuating that town. He added that the ground actions which Navarre wanted him to carry out in the area Son La–Tuan Giao–Thuan Chau—in other words, at an average distance of forty miles from Dienbienphu—were beyond him now that the enemy had cut the paved road, Route 41. That, too, was something a corporal could have told the Commander in Chief, because a corporal would have known the tracks which General Navarre and his operational deputy flew over at a great height; it is hard to see how, even without the enemy's presence, the Dienbienphu garrison, which for the moment had very few motorized vehicles at its disposal, could have carried out patrols in strength, on the ground, over a distance of thirty miles. Thirty miles on a large-scale map is only a few inches for a staff officer. For a corporal, it represents sixty thousand paces—in other words, two days' march in flat, easy country. Applied to the Dienbienphu region, such opinions verge on mental aberration.

Cogny also announced that the Vietminh had established itself strongly on the Pavie Trail, completely cutting off Laï Chau from Dienbienphu, on which two regiments from the 308th and 312th Divisions were marching. The myth of the strong offensive base was already peeling and breaking up, and long cracks covered its façade. Yet it was barely a few days since reality had lightly touched it. The dispatches settling hour by hour on General Navarre's table proved that the situation was disintegrating. Why, then, did he persist in his error?

If he had been sure that the whole enemy battle corps would concentrate at Dienbienphu, Navarre would probably not have been so rash as to provoke it just as "Operation Atlante" was building up to its main effort four hundred miles away; but he did not believe in the situation which the head of Military Intelligence at Hanoï had described to him on November 28. "In front of all the charts on which the movements of the Vietminh divisions were written up," Cogny would say later on, "I had the impression that he did not understand." But Navarre trusted nobody but himself, showed a fundamental skepticism toward all information which came to him through channels other than his own, and was particularly suspicious of Tonkin, where he was increasingly convinced Cogny was carving out an empire for himself and playing his own game. On December 3, Navarre confined himself to what he believed: there was one division in the region. It could be reinforced, but not multiplied as Cogny claimed. And yet Laï Chau was falling like a ripe fruit even before the myth had been shaken. Later, Navarre would accuse Cogny of having acted too hastily. This was a cunning or innocent game of which Cogny had been the first victim when he had played with the idea of large-scale maneuvers in a region with impracticable roads and a difficult terrain which favored the ambushes of a tireless enemy. Among the units of the Expeditionary Corps, only a few paratroop battalions were accustomed to the rigors of bush warfare. The others were incapable of covering great distances by themselves, and if the Air Force did not carry them, at least it had to supply and support them.

Now it was on the day Cogny evacuated Laï Chau by the skin of his teeth that Navarre, far from canceling his first instructions, issued a second series which increased the dangers of the first. He had decided to join battle at Dienbienphu. He knew that he would not receive the reinforcements he had asked for and that he was under orders to adapt his operations to his means, but the principal objective which he wanted to attain was the destruction of the rebel zone on the mountain plateau of Central Annam. It was to this operation, which had nothing to do with Dienbienphu, except insofar as it endangered it further, that he wanted everything to be subordinated. In spite of all opposition, his plan was to be carried out.

Blind to what was happening in the Dienbienphu region and deaf to the objections of the men of Tonkin, Navarre and Berteil would cling to their grandiose idea. What had they to fear? All the staffs subscribed to the opinion that the strength of the Vietminh had reached its ceiling.

If the enemy attacked at Dienbienphu, he would behave as he had done at Na San; the attack could not last more than a few days. After that, the exploitation of the success would begin. That was what Navarre believed and maintained.

At zero hour that day, Colonel de Castries took over command of Dienbienphu, which was referred to in military jargon as the Northwestern Operational Group, or *Groupement Opérationnel du Nord-Ouest*. It was known for short as "GONO," a medical slang term which I would have regarded as a bad omen.

Castries, who was a brilliant fighter, could not allow himself to be caught in this trap. He was probably going to tell Cogny, "General, change this mission of mine; I cannot complete it." For if military vocabulary was not to lose all meaning, he must not *try* to carry out his mission; he *must* carry it out. Five miles around the airstrip, that makes a circle with a circumference of thirty miles, which would need four or five divisions to occupy it, or else, to prevent the enemy from coming closer than five miles to the camp, Castries would have to maneuver. And he would not be able to maneuver. Bigeard, who had tried to move around on his own and now found himself hemmed in on all sides, told him so. Bigeard was not a cavalryman; he was used to dropping from the sky and returning home on foot, crossing obstacles and going up hill and down dale at a run. Here, as soon as you reached the first slopes, you had to hack your way through creepers which stifled the trees or through tall grass and undergrowth. Neither horses nor tanks would ever serve any useful purpose in this jungle.

Castries did not protest. Probably he did not know enough yet. He thought that Major Bigeard was exaggerating and that light patrols, with artillery and air protection, or patrols in strength and powerful raids would be able to destroy the enemy's weapons, whereas Bearcats were already making dive-bombing attacks in the basin itself. Perhaps, like everybody else, he thought that the enemy would never have heavy guns at his disposal, and that if by some miracle he managed to bring some up, the French artillery would soon crush them. Cogny told him so often that he was destined to be a mountain rider, leaping from crest to crest with flames shooting from his horse's nostrils, that he did not dare to doubt it.

But in a few days, the attractive concept of maneuvers in the famous triangle had collapsed. With Laï Chau gone, there was no question of venturing even six miles to the east. Nobody believed it possible any more. That didn't matter. Everybody went on pretending that they did, in the hope that there might be some madman capable of pulling off those famous patrols in strength and those swift raids into mountain country, those offensive actions which had no force except as words tapped out by typewriters. Nobody was ready to admit that Dienbienphu had already been reduced to playing the part of a super-Na San, and that the partisans to whom harrying actions were entrusted would share the fate of the partisans of Laï Chau: their columns surprised on the tracks by the Vietminh, their corpses hacked to pieces, their horses disemboweled. . . .

Gilles was glad he had gotten out of the hornets' nest and had handed over his command to Castries. Their farewells had not been particularly touching. Gilles would soon be reunited with the battalions of "Operation Castor," which would be relieved one by one to reconstitute a general reserve. Castries had struck him as being full of confidence in the future. Just the same, Gilles had felt entitled to give him a piece of advice. "Watch out," he had told him. "If you lose an inch of ground, you are done for. . . ."

December 10, 1953

That day, the Béatrice strong point was set up.

It is by way of old Route 41, which passes the foot of what remains of Béatrice and runs alongside the winding Nam Youm, that you reach Dienbienphu by land when you come from Hanoï. It was therefore that way that I arrived on November 19, 1962. Knowing the area by heart from having studied it on maps and aerial photographs, I was nonetheless astonished to find myself at Dienbienphu, though I had recognized the profile of the mountain crests from a distance before even looking down at the basin. The road, in fact, slopes gently down between the hills, and the grandiose landscape is invisible until you reach the bottom.

From the site of Béatrice, where a modest monument has been erected, if you look northeast, you command a view of the wooded hill slopes, and, not far away, the way across the rice fields around the hamlet of Him Lam. On the other hand, an enemy coming from the east, sheltered by bigger and higher hills on the other side of the road, can approach easily.

Béatrice therefore seemed a strong position, provided that it was covered by a number of other hillocks. Isolated at such a distance from

the main center of resistance, it was at the mercy of an enemy determined to take it at all costs. To believe that it could bar the way for long
to determined shock troops, you had to be deluded by legends: the
superiority of the French genius, a blind faith in firearms and the invin-
cibility of the Foreign Legion. French genius is of no value unless it
surpasses others; technical resources can always be crushed by superior
ones; and, however heroic it may be, the Foreign Legion, like all crack
units, is not a substitute for everything.

For two days, two battalions of paratroops had covered the installation
of the 3rd Battalion, 13th Demibrigade, by advancing toward the hamlet
of Na Loï, four miles away, and had then fallen back after a few
skirmishes. It would have been difficult to go any farther without organizing huge operations for which the manpower at Dienbienphu
would have been inadequate, for the skill of the Vietminh consisted of
avoiding being compelled to make a stand and of drawing the heavy
units of the Expeditionary Corps out of range of their base artillery.

But the illusion that it was possible to maneuver simply because it was
necessary would last a long time. Every vain attempt at movement, every
day wasted in trying to advance toward the crests, took thousands of
hands from the work of fortifying the basin. Besides, how could the
infantry be persuaded to abandon its natural aversion to digging shelters
and trenches in which to take cover, since everybody was convinced that
the Viets had no artillery? Moreover, as the valley of Dienbienphu was
of pure mud, it would have been necessary to go ten miles to the north,
to the ravines of the Nam Youm, or to the south, to the gorges of the
Nam Noua, to find any stone. A mere landslide, a single tree laid across
the track, and the bold men who ventured out there would have been
done for. There was no stone and no gravel. This detail would assume
tremendous importance; because of it, there would be no masonry or
concrete, and the wood cut from tree trunks for shelters would have
knots and flaws which would make it unsuitable for the construction of
adequate defense works. As it was, the beams, planks and rafters required for the building of a road bridge had had to come from Hanoï
by air. But what did that matter? The technical services were there to
overcome the difficulties produced by tactical situations. Yet Navarre
should have known that the army he had tossed into the basin of Dienbienphu was already a prisoner.

The big factory was at work. Every day sixty Dakotas dropped or
landed 150 tons of munitions, supplies, barbed wire, rubber-soled shoes

or hobnailed boots, tent canvas, medical stores or radio equipment; dozens of fighters and B-26's pierced the clouds to find the enemy and attack him; thousands of men were at work fastening packages to parachutes, folding parachute silk, loading trucks and unloading them into planes, handling bombs, loading belts for heavy machine guns and quick-firing guns, filling oil and gas tanks, and drawing up lists of names and numbers. The war-making machine could be heard a long way off, but it could still be stopped if it became known that it had gotten off to a bad start.

At dawn on June 17, 1647, Condé, who was laying siege to Lérida, gathered his generals together and summed up the situation for them: the vigor of the defense had slowed down the siege works, illness was attacking the army, the great heat and the torrents swollen by the melting snows were adding to its difficulties, and the number of desertions was growing in the regiments recruited from the south. For all these reasons, the great Condé considered that he was in an unfavorable position. To provoke an attack on the lines at the foot of a rock, with broken-down troops, in the face of a strong garrison to whose help an army of ten thousand infantrymen and three thousand cavalrymen was hurrying, meant certain defeat and possible rout. Condé decided to withdraw, even though he knew that the court at Paris expected him to send news of a victory.

That day, no apparent change was made in the troops' duties. In the evening the whole army was on the alert; during the night the batteries were dismantled; and the next morning the retreat began. A message to Mazarin opened with these words: "You will, I am sure, be not a little astonished, after all the hopes I had given you, to learn that I have lifted the siege of Lérida; you know me well enough to believe that this was not done without pain and sorrow, and that, sacrificing my honor to the King's service, I have done no small violence to my feelings. . . ." For the first time since he had taken command of the army against the enemy, braving the indignation of his generals, jeers and lampoons, the great Condé had beaten a retreat to avoid exposing his army to what he considered an exaggerated risk. Mazarin himself took the opportunity to vilify him; but soon, when everybody knew the truth, the victory which the prince had just won over himself by not fearing to be called a coward added still further to his fame.

Navarre, too, could stop. A good many colonels and generals who wanted to kill Viets would scream that victory was being snatched out of their hands, but others would end up by approving of his decision. The government, which left him at liberty to conduct operations as he wished, would praise his wisdom. Following on his decision to join battle, this withdrawal would be regarded as one of the most courageous actions that any commander in chief had ever performed. With full control over his actions, he was proud enough to impose this one and strong enough to turn it into a victory. If he wished, he could still wait a few days in order to allow the enemy divisions to advance a long way along the highland roads, and then remove his stake as he had done at Na San. He would save Laos if he forced Giap to retrace his steps and if, resting firmly on his Hanoï bases, he launched devastating raids on the enemy's rear.

At Avaricum, near Bourges, during the Gallic Wars, Caesar withdrew his legions and refrained from attacking, simply because the enemy had established himself on a hill surrounded with obstacles and marshes. And yet his soldiers were so eager to conquer that they were indignant that the enemy was able to withstand even the sight of them. One and all called for the signal to attack. Impervious to their shouts, Caesar ordered the army to turn about, convinced that the unfavorable conditions of the engagement were not worth the sacrifice in human lives which the very men who were protesting would have to pay.

For the moment, everything was against Navarre, except for the confidence his troops had in themselves. That day, the presence of the 316th Division with heavy war material was noted in the vicinity of Dienbienphu. Who had tried to prevent these forces from arriving? Nobody. Military Intelligence had collected a great deal of other, very detailed information: the Vietminh 151st Regiment of Engineers had been ordered to open Route 41 to motor traffic as far as the approaches to Dienbienphu, and instructions had gone out to widen the Ta Kho–Co Noï road to make room for the vehicles of the 351st Division; the advance military and supply headquarters for the northwest were at Muong Phan, and Giap himself was reported to be a little farther back, at Thuan Chau. He was said to have issued an order of the day to his troops; this was the mobilization order of December 6, whose text, everything considered, the French secret service may just possibly have known and Navarre may not have treated as a dead letter. Navarre himself put the number of enemy troops on the march at ten thousand. The chief of his Military Intelligence predicted that if all the elements of the 304th, 308th and 312th Divisions on the move were destined for the northwest, the enemy would be able to concentrate twenty-two battalions at Dien-bienphu by the end of the month, a figure which shattered the optimistic estimates of December 3.

The Committee of National Defense had curtly reminded the Com-mander in Chief that he had to adapt his plans to his means, and his decision to accept battle had only just arrived in Paris, where it had aroused considerable anxiety. If he failed, everybody would blame him. The government had only one idea: to bring this war to an end, if necessary by negotiation. This occupation of Dienbienphu would have been an excellent exercise for the Expeditionary Corps, the Air Force and the staffs, and Giap would always wonder what Navarre had in-tended to do and what trap he had laid for him. The enemy had given him the name of an animal to which his pointed face and sharp eyes lent him a certain resemblance: "the Fox." But he, Navarre, now knew that everything he had organized was a bluff. On a map at headquarters it looked good, but it all fell to pieces in face of the realities of country, season, men and material.

If the idea of withdrawing tempted Navarre, who would encourage him to give in to it? In his entourage, nobody. Castries, possibly the only person in whom Navarre would have trusted, because he was on the spot and could see the problem for himself, was silent. He had taken over too recently. Before putting forward suggestions or warning the High Com-mand against what was perhaps an error of judgment, he had to wait, make experiments, form a firm opinion himself before trying to persuade others of its validity. If he had been chosen, it was so that he would do his best to succeed in spite of all the difficulties. As for Cogny, all his warn-ings would remain suspect in the eyes of Navarre, who believed he was trying to bring about his downfall. Besides, Cogny, who had been to Dienbienphu the day before, had no doubt about the issue of the battle. His chief concern was that Navarre should not do anything to deplete his strength in the delta.

In the bourgeois comfort of the villa in which Navarre had established his headquarters, all was order, harmony and strength. Nothing could influence the brain working there in its air-conditioned vase. The outer air reached him only after it had been filtered and cooled, almost in cello-phane. Noise and bustle were denied entry. Navarre's reason for start-ing Dienbienphu still retained its value as a political façade: the need to bar the road to Laos to the Vietminh. Yet Navarre examined him-self, with an honesty that cannot be questioned, in the painful solitude all leaders have to endure. If he did not act like Caesar and the great Condé, it was not courage that he lacked, but knowledge of the country and its army, for he was not a man who feared braving stupidity. He lacked insight. Berteil kept telling him that they would kill Viets at Dienbienphu as they had killed them at Na San. Berteil was entitled to say what he thought. Where Navarre went wrong was in believing him.

December 15, 1953

During the night, Lieutenant Colonel Langlais, who had returned to Dienbienphu, had managed to bring back to the camp the three parachute battalions which for the past five days had been trying in vain to reach the post of Muong Pon, in the narrow ravine followed by the Pavie Trail, ten miles to the north. The 8th Assault, leaving first in independent groups to give a helping hand to the last partisans from Laï Chau, who had arrived on the heights after escaping ambush and destruction, had been encircled. Two other battalions, the 5th Vietnamese and the 1st Foreign, had gone to its assistance. They had lost a day in an engagement five miles from the airfield, at the point where the Pavie Trail entered the mountains. Once the three battalions had come together, they had been forced to fall back with heavy losses, using the 1st Foreign as a rear guard. In a dozen trips, one helicopter alone had evacuated seventy-six wounded. As for the dead, they had been buried on the spot with the prayers of a chaplain in bush kit and as bearded as a Legion drum major. In a cemetery improvised among the reeds on a crest, big clods of red earth marked the graves; planks from ammunition cases, attached to stakes, served as tombstones. A platoon of little Vietnamese soldiers, with grenades at their belts, had presented arms, grimacing in the blinding sun. The only thing distinguishing them from the men with the bamboo headgear was the shape of the American helmet, which seemed to crush them with its size and weight.

When Langlais had arrived during the night on the crests where the fighting was taking place, he had heard only confused orders and reports on the radio. At dawn, the remains of battalions emerged from the bush, with haggard, bearded faces. Langlais thought of what Castries had said to him when he had left: "Get me some prisoners."

Costly though it was, the experience would not have been in vain if the scales of illusion had dropped from the generals' eyes. Henceforth there could be no doubt about the possibilities offered by the trails in the region: they were death traps in which the Expeditionary Corps could not deploy; any advance would have to be completely covered from the heights. The Pavie Trail was simply a mountain path which followed the narrow valley of the Nam Co. Companies detached to cover the flanks made laborious progress through the vegetation and across the difficult ground, and when, exhausted by their march through the jungle and weighed down by their campaign equipment, they emerged onto the crests whose tall grass and trees obscured their view, they were fired upon at point-blank range by an enemy entrenched in his hiding places. Ambush, illusion, trickery and death were everywhere. It was impossible to tell whether it was the wind or a guerrilla moving the tall grass when it stirred. When the French fighters carried out a napalm raid, the enemy vanished, leaving behind a few roasted corpses, and established himself farther on before returning once the danger had disappeared.

It was useless for the staff officers at Saigon to get angry and tap their cigarettes irritably as, fresh from their showers, they read the incoming reports; reality was stronger than they were. The Vietminh, used to living and fighting in the highlands without food and ammunition being dropped to them by parachute, and skilled in the art of concealment, could maneuver; the Expeditionary Corps could not. Was Castries, the fiery cavalryman, pinned down on all sides in his basin, about to say that he could not carry out the mission which had been given to him? He still had hopes. Possibly he thought that everything would change with the six tanks he had been promised.

He marked out in the northwest a second strong point which was to bear the name of Anne-Marie. Anne-Marie was the heroine of a German song which the Legion used to sing as it marched along:

> Anne-Marie, tell me, where are you going?
> I'm going to town where the soldiers are. . . .

As the two Thai battalions evacuated from Laï Chau seemed to be of poor caliber, Cogny obtained eleven battalions from Dienbienphu instead of nine. He immediately gave orders for the establishment of another center of resistance, Isabelle, three miles to the south, in order to set up a support point which would not be exposed to the same fire as the main center; out of range of the guns supporting the north, Isabelle would immobilize three battalions for her protection.

Envisaged in theory on November 2, and decided on at Muong Saï on December 12 and 13 by General Bodet, Navarre's deputy, a link-up with

Laos in the southwest was arranged to install groups of partisans in the Sop Nao region, twenty-five miles from Dienbienphu, and other groups halfway, in the limestone hills of Ban Na Ti.

Cogny objected. He declared, rightly, that it was not necessary to detach three battalions for a week in order to place Intelligence units which could go off into the mountains by themselves. On the other hand, Cogny would have liked to form a satellite group, to be reinforced by parachute drops, which would radiate from Dienbienphu to harry the Vietminh in the rear. Radiate? Castries did not protest. He did not object that this was sheer fantasy and that the staff's views bordered on lunacy. The road to Sop Nao was no better than the Pavie Trail; the obstacles to progress would be the same and the equipment of the French forces had not changed. They could not manage to help some partisans a few miles to the north, and yet they wanted to organize other maneuvers far to the south, across difficult country. Nobody protested. Bigeard had left for Hanoï, his mission completed, and his battalions were going to join him. Navarre and Cogny insisted that four out of the eleven battalions at Dienbienphu should always be engaged in offensive actions. Nobody had as yet opened his eyes to the facts.

On December 14, Ho Chi Minh had addressed a message to the people of Vietnam. He had declared that if the French Government wished to arrange an armistice, the Government of the Democratic Republic was ready to enter into negotiations. M. Nguyen van Tam, the Vietnamese Prime Minister, had replied that this was an act of propaganda designed to spread discouragement among the valiant troops fighting Communism, and the French Government, assured by General Navarre that the situation would be better in the spring, had repeated that it was impossible to take any account of declarations made through the medium of the press or the radio. Eight years before, an atom bomb had been dropped on Hiroshima, but the French Cabinet was still as punctilious as ever about formalities. Diplomatic notes counted only when they were conveyed, not through the classified ads, as the French Foreign Office humorously put it, but through ambassadors, in briefcases of fine, gilt-embossed leather.

December 17, 1953

General Navarre had landed the day before in the rain at Hanoï, and had had a long conversation with Cogny. The cold weather had descended on the Tonkin plain later than usual, about ten days before. The men and women put on old woolen sweaters or padded jackets over their shirts and blouses. The children were given caps with ear flaps to wear. The drizzle had made its appearance on December 14. Navarre and Cogny, who knew what the operation toward Muong Pon had cost, studied the proposed Sop Nao expedition. Cogny argued against it. He pleaded in favor of his satellite.

In point of fact, Cogny had envisaged this satellite differently from the description of it he gives in his official notes. He wanted to maneuver light forces around Dienbienphu which, avoiding dangerous encounters, would harry the enemy incessantly and then melt into the jungle, to return when they were not expected, ready to be reinforced at the right moment by a more formidable group. The whole body would be not so much a satellite as a nebula or cloud of asteroids. Cogny thought that the Viets would have to detach an important proportion of the troops investing their camp in order to wipe out these nuisances, or, if they ignored them, run the risk of having an unexpected fight on their hands at an awkward moment.

A mixture of regulars and partisans, in imitation of the enemy organization, struck Cogny as an ideal formula, and it was indeed an attractive one. So far, only a few commando leaders had thought of copying the Vietminh organization and combat methods and had succeeded when they did. By what miracle could something impossible to improvise be suddenly accomplished? Impressed by Cogny's idea, Colonel de Crèvecoeur had spontaneously detailed one of his Laotian officers to organize this difficult game, but General Navarre refused to admit that it had any chance of success. Cogny would therefore never be able to prove to himself that his plan was utopian or to others that it was right.

How was it possible for him also to have entertained such grandiose illusions? Did Cogny, who was already complaining that the Air Force was being monopolized by Dienbienphu, want to wear it out supplying and supporting in the bush the paratroops of his satellite, whose subsequent recovery was a matter of speculation? When I come to think of it, I am not so sure that Cogny believed in his satellite. A complex and even cunning character beneath his warm exterior, bent on attaining his objective by devious means, did Cogny really think that a maneuver of this sort had any chance of success in a hilly, wooded region where the only lines of communication were mule trains? Accustomed to the vast, flat spaces of the rice fields, could the man of the delta, who was fond of vaunting his realism and who had been impatient to evacuate Na San imagine that he would be able to ask so much, for weeks and possibly months, from men who were capable of giving their all only if the effort was of short duration? With what trucks would he collect them, since the roads were unfit for motor traffic? What armor would support them? What planes would cover them or drop food and ammunition to them if the weather was bad? Who would carry their burdens in the jungle? To all these questions, there was no reply.

The explanation of these intellectual pastimes is to be found in the successful but unfinished experiment of Na San, during which some battalions had ventured more than thirty miles from the base. In time, and with the help of illusions, it was easy to forget that it had always been the same men, Bréchignac and Bigeard, the only ones, or practically the only ones, who had been capable of covering thirty miles in one night like the Viets, of marching barefoot, of using the same tricks as the enemy, of living like him and coming back with prisoners to sleep for twenty-four hours in their holes. What Bigeard and Bréchignac had done, sometimes directed by incompetent staff officers, why shouldn't others do also? Nobody remembered the conditions of the previous experiments. Nobody recalled that the enemy had been less strongly concentrated around Na San. Bigeard and Bréchignac, if they had still been there, would have had the courage to say they could not repeat at Dienbienphu the exploits they had performed at Na San. What was also forgotten was that time, fatigue and trying experiences had blunted the ardor and fighting spirit of the Expeditionary Corps, and that now, to stand up to one Vietminh battalion in open country, two or three of General Navarre's worn-out and ill-assorted forces were needed.

In the end, Navarre clung to his expedition to Sop Nao, rejected the idea of a satellite and once again refused to allow Cogny to carry out raids on Thaï Nguyen and Cho Chu, which were more practical possibilities, or on Phu Doan, which would have been a less onerous affair, on the grounds that he did not consider them strong enough to break the enemy system. The mystery about Navarre is that sense and folly should have been so closely combined in him.

One hope remained that day: in the rain, Navarre took off for Dienbienphu with Cogny, in the Dakota of General Lauzin, the officer commanding the Expeditionary Corps Air Force. Castries, who had donned his medal ribbons for the occasion, had arranged things in style. When the plane landed, at 11:30, a platoon of Moroccans, wearing turbans and blancoed spats, did the honors. The weather was fine in the highlands.

Navarre, who disliked drawn-out mess lunches, shared a cold meal he had brought from Hanoï with his hosts. Afterward, he installed himself in a jeep with the windshield let down on the hood, which Castries drove. The procession of vehicles set off for the already bare peaks of Béatrice, where they were received by Lieutenant Colonel Gaucher, the officer commanding the 13th Foreign Demibrigade. Massive, grumpy and taciturn, Gaucher had the broad face of an inquisitorial monk under his Legionnaire's cap. From the escarpments, already surrounded with barbed wire, the view extended over the whole valley, where the Nam Youm wound its glittering way at the foot of the round hills bordering it to the east. To the northwest, beyond a succession of hillocks which the garrison had not occupied, could be seen the long purple rump of Gabrielle, where the trees would soon be felled and the brushwood burnt, since it had been decided to install a fresh strong point there with an extra battalion. Facing the wild, wooded slope rising on the side from which the enemy would attack, the view was wide, but the terrain, crisscrossed with ravines and bristling with green, cone-shaped peaks as high as the highest crests, lent itself to infiltration. What did that matter? Before jumping onto the chest of Dienbienphu, the enemy would have to take that shoulder of red earth from which the Legion would spit fire and flame. Gaucher was no intellectual, but a wild boar with a solid defense system. The Viets would find him a tough proposition, and what the machine guns failed to wipe out would be reached by the curved trajectories of the mortars and 155-mm. guns.

Navarre's officers listened stiffly to Gaucher's explanations. Navarre's function here was confined to saying what he wanted, and it was not for him to go into detail. In practice Cogny had the responsibility of an army corps commander. According to Article 412 of the instructions on the tactical use of large units, he was supposed to fix the center of resistance and indicate the areas to be held at all costs. Castries, in fact, ranked as a divisional commander; it was his responsibility to establish the defense plan. Navarre would confine himself to correcting mistakes, but it was none of his business to teach his subordinates their trade. He had simply decided to help them by giving them some tanks.

A piece of information of exceptional gravity had reached him at Hanoï: the 308th Division had covered thirty miles in two days. At that rate, it would be at Dienbienphu in a week. Who could any longer doubt that this was where it was headed? But who could state for certain that the whole 308th Division was on the move and not simply a few elements of the division? In that case, the calculations on which, on December 3, Navarre had based his decision to accept battle still held good and there was no reason to make any change in the measures taken with a view to dealing with a single enemy division, the 316th, even if it was reinforced to a considerable extent.

Were there even twice as many enemy battalions, the same doctrine would hold, and nobody could go against it without being accused of mental debility: the enemy could not advance and no artillery could give him support without facing certain annihilation. The twelve French battalions in the entrenched camp, any of which would be relieved if they showed signs of weakening, were surely capable, with all their machine guns, their artillery and their ample stocks of ammunition, of wiping out twelve Vietminh battalions which would have to expose themselves to their fire to reach the basin. Who would dare to contradict Navarre? How could the gunner Cogny demur? An Air Force officer asked whether the crests overlooking Isabelle had been reconnoitered. He was told that a patrol had been sent out, and that it had taken twenty-four hours to reach the first peaks and the same time to come back. In the hills, the elephant grass reduced visibility to nil. No danger was to be expected from that quarter.

By the time he left, at five o'clock, Navarre had not taken any of Cogny's objections into account, and Cogny had not abandoned his idea of a satellite which would "nomadize" (a verb which was promptly adopted by the army) around Dienbienphu. Both men still thought it was possible to maneuver.

Generals don't dismount easily from chimeras once they have gotten astride them.

December 23, 1953

Bigeard later described the expedition toward Sop Nao as "a big bluff." Nobody, indeed, ever understood what it was supposed to achieve. The Legionnaires of the 3rd Foreign reached Muong Khoua after twenty-one days' march across the tracks of Laos, and brave Brigitte Friang, who had dropped among them by parachute, described them as looking like the inmates of a concentration camp. Their young MO had lost twenty pounds. Several typhoid victims were dying.

Brigitte Friang had continued with them, advanced at night by the light of the full moon, crossed rivers by canoe among the little horses set free to swim over, waded along ravines, slipped down wet slopes, burnt leeches off her skin with cigarettes, and slept in abandoned huts or on the black earth of scorched forests. Avoiding the villages and valleys and the Viets in them, Vaudrey's battalions finally reached the huts of Sop Nao, nestling in their rocky amphitheater.

In the afternoon of that day, they linked up with Langlais's detachment. Langlais, who was suffering from an injured ankle, and Vaudrey shook hands and drank a glass of rum together before the cameras. Brigitte Friang went on with her friends of the 8th Assault, whom Captain Tourret, a faithful disciple of Bigeard's, led through torrents which they crossed waist-deep in water, along sodden tracks and through stifling grass. The battalion MO, the handsome Lieutenant Patrice de Carfort, who also had a swollen ankle, calmly distributed injections, salts and ointments among the exhausted men. In the evening, the troops tried to dry out their clothing in front of low fires which they did not dare to allow to blaze up.

"What did it prove?" Langlais asked me later. "Only that any link-up was out of the question. The expedition to Sop Nao was a publicity operation, a stunt. It was supposed to show that Dienbienphu wasn't encircled. I'd had a hell of a job finding one bad guide from among all our Thais and Meos for twelve hundred men, whereas we really needed one good guide for every company. At headquarters in Saigon, they didn't understand why I didn't take those good roads marked in red on the maps. We weren't in France. There was rather a shortage of signposts. If I'd had to fight, I'd have lost a whole battalion in the operation. I preferred to play hide-and-seek with the Viets and avoid passes where pack horses found it hard to get through and I'd have had my throat slit; I preferred to hack my way through the jungle. Besides, Castries didn't think I ought to attempt that link-up with Laos, but he had to obey orders. In the whole Expeditionary Corps, there were only two battalions trained to deal with jungle conditions, those of Bigeard and Bréchignac. We so knocked ourselves out that in the end we wouldn't have been able to carry a man back on a stretcher. Nobody who knows what war is like in that region could ever issue orders like that."

Who could have trained and inspired this nebulous notion of Cogny's and made it a force to be reckoned with? The Viets would have wiped it out in a few days.

December 24, 1953

The big news of the night Navarre had piously thought of spending at Dienbienphu was not good news. The chief of Cogny's Military Intelligence announced it to the skeptical headquarters at Saigon: the 308th Division was already there, and its presence in the south of the basin threatened to intercept the two battalions returning from Sop Nao.

Accompanied by a silent Colonel Revol, Navarre had arrived toward the end of the afternoon with his sour look and his stick. Those who knew him praised his simplicity and goodheartedness, but admitted that the difficulty he experienced in behaving naturally with other people produced a certain clumsy shyness which made him inarticulate. He had shut himself up with Castries in the command post, and the two men had had a not very amiable discussion. He and Castries were clearly not in agreement, and there was a chilly atmosphere at the meeting of officers held at nightfall. "The military conditions for victory have been brought together." he announced. And yet he knew that the 308th Division was advancing toward the lights of the entrenched camp. According to Castries, he said, "You are going to fight for Dienbienphu." What he meant remains obscure.

Everywhere, in the trenches and shelters, singing began. The Legion knew how to celebrate Christmas fittingly; in accordance with tradition, every man received his present from the hands of his company commander or platoon leader, every officer received his from his men.

At ten o'clock in the evening, Mass was celebrated near the command post, where a Christmas tree suddenly lit up the darkness. An altar had been set up in front of the round tent of the chapel under some big panels of colored parachute silk, between torches whose flames flickered in the wind. The moon had not yet risen, but already, in the east, behind the dark mass of the mountains, the sky was turning pale. His head bowed, his eyes thoughtful, his mouth turned down slightly at the corners, Navarre stood in the front row, between Castries and Revol, with a linen tunic over his jacket, for it was a cold night. With his shaven skull, his bright eyes under bushy eyebrows, and his pointed nose and chin, Castries needed only a cloak over his shoulders to look like a soldier monk.

The strains of *"Stille Nacht, heilige Nacht,"* sung by fine German voices, rose into the darkness, in which mortar shots sounded in the distance. At the Elevation, in the midst of the impressive silence, there were two bursts of machine-gun fire and a stream of crimson tracer bullets spurted toward the hills.

After the blessing, the congregation dispersed. Navarre had hinted that the war would come to an end soon. At Castries's quarters, the Commander in Chief presided over the midnight supper party. Gaucher arrived late, slightly the worse for drink, and started telling stories about his campaigns. Irritated, Navarre left quickly. At the officers' mess of the Legion, there was a bottle of champagne for every four men. The conversations became coarser and everybody sang "Lili Marlene" and "Anne-Marie." A bunch of officers left and made their way to Castries's command post, where, dressed in his red waistcoat with gold buttons, he offered them drinks.

A tall major who was a little drunk went up to him. "You know, the Legion doesn't care much for cavalrymen, but you're different. So . . ." He took the badge of the 13th Demibrigade from his chest, and pinned it over Castries's heart, to cheers and applause. "There, Colonel. We can't say better than that."

The reporter who witnessed this scene had come from Hanoï in a Dakota full of army coffins in separate planks, ready to be fitted together.

Twelve miles away, in the bush, Langlais and Tourret celebrated Christmas with a mug of coffee heated over the flame of a candle, under the floor of a ruined hut, hoping they would succeed next day in getting back to Dienbienphu without running into the enemy, who had left recent traces of his passage everywhere.

In all the chapels and churches of Indochina, French missionaries and Vietnamese priests prepared cribs, placed statuettes of the Holy Family in them, and sprinkled the fir trees and the straw roofs with a little granulated sugar. At nightfall, poor and fervent congregations filled the churches with their litanies, plaints and hymns mingled with the crying of babies; Legionnaires, paratroops in bush uniform and officers of the Expeditionary Corps also took Communion. They needed this comfort because this distant war sometimes confronted them with questions to which they did not dare, or know how to, reply. Their enemy showed no pity, all their movements were watched, all their remarks repeated, every step they took could lead them to death. In a situation which suddenly linked them with a people whose language they did not understand, they lost for a moment the bitter impression of being foreigners whose departure nearly everybody longed for; most of the Catholics themselves, however terrified they were at the approach of Communism, knew that France would leave and hoped that she would not be forced to go sooner than expected.

In the messes, as in the secrecy of the confessionals, conversations took an unaccustomed turn. Everybody had the impression that a battle was being prepared at Dienbienphu on which the outcome of the war would depend. The atmosphere reigning over the whole of Tonkin left no doubt on that score; the effort being made on both sides surpassed everything seen so far, and the journalists who visited the camp said so. What alarmed everybody was the two hundred miles of mountains, jungle and ambushes which separated Hanoï from Dienbienphu, and which men, guns and even cigarettes and plasma had to travel. Now the season which was drawing on was unlikely to favor the use of aircraft. The Commander in Chief who had made this choice had not succeeded in winning confidence. Nothing in his career had marked him out so far; he was considered cold, distant, inexperienced in handling men, in saying those words which arouse hope or whip up energy. He failed to make contact. Nobody dared admit yet that he had bitten off more than he could chew, and yet, if victory smiled upon him, he would become the most glorious leader of Indochina; all his faults would be accounted virtues and he would be forgiven everything if, a fox conquering a tiger, he forced Giap to yield.

December 25, 1953

On Christmas morning, the basin was covered with fog, but for some days the Dakotas had been able to drop their loads thanks to a meteorological balloon which, fastened to the ground, indicated above the clouds the point where drops were to be made. In his Christmas stocking, Castries had found the first two Chaffee tanks in fighting condition. This was the only bright spot of the day, apart from the landing of the 2nd Thai Battalion, from which, for some reason or other, great things were expected on account of its knowledge of the terrain and the language.

On all the roads which the Air Force was trying to cut, the enemy trucks were moving again without any difficulty.

Langlais's battalions finally reached Dienbienphu. Near the barbed wire of a casemate, Brigitte Friang noticed a Christmas tree as sinister as one of Goya's war disasters: a stake crowned with a Vietminh helmet, and decorated with a torn boot, some disemboweled cans and an empty bottle. But, she adds, the paratroopers were already singing at the tops of their voices as they shaved.

December 31, 1953

Suddenly, perhaps as a result of his last visit to Dienbienphu, Navarre's attitude changed. It revealed signs of a gravity which nothing had previously indicated. Was he struck by the accuracy of the forecast made by Cogny's Intelligence officers about the movements of the enemy divisions? Had the idea that he might have been wrong occurred to him? The enemy's intentions were finally made clear to Navarre in the account of the situation given him by his own Military Intelligence: Giap was concentrating men and material in strength and the term "motorized vehicles" had even appeared in the decoded messages.

This was the first time that Navarre had heard the rumbling thunder of this threat. He now had to admit that the "air-land" base of Dienbienphu was completely surrounded. The Moroccans of Isabelle could no longer reach the banks of the Nam Noua, nor could the Legionnaires of Béatrice venture onto the road which rose toward the hamlet of Na Loï; and Lieutenant Colonel Louis Guth, Castries's chief of staff, had been killed on December 28 by a shot in a ravine, in the course of a patrol in the region of Gabrielle at nightfall. The battalions from Sop Nao had only just managed to avoid the 308th Division. Dienbienphu, like Na San, was encircled. Who could still believe the contrary? It was now even hard to see how it would be possible to dislodge the heavy guns, whose presence would soon be discovered along the edge of the first slopes. With the enemy encamped in depth, it was difficult to imagine a column setting off through the jungle to attack a battery. The Vietminh was not contenting itself with invading the highlands. It was sweeping toward the middle Mekong as if it intended to cut Laos in two. Thailand declared a state of emergency in her nine provinces in the north and northeast, Thakhek was evacuated by the French, and "Operation Atlante," envisaged ever since June, seemed to be justified in order to block the enemy offensive. Dienbienphu enjoyed priority for the moment, but the High Command would have to draw heavily on its reserves everywhere in order to face up to the general situation. Tonkin, like other regions, would have to provide its quota, and Cogny was alarmed at the prospect.

Using the information at his disposal, Navarre launched attacks on the enemy's lines of communication. On December 25 and 26, twenty-three fighters dropped twenty-three tons of bombs on "Mercure," one of the points where it had been decided to cut the enemy's supply lines. The next day, road traffic had been restored at that point.

From Saigon, where he had returned on Christmas Day, after a stop at Séno where he had arrived in the midst of a general panic, Navarre had wired his observations to Cogny. He had noted that there was inadequate protection against artillery bombardment, and that some of the barbed-wire defenses were not dense enough or sufficiently provided with mines and booby traps; he expressed surprise that the northern strong point, Gabrielle, which was regarded as indispensable, had not yet been begun, and finally that the political situation created by the restoration of Deo van Long's authority should have had an unfortunate effect on recruiting. In point of fact, if some of the shelters were inadequate, the fault lay as much with the contempt felt for the enemy and the consequent skimping of work as with the poor material available. Cogny would later state that the garrison had done its utmost, in view of the time and resources available; in other words, that the whole thing had been rushed.

Did Cogny really hope for a battle at Dienbienphu, as he told the special correspondent of the United Press on December 30, or did he want to trick the enemy by just appearing to hope for it? Ten years after the event, how can anybody tell? The only statements known to have been made by him at the time were in favor of a battle. What can be accepted as a document void of all pretense is the incredible report by the Inspector General of the Expeditionary Corps Artillery, who had been to Dienbienphu with Cogny two days earlier, the statement attributed to Castries that the firepower of the Dienbienphu artillery was adequate, and the conclusion that the enemy would never be able to fire by day and in good weather.

This was the essential clause of the contract signed on December 29, as if before a lawyer, in the presence of Navarre's deputy and Cogny, by Colonel de Castries and the general commanding the Air Force. The Air Force insisted on the maintenance of its landing strip in perfect condition and its protection against direct hits which would make it unserviceable, the reinforcement in the north of Gabrielle which dominated the take-off axis and the parachuting circuits, and a guarantee that the enemy should not be allowed to install antiaircraft batteries on the crests or in the basin. It asked that it should not be obliged to attack the enemy's artillery, if he had any, and that its fighter aircraft and communications should be protected. In return, it would undertake to deliver at least a hundred tons of supplies every day to Dienbienphu, and to support the defense with direct and indirect fire, reconnaissance patrols and observation. Finally, it was given an assurance that, if a crisis made the landing strip unserviceable, that crisis would last only a few days. Anxious to help Castries expose the enemy batteries, General Lauzin had suggested using an observation balloon to be brought from Versailles at great expense. Rising above the lid of clouds which sometimes closed the basin, this prehistoric device, which would probably have been shot down in no time, would have kept watch on the crests when the planes were unable to take off. This suggestion was not followed up.

In the instructions which he issued on this last day of the year, Navarre tried to show no hint of the pessimism which was beginning to affect him. He had decided to accept battle in the highlands, and if now, looking back on this decision, he began to consider it unfortunate, he nonetheless congratulated himself on it and repeated that he intended to be victorious.

As it was his duty to foresee everything, and he had already envisaged the best, there now remained the worst to be examined. He therefore pondered a hypothetical situation in which the battle, influenced by powerful resources which the enemy brought into play for the first time, went against him because artillery put the landing strip out of action and antiaircraft batteries smothered the base. He accordingly asked General Cogny and Colonel de Crèvecoeur to prepare in absolute secrecy a plan of operation to which he gave the name "Xenophon," in case the garrison of the entrenched camp was considered doomed and had to be evacuated.

One remarkable merit must be granted General Henri Navarre: that of not fearing repudiation by his direct subordinates when he made provision for defeat. Why didn't he go even further? True, he wrote that he would resign himself to withdrawing the troops from Dienbienphu only in the last extremity, but nobody in his entourage could approve of such a pessimistic view of the situation. Still less could anyone imagine that this view was already outdated, since the arrival of the 308th Division had jeopardized any attempt at escape. Like Caesar at Avaricum, like the great Condé before Lérida, Navarre thought that the situation might take a disastrous turn. Why hadn't he the courage to brave still further those who thought that they were going to make short work of Giap and were indignant that anybody could so much as doubt that victory would be theirs? Why didn't he decide to pull out? The presence of the 308th Division was a serious complication, and the evacuation of the battalions from Dienbienphu could not be carried out without loss; but the enemy artillery was not yet installed, and it would take a thrashing if it revealed its positions. There was less chance now than on December 10 of getting out unscathed, but there was still some chance. Only, the operation would take on the appearance of a rout, Navarre's prestige would be tarnished as a result, and, above all, the proof that victory had not been delusion would never be established.

⚒ 3 ⚒ The Chamber Pot

> The garrison artillery, on the other hand, should be installed in the thickness of this revetment, which should be extremely thick and in two tiers everywhere. The enemy would have to shoot very straight to put it out of action, and this would scarcely be possible since only the mouth of the cannon would project beyond the wall. . . .
>
> —PRINCE DE LIGNE

> It is known that an army can pass wherever a goat has passed; it is possible to hoist cannon with ropes onto the highest mountains, to establish platforms there, to fell the trees which have covered the summits since the beginning of the world, and to lay waste an enemy camp which did not expect to see a hail of cannon balls fall from the clouds.
>
> —PRINCE DE LIGNE

January 1, 1954

When Cogny went to Dienbienphu on December 29, he had to circle above the basin for over an hour before being able to pierce the clouds and land; the air space was already obstructed. A heavy drizzle covered the delta. Rain glistened on the roads, dripped from the roofs of the houses and obscured the car windshields and the banks of the Little Lake at Hanoï. On the airbases, the technical guiding equipment was so poor that there was an interval of fifteen minutes between one take-off and the next. At that rate, if the weather did not clear a little toward midday, it would take ten hours to send off the forty Dakotas needed to maintain life at Dienbienphu. The Air Force would succeed, that day, in landing at what henceforth must no longer be called a base for offensive and defensive operations, but an entrenched camp. The last infantry unit

98

expected there was the 5th Battalion, 7th Algerian Rifles, which had been chosen to occupy Gabrielle nearly three miles down the axis of the landing strip, on the gentle slopes of a long, wooded hill overlooking the northern entrance to the basin. About five hundred yards away, at the foot of a few rice fields, other, broader hills rose toward steep crests, covered with thick vegetation through which a skillful enemy could bring up his guns. It would be easy to get there from the dark mountain mass where Giap's army was scattered with nothing to indicate its position—not a single movement, not a single trench, not a single wisp of smoke. The only abrasions of the slope had been left by the fires lit by the Meos during the previous season in order to sow their poppies.

This strong point Gabrielle, which was so important that the Air Force itself had asked for it to be set up, could hope for no support except from the batteries in the central position. Béatrice and her Legionnaires were nearly two miles to the southeast, separated from Gabrielle by winding rivers and other hills; Anne-Marie and her Thais were over a mile to the southwest. Gabrielle and her leader would need not only machine guns and mortars to hold fast, but cast-iron morale, for the men there would feel isolated; they would even lack the comforts which the main center of resistance enjoyed: the electricity provided by the engineers' generators, the parachute drops on the spot and the reassuring impression created by the number of men and the accumulation of weapons. The few officers in command of the Algerians at Gabrielle would have wondered what fate was being prepared for them if they could have read the document General Bodet carried that day in his briefcase in the plane taking him to Paris.

This was a long letter from General Navarre which bore the number "1" of the official correspondence of the New Year, already darkened by the prospects which the secret instructions of December 31 would create. The copy I have seen contained grammatical errors, but that was of secondary importance. The main thing was the substance, and the substance would plunge the recipients of that document into a perplexity they would not know how to dispel.

How could they understand that the man who five weeks before had replied with a categorical "no" to the timid proposals to open negotiations could now envisage the failure of an enterprise into which he had thrown himself without asking the government's opinion or in spite of that opinion? How, at such a distance, could they follow the process which had led Navarre from blind optimism to hopeless pessimism?

Above all, how could they feel obliged to rescue him from the predicament in which he seemed to have lightheartedly landed himself? *"Un roman noir"* was the phrase which went round official circles as soon as General Bodet had opened his briefcase. They would wince at a few poker player's expressions which studded the text: "a stake which could bring in considerable revenue"; "sweeping the board"; "raising a bid." They would ask themselves whether Navarre, too, did not imagine that he was sitting at a table where the stake was Indochina. Doubts arose as to the value of the hero whose prudence and sagacity had been praised so highly.

"That report," General Navarre told me nine years later, "was not so very pessimistic. Obviously, I didn't claim that the battle was already won, but that didn't mean that it was going to be lost. I added that, whatever happened, Dienbienphu would have diverted the Vietminh from a general attack on the delta. I pointed out that the enemy's supplies were assuming alarming proportions and that China was sending trucks, artillery and ammunition. But I showed no undue anxiety."

A *roman noir?* Navarre scrupulously reported the arrival of enemy antiaircraft guns and possibly heavy artillery and motorized vehicles. According to him, if the Air Force had succeeded in preventing these resources from arriving, the battle would have been won; if the enemy managed to put them in position, success could no longer be guaranteed. This was such a new style that the members of the government, accustomed to optimistic estimates, found it hard to believe their eyes. After the fanfares of Lang Son and the songs of victory of November 20, ministers who did not know Colonel Nicot's report against the principle of "Operation Castor" found it impossible to imagine that a commander in chief could have exposed the Expeditionary Corps to such dangers and could make the fate of such a battle dependent on a few bombers more or less. The first officer to be informed of both the importance of the Air Force's role in this affair and the inadequacy of the resources at his disposal had been General Navarre himself. It was for no other reason that he had been asked several times to revise his plans, and it was with full knowledge of the facts that he had decided to fight at Dienbienphu. Nobody in Paris could believe that the fate of twelve thousand men, penned in the entrenched camp, had been left to luck. At Dienbienphu itself, nobody knew anything about the enemy's reinforcements and the approaching battle except Castries, whom Cogny had come to alert that day.

January 2, 1954

From Hanoï, the permanent special correspondent of the Associated Press reported this fresh statement by General Cogny: "The French Command is sure of inflicting a serious defeat on the Vietminh at Dienbienphu. We expect a long, hard fight. We shall win."

In Cogny too, the tone had changed and the confidence had become slightly qualified. Cogny had been the first to say that Dienbienphu, as a barrier on the road to Laos, was practically worthless, but Cogny thought that at least at present the dice were still rolling and that it would not take a great deal for Giap to be the loser. For his part, he could not stop anything.

Navarre could do everything. Why hadn't he decided to retreat when the 308th Division was not yet ready to fight? Caesar at Avaricum and Condé before Lérida were not the only precedents. Other generals in the history of war had refused battle when the enemy had not offered himself as they expected, and if there had been no example, Navarre could have set one, to his credit. Finding himself in such trouble, de Lattre would not have hesitated to evacuate those twelve battalions which represented a poker stake in order to drop them near Hanoï, in the enemy's rear, and spread disorder there, while boasting to the whole world of the trick he had played on the Viets.

If Navarre thought of this now, it was too late. The drizzle was going to cover the delta and the transport aircraft would have found it hard to evacuate one battalion a day. Even if he decided to pull out, Navarre could no longer have done so, and nobody in Indochina would have forgiven him this disgrace. He did not have enough prestige to be taken at his word and obeyed. He would have been covered with ridicule.

From the crests dominating the gray basin of Dienbienphu, thousands of soldiers wearing latania-palm and bamboo helmets looked down at the smoke rising from the entrenched camp and guessed that they would not reach the valley alive. But Giap would never have dared to compare them to a stake on a card table; they were the Vietnamese Army of Liberation and knew that they were fighting for their independence against a colonialism in the process of disappearing from the surface of the earth. If they died, it would be with the cry of liberty on their lips.

For Navarre, nothing was lost if he refused battle, since he knew the risks he was running. Faced with the pawns his adversary had unexpectedly moved, Navarre had seen his own plan upset; the general battle which he had wanted to avoid was now forced upon him and he could no longer escape, caught in the net he had tried to cast. Like him, however, Giap was unable to raise and train fresh divisions to throw into the current campaign; however much his means of supplying his troops with rice, heavy guns and ammunition had improved, he would end up running short of the time and forces that conquer space. At the worst, Dienbienphu might meet the same fate as Na San, which Giap had been unable to swallow because his teeth had not been sharp enough nor his belly hollow enough. At Dienbienphu too, the time would come when the rains would interrupt operations; if Dienbienphu held out, Giap would then have to send his divisions to lick their wounds in their summer quarters; the garrison of the entrenched camp would be able to disappear, as at Na San, and slip through his fingers. Navarre could still bring to this battle, however ill prepared it was, resources far exceeding those of the enemy.

Navarre was going to throw everything into Dienbienphu; nobody had any doubt about that, except for the few officers, of whom Cogny was not one, who had read the January 1 letter to the government. Navarre stuck obstinately to his lofty plan. He regarded "Operation Atlante," the offensive he wanted to launch in the south and in Central Annam, as his strongest card, though without being sure that it would bring him victory, for he had written about it: "If it succeeds." In that case, it would be what he called a trump card. On the other hand, Navarre did not understand that if the battle of Dienbienphu were lost, he would be defeated. For his part, Giap had no doubts. His offensive on the mountain plateau of the south was simply a trick. He knew that the decisive struggle was taking place at Dienbienphu, and it was a few miles from there, in the forest of Muong Phan, that he had established his headquarters a month earlier in order to direct it.

In the late morning, at Hanoï, the weather cleared. Cogny left for Dienbienphu, where he lunched in Castries's mess. At 1305, Navarre arrived with the Commissioner General, M. Dejean. The letter Navarre had sent the government on January 1 had plunged him into the depths of perplexity, for in Saigon he knew no more than M. Jacquet did in

Paris. His chief desire was to discover the generals' intentions, without annoying them too much, and to get some dispatches out of them for his department.

However, he was not so incompetent as the generals imagined, and he asked what would happen if the enemy artillery established itself along the crests or on the slopes. He was told that it would be difficult enough for the Viets even to bring up artillery of any importance and move ammunition through the highland jungle, that the Air Force was watching the approaches, and that the counterbatteries of the entrenched camp would destroy the enemy's guns, which were bound to reveal their positions when they opened fire. The enemy artillery had never been used to any significant extent. It had opened fire only on rare occasions, in the delta or on posts close to the Chinese frontier. The calibers used had been the Japanese 75-mm., and the Chinese 75-mm. and 57-mm. No use had been made so far of 105-mm. guns.

M. Dejean, who perhaps remembered the old saying "Valleys attract cannon balls," did not appear convinced. He was assured that the Viets had no gunners capable of maintaining effective antiaircraft fire or jeopardizing the operation of the airlift. Up till 1953, low-caliber antiaircraft guns had inconvenienced only observation or transport aircraft on the approaches to dropping zones in the mountains. At Hoa Binh, however, the first direct hits had been registered.

The commissioner general had accepted these assurances. At 1530, he set off again for Vientiane and Saigon in his personal Dakota. Yet Navarre's letter to the government had led M. Maurice Dejean to understand that misfortunes for which he was unprepared could befall the territory that had been entrusted to him. What he had seen—the extent of the basin, the number of units installed, the guns in their circular pits, the fighter aircraft taking off from the airstrip in a cloud of dust, the trucks, the organization of the defense works, the distances he had covered in a jeep from one strong point to another, the barbed-wire defenses and the officers' behavior—all this had left him with the impression that the enemy, if he dared to venture into the basin, would never get near the command post of Castries, that imposing leader with the disdainful mouth and the handsome swagger stick.

Two days later, the commissioner general would enlighten his minister as to the High Command's intentions in a cable which would offset the unfortunate effect of the letter of January 1: "Our command considers that the battle, if joined by the enemy, will be very hard but offers us genuine chances of success. So far, General Giap's army has never faced a mission as formidable as that of attacking Dienbienphu."

This was the first time that the title of general without the insulting quotation marks had been granted to Vo nguyen Giap in an official document. Weight of arms brings courtesy in its train.

". . . the battle, if joined by the enemy . . ." cabled the commissioner general. Only a year after Na San, the French Command could still raise this question. They were almost certain that Giap would not attack, for Giap had not been through Staff College. In cases of doubt, they put their trust in another article of the Expeditionary Corps catechism which stated that the Viets never attacked when they found themselves equally matched or faced with serious difficulties. Together with the premise that Giap had no artillery, that if he had any he would not know how to use it, and that his resources and his concept of logistics did not allow him to spend more than a month in the highlands, this article of faith made up the doctrine of both officers and men.

Who could imagine that that forty-two-year-old amateur, compared with the geniuses who were trained in the Place Joffre, could represent the shadow of a threat to real generals appointed by the Cabinet and to a colonel fresh from the Course of Advanced Military Studies, the modern school for marshals? And yet, at the time of Na San it had already been reasonable to assume that the ambition to destroy the entrenched camp would offer Giap a chance to finish the war to his advantage by preferring a large-scale sacrifice to endless fighting and isolated deaths. A victory over the Expeditionary Corps in such circumstances would have consecrated the triumph of the Vietminh regime in public opinion and forced France to negotiate. Now, once again, the only question facing Giap, as he set about his task of carrying out the Party's orders, was this: "What do I need in order to swallow Dienbienphu?" The Air Force obstructed him because it saw, destroyed and supplied. If it saw nothing, if its blows missed their target or its striking power were limited, and if it were smashed in the air and on its bases, the problem would be solved. The garrison of Dienbienphu would die of suffocation. To imagine, even for a moment, that Giap could fail to be tempted to spring upon such a prey was sheer lunacy.

However, just as he had given up the attack on Na San after realizing that it could not succeed, so he might give up the attack on Dienbienphu if Dienbienphu struck him as being out of reach. Giap had never yet been faced with such a risk; but every year that passed increased his forces, opened fresh roads from China, added to his fleet of vehicles and enlarged his stocks of guns and ammunition. Why should the French take him for a fool? Why should they imagine that he would not know how to use antiaircraft guns? And what was the purpose of those two thousand bicycles which an intercepted message had reported on their way to Dienbienphu around Christmas?

The bicycles, as Military Intelligence had known for three years, served as transport. It was calculated that a bicycle could carry between two and two and a half times the weight of the man pushing it. But those men did not weigh very much. In point of fact, the load of a bicycle could go up to five hundred pounds, more than an elephant could carry. Wooden struts to strengthen the frame and the front fork, and bamboo poles to extend one handlebar and the brake levers, formed the basis of an outfit which each cyclist did his best to improve. Camouflaged and split up into several bundles, the load was ten or twelve times as big as that of a coolie, and there were thousands of bicycles in service. With these bicycles, it was no longer a question of counting in pounds, but in tons. This was pointed out to Navarre, who did not deign to worry about it.

That day, Navarre probably gave Castries what information he possessed about the enemy. Castries learned that he had to expect to see his planes shot down and motorized vehicles come down the slopes. Did Cogny worry about the gaps which existed in the defenses and those two strong points isolated miles from the central position, Béatrice to the northeast and Gabrielle to the north? Did Cogny and Castries insist on telling Navarre that the defenses as a whole would not stand up to the attack being prepared? I don't know, but I think that in similar circumstances I would have seen that I was told. It seems clear that if these problems were studied, they were not solved.

At 1700 hours, another platoon presented arms to Navarre when he left for Hanoï. The atmosphere was impressive. The factory was rumbling. Packages were raining from the sky. Faces and clothes were still covered with dust. Cogny went and sat beside Navarre, in the front of the plane's cabin, near a small desk. Farther back, the officers in their suites watched each other warily; the noise of the engines drowned out the conversation.

Cogny respectfully asked Navarre whether he intended to launch "Operation Atlante," preparations for which were beginning to act as a drain on the Expeditionary Corps. For anybody who knew Navarre this was not the sort of question to ask. Navarre replied in a curt, confident manner: "Operation Atlante," which he had conceived and planned, was the only large-scale offensive operation in a campaign cast in a defensive mold; it would take place. Then Cogny put forward, one after another, all the arguments against it: the terrain which would require large forces, the evasive tactics of the enemy who would refuse to make a stand, and the reinforcements which could not be sent to Dienbienphu if the attack took place. He did not tell him that the entrenched camp was not strong enough, that he had to confront the enemy with greater obstacles, and that he would need the battalions Navarre was in the process of taking from him to use in "Operation Atlante." In short, and probably because he himself was not frightened enough of a battle, he did not frighten Navarre, even though since Christmas the latter seemed to have become aware of the growing dangers. In any case, why should he have tried, in connection with Dienbienphu, to frighten a man who had just instructed him to study "Operation Xenophon" and who had foreseen everything?

Wrapped in his raincoat as in a toga, Navarre remained impassive and aloof. He listened condescendingly to Cogny giving him a lesson in strategy; let him tire himself out, repeat himself, return to the idea of his nebula, demonstrate that "Operation Atlante" was going to reduce his freedom of maneuver at Dienbienphu and then cut him short.

"If I couldn't carry out 'Operation Atlante' as I wish, I would ask the government to relieve me," he said, to put an end to the conversation.

Resigned, Cogny fell silent. He did not know what to do with his big body, and hunched up slightly in his armchair. Navarre turned his head toward the window, and Cogny felt something akin to aversion. He felt isolated and yearned nostalgically for the cunning Salan. Salan, too, was capable of making mistakes, but you could get at him, take him up, win him over. Navarre did not seem to give you a handle to anything, least of all to friendship.

January 5, 1954

Graham Greene, who visited the camp that day, was invited to lunch with Castries. At the table Colonel Piroth was talking about Na San when Colonel de Castries interrupted him by banging his fist on the table and exclaiming with what Greene calls a sort of Shakespearean frenzy, "Shut up! I don't want to hear the name of Na San spoken here. Na San was an entrenched camp. We are on an offensive base."

These words, Greene adds, were followed by an embarrassed silence which one of Castries's adjutants, probably Séguins-Pazzis, broke to ask the novelist whether he had seen Claudel's *Christopher Columbus* in Paris.

During the tour of the strong points which followed, Graham Greene asked his guide, "What did the colonel mean by 'an offensive base'?"

With a sweeping gesture, the officer pointed to the crests. "To be capable of taking the offensive, it isn't a squadron of tanks we would need, but a thousand mules."

According to Colonel de Castries, his exclamation had been intended to deceive the enemy through Graham Greene.

January 15, 1954

As far as he was concerned, Cogny seemed to have no doubts. Returning that day from inspecting the northern and southern defenses of the entrenched camp, he told the United Press correspondent at Hanoï, "I am hoping for a fight at Dienbienphu. Admittedly, the Vietminh artillery may bother us for a while, but we shall silence it. As he can't go to Laos in force for fear that our forces will close in behind him, Giap is obliged to attack. I shall do everything to make him bite the dust and cure him of the desire to try his hand at grand strategy."

Colonel de Castries, with the High Command's consent, sent planes to drop leaflets on the enemy positions and on the roads, or else he had messages broadcast on the wavelength of the enemy command in which he taunted the Viets: "What are you waiting for? Why don't you attack if you aren't cowards? We are waiting for you." Or again: "We are ready. If you are as strong as you say, come on." After all, Hector called Achilles a poor fool, an expression which we would translate today by a stronger term, while Achilles insulted Hector by calling him a "dog." I have been unable to find any authentic record of Castries's challenges, but that was the gist of them. Among other things, they mentioned cowardice. According to one Viet prisoner, the dropping of these leaflets produced an explosion of joy in the ranks of the People's Army, and Giap exclaimed, "They are staying. This time I have them."

One or two nights' journey away by jeep, in a hut which was indistinguishable from the forest, a man turned a pith helmet upside down and, putting inside it a hand so emaciated that it was almost transparent, said, "The French are there. . . ." Then, running a finger around the rim, he added, "We are here." This was Comrade President Ho Chi Minh, alias

Nguyen tat Thanh, alias Nguyen aï Quoc, whose father, a mandarin in a province of Annam, was relieved of his post because he refused to teach French and distributed the "letter written from abroad with blood" by the nationalist leader Phan boï Chau. With his huge forehead and his tuft of gray hair, his alternately ironical and fierce gaze, his straight nose, his projecting ears and his debonair little goatee, Ho Chi Minh seemed ageless, just as his fleshless body seemed the frail dwelling of an intrepid and indomitable soul. He had worked as a steward on boats, as a bottle washer in the great restaurants of Paris and as a road sweeper in London. Divided after that between prison, underground activity and political warfare, his life had led him to use all means to achieve his end: the independence of Vietnam. A confirmed bachelor, now playing the part of a kindly old uncle and pensive sage, and yet an intransigent and incorruptible revolutionary, dressed the year round in the same military uniform with no insignia of rank, he was a combination, as Jean Lacouture put it, of a Communist *poverello*, a sawdust Caesar, a Chinese pimp and a Franciscan Gandhi, mingling the studied charm of his clumsiness with a deliberate mildness which could be suddenly pulverized by an indignant accent, quickly covered in turn by a moist, indulgent smile. He was one of the most curious characters in world politics.

It was a far cry from Ho Chi Minh to the high commissioners who gave a dinner every evening at the Norodom Palace. Out of their sight, and yet facing them across nearly a thousand miles of jungle, were the wrinkled features and the long, straggly goatee of that dried-up little man, lost in his unimpressive clothes: Uncle Ho, who had forgotten his real name and everything which formed his personality in order to become the embodiment of his country. Assisted by the gaze which flashed beneath his powerful brow, he would use a language which thundered in the ears of his people and knew how to call to arms this nation to which he wanted to restore existence and honor. But, like many other men to whom he would later become an example and a guide, he had dreamed for a while of cooperation with what he knew of France, where he had succeeded in distinguishing the ambitious and dangerous from the wise and generous. For him, Leclerc was "a decent fellow," Sainteny a man he trusted. His chief crime was in wanting to be ahead of his time, when nobody in Europe imagined that the era of colonialism was over and that the empires were going to break up one after another if they refused to open their doors to the former colonial peoples.

The world that separated Uncle Ho from the representatives of France was not simply a means of expression or comprehension, a language or a civilization, for if Uncle Ho's civilization was not yet industrial, it had nothing to learn from that of M. Letourneau or M. Dejean. It was the same world which would later separate M. Lacoste from Belkacem Krim in Algeria: that of men who fought, not for portfolios, mandates or constituencies, but for the freedom of their people.

About this time, the French High Command learned that a meeting of the Vietminh Government was going to be held at Thaï Nguyen; the date and time of the meeting were known, but the locality of Thaï Nguyen consisted of a large number of villages and hamlets. In which straw hut were the members of the Central Committee going to meet? To wipe out the whole township, so as not to miss Ho Chi Minh, Vo nguyen Giap and Pham van Dong, the French needed hundreds of B-26's, following one another in several waves at intervals of a few minutes. They did not have them. So as not to give away the agent who had provided the information, no action was taken. This was why Giap had established his headquarters away from any center of population, in the depths of narrow ravines, among fallen rocks. With his maps spread out on blocks of stone in the shape of tables, surrounded by a staff of young men, Giap, dressed in dark clothes, bare-headed, his hair brushed back over his left temple to reveal his powerful forehead, analyzed Navarre's mistakes and decided on his rejoinder.

Cogny had submitted to Navarre, by way of a report, a copy of the instructions he had sent Castries, following the Commander in Chief's somber directive. He had used the device of an offensive plan, which in any case he believed to be plausible in the context of the nebula, and disguised the plan for the evacuation of the Dienbienphu garrison as a vigorous operation toward Laos, so as to avoid dealing a disastrous blow to the morale of the officer responsible, Colonel de Castries.

By what right was the truth concealed from Colonel de Castries? Why was he not told what lay ahead of him? Far from being frightened, if he was what he could not help being, he would be stimulated by the information. He would realize—for he was not surrounded simply by officers reciting the articles of their catechism—that Gabrielle and Béatrice were not enough to break the enemy's furious waves, miles from the central position. Battalion commanders to whom he had entrusted the defense of certain strong points had not failed to tell him so, and he remembered Gilles's remark: "If you lose an inch of ground, you are done for." Did he not at least know that the Vietminh High Command had insisted that all the crossroads along Route 41 should be able to bear a weight of twelve tons? Had Navarre informed him of the situation during that dark Christmas night? The answer to these questions is "yes." Castries knew everything about the enemy. Cogny sent him all his Intelligence reports. But the French High Command did not want to risk damaging his morale by telling him that one day, perhaps, they would have to move out. They simply counted on him to kill Viets when the time came.

Cogny therefore asked him to study the possibilities of a movement southwest toward Muong Khoua and a thrust in the direction of Son La in conjunction with a group which would be dropped by parachute at Na San, a request which, contrary to the High Command's secret intentions, could confirm Castries's sense of superiority.

Castries sent for Langlais.

"Would you be able to find your way again along those tracks you took to Sop Nao?"

"Why?" asked an amazed Langlais.

"You might well find yourself back on them one of these days."

Navarre was annoyed with the Air Force, which, contrary to what he had thought on November 28, was failing to stop the Vietminh divisions from pouring toward Dienbienphu. His deputy, General Bodet, considered that the fault lay with the officers at the top, but the means of reconnaissance and attack at the pilots' disposal were limited, they were hampered by the weather conditions, and the enemy was taking advantage of darkness and clouds to carry out his movements. What is more, he never, or scarcely ever, moved except under cover. The tens of thousands of coolies pushing their bicycles along or carrying on poles balanced on their shoulders mortar shells or machine-gun bullets, or the rice, salt or dried fish on which both officers and men lived, and the peasants who repaired the bombed roads or made new ones under the supervision of engineers, scattered as soon as the sound of planes was reported, and the foliage which they fastened to their equipment helped them to merge into the jungle. The trucks drove at night. During the day, they disappeared without a trace into the jungle tunnels, where workshops, messes and rest rooms were hidden. No smoke rose from these hiding places, for the cook, Hoang Cam, who was to become a national hero, had invented a smokeless oven. In order to strike, it was necessary to see, and the French Air Force saw nothing.

Navarre remained skeptical and thought that somebody was at fault.

He urged Cogny to give the battle a personal stamp and suggested that his liaison with the Air Command was inefficient.

January 19, 1954

In spite of the clouds which blotted out the highland valleys and the delta plain, the pilots of both the Air Force and the Fleet Air Arm attacked roads and depots. By this date, 127 tons of bombs had been dropped on "Mercure" alone. Forty-eight hours at the latest after a road had been cut, the enemy trucks were on the move again, and the weather conditions, which were getting steadily worse, made raids less frequent. Since November, over a score of targets of this sort had been kept under attack with just as much difficulty and just as paltry a result.

The Vietminh had perfected a method of repairing roads. In the vicinity of danger points it grouped the inhabitants of the neighboring villages, over ten thousand altogether along Routes 13B and 41. After the bombers had passed, the band of villagers, which helped with the reloading if necessary, came out of the thickets with shovels, pickaxes and baskets. To remove delayed-action bombs which had not yet exploded, the political commissar would call for volunteers. The smallest among them would crawl into the holes leading to the bombs and fasten the hook of a cable to their fins. A roped party would then pull out the bombs and roll them away to be exploded. To deal with the butterfly bombs which exploded on the ground only when they were touched, herds of buffaloes were driven up and down.

The staffs of the Expeditionary Corps learned that the Vietminh High Command had just given absolute priority to the transport by all possible means of 105-mm. shells and 81-mm. mortars.

January 20, 1954

That day, the interception and decoding of a fresh message provided an explanation of this order: the attack on Dienbienphu was to take place during the night of January 25-26, by the light of the moon in its second quarter. A feverish joy took hold of the operational officers at Hanoï and Saigon, and Navarre received the news calmly. Nevertheless, he did not cancel the launching of the first phase of "Operation Atlante"; it was to last over a month and involve twenty-five battalions in the Savannakhet zone where Navarre wanted to destroy the rebel forces, between the

Mekong and the coast. The Vietminh withdrew from the Mekong and took refuge in the inland jungle and the mountain plateaus. A new front was formed which would have to be supplied by the Air Force.

At Dienbienphu, Lieutenant Colonel Langlais, the commander of the two reserve battalions of paratroops, continued his study of the counter-attacks intended to recover any ground the enemy might succeed in winning. There were so many possibilities that the speediest measures were laid down: Gabrielle or Béatrice, the most distant strong points, were to be reoccupied first of all. It would be necessary to plot the routes in detail, to use the slopes, to avoid the obstacles formed by the barbed-wire defenses and the watercourses, to keep up a steady covering fire, to check the time needed for each movement and to fix the extent of supporting fire from neighboring units. Already it was clear that no counterattack would be possible by night because the troops of the entrenched camp were not accustomed to maneuvering in darkness. As in a well-organized film, the exercise would have to be rehearsed, with real shelling, as long as any faults in its execution could be found.

January 23, 1954

Cogny had sent Navarre his study of "Operation Xenophon," the plan for evacuation of the entrenched camp in the event of a disaster. He made no secret of his opinion that the enterprise was so hazardous that it seemed impossible. Colonel de Crèvecoeur had done the same. Navarre would never deign to communicate to his subordinates whatever conclusion he drew from these two studies. In Cogny's opinion, the investment of Dienbienphu by the enemy was such that enormous resources would be needed to open a breach through which even light elements could pass. Writing the word "disaster" for the first time, he at last shed a light on the facts which left no more hope for the strategic concepts by which he had allowed himself to be deluded too long. "Away from the tracks," he wrote, "it is impossible to move large columns." He suggested using the old road from Dienbienphu to Sop Nao, along which tracked vehicles could move, though only provided certain passages were cut out along the way. Yet the terrain had not changed since the High Command had dreamed of making it a theater for offensive operations, and it was there that they had installed a cavalryman.

Cogny therefore insisted that the 13,500 men which made up the garrison should not be doomed by an attempt to escape and that Dienbienphu should be held at all costs. He added, to reassure Navarre, that nobody at Dienbienphu had known of the real intentions of the operations. But who could have made any mistake about the name it had been given? Xenophon was the author of the *Anabasis,* and the Anabasis was the retreat of the ten thousand.

In anticipation of the expected attack, Navarre outlined two hypotheses in further secret instructions: either the enemy would hurl all his forces at the entrenched camp or else he would content himself with neutralizing it and transfer some of his forces elsewhere. In the latter case, Navarre estimated that only about ten Vietminh battalions would be able to invade Laos, for all the others would be held up by the vigorous resistance of the entrenched camp, whose blows would destroy both men and batteries. He even ventured to add that, if the balance of forces permitted, an attack should be made upon the base of Tuan Giao.

It can be seen that once again the concepts the two generals held of the battle were suddenly separated by a wide disparity. Navarre and his staff were still drawing arrows on their maps at headquarters, when reconnaissance patrols found it almost impossible to cross the borders of the entrenched camp. To mount a land attack on the base of Tuan Giao was sheer lunacy; and to imagine that Langlais's battalions would be able to attack the crests to destroy the enemy batteries showed that either Langlais had never been asked about the difficulties he had experienced or that he was regarded as incompetent—in which case he should have been relieved of his post.

Cogny, however, had taken the measure of the enemy and the terrain. The instructions which he in his turn gave to Colonel de Castries and which he would subsequently consider as the basic defense plan did not wander off into the realm of imagination. He had gone back, the day before, to Dienbienphu. He listed the means of defense, defined the mission of the entrenched camp, and hinted that success was not certain and that it would be necessary to recapture lost ground. But it seems clear that in his mind Béatrice and Gabrielle were already doomed, since they were not included in the list of strong points to be held at all costs. In that case, how could he imagine that he could still win if the airstrip became unusable? Because of his artillery. Not for one moment did Cogny the gunner imagine that Viet batteries could stand up to the fire of Colonel Piroth's guns. Like all gunners in the Expeditionary Corps, Cogny was convinced that Giap would be unable to use his guns behind the crests on account of the range and the form of the trajectory, or in front of the crests because they would be seen firing and so destroyed. And Castries did not imagine for one moment that the Viet infantry would be able to advance under shellfire and gain a footing on the conquered positions.

That day, it was learned that a regiment of the "Iron Division," the 304th, whose departure had been reported earlier, had reached Dienbienphu. This was the 57th Regiment, whose chief of staff was called Nguyen Hien and marched with a mortar splinter near his heart.

For the three battalions of this regiment, the three hundred miles from Yen Bay to Dienbien were sheer hell. Day and night, the shout "Planes!" would be raised and the columns would throw themselves into the thickets to avoid being seen from the air. The men ate as best they could, more often than not a-ball of cold rice kept from the previous day's meal in a latania leaf; it was forbidden to light fires, except at halts, in smokeless ovens, and after a few hours on the march, arms and equipment grew heavy.

The hardest part of the journey was the crossing, between Thuan Chau and Tuan Giao, of the Fa Dinh Pass, so called because its heights, which were often in the clouds, seemed to touch the sky. On the French map it bore the name of Meos Pass. As it was always threatened with air attack, in spite of the antiaircraft batteries which had been installed there, the Viet troops had to cover its twenty miles, along a winding path across one of the few bare mountains in the region, at one go, almost at a run, in the same night, often in the light of flares dropped by the French planes. Some parts of the route, which were bombed every day, were destroyed to such an extent that it was difficult to get through on foot and lines of trucks were often held up for hours. Sometimes, too, the engineers had to cut a way through fresh walls of rock.

When I asked Captain Hien whether the French Air Force had given them trouble, he replied that the only people who could doubt that were those who had not fought on their side. But he added that if it had been a hundred times stronger, it would still not have prevented them from crossing. As they approached the pass, a sort of holy frenzy took hold of the soldiers and the wave of men, women and vehicles who were advancing toward Dienbienphu on the ravaged Route 41 or who were coming back to fetch fresh loads.

It was only one hour after daybreak when they reached the foot of the pass, and, as usual, dug some trenches to sleep in. Before lying down, the platoon leaders made sure that the men's mosquito nets were properly arranged. At Tuan Giao, where the rations were shared out, the necessity of checking the weight of the loads led to furious quarrels between those who had to light lamps to verify their accounts and those who were afraid that, however small they might be, these lights might attract the bombers.

From the base of Tuan Giao to Dienbienphu, it took three consecutive nights on the march to cover fifty miles. To begin with, the road ran along a valley which I saw in a smiling mood when I passed that way, in the daytime, nine years later. The big wheels of the water mills were bringing water up from the river into the irrigation canals. Herds of buffalo gleaming with mud were grazing in the stubble and bathing in the pools; rice was being threshed near the ricks. Peasants kept passing us on little horses with long, fair manes.

Here and there, limestone rocks pierced the gray skin of the rice fields with their bare bones and suddenly barred the way, leaving only a single passage between their black cliffs. Then the valley narrowed, the villages became fewer and finally disappeared, the landscape turned wild and stifling, and the river flowed in full force under a vault of bamboos.

Suddenly, at the foot of a rock, the road, which throughout the whole of its length the Viets were trying to widen, assumed a terrifying appearance —though, on reflection, neither more nor less terrifying than all the highland roads which the generals chose for their maneuvers. Bold engineers had traced them out at a time when government officials traveled without escorts through a peaceful country. Full of holes and furrows, they were roads in name only and on maps. Plunging up and down ravines and fording rivers next to ruined works of art, they made engines scream and broke springs and backs; the trucks in front raised clouds of thick dust which clung to the face. They were even worse when the convoys advanced under the threat of air attack across huge quagmires made by hastily repaired bomb damage, overflowing, in rainy weather, with a sticky mud which the wheels splashed over the infantry. As the convoys could pass only at certain points, on account of the narrowness of the roads, vehicles which broke down were hooked onto those in front until the next turnout.

About twelve miles from Dienbienphu, road junctions suddenly appeared in the forest. The guide shunted the 57th Regiment toward the north, along other roads in the vast network laid out by Giap, in order to bring up his artillery. Covered with branches like the trucks that towed them, and looking like thick bushes, the 105-mm. guns of the 351st Heavy Division had passed that way and were still passing. Hidden during the day in jungle tunnels, they had reached the heights of Dienbienphu,

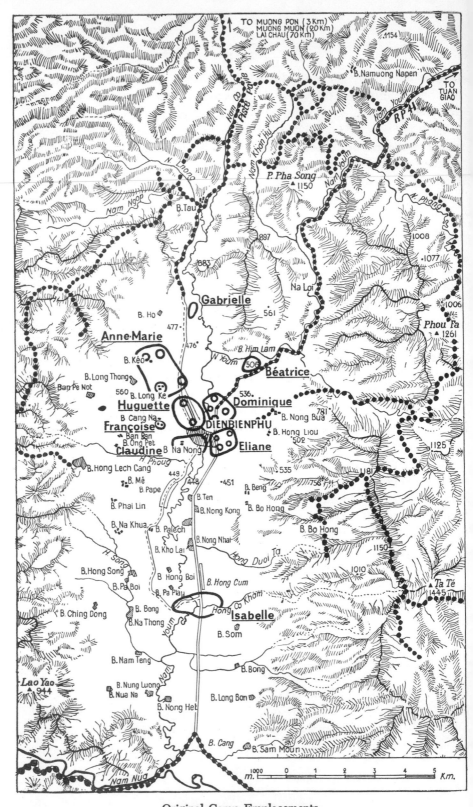

TO MUONG PON (3 Km)
MUONG MUON (20 Km)
LAI CHAU (70 Km)

.1154

B. Namuong Napen

TO TUAN GIAO

RP 41

P. Pha Song
▲ 1150

Na Loi

.897

.683

1008

.1077

1006

Phou Fa
▲ 1261

B. Ho

Gabrielle

.561

477·

476°

Anne·Marie

B. Kéo

B. Long Thong

Ban Pe Not

560

B. Long Ke

Huguette

B Cang Na

Françoise

Ban Ban

B. Ong Pet

Claudine

B Na Nong

B.Hong Lech Cang

·B. Mé

B. Pape

B. Phai Lin

B. Na Khua

B. Palech

B.Hong Song

B. Hong Bai

B.Pa Boi

B. Pa Play

B. Ching Dong

B.Na Thong

B. Bong

B. Nam Teng

B. Nung Luong

Lao Yao
944

B. Nua Na

B. Nong Heb

W Youm

B. Him Lam

506

Béatrice

536.

Dominique

781·

B. Nong Bua

DIENBIENPHU

B. Hong Liou

·502

1125

Eliane

H. Phoug

449·

.535

756

1181

448

·451

B. Beng

B. Ten

B. Nong Kong

B. Bo Hong

B. Nong Nhai

Hong Duoi Ta

B. Bo Hong

1150

B. Kho Lai

1010

B. Hong Cum

Ta Té
▲ 1445

Hong Co Kham

Isabelle

B. Som

B. Bong

B. Long Bon

B. Cang

B. Sam Moun

1000 m.   0   1   2   3   4   5 Km.

Nam Nua

Original Camp Emplacements

•••••=Enemy road network.   Ban or B.=Village.   Nam or N.=River.

thanks to huge trenches cut into the limestone massif. In most cases, it had been sufficient to adapt the Meos' tracks or the forest paths made by the French.

The task was made more enormous because of the primitive methods employed. To reduce the distance, the slopes had been tackled at dizzy angles; with no thought of saving trouble, the tree trunks used for bridge-building were carried on men's backs, and the roads went up sheer cliff faces, without handrails, camouflaged, when they were exposed to view, with wild banana trees and bamboos with long curved stalks, which had been transplanted there, roots and all.

The workings had not yet pierced the mountain. Hundreds of men, women and girls were still attacking the ground with pickaxes, scraping the road walls, taking the earth away in round baskets, wheelbarrows and little two-wheeled carts, carefully sifting the stones, which were used for surfacing the road, or sometimes going for miles to fetch some.

The men of the 57th Regiment were singing. They no longer felt the weight of the weapons on their shoulders. They exchanged greetings and jokes with the teams who had been living for weeks in those woods, with thickets covered with leeches just waiting for men to pass in order to fasten onto their flesh. Day and night, the forest rang unceasingly with the noise of pickaxes mingled with the cry of birds, the obsessive tapping of woodpeckers and the roaring of uneasy wild beasts. This mobilization of a whole people, set in motion by a decision of the Central Committee in order to seize victory in spite of every obstacle, had taken them out of themselves. They were dimly aware that they were taking part in a momentous event, an event which had penetrated to their very bones, giving them the conviction that they were going to win and that what had so far been so much blind effort was about to culminate in dazzling light. Step by step, day after day and night after night, the longed-for battle had come within their reach, and its issue now depended only on their courage.

January 25, 1954

In Hanoï, M. Jacquet, who had been back in Indochina for a week, was listening to General Cogny outlining to him and the Army Chief of Staff, who had arrived a week earlier, the threats accumulating over Dienbien-phu. Navarre was there, and Cogny did not let him down.

The minister, uneasy to begin with, suddenly pricked up his ears.

Rugged in build, smooth in manner, his crew-cut gray hair accentuating the rough side of his face, he silently filled a fresh pipe and then abruptly asked Navarre whether he was absolutely certain of victory.

Navarre drily repeated the arguments on which his plan was based, insisted on the necessity under which he had found himself of defending Laos, recalled the pressure that had been exerted on him to occupy Dienbienphu, and concluded with an impressive enumeration of the forces in the entrenched camp in the face of an adversary who had been halted in his progress toward Laos and who was showing no reaction in the delta. M. Jacquet did not feel qualified to reply. Besides, in whose name could M. Jacquet have raised a protest?

"How would the Tonkin troops take a reverse at Dienbienphu?" he asked Cogny all the same.

"They would take it," said Cogny. "But what about Paris?"

"I sincerely hope that Paris will not have to face such an eventuality," said M. Jacquet before a silent Navarre.

Everywhere, it was hoped that the expected attack would be launched before long. Every evening in the trenches of Dienbienphu, where the yellow dust raised by planes, vehicles and tanks fell and settled, weapons were cleaned when the guns let off their first salvos which lit fires in the mountains. The succession of alarms was nerve-racking. All these bored young men dreamed of frothy beers on café terraces, of showers and women, and indulged in the eccentricities of morose schoolboys. The filtered water of the Nam Youm and the dark rotgut which was issued to them under the name of *vinogel* made them sad; sometimes, with a macabre sense of humor, beer was smuggled into the camp in coffins. Castries's beautiful secretary, the appearance of the air convoy girls, Brigitte Friang, whose lipstick-stained cigarette stubs were piously collected, and the bronze faces of the Arab Ouled Naïls of the military brothel of Laï Chau, which had been moved at the same time as the garrison, and of another brothel which had been brought from Hanoï, turned their thoughts to love. On Béatrice, indeed, shelters had been ingeniously arranged for these ladies, who in the end had been moved a little further away from the enemy.

The hospital of the entrenched camp had played its part in evacuating the sick, the wounded and the dead. In a single month, 207 wounded, 75 victims of accidents and 354 cases of illness had been moved to Hanoï. The surgical unit had only forty-two beds. There were only seven in the resuscitation ward. "That doesn't matter," Castries told Brigitte Friang. "In the event of an attack, we'll put the wounded everywhere." To bring them in, there were only one ambulance and two jeeps. The morgue had been dug out near the hospital. The output of the water-purifying plant was inadequate, and not all the units had tankers. There was a shortage of individual mosquito nets, and malaria was rife in all the surrounding villages.

When night came, the waiting would begin again. A Dakota circled above the camp, ready to drop flares. The moon lasted ten days. It had risen before sunset, a huge yellow paving stone in the sky. Nobody knew how, if it came, the attack would start. Probably, as at Na San, with a concentration of mortar fire on Béatrice or Gabrielle, the two advance redans of the fortress. Fifty or a hundred mortars would spit 81-mm. shells in one blast. To the north or the northeast on the hills, the night would abruptly split open, steel would rain down on the men, and the earth would open under the hammering of an invisible enemy. Behind the loopholes in the casemates, snipers would press the triggers of automatic rifles; then the artillery of the entrenched camp would go into action, and death would fall upon the crests where the enemy troops were massed for attack. In all the surrounding villages, people would come out of the huts and watch the glows and flashes of battle. Children would start crying. The animals in the jungle would take flight. Then four or ten Vietminh battalions would rush toward the peaks of Béatrice or the hillocks of Gabrielle, wave after wave of them, preceded by a group of dynamiters with orders to make openings in the barbed-wire defenses and destroy the blockhouses, blowing themselves up with them. Thousands of soldiers in latania and bamboo helmets, with pieces of tires on their feet and strings of grenades round their waists, would be crushed under Colonel Piroth's iron fist or under the bursts of fire from Béatrice and Gabrielle.

If only the battle would begin and put an end to the unbearable anticipation of an event which might determine the fate of the war! The imaginations of the men of the Expeditionary Corps carried them thousands of miles away, where women waited for them, under soft skies, in houses and on soil which were not like these.

In his shelter with its walls lined with sandbags and matting, Colonel de Castries listened to the night, sitting at his table. Light poured from the naked bulbs hanging from the ceiling. A clattering typewriter and the ringing of a telephone were muffled by the walls. Practically the whole of one wall was taken up by a large-scale map of the entrenched camp, covered with a sheet of cellophane on which conventional symbols had been traced with a crayon.

This was a strange fate for a cavalryman—to spend his nights and part of his days six feet underground, encircled. A jeep waited at the end of the sap or trench which came out on an inclined plane under the stars. If the Viets attacked that night, Castries might learn where this adventure which could win him glory or contempt was taking him. At any rate, he was fighting for two silver stars, which he would have obtained in any case, and a higher rank in the Legion of Honor. Failure was impossible with the Air Force supporting him, the twelve battalions entrenched in the basin, his twenty-eight guns and sixteen heavy mortars ready to open fire, and Cogny watching over him from Hanoï, to whom he could speak frankly whenever he wanted to, thanks to a radiotelephone which scrambled the waves at the transmitter and unscrambled them at the receiver. Toward the end of the day, the planes had searched the crests, looking for any signs of preparations for attack. There had been nothing, or scarcely anything: a few movements which the artillery had dealt with, and which would not have meant much without the foreknowledge that an attack was due to take place.

Yet Castries knew that his enemy was strong and that his weapon was secrecy; nobody saw him coming and, once the fighting was over, he disappeared with the same skill, to escape retaliation. He would unleash an action in an instant, in the darkness. When dawn came, he would be far away, or have disappeared into the heart of the jungle, across the rice fields, into the marshes or into the underground passages beneath the villages. In the delta, which he knew well, Castries had succeeded more than once in surrounding and destroying him with his armored formations. Here, Castries had looked for him in vain. Almost every day, he had flown over the mountains in an observation plane with Piroth, his gunner, to try to discover signs of occupation. Castries wanted to convince himself that the Viets would simply have to show themselves. And then the guns of the entrenched camp would reduce them to dust.

He loosened his red scarf a little and stubbed out his cigarette in the ashtray. For his part, if the attack took place, he hoped that it would be violent and short. For the moment, he would like a game of bridge if he could find three partners: his new chief of staff, for example, Major Keller, the only person to read Cogny's Intelligence reports with him; the

Legionnaire Lieutenant Colonel Gaucher, the officer with the buccaneer's face who was in command of the central subsector; and Langlais, whose command post was not far away and who had put in a state of readiness the two parachute battalions reserved for counterattacks. Reserved? Not completely. Under normal circumstances they covered one side of Claudine, but it was expected that there would be very little time to get them together. Castries rang for his secretary, Paule Bourgeade, that girl of twenty-eight with the hazel eyes whom he had met in the south of the delta, where she had been serving for five years with a courage many men could envy.

Like the frail and charming Brigitte Friang, she belonged to that class of women you were surprised to find in the army and who liked the life because they had suffered experiences in Europe which they were trying to forget, more at ease among men who risked their skin than in cowardly bourgeois comfort. Nobody had any doubt that there had been drama in their lives, as in the lives of the other girls who had come out to the Far East, but nobody tried to find out anything about that drama. For them, the Expeditionary Corps symbolized what the Foreign Legion offers those men whom an unhappy love affair or banishment by society leads one day to a recruiting office. Castries had attached this one to himself, and it was easy to see why. He took her with him in his jeep when he visited the strong points; she noted his remarks on her shorthand pad and left behind her dreams and a faint whiff of Dior perfume, the only luxury she possessed, just as Brigitte Friang jumped by parachute with her set of face lotions, powder and lipstick. Wasn't there something improper about a secretary of this sort? In Indochina, since de Lattre's time, free morals had been common currency. After all, wasn't this war rather like Atlantis?

Paule Bourgeade appeared in her heavy clothing and army boots, which added a spicy charm to the situation. She smiled. She was beautiful and strange, and must have turned the heads of a great many Legionnaires and paratroopers. She was worthy, in fact, of a marshal in the field.

"A game of bridge," said Castries. "Try to find me some enthusiasts."

Mademoiselle Bourgeade went off. She liked this life and the danger that went with it. This was her right, and indeed her nobility. The only thing that can be held against her is that she allowed herself to be decorated with the *Croix de guerre* at Dienbienphu, in front of the troops.

The attack did not take place, and it was the first time that a piece of information of such importance seemed to have been proved wrong. Possibly the counterorder had been entrusted to more reliable methods of communication than the radio.

M. Jacquet landed at Dienbienphu at 1350, accompanied by M. Dejean, General Blanc, Navarre and Cogny. The usual ceremonial was ready.

Castries installed Jacquet in the jeep he was driving, and, followed by the usual procession, with the vehicles a good distance from one another to avoid the dust, took him first to Béatrice, where the Legionnaires' beards made a lasting impression on the visitors; Béatrice, if necessary, would be another Camerone. It had a lookout post with a magnificent view of the whole entrenched camp and the dark crests which dominated it. Field glasses were fixed to a stand on the hillock which surmounted the command post. Monsieur Jacquet climbed onto it and suddenly sank up to his knees in the loose soil.

Lieutenant Colonel Gaucher helped him out. Smart, shrewd, silent and watchful, the head of the commissioner general's information service smiled.

"Say, Colonel," said M. Jacquet, "what about the people underneath?"

"Oh," replied Gaucher, "there's fifteen feet of rubble and logs above them. Don't worry, M. Minister, it will hold."

Who could doubt it? A battalion of the Foreign Legion, clinging to the three peaks of Béatrice, and eleven other battalions with their guns in the valley where smoke was rising from the messes and from the undergrowth which was still being burnt—it looked like a tough proposition. To complete the tour and impress the visitors with a sight which would win their admiration, they were taken to the command post of Piroth, the gunner. He had lost his left arm in Italy and had the empty sleeve tucked into his belt. His big forage cap jutted out over his shaven skull. His turned-up nose, his little eyes buried under his forehead, his thin lips and the wart on one cheek gave him the face of a wrestler or a football player. With a single gesture, he could make his guns spit wherever he wished, and his battery of 155's would destroy the enemy batteries behind the crests with their plunging fire. His ugly mug and his crusty temper were reassuring. Everybody liked the man his reputation had made him. Victory depended on his crushing retorts, his clear-sightedness, his lookout posts, his toughness.

A captain in the Air Force Reserve, M. Jacquet thought about the runways of the airfield and felt a certain uneasiness about them. If, in spite of everything, the enemy succeeded in hitting them, even if it were only with heavy mortar shells, the whole situation would be complicated. Twenty-four 105's, a battery of 155's and sixteen heavy mortars did not strike him as terribly impressive. In Korea, the Americans had massed thousands of guns behind their lines.

"Colonel," he said to Piroth as he was leaving, "I know that there are hundreds of guns lying idle at Hanoï. You ought to take advantage of a minister's visit to get a few sent you on the side."

"What!" exclaimed the shocked Piroth. "Look at my plan of fire, M. Minister. I've got more guns than I need."

To General Blanc, who had been trained in one of France's great technical schools, the École Polytechnique, and who, as a gunner, had had him under his command and had asked him if he had everything he needed, Piroth replied, "If I have thirty minutes' warning, my counterbattery will be effective."

And what if he didn't have those thirty minutes? What if he never had them? It was known that the Viets on their side had brought up twenty-four 105-mm. guns which nobody had managed to locate. The French were waiting patiently for them to reveal themselves, in order to destroy them.

When the afternoon was drawing to a close, Navarre went up to M. Jacquet.

"We have the impression they are going to attack tonight," he told him in an undertone. "I would prefer not to expose a minister to any risks."

The official Dakotas took off at 1645 for Hanoï.

Three hours was not long to size up a situation like that, even for General Blanc. As far as he was concerned, however, it was enough for him to fear the worst. In his opinion, this was not Verdun, as he has been reported as saying, but the Somme, and the artillery was going to decide the outcome of the battle. But Navarre, who was irritated by the slightest reservation, displayed his cold confidence, which became mocking or faintly contemptuous when he was correcting people's errors of appraisal or answering questions which he considered puerile.

"I asked my visitors several questions about Dienbienphu," M. Dejean would write later.

I did not find the same enthusiasm in them all. Two of them would have preferred Dienbienphu not to be attacked. One of them referred to the disadvantages of a position overlooked by the enemy. But none of them expressed the opinion that the position was a dangerous one and that it was essential to pull out as quickly as possible. None of them seemed seriously uneasy. A few days before the enemy offensive, the chief fear of our command in Indochina was still that the Vietminh might call off the attack on the entrenched camp.

A dispatch from Paris anounced that a mission was coming to Indochina with the Minister of National Defense to study the military situation.

January 27, 1954

M. Jacquet phoned the Commander in Chief early in the day.
"Well?"
"They haven't attacked," Navarre replied in a disappointed voice.

It seems clear that Ho Chi Minh had summoned the Central Committee of the Party the day before the attack to make a joint decision. The Viets wanted to take advantage of the fact that the defense system of the entrenched camp had not been finished and penetrate the area along several axes, cutting it into pieces and crushing the zones of resistance one after another. Although he was prepared to go into action if ordered to do so, Giap nonetheless observed that he could not guarantee victory on account of the heavy losses which might be suffered and his units' lack of experience in operations on so large a scale. What is more, not all the battery emplacements were satisfactory; some guns had not yet reached their casemates, others would have to change position, and the plan of fire would have to be altered slightly. A quick victory struck him as doubtful; he preferred to continue with his preparations and make steady progress. "Attack to conquer" was the motto of the People's Army. The Central Committee gave its support to this principle of revolutionary war and modified it slightly so that it read: "Attack only when victory is certain, otherwise hold back." The action planned for the night of January 25-26 was accordingly called off.

The Central Committee went further. It decided that the Dienbienphu operation was not to be regarded simply as an attack on a fortified position, carried out over a comparatively short period, but as a campaign of long duration, lasting until the rainy season and consisting of a whole series of separate phases culminating in the annihilation of the enemy. In order to gain possession of all the approaches to the basin, Béatrice and Gabrielle were to be attacked first, then the main center, in a series of attacks in strength and offensive patrols, while Isabelle would be neutralized. Each attack, carried out with heavy artillery support and a mass of infantry, would aim at swamping the enemy from the very first night. The assault units would be relieved before they were worn out and would leave the battlefield in turn to rest. While the road system around Dienbienphu was being perfected and supplies of all sorts were being accumulated, the 308th Division supported by two battalions of the 148th Regiment would leave the vicinity of the entrenched camp to trick General Navarre and would move toward the southwest. As for the French Air Force, its parachute drops would be hampered and its planes destroyed by the installation on the lower slopes and then in the valley itself of skillfully camouflaged antiaircraft guns. Contrary to what was later stated on the French side, the decision to postpone the attack was taken without any Chinese or Soviet representative present. While there were some foreign military advisers in the ranks of the People's Army, they had no power.

What Navarre and Cogny did not know that day was that the greater part of the Vietminh artillery was already in position. The regiment of 105-mm. guns of the 351st Heavy Division had installed most of its twenty-four guns under yards of rock without being observed. Giap even treated himself to the luxury of establishing dummy emplacements to draw French fire. If Cogny had known this, he would immediately have given orders for the guns of the entrenched camp, which were installed out in the open, to be buried, and Piroth would no longer have answered M. Jacquet that he had too many guns; he would have asked for three times as many. Castries was suspicious, but his gunner swept his fears aside. Never for a moment did anybody imagine that the Viets might install their artillery on the slopes facing Dienbienphu; nobody had done that since Napoleon. Batteries were always set up out of the enemy's sight, on the reverse slope, and they fired from that position, according to classic calculations. In the case of Dienbienphu, the gunners of the Expeditionary Corps were unanimous in believing that the height of the crests made it impossible for a trajectory to reach the center of the basin. The Viets would therefore be obliged to fire from the slopes facing Dienbienphu, which was impossible, since they would then be seen and destroyed.

Besides, the French continued to express considerable skepticism as to the possibility of the enemy bringing up, over mountainous terrain devoid of tracks, anything but mortars and 75-mm. guns. It had, in fact, been 75-mm. mountain guns which had harried the entrenched camp the night before. It never occurred to the French that Giap had intended to put them on the wrong scent. In the opinion of the French technicians, artillery of 75-mm. range would be incapable of maintaining a concentrated barrage and the shelters could easily stand up to its fire. To be suspicious of such conclusions one would have to have the realistic mind of a Gilles or a Bigeard. As for General Navarre, he was beginning to have such doubts about the judgment of his subordinates that nothing would have surprised him, but even so he would not change his plan.

January 31, 1954

Speaking of an operation which had just taken place against a Viet battery, and of those which he had carried out earlier, Langlais used the phrase "bloody reverses." And yet the French were "going to show them. . . ." Robert Guillain heard that expression everywhere. "We're going to show them who we are, the Viets and all the others." That was the explanation given by the special correspondent of *Le Monde*. "All the others?" The onlookers in Paris and elsewhere.

"To get the Viets down into the basin" was the dream of Colonel de Castries and the entire staff. "If he comes down, we've got him. It may be a tough fight, but we shall halt him. And we shall at last have what we have always lacked: a concentrated target that we can smash." Here Robert Guillain records remarks whose authenticity cannot be doubted. He told Castries how astonished he was to see him leave the crests to the enemy.

"You don't know anything about modern tactics," replied the commander of GONO, who cut short the conversation with a contemptuous sneer, and later stated that he had been trying to deceive the enemy through the journalists.

Before he had left Paris, a high-ranking officer belonging to one of the Saigon staffs had already told Robert Guillain that the situation had never been better and that he was going to arrive out there at the right moment.

The 308th Division, which suddenly went off toward Laos, causing considerable surprise among the strategists, could only be bothered, if at all, by the troops it met on its way. How could it be pursued, and with what forces? Navarre hurriedly sent extra barbed wire and armored formations to Luang Prabang, where the decrepit old king took to his bed, and while in the theater of "Operation Atlante" Navarre's offensive marked time, Giap retaliated by attacking on the plateaus of Central Annam.

February 3, 1954

Throughout Vietnam, the people were celebrating the *Tet*, the New Year's Day of the lunar calendar and the first moon of January. In Saigon, Hanoï and the whole country, gifts were exchanged, houses were decorated with dragons and huge paper carps on which the household god left for heaven, and fireworks were set off. Usually it was the coldest day in the year; but spring was close and in the north the peach trees were in blossom.

During the previous evening, the command liaison officer had brought the chief of staff of the 57th Viet Regiment an order to move at once toward the north of the Dienbienphu basin. It was a dark night and the men could not see where they were going. On the steep slope, their feet slipped and stubbed against stones so sharp that Captain Hien compared them to cats' ears. At midnight, the French Dakota dropped flares which brought progress to a halt. The regiment advanced at barely half a mile an hour.

At midday, in honor of the *Tet*, some 75-mm. shells were fired from the lower slopes in the northeast at the planes and the airstrip. A single battery, installed and camouflaged in special trenches, fired 103 shells for half an hour from the mobile American 75-mm. guns captured at Hoa Binh.

Three guns, fifty yards apart and two and a half miles from their target, fired in salvos of nine shots each. At the second salvo, Piroth's artillery replied, guided by a lookout post on Éliane, but its shells fell on the dummy emplacements where two men were letting off explosives to imitate shots. In all it would fire 1,650 105-mm. shells. The fighters and B-26's dropped 158 bombs on the dummy emplacements and then on the real ones; rockets wounded three men seriously, and a few others slightly, and hit a field kitchen. The tanks came up and fired into what they took to be the embrasures of the guns. At Castries's command post, they thought that everything had been destroyed.

In the afternoon, the Viets sang, danced and played the flute or the harmonica in the valleys hidden from sight. Porters came and congratulated the gun crew of the battery, about whom Giap wired a mention in dispatches. Porters and soldiers shared the sweets and rice loaves with spices and meat balls traditionally eaten on this feast day.

Like the ten drivers in his group, the soldier Tran van Tha, who was as nimble as quicksilver, had filled his truck up with gas at five in the afternoon, put five twenty-liter cans of gas in the trunk, and changed the branches which made up his camouflage. Tha was the very opposite of gunner Tu; nobody in his family was tall but he measured only five feet. His small stature did not bother him, except for driving his GMC truck, when he put a cushion behind his back to wedge him in his seat and bring him closer to the controls.

At nightfall, he set off with his convoy, empty, for Tuan Giao, giving a lift to some porters, for he liked exchanging ideas. Empty, the GMC, which he found heavier than a Molotova, was quite manageable, and the road in that direction easy. He arrived at Tuan Giao at about one o'clock in the morning, stopped for twenty minutes at the canteen to drink some tea and a bowl of sugared soup, and reached Son La at nine o'clock, just as the fog was lifting, after crossing the Fa Dinh Pass without any trouble, with all his lights on because of the clouds. He had remembered the night he had been driving with his parking lights when, nobody having warned the convoy that there were planes overhead, the thunder and flashes of a raid had taken him by surprise. Then, as laid down by regulations, the driver of the leading truck had driven on at top speed, switching on his headlights, and the others had stopped behind, dowsing all their lights.

At Son La he stopped his GMC in the forest where the supply base was installed, drained his gas tank so that his truck would not burn if it were hit by a bomb, checked his oil and water, and went to get something to eat and rest. In the meantime his truck would be loaded with what the convoy from Yen Bay had brought.

February 4, 1954

That morning, at 0730, after a third night on the march, the 57th Regiment arrived at its new quarters on a northern peak, three miles as the crow flies from the Tays, who could not be seen yet. Probably on the slopes of the Pha Song, near the hamlet of Na Khauhu. It then learned its mission: to pull some 105-mm. guns to their emplacements.

Captain Hien was surprised to find himself in the midst of a considerable number of antiaircraft batteries, whose guns, as long and narrow as poles, poked out of the bushes in which they were hidden. After remaining so far on the outskirts of the battle zone, the 57th Regiment now found itself in the very heart of the operation, in the cross-current of armed combatants and porters trotting along under their load of supplies and ammunition. "Shoot down Navarre!" they shouted to the gun crews of the antiaircraft batteries crowded around their mountings. Half a pound of rice, a little meat and a spoonful of sugar for dinner, together with some applause, was not much with which to celebrate the *Tet* and spring. There was a rumor that the delivery of a lot of letters and presents from the delta had been delayed by more important traffic, but what a joy it was to spend the evening in the midst of those guns which had not yet spoken and which some men went and touched as if they could not believe their eyes.

When the crescent of the new moon had disappeared behind the western crests, the regiment went over to the 105-mm. guns, which had to be hoisted into the casemates sappers had been digging out of the mountainside day and night, under a net of creepers which concealed their work from the air, while getting rid of all traces of digging as they went along. A few legends were already in existence, which were constantly repeated. One was of a soldier who, when all the ropes had broken, had used his body to wedge the wheels of a gun that was beginning to roll down the slope. Everybody was singing a song which had become famous in a few weeks, "*Ho kéo phao*":

> The ravines are deep,
> But none of them deeper than our hatred.
> Let us pull the gun behind us
> And the battlefield will become the graveyard of our enemies.

Now the 57th Regiment's turn had come, just as several salvos of 105-mm. shells from Colonel Piroth's batteries were falling, perhaps not accidentally, quite close and making the forest tremble and groan.

On a slope of 45 degrees which followed a ravine, the platoons harnessed themselves to ropes while the gunners, leaning against the wheels, pushed huge wedges under the tires.

Its twin shafts pointing upward, the gun moved a few inches forward, stopped, moved up again. At an average of a yard a minute on the steepest slopes, that made only fifty yards an hour, and, counting pauses for rest, half a mile a day. Only half that distance at night. By dawn, the gun had to be secured and merged into the landscape, and all traces of the haul obliterated, so that observers and aerial photographs could discern nothing.

February 5, 1954

At that moment, who could imagine that the Vietminh would ever decide to attack? The departure of the 308th Division seemed to prove that Giap would not dare to. The only person to take a correct view of the situation and scent a ruse was Cogny. On February 3, in his instructions to Castries, he had suggested that the enemy's intention might be to go spread disorder in the direction of Luang Prabang, then bring the 308th Division back to Dienbienphu. Strongly opposed to Navarre's plan to cut down the garrison of the entrenched camp, he refused to believe that Giap had given up the idea of attacking until the 312th Division and the artillery followed the 308th. Cogny remained convinced that even then Giap might be trying to put them on a false scent.

That day, Navarre wrote Cogny that he had asked him to plan "Operation Xenophon" only in order to prepare for the worst. In his opinion, the possibility that "Xenophon" might be needed had ceased to exist, for Giap could no longer feel capable of attacking Dienbienphu. But, of course, it was Cogny who was right.

When I asked Giap why he had sent the 308th Division toward Laos, he replied, "To create a diversion and sweep away the units you had over there. To be more precise," he added, "with a view to wiping out the few mobile battalions which the Expeditionary Corps had perched up in the mountains, to disguise our preparations for the attack and to cooperate with the Pathet Lao's units in order to cut off General Navarre's retreat in the direction of Laos."

In that case, Cogny was right in still another respect: his satellite, if it had been strong enough and if he had been able to put it into orbit, could have proved very troublesome to Giap. Nobody doubted that at the time, except perhaps Navarre. What was doubted was the possibility of breathing into that group of corpuscles within a few days qualities that cannot be improvised: unity, faith, the desire and the will to fight.

But what would that have mattered if their mere presence could have created in Giap that feeling of insecurity of which Cogny dreamed and which would have prevented him from attacking? Here again we are back in the realm of hypotheses. Giap would have had no more trouble in sweeping away the satellite than he had in cleaning up Laos; a Viet division moves and fights in the jungle; against it, a hypothesis is powerless. Besides, was Cogny afraid of Giap attacking the entrenched camp? The answer is "no." "No" for the public, "no" in order to bolster Castries's morale, or "no" in the secrecy of his private reflection? With Cogny it is difficult to say for sure. With Cogny, it was never "yes *or* no"; it was "yes *and* no." Of what Cogny really thought at that time, no trace remains, and that would not have been the case had Cogny thought Dienbienphu was going to end in disaster.

February 6, 1954

In Paris, a meeting was held of the Committee of National Defense. M. Pleven observed that the situation in Laos was critical and that General Navarre might ask him a question which two cables, from the Commander in Chief and from M. Dejean, seemed to foreshadow: Was the defense of Laos still part of the government's policy? Marshal Juin's opinion was that the fate of the Expeditionary Corps must come before that of Laos, and the committee expressed unanimous agreement.

M. Pleven, the Minister of Defense, was leaving by air for Indochina the next day. The committee gave him full liberty, except insofar as negotiations with the enemy were concerned, to take what military decisions he thought appropriate if time did not permit him to consult the government. In fact, M. Pleven was going to be accompanied by the Committee of the Chiefs of Staffs, presided over by General Ely, which would examine the situation on the spot and rectify whatever errors had been committed. M. Pleven, who had complained of being nothing but a blood donor, suddenly found himself in possession of powers which few politicians before him had ever been given.

February 7, 1954

Coming from Saigon and Séno in General Navarre's Dakota, M. de Chevigné, Secretary of State at the Ministry of War, landed at Dienbienphu. A few moments before landing, the pilot, who was forced to dive fairly steeply into the basin to avoid the enemy's antiaircraft batteries, had asked the minister to fasten his seat belt. M. de Chevigné, who had been unaware of the very existence of those antiaircraft batteries, was astonished. His astonishment increased when the radio operator handed him a message from General Cogny and Colonel de Castries informing him that there would be no guard of honor to meet him on the airstrip, which was under fire from the enemy's mortars, and asked him to leave the plane quickly as soon as it came to a stop, and immediately get into the jeep which would be waiting for him.

M. de Chevigné would speak later of the shock he had received. He would even say, "Not since Roland at Roncevaux have foot soldiers ever been placed in such a defile." Even though he had already learned from Air Force personnel the name given to the basin of Dienbienphu, the impression he obtained when he jumped into the jeep next to Castries, with General Cogny behind them, was deplorable. Dienbienphu was indeed a chamber pot, with the garrison occupying its bottom and the Vietminh its rim.

Former commander of a colonial brigade of the Free French Forces in the Middle East, former leader of General de Gaulle's military mission in Washington, a war casualty, former High Commissioner in Madagascar, which he had pacified after the war, and a relative of the Castries family, M. de Chevigné, who had the build and voice of a kindly butcher, decided to spend two days at Dienbienphu to get some idea of the situation before M. Pleven arrived. He spent hours with the colonels and majors in order to see and understand everything. Perhaps it was there that, after accidentally setting off a booby-trapped grenade which was being shown to him, he asked that scratches be classified as war wounds. One evening, disguised as a private, he took part in a patrol. But what conclusions could a minister draw from officers who were constantly on their guard with him, even when, like Gaucher or Piroth, they had graduated from the Saint-Cyr military academy the same year as himself? Or when, like Langlais, they had been in the same army class preparing for Saint-Cyr? What M. de Chevigné knew when he left Dienbienphu was that the position seemed strong in spite of an organization which was in certain respects inadequate, and that the garrison was violently repulsed as soon as it tried to climb onto the rim of the pot in which it was stuck. Castries had turned out two very good battalions for him with artillery and air support, which had been unable to go more than a mile beyond the basin; but the battle had not yet been joined and nobody expressed any doubts as to its outcome. Everybody told him, like Castries and Cogny, "Dienbienphu will be Na San multiplied by ten. We shall crush not one division, but four."

February 8, 1954

In Saigon, three days earlier, General Blanc had given M. Jacquet a rather gloomy picture of the political and military situation. Behind his debonair attitude and his Catalan accent, General Blanc saw clearly, judged quickly and gave his opinion even when people didn't want to hear it. His character had barred him for a while from posts for which obsequious colleagues had proved more amenable than he was, and then marked him out to play a difficult role. Considered for a long time incapable of obeying, he had proved that he was born to command. On the subject of Indochina, he held realistic views: in 1950, foreseeing the approaching disaster, he had advocated the evacuation of Cao Bang. China, the Vietminh, the flabbiness of the Vietnamese Army and the ineptness of its leaders filled him with serious anxiety about Dienbienphu. In his opinion, the French ought to evacuate Tonkin in order to be better able to hold Annam and Cochin China, and, to achieve this aim, open negotiations to put an honorable end to a war which was going to lead to the loss of North Africa. He considered that to go on sacrificing the Expeditionary Corps, whose reserves were dwindling, was a crime. The minister had listened to him without taking any notes, drawing on his pipe and nodding his head.

That evening at Nice, M. Jacquet, who was returning to Paris, met the Pleven mission on its way out. In a lounge at the air terminal, he exchanged views with M. Pleven and General Ely.

"I'm very pessimistic," said M. Jacquet.

"We're even more pessimistic," answered M. Pleven. "That's why we're going out there."

February 9, 1954

The day before, for the first time, the soldiers of the 57th Regiment, who were resting after they had hoisted a few guns into the mountains, had been able to see the basin of Dienbienphu. So tired that they dreamed of sleeping twenty-four hours at a stretch and of eating a few precious lumps of sugar, they had gazed for a long time, in moonlight which glinted on a piece of steel here and there, at the black expanse of the valley where twelve battalions, entrenched behind their blockhouses, were waiting for them. What most stirred Captain Hien, who had been accustomed for years to living like a hunted wolf, were the lights of the airfield and its torches flickering in the wind, which reminded him of the flames of the little faggots it was customary to light on the thresholds of houses in honor of the dead.

So many steps and so much suffering had finally brought them to the camp where the assembled enemy defied them. They recalled the words they had repeated over and over, in regiment after regiment, from the leaflets in which Castries had called them cowards. "Coward" was really the last word the French should have chosen. They were naïve, submissive, fanatical to the point of aberration, prepared for any servitude to come—anything but cowardly. This showed how much their enemy misjudged or wanted to insult them. They had approached in their silent, stubborn way, like featherweights hopping about in front of a heavyweight without daring to face up to him, had driven their powerful opponent onto the ropes and, after so many dodges and feints, were preparing to deal him a crippling blow with guns some of which had formerly been fired at them.

All the men of the 57th Regiment had remained silent before the huge black crater above which floated wisps of smoke rising toward the milky crests. It was down there that they would have to go to wash away insults and injustices, and plant the red flag with the gold star which was finally going to give them a country.

February 15, 1954

All the visitors to the entrenched camp showed the same astonishment at the landscape and the situation. Blurred by the network of tracks and the trails of dust which the vehicles left behind them, the basin was agog with the life of a little army which waited for the attack, hid its weapons, picked up the food which was thrown to it, surrounded itself with protective obstacles, cooked its meals and bathed in the river which flowed from the nearest bare peaks. Farther off, the crests followed one after another, up to those which bristled along the horizon, where nothing betrayed the presence of an enemy who merged into the forests and watched every movement in the valley. A stadium, to quote Robert Guillain's phrase, in which the Vietminh occupied the tiers.

"Naturally," a captain said to Henri Amouroux, the special correspondent of *Sud-Ouest*, "they can see us clearly, fire at us now and then, and get the range of the airfield. But there's nothing very serious about all that."

"So you're a journalist," said Castries with a grimace in the direction of *Le Monde* and the press clippings which had just landed on his table. "Still another one. You know, if M. Guillain comes back here, he won't even get off the plane. I'll put a guard on him. And to think that he drank our brandy!"

"Colonel, I know Guillain. . . ."

"To write that Dienbienphu was a lion pit!"

"A metaphor. A mere metaphor. Besides, it doesn't strike me as so unsuitable."

"So you're like the others, are you!" cried Castries. "Why don't you let us get on with our work in peace? If the Viets attack, you'll see the sort of welcome we'll give them. Everything is ready, Monsieur Amouroux, everything. Take a jeep. Go and see for yourself."

From what he saw, Henri Amouroux obtained a curious impression, in which confidence was mingled with uneasiness. He had been to Anne-Marie to meet Lieutenant Makowiak, adjutant to Captain Guilleminot, who was in command of the 3rd Thai Battalion, had taken refuge with them in a shelter which resembled a tomb and shared their meal.

"We came here to maneuver, and we shall maneuver," Guilleminot said calmly.

"But where, Captain?" asked the astonished Amouroux.

Guilleminot made a vague gesture.

"We shall maneuver."

In the evening, after Guilleminot had consulted the almanac he had brought with him, while Amouroux was trying to sleep on his bunk, the Viets opened fire again with their 75-mm. guns. The officers got dressed in the dark and went out. Birds were beating the darkness with their wings —possibly those crows which I later saw crossing the basin from east to west every evening and from west to east every morning, in great black croaking flocks. All of a sudden, in the white light of the flares dropped by the on-duty Dakota, machine guns started rattling, and the artillery of the entrenched camp lobbed shells onto the approaches of one strong point and onto the crests, where fires lit by napalm bombs were still burning. Then silence returned and everybody went back to bed.

That day, in the fog of dawn, Henri Amouroux took part in a fresh operation mounted by Lieutenant Colonel Langlais with three battalions. Guilleminot acted as his guide as far as the village of Ban Ta Po, one and a half miles away at the foot of the three peaks of Béatrice. The villagers, still drowsy with sleep, were coming out of their huts, yawning; the women were already pounding rice.

Searching for the truth, Henri Amouroux wondered about these apparently indifferent peasants and about himself, who was perhaps about to face needless perils. He walked on through the high grass toward the Nam Youm, which the troops crossed by a ford. Suddenly bullets whistled through the air, shells fell, a chaplain bent over a dead lieutenant whose face was already covered with flies, while a captain radioed for the heli-copter: "Soleil calling Grand Soleil, send Alouette," and the wounded came out of the jungle, leaning on one another's shoulders. One unit of the 1st BEP (1st Battalion, Foreign Paratroops) had been practically wiped out, and a platoon leader who had lost one eye arrived covered with blood, resting his hand, like King Creon, on his guide's shoulder. Mortar shells rained down just as the helicopter was about to land, and the wounded were sent back toward the village. On the chaplain's advice, Henri Amouroux went with them, helping an Italian to walk.

"I'll get the Military Medal for this," the platoon leader said by way of consolation. Somebody had spread a pink handkerchief over the face of the lieutenant, who was being carried back on a stretcher.

Once again, the object of the operation had not been attained and the Viet 75 was firing at the camp.

"Why, yes, Monsieur Amouroux," said Castries, "they're firing at us. What of it? I wear my red forage cap so that they can see me better."

At lunch, the conversation was still all about Robert Guillain's article and the expression "lion pit," which had shocked everybody there. Hadn't they understood that it referred to the pit where the lions of ancient Rome waited before the fight? To be compared to lions, even lions in captivity, has never been an insult.

"It's true," a major said sarcastically to Henri Amouroux, "that soldiers aren't very intelligent."

After the morning's dead had been sent off under shellfire in front of a ragged guard of honor in a hurry to have done with it, Amouroux re-turned with sixteen wounded men. In the Curtiss Commando flown by Henri Bourdens, blood was streaming from the coffins.

February 16, 1954

Every evening in the entrenched camp, the troops went swimming and there were games of volleyball everywhere. Captain Capeyron, who was in command of Claudine 5 with a company of the 1st Battalion, 13th Demibrigade, thought that nothing would ever happen. Like his com-rades, he even had the growing impression that the war was over and that the Viets were going away. When Piroth's guns suddenly shattered the silence to get the range for a routine exercise, he didn't even jump. An-other night began to the purring of the on-duty Dakotas, with sentries ready to revolve their flashlights about the ramparts in order to reveal the enemy. If the sirens wailed, Captain Capeyron knew that it was for another alert. But if it was the attack, wouldn't they rejoice? What a shout of joy and relief would go up from the poor shelters of Dienbienphu!

In Hanoï, M. Pleven summoned Cogny to the Maison de France at the end of the day, to ask him in private what he thought about the possibility of halting the conflict. Cogny argued against Navarre's strategy and "Operation Atlante."

February 18, 1954

The day before, Major Paul Grauwin of the medical services had arrived at Dienbienphu to act as a replacement in Field Hospital 29. He was a surgeon of considerable virtuosity whom a taste for adventure had brought into the ranks of the Expeditionary Corps.

This Flemish giant was as famous for the physical energy he expended as for his kindness. Above the neck and torso of a bull, his face, lit by gentle blue eyes behind spectacles, seemed steeped in pity. He was one of those rare men whom you cannot meet without loving. Grauwin never refused anything to those who suffered, and the only enemy he recognized was pain. Fortunately, Dr. Grauwin also knew how to see and how to take notes.

Guided by his predecessor, he visited the operating theater, the doctor's shelter lined in shroud material, the resuscitation ward, the X-ray room and the stocks of drugs and material. Like Brigitte Friang, he counted only forty-two beds on the way.

"If a hundred wounded came in, what would you do?" he asked the doctor he was relieving.

"There are always the planes."

"And what if the airfield were put out of action?"

"Then you would use the quarters of the GCMA."

The GCMA, on the other side of the road and a barbed-wire barrier, with no covered passage leading to it, was the Group of Mixed Airborne Commandos whose task it was to interrogate prisoners. Langlais contemptuously referred to this group as a lousy bunch of Thais and Meos mixed with a dozen Europeans and commanded by a former captain of the Special Section of the Second World War, whom Langlais had ordered to remove his red beret.

"The field hospital strikes me as too close to the command post," Grauwin added.

"It was Colonel Terramorsi of the medical services who put it here for greater convenience."

"In case of bombardment?"

"You're joking," said an officer. "What would they bombard us with?"

"And what if you have three hundred wounded?" Grauwin in his turn was asked that day by General Jeansotte of the medical services, who was accompanying Navarre on a fresh inspection of Dienbienphu.

Grauwin made no reply. That was a problem for the presiding geniuses of the medical services to solve.

The general shook his head over the figures he was given regarding the thickness of the ceiling, and expressed astonishment that the communication trench leading to the field hospital was not covered. Climbing back onto the superstructure of the installations, and looking out across the whole of the entrenched camp, he said to Grauwin, "If there's a big scrap here, my friend, it will set you back forty years, and you won't be able to cope with it by yourself."

That day, the Commander in Chief received two pieces of bad news. The listening posts had intercepted an order increasing the Vietminh transport flow to Dienbienphu from fifty to seventy tons a day, and the plans for a gun emplacement had been found on a prisoner. General Cogny mentioned this to Colonel Berteil, who, like Cogny himself, was extremely impressed, for a close study of aerial photographs had revealed nothing of this sort. The weather conditions, the big, leafy trees of the jungle and the narrow valleys complicated everything. Bearcat pilots had taken considerable risks skimming the ground to photograph those zones where it was feared batteries might have been installed. In spite of the help of specialists who had come from Korea, and who had recommended the simultaneous taking of photographs in both color and black and white, or the use of infrared cameras, all their efforts had been in vain. They had as yet no proof of the presence of enemy batteries.

Berteil replied thoughtfully, "If the information is accurate, the counterbattery is in trouble."

Piroth shrugged his shoulders when he was told.

"Watch out for the enemy's artillery," Berteil said to him. "The Viets may use it like the Chinese in Korea, under casemates and with direct fire. It might be a good idea to put your guns under cover."

"Colonel de Castries has thought of that," replied Piroth.

The idea had been considered. To carry it out, twice as many guns would have been necessary, and large-scale earthworks would have had

On the 5th of August, 1953, Navarre decorated the giant Cogny, with Gilles in the background. Seven months later, the two generals will not even shake hands.

Shortly after 10 o'clock on the morning of November 20th, the first wave of paratroopers began Operator Castor, the occupation of Dienbienphu.

Ho Chi Minh, leader of North Vietnam, during negotiations with the French in 1946.

General Vo nguyen Giap, Commander in Chief of the Viet forces, instructing his lieutenants in strategy on a mountain dominating Dienbienphu.

Christmas night, 1953. The officer on the left, holding his cap and flashlight, has only three more months to live. This evening the news is bad, and the garrison is almost entirely surrounded. Castries and Navarre (second and third from left) are the only ones who know it.

French observation point, looking over into Viet territory.

Bigeard: "If it's possible, it's done; if it's impossible, it will be done."

Generals Navarre and Cogny come to inspect Dienbienphu shortly after Castries has taken command.

November 22nd: Cogny is shown the new encampment at Dienbienphu by Gilles (right), who is about to depart.

Gilles's replacement, Castries, explains to Cogny: "We'll demolish the Viets when they come down from the hills.

Viet construction workers building roads which will allow provisions to get through to the guerillas.

Bicycles, each loaded with more than 440 pounds of rice and munitions, supply the Viet army.

The Vietminh arrive at Dienbienphu, May, 1954.

Viet soldiers, prisoners of the French.

French counterattack on Éliane, after it had fallen to the Viets. Viet soldiers are in the foreground.

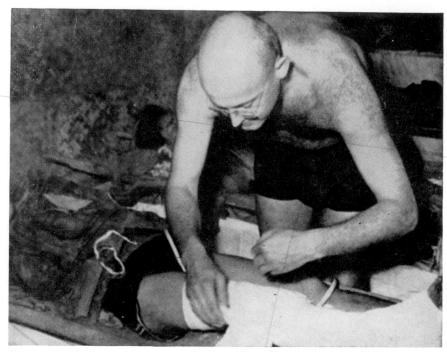

Doctor Grauwin at work in the French "hospital."

Helicopters evacuate French wounded under heavy Viet mortar fire.

A ceremony honoring French soldiers killed during the attack on Hill 1145.

French and Viet dead after the battle for Dominique, finally captured by the Viets.

The remains of a French B-26 shot down by the Viets.

The taking of Dienbienphu: Algerians and Moroccans surrender.

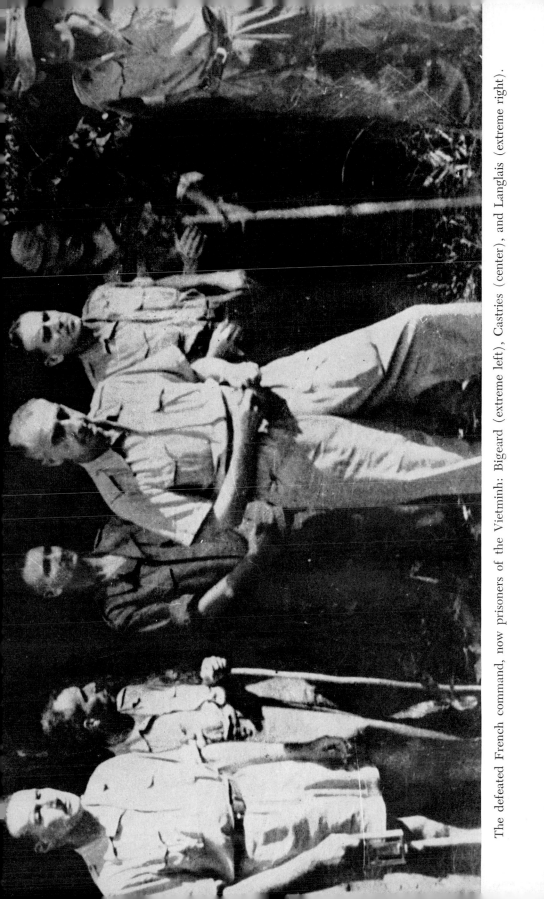

The defeated French command, now prisoners of the Vietminh: Bigeard (extreme left), Castries (center), and Langlais (extreme right).

to be constructed. At Na San, the base artillery had been used in the open and had reduced the few enemy guns to silence; the same would be done at Dienbienphu. The Viets were formidable infantrymen, but their artillery was laughable. But what if that artillery existed? What if it were already in position? "If you can't see it, what are you going to fire at?" Castries had frequently asked Piroth. "We shall at least see it when it opens fire," Piroth had always replied. "And then I'll smash it." Castries, who was not a gunner, believed him, but each time he pursed his lips in irritation. For reassurance, he kept telling himself that the Air Force would make up for the deficiencies of the counterbattery, and that the attack would not last long.

Gaucher, if he learned of the existence of those casemates, probably laughed. Besides, the French told themselves, if the document found on the prisoner was genuine, the enemy must be carrying out work on such a scale that it could not escape notice from the air, and he would have neither the time nor the resources to complete it. Nobody suspected, even by reductio ad absurdum reasoning, that this work was largely finished. And even if the Viets succeeded in putting some guns in position, how many shells would they have to fire? Only a small number. All the French had to do was to wait until the enemy ran out of ammunition. On this point it seems that complete agreement was reached in the course of a two-hour conversation between Navarre, Cogny and Castries.

In Berlin, it was announced that an international conference would open in May, in Geneva, to consider Asian problems. No one could have been foolish enough to think that things were going to change almost miraculously, that the announcement of a conference would load the dice which were being rolled, or alter the structure of the shelters in the entrenched camp, the caliber of Colonel Piroth's guns or the determination of the men living in and around the basin. That day, John Foster Dulles had a private conversation with M. Bidault, and asked him to be prepared for a general offensive in Indochina. Even this would not affect General Navarre, who had wanted Dienbienphu and had agreed to join battle there. It was still there that everybody was hoping to tackle the enemy. If there were certain disagreements in the garrison, it was because a great many young officers blamed the High Command for its lack of spirit. Conferences have never worried military men when they hold victory in their grasp, or declare, like Navarre, that they know how to impose it.

To Democratic Senator Mike Mansfield, who had asked whether the

United States would send naval or air units to Indochina if the French were subjected to greater pressure there, Charles E. Wilson, the Defense Secretary, had said in reply, "For the moment there is no justification for raising United States aid above its present level." And President Eisenhower himself had stated, "Nobody is more opposed to intervention than I am. Nothing would be more tragic for us than to be engaged in open war in Indochina." Planes, weapons, mechanics and civilian teams— that was all that could be expected from America to help France. From China, the Vietminh did not receive a tenth of this help; it had no tanks, its soldiers traveled on foot, and thousands of bicycles increased tenfold the loads of the porters pushing them. But which side had faith and which side was prepared to die for something? The name of H.M. Bao Dai was not one that men uttered to conquer hunger, thirst or pain. Nor was that of M. Joseph Laniel.

At Dienbienphu, a huge fire lit by fighter planes in the mountains blazed in the dark. To René Mauriès, the special correspondent of the *Dépêche du Midi,* some troops said, "What the hell are they up to? We're fed up with waiting for them. Let's get it over with!"

February 19, 1954

At 1100 hours, the planes carrying the Pleven mission and the suite of the Chiefs of Staff took off from the airfield at Hanoï. A current of icy air had produced a sudden worsening of the weather in the delta, where the drizzle, which had disappeared for a few days, had started falling again. In the highlands, on the other hand, it was fine. A few minutes after take-off, the Dakotas emerged above the pimply surface of the stratus clouds pierced by the black ridges of the mountains. Little by little, the valleys came into view, bathed in sunshine, still linked together by a few threads of mist which the heat was dissipating. Lunch was served on board and the omens were good. General O'Daniel, the leader of the American mission to Indochina and President Eisenhower's military adviser, had told Washington that he was enthusiastic about the entrenched camp. Castries had made a hit.

At Dienbienphu, the unit detailed to receive the ministers was the 3rd Company of the 1st Battalion, 13th Demibrigade, commanded by Captain Capeyron, who was wearing the Demibrigade's proud insignia: a blue Cross of Lorraine on the legendary grenade. One hour before the plane was due, the four platoons of Legionnaires took up position, spick-

and-span, with all their medals on. Captain Capeyron saw a swagger stick, a pink silk neckerchief and a red forage cap getting out of a jeep flying a pennant. As he had caught only a glimpse of the commander of GONO on that Christmas Eve when Navarre had gathered the officers together to tell them that the war was probably going to end there, he said to himself, "That must be Colonel de Castries," went toward him and saluted.

"Colonel," he said, "may I present my company to you?"

"No," replied Castries, shaking hands with him. "You've got enough to do as it is. Keep your arms drill for later."

"He's a good guy," thought Capeyron. "He doesn't put on airs."

The cavalcade of vehicles was drawn up, and the escort was ready. Sure enough, big shots and brass hats emerged from the two Dakotas. M. de Chevigné had come back as an old acquaintance.

The special correspondent of the *Dépêche du Midi* heard M. Pleven say to Castries, "Do you realize, Colonel, that France has her eyes fixed upon you?" Out of a sense of discretion, Navarre had stayed away. His absence indicated his desire to avoid influencing the visitors' judgment in any way. To represent him, he had appointed his deputy, General Bodet, who was wearing a cap with a white peak and had a cigarette jutting out from under his mustache. Leaning on his stick, a cigarette between his lips, one arm stretched out toward the enemy, Castries, who under the Empire might have hoped to become Duke of Dienbienphu, explained to General Ely, with his five-starred cap, and to M. Pleven, who was dressed like a crab fisherman with a panama hat pulled down over his ears, the organization of the entrenched camp. In front of the sandbag barriers and the hillocks from which heavy machine guns were poking, Castries, the cavalryman famous for his disciplinary offenses in garrison and his feats of arms in the field, listed his forces, and referred to the strong points by their romantic Christian names. Béatrice, Anne-Marie, Gabrielle and Éliane, whom his audience pictured as beauties and to whom each lent the face of a beloved woman, rose above the pock-marked peaks where Legionnaires, Algerians and Moroccans had taken up their positions. Behind him stood Langlais, sharp-faced and wearing his red beret, the commander of two parachute battalions. Who could have any doubts?

Some of the visitors expressed astonishment at seeing gashes in the shoulder of the command post.

"Don't worry," said Castries, "it's very solid."

On Béatrice, where part of the 3rd Battalion, 13th Demibrigade was gathered, the Legion played its usual part. Only the band was missing. General Ely quietly drew his minister's attention to the fragility of the shelters.

"Colonel," M. Pleven asked Gaucher, as if he were treading on thin ice, "isn't it true, unfortunately, that we have to reckon with the Viet artillery, since I gather that they have some?"

Gaucher threw out his chest, tightened his scarf around his neck, narrowed the thick black eyebrows which concealed his eyes and stood at attention.

"M. Minister," he retorted, "we shall fight as at Verdun."

To everybody's astonishment, the lieutenant in command of the company they were inspecting spoke up without being asked.

"M. Minister," he said forcefully, "it would be a catastrophe if we didn't fight. We've got a unique opportunity to crush the Viets."

As unprepossessing as a block of stone, but skilled at appearing affable and unctuous, ready to hear every sort of confession as well as give every sort of absolution, his gaze protected by sunglasses and unlimited powers, M. Pleven turned away, intimidated in spite of his tall stature and his authority. General Ely did not bat an eyelid. The commission continued on its way for a while in silence.

"Just the same," the special correspondent of the *Dépêche du Midi* said to an officer on Castries's staff, "if the Viets have got some artillery . . ."

"Remember that it takes a whole regiment to hoist a 75-mm. gun onto a crest. So to bring it here over hundreds of miles, think of the swarm of coolies that would be necessary."

However, Major de Mecquenem, who was in command of the Battalion of the 7th Algerian Rifles on Gabrielle, asked for an interview with General Ely, whom he had served under on the military mission in Washington; and Major Keller, Castries's chief of staff, had asked to be relieved. Something was wrong.

"I'll see you this evening," General Ely told Mecquenem.

At Isabelle, after a discreet explanation of the situation by Lieutenant Colonel Lalande, whose Legionnaire's cap sheltered a gentle, respectful and obedient face, M. Pleven looked around him for arguments to support the optimism which, little by little, in timid waves, was submerging the anxieties tormenting him. On his return to Castries's command post, he turned to the Secretary of State for War and the generals. Their replies were evasive, prudent or solemn. Who could express an opinion under such circumstances? The weather was fine, and it was already as warm as a spring day. A great many eyes were protected by sunglasses. It was no time to demoralize the garrison, to repudiate the work of those responsible for the conduct of operations or to ask questions about what could and could not be seen. Silence was golden, and any word spoken risked rebounding later to the discomfiture of the speaker. M. Pleven was too shrewd a politician to be unaware that an exchange of ideas of this sort could not help showing the satisfaction which he felt and which reassured him.

There remained one last general whose acquiescence was needed to complete the unanimity which had brought a glow of pleasure to M. Dejean's chiseled features: General Fay, the Chief of Air Staff, who had so far remained silent and, indeed, almost sulky.

"And what about you, General?" asked M. Pleven.

General Fay was not very tall. He was a quiet, calm, thoughtful man, who was scrupulously careful to carry out the tasks entrusted to him and who shunned all emotion. Behind a cold manner, his round face was full of kindness; certain weaknesses could be held against him which were due to the care he took not to cause needless conflict. He weighed his words, hated outbursts of anger and measured his gestures, but his blue eyes could express a determination from which there was no appeal. General Navarre had been asked to adapt his plans to his means because Fay could no longer meet his requirements; he did not have enough air crews to wear them out on missions which served no useful purpose, and the government was too parsimonious with its money for him to waste it.

"Minister," Fay said gently, "I am afraid I cannot join in today's concert. What I have seen has only confirmed me in an opinion which I shall express bluntly, in full awareness of my responsibilities. This is it: I shall advise General Navarre to take advantage of the respite available to him and the fact that he can still use his two airfields, to evacuate all the men he can, for he is done for. That is all."

Fay fell silent and refused to add a single word. Consternation descended upon M. Pleven and the army officers, who abruptly turned away. The long, austere face of General Ely remained impassive. Cogny shrugged his shoulders and snickered. The party hurried away toward the jeeps and a dismal take-off. Castries's mask suddenly seemed as rumpled as his pink scarf. In the plane, M. Pleven leaned toward General Ely, who had decided not to see Major de Mecquenem, and ventured a confidential remark: "What admirable men! They want the enemy to attack them. I must admit that I hope he doesn't."

"So do I," said General Ely.

In the evening, at Dienbienphu, the special correspondent of the *Dépêche du Midi* repeated M. Pleven's words: "France has her eyes fixed upon you."

"That," somebody quipped, "is probably why we were told not to hang our wash on the barbed wire today."

In Hanoï, a few journalists were received at the Maison de France. To Brigitte Friang, who asked him whether he was not afraid of difficulties arising from the announcement of the Geneva Conference, M. Pleven replied that a Vietminh victory was impossible. As she pressed him mercilessly, he broke off the conversation with these words: "Mademoiselle, if I were in Giap's place, I would be extremely worried precisely on account of the announcement of the Geneva Conference."

In Saigon, Navarre also summoned the journalists, whom, after having humiliated them, he now tried to charm. That day, General Navarre stated with cold authority, "The Vietminh has reached the highest point of its pretensions and has just furnished proof that it has exceeded its logistic possibilities."

Robert Guillain, special correspondent of *Le Monde*, who had just published a series of impressive articles on Dienbienphu, after traveling by rail across Siam to reach Laos and Hanoï, was, like most of the audience, very dubious. "Ours is a wonderful profession," he exclaimed in the presence of a few colleagues. "The Commander in Chief has just explained everything to us dogmatically, and I, an humble journalist, would stake my life on it that he is either making a terrible mistake or lying to us. I would be ready to swear that the situation he has described has nothing in common with reality. What the Commander in Chief lacks, like his entourage, is our fresh, unbiased view of events."

February 25, 1954

M. Pleven had returned to Saigon on February 19 and had retired with General Ely to Cap Saint-Jacques under the pretext of working on a report which everybody already knew would lead nowhere; in fact, it was intended to provide the Vietminh with the chance, which he had been told it wanted, to bring the conflict to an end by means of a secret meeting.

Later on, Navarre would regard as disastrous for his plans the announcement of the Geneva Conference, which M. Pleven had at first seen simply as a convenient method of reaching a peaceful settlement. The announcement in no way altered the strategy of the Vietminh any more than the Berlin Conference had inspired Giap with the idea of catching Navarre in his own trap. The preparations for the investment of Dienbienphu dated from November 25, 1953, and the decision to destroy the garrison of the Expeditionary Corps there dated from the following December 6.

In order to dispel any anxiety General Ely might have felt, Navarre had relegated General Fay's objections to a technical level, and feigned astonishment that they had never been raised before. According to Navarre, General Fay was afraid that the runways at Dienbienphu would be unusable in the rainy season, but an investigation had established that in the past those runways had never been out of action for more than two or three days; the drainage canals and grids reduced that risk still further. In any case, it was henceforth impossible to evacuate the Dienbienphu garrison without suffering huge losses.

General Fay did not press the point, although his objections were of a tactical and strategic nature. In front of General Ely, Navarre told General Fay, "Dienbienphu was chosen deliberately, and it is there that we shall win the battle."

Fay did not consider himself beaten. He returned to see Navarre in private.

"Think it over," he told him. "I am willing to stay here a week and assume personal responsibility for the operation. I promise you we shall fly out everything we can. And I'll give you all the support you need."

Navarre smiled and turned down the offer. Once again, in his eyes, an airman's opinion was not worth considering. If M. Pleven's memory retained nothing of General Fay's opposition to the maintenance of Dienbienphu, and if General Ely did not give the attention it deserved to the opinion of the Chief of Air Staff, it was because that opinion was not expressed with the force such an attitude required. At Dienbienphu, the Chief of Air Staff had spoken his mind to the minister. He considered that it was for the minister to show a desire to pursue the matter, and did not dare to by-pass General Ely in order to express his disagreement more emphatically than he had already done, or to criticize his comrade Navarre to an unseemly degree. Dogs may bare their teeth at one another; it requires graver circumstances for them to bite.

In the Pleven report drawn up by General Ely, no reference remained of General Blanc's solution of a withdrawal or to General Fay's objections. It was a document intended for the government and designed to show that the Minister of the Armed Forces and the Chief of Staff, united in the same line of thought, were following the same line of conduct. Diluted in the text, the ideas expressed by the members of the commission or by the officials it had encountered only served to show that no solution by force of arms was possible. M. de Chevigné was mistaken when he insisted on the inclusion of this statement: "At Dienbienphu, the military are hoping for an attack. The Secretary of State for War and I do not share that point of view." And although General Ely did not give his support to Navarre's fantasies, he did not have the courage to denounce them. The report did not conceal the fact that the situation was disturbing, but it was reassuring in the impression it gave of the Commander in Chief: Navarre was in command of the situation. Later on, General Ely would whisper, "In a word, Navarre convinced us all."

Accordingly, M. Pleven, with his adviser Ely, nourished new long-term fantasies which would assure him for a time a comfortable majority in the National Assembly: a Vietnamese Army of eight hundred thousand enthusiastic soldiers and American aid on a torrential scale. When M. Pleven later declared that there existed no report by a general criticizing Dienbienphu, he would not really be lying; General Fay's opinion was given orally. The only strongly unfavorable report never reached government level and was signed only by a colonel, Nicot.

Speaking of General Ely, everybody praised his modesty and self-effacement. This product of Saint-Cyr, who had taken twenty years to rise from the rank of lieutenant to that of major, had succeeded, by effacing himself all his life, in attaining the highest post in the military hierarchy. What virtues did he lack? He drank only water, expressed nothing but moderate opinions, never condemned anything or anybody. In a profession where men of character have no future except under stormy circumstances he did not dare to ask for anything and did not know how to refuse anything. If another star appeared on his sleeves—and four suddenly did appear in four years—it was in spite of himself. If he showed any desire, it was the desire to express none. He merely served. A fine figure of a traditional soldier, he lived on legends and slipped underneath the armor of others. His noble stature and slim figure were impressive; his right arm half-paralyzed by a war wound, he saluted with his left hand, whose thumb appeared to be broken; in his face, with its complexion as gray and diaphanous as frosted glass, could be read the self-abnegation, the dignity, the self-control and the loftiness of mind which characterized him. Who could believe that there was any ambition in him? He did not fight to conquer, and he obtained advancement only by a process of elimination. When there was nobody left to accept a mission, somebody would find Ely. He had represented the French Army on the Standing Group at the Pentagon because nobody else had wanted a post so far from the sun, and he had become Chief of Staff of the Armed Forces at a time when no candidate had come forward to perform the funeral rites of the Indochinese War.

Born in 1897 in Salonica, where his father had represented French interests among the Turks, he had retained from his childhood a certain Levantine unctuousness which could have led him, if he had had a religious vocation, to become a Cardinal in the Roman Curia. He knew how to wait, how to feign indifference, how to avoid adversity at the right moment and return stealthily when all danger seemed to have passed. If he ever wrote his memoirs they would never be anything more than a roll of honor, for he regarded himself as the guardian of rights and traditions. A standardbearer who had wrapped himself in the folds of the national flag, he believed it to be his mission to unite warring brothers and to reconcile the irreconcilable. Serving all governments with the same devotion and the same self-abnegation, he did not know how to contradict; holding his hands out to one and all, he would never venture to express an opinion except if it criticized no one; wanting to spare others any risks to their careers, he did not consider himself entitled to take any which might endanger his own. If he sinned, it would therefore be only by mental reservation, and since he did not dare to criticize Navarre, he would refuse to worry about General Fay's firm stand and would prefer to forget what struck him as excessive opposition. Words are carried away on the wind, and out of weakness General Fay had written nothing down. Ely was safeguarding the future, and M. Pleven, who thought that he was accompanied by a generalissimo, really had only the General of the Company of Jesus beside him. But which of the two men was the more skilled in casuistry? Which was the better at disguising the truth?

February 28, 1954

Without having obtained the secret contacts it had been hoping for, the Pleven mission set off again for Paris, the promise of springtime, the soft air, the boulevard cinemas and cafés. Of the visit of a minister who had arrived with full powers, nothing remained but the star of a Grand Officer of the Legion of Honor pinned on General Navarre's chest.

"What do you want of me?" Christ asked the blind man in the Sunday Gospel. "Lord, make me see!" And Jesus said to him; "See! Your faith has saved you."

But who had faith? Before going to the front, each battalion in the People's Army had received the political education which preceded any military training. Gathered together in companies, the troops were invited to tell the story of their lives, and they realized that they were linked by one and the same destiny. Apart from a few sons of townspeople and intellectuals who were ready to die for the independence of Vietnam, and who were convinced, more than the others, of the necessity of the revolution, they were nearly all poor peasants. Their fathers had worked to avoid dying of hunger, had been deported or imprisoned. Certain soldiers who had worked as servants in the past had been beaten, and angry farmers had pushed their faces into dung heaps. In the religious atmosphere which reigned over these evening classes, it sometimes happened that somebody would burst into song and hardened veterans would find it impossible to hold back their tears. They all belonged to the same body of humiliated human beings ready to give their lives for honor to the same suffering church marching toward victory. And if that victory was only a fresh servitude whose evils they could not foresee, they had at least chosen it themselves.

March 2, 1954

M. Pleven, who had landed at Orly the day before, immediately went with M. de Chevigné to see M. Laniel, who had summoned a meeting of ministers. M. Pleven's statement to the press made reference to the universal confidence inspired by a commander in chief convinced that the winter would come to an end without any positive gain for the enemy. A rumor rapidly spread that, for fear of leaks, there would be no official report and that the commission's findings would be given only to restricted bodies and the Committee of National Defense. Alarming rumors, however, began to circulate in the corridors of the National Assembly.

M. Pleven sent for General Salan, Inspector of National Defense since his departure from Indochina, gave him his report to read and asked him, "What can be done to save Dienbienphu?"

At about that date, in Hanoï, a chivalrous gathering took place at the airport of Gia Lam, where Gilles was taking his leave of the airborne troops of the Expeditionary Corps. He was broken in health; an infarct of the myocardium had rendered him incapable of any violent activity and was forcing him to return to France.

Old Gilles had few illusions. He knew that he was henceforth condemned to staff posts and that he would not do many more jumps from a Dakota. To conceal his emotion, he coughed, spat, exchanged dirty jokes with his neighbors and played the indifferent brute. He did not know that he had put on his bush uniform and red beret for the last time in his life. He beckoned with sweeping gestures to Lieutenant Colonel Langlais, who had come up from Dienbienphu for the occasion and who seemed more tense and wiry than ever. With his blue eyes, crackled face, protruding ears and three vertical creases in the middle of a tightly stretched forehead, Langlais looked like a Breton sailor disguised as a paratrooper. The remarks he made were anything but gentle. Langlais confirmed Gilles's suspicions that they had done some damned silly things with his men.

"But," asked Gilles, "if the Viets attack, will the camp hold out?"

Langlais burst out laughing. The question was meaningless. "We're there," he said. And he gestured toward the battalions drawn up in a square under the lowering sky, in a drizzle which was making the runways of the airfield shine.

One after another, Dakotas rolled slowly toward the take-off point, revved up their engines, rose clumsily into the air and disappeared into the clouds in the direction of Dienbienphu. Gilles inspected the troops, saluted the flags and stopped in front of every officer and every pennant, looking into each face with one moist and hazy eye which nobody could ever quite tell from the other, motionless in its socket. A gentle Cyclops with a great bovine brow, Gilles growled, touched arms and filled his heart with these images of young men ready to kill themselves for his sake.

A chivalrous gathering? If you asked those boys, few of them would have been able to reply, and a few officers would have shrugged their shoulders. Chivalry, the defense of the widowed and the oppressed, the old stories of an army on the march toward the Tomb of Christ—all that had been shattered by the atom bomb at Hiroshima and the Nazi extermination camps. Most of the men there had chosen the paratroops out of vocation or by chance, and their comrades took the place of religion in their lives. They did not jump for the sake of H. M. Bao Dai, whom they

despised or about whom they knew nothing. Langlais, Bigeard, Bréchignac, Botella, Tourret and all the captains with cantankerous characters and
biting wit who stiffened to attention as old Gilles went past fought simply
to prevent France from going under. They had not yet been taught how
to torture, and they respected and even envied their enemy, for he had
the advantage over them of getting himself killed for the goal of substi-
tuting his flag for theirs. That was his right. The duty of the paratroops
was to refuse to give way. They went no further in their reasoning, and
that was as it should be; reasoning was not supposed to be their province.
It was not they who had launched the Indochinese War or defined the
cause to be defended. They adopted the rights and wrongs of the nation
whose sons they were, even if they sometimes felt as if they were bastards. They went because their leaders told them to go. Their morality did
not surpass that of the centurion in the Gospel, who cannot, indeed, have
been very intelligent, since he was only a centurion and not a consul or a
teacher. What distinguished them from the rest was that they did not stop
before they were told to stop.

That night, the 57th Regiment had crept down the west slope of the
basin to take up its position around Isabelle. Captain Hien had crossed
the village of Ban Phuong, which had been razed to the ground. He had
stopped near a few pompelmous trees which had been miraculously preserved. In the old days in his family, as everywhere on the plain, they had
used to bake little loaves scented with pumelo blossoms, and this
sudden memory had almost brought tears to his eyes. He had sworn to
fight to the end to restore life to this village and to make sure that the
scent of orchards in springtime replaced the stench of napalm.

After the parade at Gia Lam, the paratroopers, as usual, had a drink
with the officers of the other services, the chaplains and the generals.
Langlais did not stay long. In the plane taking him back to Dienbienphu,
something worried him. Lieutenant Colonel Denef, Cogny's operational
second-in-command, another paratrooper who had joined the staff, whom
he regarded as conceited and who didn't like him either, had shaken
hands with him effusively. Langlais wondered what could be the explanation of this unexpected friendliness on the part of a comrade with whom
he had nothing in common, and then suddenly realized that Denef had
behaved as if he were never going to see him again. "So," thought Langlais, "they all think that we're done for at Dienbienphu, do they?"

March 4, 1954

In the afternoon, at Dienbienphu, Navarre and Cogny inspected the principal strong points. They questioned the unit commanders, and the answers were unanimous: they were waiting resolutely, and without the slightest apprehension, for the Viets.

Navarre could not say the same for himself. The day before, he had rejected Cogny's request for a fresh operation toward Lang Son, for he was afraid of wasting his remaining resources and preferred to keep them all at hand, intact, in case of need. In his opinion, a success at Lang Son would have no perceptible effect on Dienbienphu, and a reverse would dangerously weaken the entrenched camp. Moreover, if he was impressed by the optimism of the battalion and group commanders, who did not know everything, he who possessed all available information about the enemy did not want a battle. Information suggested that the enemy had some heavy artillery. Being determined to give battle and win it, as he had written on several occasions, did not necessarily mean that he wanted it. So far he had dismissed all suggestions that he should force Giap to attack. But if Giap attacked, Navarre would retaliate.

Tormented by a final scruple, Navarre, who seemed to be more and more afraid of having let himself be pushed into this position, considered that the organization of the entrenched camp was not strong enough, and suggested to Cogny and Castries that a new center of resistance should be established between Claudine and Isabelle and that the garrison should be reinforced with two or three battalions. Isabelle was three miles to the south of Claudine; her artillery fire could barely support Gabrielle. Over that distance, counterattacks based on Isabelle would find it difficult to reach the other strong points.

In order to discuss all this freely without any danger of their remarks being overheard, Navarre had left the command post with Cogny, Castries and Colonel Revol. They had gotten into a jeep and, with Castries at the wheel, had driven off.

It seemed advisable, in fact, Navarre went on, if not to insert forces in that three-mile gap, at least to plant fresh obstacles to the northeast, to bolster up the Thais, who were good at marching but poor in defense, and to support Béatrice, which would be bound to suffer the first attack. If General Cogny had hesitated so far to establish new strong points in order to avoid squandering his Tonkin forces, hadn't the moment come to make a decision? In fact, Cogny placed more reliance on vigorous counterattacks than on the usefulness of new defenses. There was already such a tangle of barbed-wire defenses that people were tripping over them. Where, under these circumstances, were they to find room for two or three extra battalions? Wasn't the commander of the entrenched camp a cavalryman famous for his unexpected counterthrusts and his sure eye? In Cogny's opinion, that was where the irresistible strength of Dienbienphu was to be found. What is more, Transport Command had undertaken to provide supplies for six battalions, then nine, and now twelve. It could not do more or it would fail to meet its obligations, and the whole logistic support of Dienbienphu would be upset. Estimated at fourteen pounds a head a day, the scale of maintenance had already risen to eighteen pounds. They could rely on Langlais, who was in command of the two parachute battalions of the mobile reserves, and conclude that a new center of resistance would place a heavy burden on the fortress as a whole. That did not mean that the garrison did not feel the slightest anxiety, but when the Viets were entangled in the barbed wire, the French would smash them. That was what Castries himself replied.

Navarre was insistent. If the Viets saw that a new center of resistance was being installed, they would postpone the attack in order to modify their plan, and if, with one postponement after another, they reached the rainy season, the attack on Dienbienphu would not take place.

Castries, who did not believe that Giap would postpone his attack, is said to have replied, "They risk not coming at all, and we must push them into attacking so as to get it over with quickly."

"Can you hold out?" asked Navarre.

"It will be a tough fight, but we can hold out if you've got two or three battalions you can send me."

And Cogny added, "We mustn't let the Viets change their minds. For the entrenched camp, this fight offers the prospect of a great defensive victory. It would be a catastrophe from the point of view of morale if the Viets failed to attack."

Cogny has never denied that he made this last remark. However, maintaining that he did not want Castries to suppose he felt the slightest doubt about the solidity of the camp's defenses or that he did not share his desire to see the Viets attack, he claims that he made it only because Castries was listening. He would have liked, too, to upset Giap's plans by giving a few kicks to the ant heaps of his bases in the rear, and by cutting one or more of his vital supply arteries north of Hanoï, an idea which

Navarre stubbornly rejected because he did not believe in it, and because, with "Operation Atlante" immobilizing too many reserves, he no longer had enough parachute battalions and mobile groups at his disposal to take the risk.

Cogny therefore made that remark. He states in addition that Navarre could not have been deceived by the fake optimism he displayed. According to Cogny, pretending to take him literally on that level was sheer infamy. But did he return to the subject in order to dispel any ambiguity? Did he go over to Navarre when they were once again alone in the plane? Did he say, "Naturally, General, my remarks earlier were meant for Castries. You know what I think. We must do everything we can to prevent Giap from attacking"? No. He said nothing because it was no longer possible to get out of the trap, and because Cogny believed the French were going to win.

It was not hatred that existed between Navarre and Cogny; it was something worse. Hatred can be read in human faces and breaks everything up. When two people hate each other, each knows what the other is trying to do. At this moment in their relationship, Navarre and Cogny were trying to destroy each other without either of them admitting the fact to himself. On the surface of Navarre, who was forever imagining that he could hear Cogny reproaching him with being nothing but a shadow of de Lattre, you could make out strong undercurrents of jealousy, of contemptuous condescension and of fear of betrayal. On Cogny's side, the wounds that had been inflicted on his vanity, together with suspicion of a leader who lacked experience and cloaked himself in icy mystery, created between them what is known in divorce cases as psychological incompatibility. The bull Cogny loathed the catlike Navarre. His chief mistake was not to have followed Salan and the de Lattre team into retirement; at that level a man cannot change his boss when they don't know each other and quickly discover that they don't like each other. Undecided, mulling over gloomy thoughts and not knowing what attitude to adopt, Cogny said nothing, concealing his uneasiness and shutting himself up in a hostility that assumed the guise of respect.

For his part, Navarre could have asked Cogny if he stood by everything he had said in his reply or if that reply had been intended more for Castries than for him. But he, too, said nothing, only too happy, if he detected some ambiguity, at being able to blame Cogny for it later. Silence fell between the two generals. Although they still invited one another to dinner on the occasion of a ministerial visit, they no longer communicated with each other except in letters and dispatches scrupulously respecting the hierarchical formulas of military correspondence.

March 10, 1954

The interception of Vietminh messages revealed a plan for supplying rice to ninety thousand men in the highlands, seventy thousand of them around Dienbienphu. Another piece of information informed Navarre that the attack on the entrenched camp was to take place during the night of March 13-14. The count of Giap's forces and resources had been completed: 27 infantry battalions, 20 105-mm. guns, 18 75-mm. guns, 16 and soon 80 37-mm. guns and 100 12.7 antiaircraft guns, not counting the mortars. The figures of shells were known only by their guaranteed minimums: 5,000 75-mm. shells, 15,000 105-mm. shells, 44,000 37-mm. antiaircraft shells and 24,000 mortar shells, of which 3,000 were of 120-mm. caliber. It was known, too, that two hundred tons of ammunition were due to arrive between March 8 and 15. As for the scale of food supplies, it had reached seventy tons a day. The director of supplies was also sending two tons of pharmaceutical products and stretchers.

Did Navarre feel any doubts about the retaliatory capability of Colonel Piroth's 155-mm. guns, which had destroyed none of the guns already firing at the entrenched camp, or about the Air Force, which had failed to detect any emplacement for certain? He revealed no such doubts. In any case, Giap had already won a logistic battle with those coolies of his, who, according to the calculations of the French Command, were bound to eat four-fifths of their load on the way, and he seemed to be planning to destroy the Air Force on its bases and over Dienbienphu with arms whose arrival the French had been unable to prevent. But perhaps, as Lieutenant Colonel Gaucher said, the 105-mm. guns were made of wood.

March 11, 1954

Captain Capeyron was in Hanoï, where he had gone for treatment for some metal dust in his eye. His comrades asked him what he thought of the Viet artillery.

"They must have a gun or two," he replied, "but most of time the shells don't even explode. It's a farce."

He flew back to Dienbienphu, where during the day the two parachute battalions had attacked Hill 555, less than a mile to the east of Béatrice, come up against strong opposition and fallen back.

Captain Capeyron had scarcely rejoined his company on Claudine 5, at five in the afternoon, when the enemy's artillery opened fire on the airstrip. At the third shot, a Packet which had been forced to land a few days earlier with one engine on fire and on which repairs were nearly finished, sitting a little distance from the other planes, sustained a direct hit and tipped up on its nose, with its twin tail pointing toward the hills. At the twelfth shot, it burst into flames. A single gun, that of Gun Crew Commander Tu, with a stock of only thirty shells, which were not all used, had been detailed to destroy it. Another transport plane, a Curtiss Commando belonging to the Blue Eagle Company, which had been out of service for two weeks, was spared. Some fighters took off toward the slopes where the gun was installed, machine-gunned at random, circled around in the hollows and over the crests, and then returned to their sandbagged pits, covered by the black cloud of the fire. The Dakotas which had landed lost no time returning to Hanoï. The battery to which Tu's gun belonged was firmly installed on the slopes which the Viets called the Green Hill, two and a half miles from the airstrip. Its guns were covered by over six feet of earth; before and after firing, the embrasure of their shelter was stopped up with sandbags and camouflaged.

If Castries had taken the trouble, he could have consulted his files on the conclusions of the American mission which had come from Korea two months earlier to appraise the position of Dienbienphu. He would have found a sentence in the report whose optimism would have comforted him: "The situation makes it possible to envisage with confidence the continued maintenance of this center from the air."

While the flames from the Packet were lighting up the night sky over Dienbienphu, the Committee of National Defense was meeting in Paris. M. Pleven completed his report in a monotonous voice, and proposed sending General Ely on an information mission to the United States, at the invitation of Admiral Radford. In M. Pleven's opinion, the war could still be won. In response to Ho Chi Minh's statements in February, M. Laniel had demanded population regroupings which the Vietminh regarded as unacceptable. The Foreign Minister, M. Georges Bidault, instructed General Ely to ask Washington for American intervention in the case of any use of aircraft against the Expeditionary Corps. Can anyone doubt that General Fay repeated the frank advice he had given General Navarre? Even if the phrase "In my opinion, at Dienbienphu we are heading for disaster" is not to be found in the minutes, the Prime Minister and his colleagues cannot have failed to hear it. It is nonetheless strange that nobody remembers it, for a witness like General Fay weighs his words and does not tell lies. M. Pleven proposed setting up a restricted war committee which would be entrusted with the conduct of the war, under the authority of the Prime Minister. These conclusions were unanimously approved.

For the first time since the beginning of the conflict, a government, admittedly under the pressure of events, had taken the trouble to appraise the suitability and the consequences of the Commander in Chief's operational plans, and to study with him the means of carrying out or scrapping those plans in relation to its over-all policy. Ely's prudence and M. Pleven's unctuousness had been unable to stifle the voice of General Fay. It was no longer possible to withdraw from Dienbienphu. That was a fact. But to state that nobody, in spite of everything, had made such a desperate assertion would later constitute a remarkable distortion of the truth.

In the vast shelters installed deep underground, in the dining rooms of the service stations along Route 41 and in the villages where the inhabitants waited for the planes to pass before rushing out to repair the bomb-damaged road with their shovels, pickaxes and baskets, the political commissars had for some days been reading over and over, as it made its way from one place to the next, a proclamation by the Commander in Chief of the People's Army. Men and women listened to it standing, and the yellow glow of an oil lamp sometimes lit up their impassive faces.

"*Hoi toan thê can bo va Chien si, tran Dienbienphu sap bat dau.* . . . Officers and troops, the battle of Dienbienphu is about to begin. . . . The hour has come for you to go into action."

The reader uttered these words in a loud voice, then studied their effect on his audience, which had grown suddenly tense. This battle for which so much sweat and blood had already been expended was almost upon them, and the crimson curtains of the sky were opening to reveal it.

"Winning the battle of Dienbienphu means exterminating the major part of the best enemy forces, liberating the northwest of the country, and strengthening our rear areas, things which will guarantee the success of our reforms. Winning the battle of Dienbienphu means smashing the Navarre Plan, which has already suffered serious setbacks, and dealing a terrible blow to the schemes of the Franco-American capitalists who are financing the war. The victory of Dienbienphu will have immense consequences both at home and abroad, and will help the world-wide movement for peace in Indochina, especially at a moment when, after a series of reverses, the French Government is at last trying to negotiate to end the conflict. Here are the orders of President Ho, the Party and the government. . . . "

The voice reading the staccato words and syllables, which sometimes whined like bullets, suddenly trembled, then paused for a moment.

"While our troops on all fronts are bravely attacking the enemy in order to act in concert with us, I address this appeal to all the officers and troops of all the units of all services in the Dienbienphu sector. Remember that it will be an honor to have taken part in this historic battle. Determined to destroy the adversary, keep in mind the motto: 'Always attack, always advance.' Master fear and pain, overcome obstacles, unite your efforts, fight to the very end, annihilate the enemy at Dienbienphu, win a great victory! The hour of glory has come. Officers and troops of all the units of all services, forward to win President Ho's victory flag!"

The voice suddenly fell silent, then the commissar decided to go on to the end.

"The Commander in Chief of the People's Army of Vietnam, signed: General Vo nguyen Giap."

After a moment's pause, when it was clear that the political commissar had finished, shouts and cheers burst forth.

"You will know before tomorrow night whether France or the Vietminh is to rule over your people. It is not Dienbienphu or Hanoï, but the whole of Vietnam which is the prize in this battle. The vanquished share the same risks; the victor will reap the same reward." If the names of towns and countries were replaced by those of Rome, Carthage, Africa or Italy, this would be Hannibal's speech, as reported by Livy, on the eve of the Battle of Zama, two centuries before the birth of Christ.

If it was aware of the threat of an attack on Dienbienphu, the restricted war committee which had just been set up in Paris could have begun by asking General Navarre whether he should not install his headquarters at Hanoï. But no, the Pleven report was reassuring on that point: Navarre was in full control of the situation. General Fay's shocking comment would not keep anyone awake at night.

March 12, 1954

It was a Friday like any other for Sergeant Sammarco and Captain Capeyron. The weather was so fine that everyone was filled with the joy of living. Sergeant Sammarco was waiting for the arrival of the first Dakotas with his fatigue party of prisoners of war. The trucks were ready to carry the supplies to the stores. At eight o'clock, the operation started. Now and then the parachutes fell on the barbed-wire defenses, which tore holes in them, and time was lost retrieving the packages. Sammarco went to the air traffic control center near the still smoking wreckage of the Packet and complained. The pilots knew they were supposed to avoid giving the ground teams this extra work, but sometimes a careless dropper or a gust of wind was enough to scatter the loads. For form's sake the officer picked up his microphone.

"Torri Rouge calling François Hector," he said. "Watch your dropping point. You're a bit slow."

Grauwin received drugs, battle dress and new canvas shoes. Dakotas landed, disgorged convalescents and men returning from leave without stopping their engines and took off again. One of them taxied to one side and switched off. Cogny got out clumsily, his eyes buried beneath his brows, his jacket and his face creased, and hoisted himself into Colonel de Castries's jeep, which drove off. The circus was in full swing, humming, raising clouds of dust, firing field guns and machine guns, opening tins of sardines and drinking *vinogel* mixed with the filtered water of the Nam Youm.

At Isabelle, the 8th Assault and the Legion carried out a patrol to the south of the basin without meeting any resistance. On the other hand, they discovered that half a mile of trenches had been dug in the rice fields nearly a mile to the east. Covered by Lieutenant Préaud's three tanks, the Algerians of the 1st Rifles filled them in again without incident.

Captain Capeyron was no strategist. He had not been through Staff College and had no desire to go there. The Legion was enough for him. The rumors which had been circulating since morning had already circulated in January, when one alert had followed another without any result. To attack, the Viets would have to be mad, and they were not mad. The destruction of the Packet, whose blackened carcass stood like a gibbet at the end of the runway, was simply a stroke of luck. How could the Viets have failed to be tempted to hit such an inviting target? They had left it at that because they probably had only two or three 75-mm. guns.

Cogny had come to make sure that good use was being made of the two parachute battalions he was relying on for counterattacks. This question had obsessed him ever since he had refused to reinforce the garrison of the entrenched camp; the reaction of Castries's mobile forces justified his view. If Béatrice, which was known to be invested, fell, where would the operation to recapture it start from? What artillery support would it be given? Cogny went up to Béatrice, where a few mortar shells fell at about 1300 hours, and asked for all the details of the proposed counterattack. He was being unduly pessimistic in imagining such an eventuality, but Cogny wanted to guard against the worst. He knew that Castries normally used the two battalions intended for counterattacks to cover certain sides of Claudine, and that they were not immediately available. How much time would be needed to regroup them and put them in position? A few hours. How many hours? Nobody knew. Cogny asked Castries to find out but felt no real anxiety; the attack would be launched at night and they would have to wait until dawn before being able to maneuver. If the situation deteriorated during the night, they would therefore have time to get their balance. Cogny asked to see where the reserves were quartered; it looked as though they would be easy to assemble.

He felt reassured when he returned to his Dakota, and impatient to get back to his Hanoï headquarters. The delta worried him, for in his eyes it remained the chief potential battlefield and the source of Giap's troops and supplies. The enemy commander was conducting operations on that basis. Contrary to appearances, the campaigns in the highlands served only to draw off the Expeditionary Corps and wear it out away from the delta. Every night, the railway between Hanoï and Haiphong was sabotaged with booby-trapped shells and mines which exploded when the first train went through. In spite of the derailments, General Masson, Cogny's deputy, had orders to send six trains through every day, along a line strewn with overturned trucks. For ammunition, gas and food supplies to reach Dienbienphu, they had to reach Hanoï first. Bigeard, who had just returned with his battalion to the capital from Tonkin, had passed villages and stores in flames.

It was nearly 1530. Cogny shook hands and climbed into his Dakota, whose engines were warming up. He was giving a farewell wave to Castries through his window when some shells exploded on the airstrip and everybody threw himself to the ground. One Morane went up in flames and another had its left wing broken. Cogny's pilot opened out the throttle and took off. Behind him, the fighters rose from the airstrip and vainly machine-gunned the crests. Where had those 105-mm. shells come from, fired for the first time at a waiting plane, the sign of an important visitor? In the air-traffic shelter, a shell splinter was added to a collection fastened to a board. It was the seventh since February 1.

At 1730 a Bearcat was hit by antiaircraft fire. At the evening conference, when he met all his staff officers and the commanders of the subsectors and strong points, Castries read out the dispatch General Lauzin, head of the Air Force, had sent to the formations under his command: "The situation at Dienbienphu depends on today's air activity. You are permitted to take exceptional risks." Everybody turned with a laugh toward the commander of the entrenched camp's air base. The pilots had been taking exceptional risks for a long time. . . . Castries closed the meeting with these words: "Gentlemen, it will be tomorrow at 1700 hours."

Captain Noël, Chief of Military Intelligence in the entrenched camp, had just learned that the evacuation of the villages by their inhabitants had been fixed for the morning of the following day, Saturday. The Viets' big operations usually began on a Saturday evening. The estimated hour seemed to be the most auspicious; it would still be light enough for the gunners to get the range and the Air Force would not have much time to intervene. The new moon would be eight days old and the greater part of the night would be dark.

As they separated, the officers exchanged cynical remarks. Most of them believed that this was just another feint. Many were showing obvious signs of fatigue. The losses suffered on patrol had created gaps in the units, and the announcement of the attack did not inspire the companies with the joy the same news would have evoked in January. Captain Capeyron told himself that they could say what they liked, but if the Viets came down into the basin, well . . . When he saw his platoon leaders, he could tell that they were determined to make the enemy pay dearly for this audacity. At last they were going to lay their hands on those bands which always slipped through their fingers before dawn after attacking an outpost, taking their dead and wounded with them! They were going to mow down those battalions which disappeared into the rice fields and the mountains as soon as the dust kicked up by the GMC's rose from the roads. And they would be able to avenge, not only their comrades who had been caught in traps, but all their failures, the vain searches in burnt villages for those responsible for the cutting of railway lines, the laying of mines and the killing of important men.

Since November 20, 7 officers, 19 NCO's and 125 men had been killed; 2 officers, 9 NCO's and 77 men had disappeared; and 29 officers, nearly 100 NCO's and 675 men had been wounded. For what and for whom? On the enemy's side, this question was never asked. In his order of the day, Giap had not even referred to the death which awaited many of those who were preparing to face the fire of the guns, planes and automatic weapons of the entrenched camp; that went without saying. All the men in the People's National Army had agreed to lay down their lives for Uncle Ho and the country. "A thousand years of life for Uncle Ho!" They themselves were only the grains of sand on the beaches, the leaves on the trees, the clods of earth in the rice fields of a nation which was coming to life and which needed their bones upon which to build its destiny. They agreed to die and to serve as manure for future harvests which would no longer belong to a few mandarins but to the people. The region of Nam Dinh–Thaï Binh alone was in the hands of thirteen landed proprietors. A thousand years of life for Uncle Ho the Liberator!

In Saigon, Navarre said nothing, probably because he did not realize that the fate of Indochina was going to depend on Dienbienphu and because he believed that he had already said everything in his letters published in *Caravelle,* letters which the troops read without much enthusiasm, preferring the naughty drawings intended for the warrior' intellectual relaxation.

During the night, a Vietminh commando got through to the Dienbienphu airfield, sabotaged the landing strip by letting off explosive charges under the grids and left leaflets in the vicinity. On some of them these words were written in French and German: "Dienbienphu will be your grave." On others, a crude caricature showed Navarre's hand pushing soldiers of the Expeditionary Corps toward a line of daggers.

4 The Match

The less one has foreseen something, whatever it may be, pleasant or dreadful, the more pleasure or terror it causes. Nowhere is that seen more clearly than in war, in which any surprise strikes terror into even the stoutest hearts.

—XENOPHON

There are some who say that a governor must never risk his person, and maintain that if he dies all is lost. I agree that he should not risk his life in all encounters like an ordinary captain, but since it is a question of the loss of everything, what will become of you, the King's governors and lieutenants, and how many arguments will there be about your honor and fame? Do you think you will get off by saying, "I did not want to risk my life in battle for fear that if I were killed, all would be lost, or I did not want to endanger myself protecting a fort or a citadel, for I had to defend the town"? That will not save you. The taking of a fort is of such consequence that your enemy then has his foot on your throat. You must rather die or recapture what you have lost, as I did, when I closed the gate behind me in order to deprive us of all hope of retreat, in my determination to repel the enemy or die. For, if I had left him where he was, it was I who would have been doomed. . . .

I want to warn you of one thing, and that is that when adversity presses you hard, you must not remain shut up in your room, but show yourself to the captains and the soldiers, and even to the people, with a confident face; your mere presence will encourage them.

—MONTLUC
Memoirs, Book III

At dawn the enemy artillery barrage began again. In spite of the smoke screen which the French tried to lay down to hide the airfield from the Viets, a Dakota was destroyed on the ground on the main airstrip and another on the southern airstrip near Isabelle. Led by its chief, Captain Maurel, the crew set off on foot toward Dienbienphu, lost its way and had difficulty in getting back to the air command post. At 0830 hours, the Curtiss Commando of the Blue Eagle Company, which a pilot had come to fly back to Hanoï because it needed an engine change, was hit just as the mechanic was starting her up and burst into flames. It was on to that plane that M. Bidault had put the Sultan of Morroco when he had sent him to Corsica. The information service reporters Martinoff and André Lebon were filming the fire when a mortar salvo hit them. Martinoff was killed. André Lebon had one foot practically blown off. Dr. Grauwin finished the amputation and sent the wounded man off to Hanoï. At eleven o'clock, a third Dakota was badly damaged.

At 1500 hours, Major Phuc was ordered to get ready to open fire on the planes with his heavy 12.7-mm. machine guns. At 1530 he brought down his first Bearcat, which crashed near Béatrice. The artillery of the entrenched camp replied at random, for the lookout posts were unable to locate the Viet guns. Most of the fighters and bombers in the delta were grounded by the rain. On the Dienbienphu airstrip, five Moranes, one helicopter and six fighters were unable to take off; the gas in their tanks had been mixed with water.

Castries kept looking at his wristwatch. Before 1700 hours, he was in his command post, sitting at his table, ready to call Cogny on the radio-telephone. He was smoking. Everything was in order. If he had dared, he would have started a game of bridge. The photographer Daniel Camus saw him elegantly dressed and as courteous as if he had just come from a social function.

The time arrived. Castries pricked up his ears. He could hear the background noise of the planes, mingled with the voice of his secretary Paule Bourgeade and laughter in the next room. 1705 hours. Nothing. Over the hills floated wreaths of thick mist which the sun could scarcely penetrate. He lit another cigarette. Those damned Viets were not going to attack. 1710 hours. It was a washout. They had called it off. He felt like ringing up Captain Noël and saying to him, "A dud, my friend. You were wrong."

Major Phuc received a telephone call congratulating him on shooting down the Bearcat. He could scarcely believe his ears; it was Giap, quite near, who was speaking to him. Some shells fell on the gun crews sheltering in deep trenches. Another antiaircraft battery had fired from Ban Na Tan; Gun Crew Commander Hoang da Hung, a little peasant with a high forehead and a flat nose, fired unsuccessfully at the planes with his 37-mm. American guns which had come from Korea.

Langlais was taking a shower in the cubicle which had been fitted up in the trench connecting the command posts, when a thunderous roar as if the sky were opening sent him rushing into his shelter. He pulled on his battle dress. The floor was shaking under his feet, and earth was raining down. Shots were shaking the wall, and the noise was like that of a ship breaking in two and sinking. The light went out. Langlais no longer had any doubts; the Viets were on time, and the din was that of heavy shells. His adjutants came running down into the command post with flashlights in their hands.

"All right?" asked Langlais.

The officers tried the telephones. The lines had been cut. They could no longer get through to the commanders of the reserve battalions.

"The radio," said Langlais.

One of them went to the transmitter and turned a knob.

"Young Pierre calling Pierrot, Young Pierre calling Pierrot, can you hear me?"

"Pierrot calling Young Pierre, I can hear you loud and clear. Over."

The voice of Tourret, who was in command of the 8th Assault, answered Langlais calmly. So did the voice of Guiraud of the 1st BEP. The men were safe. Everything was all right. Langlais switched off. Was it the transmitter that exploded or the sky that fell with all its stars on the roof of the shelter, taking the men's breath away? Not all the stars had fallen, since some could be seen between the exposed logs, in the brand-new night. Another 105-mm. shell embedded itself in the wall, without exploding, just above the adjutant's shoulder, like a terrible ax blow, while a telephone started ringing. The ray of an electric flashlight was turned on it: it was the direct line to Castries.

In one of the four rooms which formed Lieutenant Colonel Gaucher's command post, Lieutenant de Veyes, the chief signals officer of the central subsector, was listening in to Béatrice. Near him was the Abbé Trinquand, a priest of the diocese of Meaux, who had come to Indochina to serve as a chaplain to the 13th Demibrigade of the Legion. He was a tall, well-built man of thirty-eight, intelligent and kind, with a handsome Roman face, thinning hair and thin lips. Like the Viets, he had a mania for statistics and was counting the shells which he could hear whistling and exploding: fifteen to eighteen a minute. All of a sudden, a voice made a loudspeaker vibrate. They could not make out much of what it said, except for the word "dead."

Lieutenant de Veyes informed Lieutenant Colonel Gaucher, who took the microphone, bawled out the man at the other end of the line, and told him to calm down and use the terms of the conventional vocabulary. Major Pégeaux, the commander of the 3rd Battalion, 13th Demibrigade, and his adjutants had just been killed in their shelter. For the benefit of his own officers, a furious Gaucher growled as he stalked off, "I always said those shelters were too flimsy."

One of the companies on Béatrice was no longer answering and the whole of the strong point was under fire. After a fresh salvo of 105-mm. shells which shook the ground, the electric light went out. In the beam of a flashlight, a white specter, leaning on a prop, appeared in the doorway; huge, livid, his clothes in rags, his hair tousled and his face covered with dust, Vadot looked like a Templar returning from hell.

"The colonel is wounded," he said.

Chaplain Trinquand tried to call Captain Le Damany of the medical service on the telephone, but the lines were dead. He left the shelter, and ran a few dozen yards to the doctor's shelter, where he found Le Damany reading. Lieutenant Colonel Gaucher had lost both arms and was bleeding to death. He said to his batman, "Wipe my face and give me something to drink. . . . "

Langlais spat out the earth in his mouth, detached himself from the wall against which he had been flattened and put the receiver to his ear.

"Is that you, Langlais?"

"Yes."

"Gaucher has just been killed. You take his place immediately as commander of the central subsector. Transfer command of the reserves to Pazzis."

There was a faint click; Castries had switched off. Langlais extricated himself from the ruined shelter and went up to the trench, which had half-fallen in. Beyond the lacerated logs, the darkness was vibrating and thundering under the gigantic hammering being given the heart of the entrenched camp, where the command posts and the field hospital were huddled only a few dozen yards from one another. Behind the dark hill of Dominique, sudden flashes furrowed the red sky above Béatrice. Where had the Viets gotten all those guns? Where was this blinding thunderbolt, this steel whistling like whips, coming from?

In the trenches which had been dug for the attack, thousands of men did not know whether they should hold their breath or give free rein to their joy. They had been waiting years for this moment. Piroth's guns were now answering, but without the massive and terrifying majesty they had had during the last few days. Crimson streams of tracer bullets soared toward the crests. Near the airstrip, great flames gushed into the air, lighting up the belly of the basin like the crater of a volcano, as the gasoline and napalm stores suddenly exploded among geysers of sparks. In the darkness, the assault units went forward, crudely lit up by the flashes from bangalores.

For the moment, it seemed to Langlais that only Béatrice was being attacked, while the Viets neutralized the central position with their fire. Langlais analyzed the situation calmly, called the strong point commanders one by one on the radio, stopped the startled, ragged fire which was coming from all sides and wasting ammunition, restored calm, and learned that a Dakota pilot had taken off under shellfire to escape the unforeseen bombardment.

In the field hospital, the wounded suddenly came flooding into the casualty clearing station, and overflowed into the mess and the dormitory. Dr. Grauwin bent along with Chaplain Heinrich over the shattered body of the dying Gaucher, then straightened up, pulled a sheet over it and had the corpse carried to the morgue, where the dead were already piling up.

At last some information came in from Béatrice: each strong point was fighting separately. Six Viet battalions, pouring in along three axes from the northwest, the north and the northeast, had already gained a footing in the inner defenses. Langlais asked Piroth to lay down barrages on the barbed-wire defenses destroyed by the Viet guns, but Piroth's batteries, under enemy fire, were suffering terrible losses.

To dismantle obstacles, the first waves of the Viet troops were preceded by squads of dynamiters. One by one, under continuous fire from the machine guns, these men went forward, laying down their long bamboo poles stuffed with explosive and igniting the fuses with their gas lighters. Each bangalore cleared an area of four square yards. The losses were so heavy that the division was asked for reinforcements. The attack from the northwest was hanging fire. It was then that the young section commander, Phan dinh Giot, who had already blown up the last few yards of barbed wire, crawled toward the blockhouse which was holding out, threw himself on the embrasure and stopped it up with his body. The advance continued. Within ten minutes of each other, two of Béatrice's peaks fell, submerged by infantrymen who encircled them and crossed the trenches in screaming waves. Disaster loomed.

Disaster is reduced by half when one refuses to submit to it. Two of Béatrice's peaks were no longer answering on the radio, but they must still be resisting, and the center was holding well. Five hundred Legionnaires of a demibrigade whose flag bore the name of Bir Hakeim couldn't give in as quickly as that. A lull would allow them to get their breath back. At about 2100 hours, the firing slackened. The central peak had probably halted the attack. Once the night was over, the two battalions of Guiraud and Tourret would descend the northern slopes of Dominique with the tanks and set off to recapture the lost ground. Major de Séguins-Pazzis, whom Castries had kept with him, studied the order of battle for the counterattack and the support his units would need.

Suddenly, at 2300 hours the attack was renewed, and the central peak fell fifteen minutes after midnight. The Viets touched on Gabrielle and pushed on as far as the foot of Dominique. In the white light of the flares dropped by the French "firefly" plane, they could be seen digging holes. To dislodge them and reach the cemetery which Béatrice had become, Castries now knew that two battalions would not be enough. Nor would twenty-eight guns. At the field hospital, Grauwin, stripped to the waist, operated on stomach wounds, broken limbs, chests and skulls. One hundred and fifty wounded men were groaning around him.

It was a soldier named Nguyen hum Oanh who planted on Béatrice the victorious red flag with the gold star entrusted to his unit by Uncle Ho.

"Didn't it surprise you," I asked Major Le hong Duc, "to see a unit of the Foreign Legion fall so quickly?"

"We had seen others fall before that one," he replied. "We had observed everything and made a minute study of the terrain several nights before the attack, using models too. Every evening, we came up and took the opportunity to cut barbed wire and remove mines. Our jumping-off point was moved up to only two hundred yards from the peaks of Béatrice, and to our surprise your artillery didn't know where we were. Finally, some Thai deserters had given us a lot of information."

In place of his left hand, Major Le hong Duc had only a stump, but he was smiling and his upper lip bared his incisors as far as the gums. A brown plume on top of his high forehead gave him the look of a tragic clown.

Was there, as Duc told me, an officer of the Legion who presented himself, at dawn that day, to the advance sentry of a peak to the north of Béatrice and told a political commissar that he was giving himself up because he had had enough? I don't believe so. A Legionnaire may desert on account of some woman, but no officer of the Legion ever commits treason. It may be that a soldier captured in an ambush tried to pass himself off as an officer and was taken at his word; he is said to have advised the Viets not to attack so as not to suffer a defeat. Major Le hong Duc alleges that he replied, "We shall attack, and we shall take all the officers and troops on Béatrice prisoners." When this had been done, the Legionnaire is said to have exclaimed, "If you can do that, then Dienbienphu is yours."

March 14, 1954

There was no rest between the two days, not a moment's peace in the night full of shouts and explosions, with the gasoline and napalm stores burning like a huge torch and casting their red glow as far as the crests. Two more Bearcats had been destroyed on the ground. The airfield control tower was in ruins, the frame of the direction finder was destroyed, the aerials were down, and the battalion dressing stations were overflowing with dead and wounded. At the field hospital where Lieutenant Gindrey of the medical service was busy amputating, the resuscitation ward was covered with splashes of blood. Most of the shelters had collapsed and the men were crowded in holes. Grauwin sent an urgent message asking for ten liters of blood, fifty million units of penicillin and five hundred grams of streptomycin.

Celebrating the Mass of Reminiscere Sunday, Chaplain Trinquand suddenly remembered what he had read in Daniel the day before about the three young Hebrews in the furnace, who remained unscathed in the midst of the flames. The flames were here with a vengeance.

At daybreak, the bodies ripped apart by the shells were brought out of the shelters under tent material; three pilots succeeded in taking off in their Bearcats, which the mechanics had somehow or other made airworthy, and returned to Hanoï in the rain. Survivors from Béatrice arrived in a dazed condition, their clothes in rags. A wounded lieutenant told

Grauwin that the Viets had released him with an important message, which was taken to Colonel de Castries. Castries called Cogny's chief of staff at 0745.

"The Viets have offered to grant me a truce from eight o'clock to midday to pick up our dead and wounded. Should I accept? What I'd like first of all is to see a battalion of reinforcements dropped by parachute."

In his messages during the night, Castries had appeared pessimistic and depressed. Cogny got in touch with General Gambiez, in Saigon, who gave the Commander in Chief's permission.

"And what about your counterattack?" asked Cogny.

Through the static and background noises, Castries's voice seemed shriller.

"The enemy has been on Béatrice since midnight. The stocks of ammunition are down. My artillery has fired six thousand 105-mm. shells. That leaves me just over twenty thousand, and with the weather as it is down there how many can you send me if you are dropping a battalion here as well? The reserve units are dazed by the shelling they have had all night. What do you expect me to do?"

"All right," said Cogny. "Accept the truce; it's all right by me. You can launch your counterattack with your reinforcements later."

In Hanoï, the weather was so bad that a wait of thirty minutes was imposed between the take-off of each pair of Dakotas, so that the pilots would not have to circle too long over the bases while awaiting their turn to land.

In the zone of the command posts there was an atmosphere of consternation and nervousness. Castries did not leave his shelter. His chief of staff wore a helmet in his office and urinated into empty tins, arousing the hilarity of certain paratroopers. Langlais had his shelter cleared of debris and the roof buried under six feet of earth and logs. Signal teams fastened the telephone wires, which nobody had bothered to protect, to the sides of the trenches.

"Pack your bags," Castries told Paule Bourgeade, who had served coffee all night long, smiling in the midst of the turmoil and the shouting. "You're leaving by the first plane." And as she protested, he added, "That's an order."

But how could a plane land under fire? The airstrip was in chaos, pitted with holes and bristling with pieces of broken grids sticking up like daggers or the teeth of a saw. The grids were fastened in such a way that separate units could not be changed, and they had to be repaired on the spot by being cut with a blowtorch and soldered with an arc lamp. Yet it was absolutely essential for a plane to come and fetch the wounded who were in danger of death and bring the blood which could not be dropped by parachute. Squadron Leader Claude Devoucoux volunteered for this mission, which called for courage, *sang-froid* and virtuosity. At eight o'clock he landed a twin-engined Siebel at Dienbienphu with six liters of blood for Grauwin, picked up four wounded men and Paule Bourgeade and took off again immediately under artillery fire.

Nine years later, on the Vietminh side, nobody any longer remembered this truce. Most of the officers who had taken part in the attack on Béatrice, which now bore the name of the neighboring village, Him Lam, even denied that it had ever existed.

"Why should we have granted a truce? We had been victorious at Him Lam, and we were getting ready to attack Doc Lap [Gabrielle] that same evening. When we attack, we attack until victory is ours; fighting and then offering a truce isn't our way."

And yet that truce existed. Therefore it was granted by the local commander.

At Dienbienphu and in Hanoï, it was regarded as a maneuver on the part of the Vietminh, which benefited from every hour of respite; once a truce had been accepted, it would be impossible to dislodge the enemy from Béatrice. Did he on his side misjudge the offensive power of the entrenched camp? At dawn, the two parachute battalions of Tourret and Guiraud, dazed by the thousands of 105-mm. shells fired by Giap's batteries, were unable even to cover the distance separating them from their jumping-off place, just as the tanks were unable to get out of the barbed-wire defenses to support them. Gunner Piroth was no longer capable of establishing a fire plan and putting it into operation, and the bad weather prevented the Air Force from getting through. It seems certain that there was a semblance of a counterattack with two companies which Major Duc later told me were wiped out as soon as they emerged.

Chaplain Trinquand went to see the wounded lieutenant who had brought the message offering the truce. In the state in which they had found him, the Viets had failed to distinguish him from the other Legionnaires. As he was the only one who could speak French, they had told him, "Take this message to your headquarters and you can come back to fetch your wounded whom we can't move." Followed by an ambulance carrying Chaplain Trinquand and a Dodge truck carrying twenty stretcher-bearers, Captain Le Damany of the medical service, wearing his cap with the scarlet velvet band, set off in a jeep with the Red Cross flag fluttering from its windshield. About eleven o'clock, after crossing a deserted and menacing landscape, the little convoy arrived without incident at Béatrice. At the foot of the first southeastern peak, not far from the straw hut containing the chapel, which was still intact, two huge craters gaped wide. A patrol under a Vietminh officer wearing leather boots met Captain Le Damany and escorted him to the western peak, in the middle of a tragic desert, while Chaplain Trinquand climbed to the top of the slope, which the garrison used to descend to fetch water from the Nam Youm. There he helped a Legionnaire in a coma, before going to the northern peak.

The legs of a member of the garrison were sticking out of one of the smashed blockhouses. From his distinctive footwear and the color of his trousers, the chaplain recognized the body of Lieutenant Carrière, a company commander. It was obvious that fighting had taken place, but the chaplain was surprised to find the position in a less ravaged state than he had expected. Twelve Legionnaires, most of them in a hopeless condition, and three corpses were carried to the waiting vehicles. The rest of the battalion had disappeared, apart from the hundred or so men who had managed to escape when they had seen that all was lost, and had reached the French lines at dawn with Second Lieutenant Makowiak, by way of Dominique, where they had made themselves known. Of the enemy's losses, no trace remained in the barbed-wire defenses, until, at the beginning of a trench which the Vietminh had dug as far as the summit of the narrow ravine separating two peaks, the chaplain discovered, among a few abandoned light weapons, remains of human bodies forgotten by the teams of corpse collectors. One of the Legionnaires in the convoy, Sergeant Kubiak, voiced the opinion that the Viets would not attack the entrenched camp again in a hurry.

At the beginning of the afternoon, Navarre set off for Hanoï with General Lauzin to see how many reinforcements should be dropped. Before leaving Saigon, Colonel Revol told the press correspondents that the French Command had granted a truce to the Vietminh, which had asked for it. That was what M. Bidault would later repeat in the National Assembly.

I questioned Giap on this point. It was a question which he evaded, like many others, referring me to a vaguely worded statement: "Strictly speaking, there was no local truce on March 14 after the fall of Him Lam. Out of humanity, we unilaterally granted permission that day to the commander of the entrenched camp to pick up his wounded."

So who is lying? Everybody. Except for the witnesses who went to Béatrice.

That same morning, Grauwin met Piroth in the command post trench.

"You remember Thaï Binh?" Piroth asked him, holding out his only hand. "I land up in all the dirty messes."

At Thaï Binh, the operational command post of the division had been attacked by commandos during the night of December 3-4, just when Castries was arriving at Dienbienphu. Grauwin, Paule Bourgeade and he had made a miraculous escape.

"Is everything all right?" asked Langlais, going past just then.

Piroth did not reply and turned away so abruptly that his forage cap fell off, revealing his shaven skull and his neck with wrinkles that looked like the marks of a harrow. He bent down to pick it up, and Langlais noticed that tears were running down his cheeks. Then, straightening up and holding Langlais back with his single arm, he said, "We're done for. I've told Castries he must put a stop to it all. We're heading for a massacre, and it's my fault."

And he suddenly walked away, with the jerky steps of an automaton.

The entrenched camp was in the grip of boundless stupefaction. The sudden fall of Béatrice, the absence of any reaction on the part of Colonel de Castries and Gaucher's death had dealt a terrible blow to the garrison's morale. Sergeant Sammarco, who was watching over his colonel's coffin with four armed Legionnaires, above the hole of the morgue in which the bodies were beginning to pile up on top of one another, sometimes tied up in blankets or parachute material, also thought that Béatrice had been taken by surprise and that the Viets would pay dearly for their victory. When a volley of shells straddled the zone of the command post, Sammarco and the guard threw themselves into a trench, and then, when calm had been restored, returned to their posts at the four corners of the grave, on the terreplein. That day for the first time, Sergeant Sammarco asked himself aloud the question which had been tormenting him since dawn: "I wonder if we aren't going to end up eating rice." He darted a quick look around. Nobody had heard him.

In Hanoï, Brigitte Friang asked for permission to jump with the battalions that were waiting for the order to enplane.

"A woman at Dienbienphu?" exclaimed Cogny's adjutant. "This isn't the time for that. Castries has just sent back the only woman who was out there."

This was not strictly true. The prostitutes from the Laï Chau brothel were still there, as well as those who had been brought from the brothel in Hanoï to amuse the Legionnaires in the main center. For some time to come, Chaplain Trinquand would go on seeing their bronze faces and purple tunics.

Without folding his parachute, which he left among all the others littering the battlefield, Second Lieutenant Jean-Claude Thélot, who had just jumped with the 5th Battalion, Vietnamese Paratroops, regrouped his platoon and in a series of rushes reached a strong point. One of his men, thrown into the air by a mortar shell just as he was landing, died with one leg blown off. Another could no longer walk. Thélot took him on his back and, stopping now and then to catch his breath, carried him to an ambulance. Without guides, hampered by the wounded and stragglers, he finally arrived in a jeep at Dominique, where he found his men among the Algerians occupying the peak. He installed his troops in holes and did honor to the dinner which the battalion commander offered him in his dugout. A succession of storms broke out and swamped the entrenched camp in mud.

At 1600 hours, Navarre landed at Hanoï, where he was met by Cogny. The two generals barely exchanged a few words.

At the end of the afternoon, the alarm was given at Gabrielle, which the Viets call Doc Lap, "the lonely one": the Viets were rushing down the opposite slopes. At 1730, the enemy artillery opened up again. A Morane blazed up in its pit, and the flames from it rose into the new night. Under the deluge of steel pounding the earth, the gun crews on Gabrielle, caught in the fire of 75-mm. nonrecoiling guns and mortars brought within close range, were incapable of retaliating. At 1830, Major de Mecquenem, whom General Ely had not heard, announced that he was under attack; having come to the end of his tour of duty, he was handing his command over to Major Kah, who had just arrived in Indochina.

The first attack took place at 2000 hours, and the fireworks started again. Castries ordered Séguins-Pazzis to prepare a counterattack right away. Gabrielle, whose command post, like that of Béatrice the night before, had just been crushed by a 105-mm. shell, suddenly fell silent. The Viets stormed up the steep slope bristling with barbed wire, which was defended by the 4th Company of the battalion of Algerian Rifles, and the men mown down by the machine guns were replaced by others who seemed invulnerable. Listening to the radio on the inside wavelength of the battalion, Castries heard the calls from the company commander: "The Viets have got a foothold on the summit. . . . The mortars are giving us a hammering, but morale is terrific. Fire quickly!" The moon, the "firefly" plane and the flashes of the explosions lit up the north end of the basin where Gabrielle stood guard over the outlet of the Nam Co and the Pavie Trail. Yet at 2200 hours the attack seemed to have come to a halt.

Relieved every hour, a B-26 had been machine-gunning and bombing the attackers "blind" since the end of the day.

Langlais, who remembered the tears he had seen that morning in Piroth's eyes, had questioned the artillery commander several times.

"Do you know where the Viet guns are?"

"They may be there," Piroth replied, pointing to a zone on the map. "Or there . . ."

"Can you silence them?"

Piroth shrugged his shoulders. Of course he was going to silence them. He had never been known to fail. At the conference, where Castries reproached him with blaming himself for everything and demoralizing everybody, and then sent him to get some rest, Piroth walked out abruptly. He had become a shadow of his former self and refused to eat anything. Castries had a meal sent to him in his shelter and asked Father Heinrich to look after him. The chaplain came back with the report that Piroth seemed to be feeling better.

For twenty-four hours he had been brooding over everything he had said: "We know to the nearest gun what they have got. We shall win because we have some 155's with plunging fire. We shall hit them behind the crests where they will have to put their batteries because they can't install them on these slopes." And to the Minister Jacquet, who had offered him some extra guns, he had said, "I have more than I need." He had even refused to dig his own guns in to provide shelter for their crews. Who could hit them? To fire in all directions he needed open emplacements. At the very most he had agreed to install his guns in pits with sandbag walls to protect them against mortar shells. He remembered his old arguments with Bigeard, who kept telling him that the Viets were capable of anything, and the reproach he had flung at him one day, to cut him short: "What you're saying is scandalous, Bigeard! Nobody has any right to praise the enemy." Piroth, who knew virtually nothing about the enemy's positions and had failed to destroy anything but a truck with his 155's, realized that Bigeard and Castries had been right, and he felt responsible for the loss of Béatrice and the death of Gaucher and the others. Had he any right to go on living, he, the righteous Piroth, who refused to keep going, as others did, on double brandies? Huddled at the back of his shelter, he took the grenade which he carried in his belt, pulled out the pin with his teeth and held it close to his heart.

March 15, 1954

After the moon had gone down, the attack was resumed at 0330. The defenders of Gabrielle asked that the command post be fired on by their own artillery. With all his reserves in action, Major de Mecquenem was wounded and Major Kah, at his side, had one leg blown off. Part of the garrison fell back toward the south; they already knew that Séguins-Pazzis was coming to the rescue and that he would not succeed in dislodging the Viets, who were too many and too strong.

Piroth's Senegalese batman rushed like a madman into the adjutants' office and called for help.

In his shelter, Piroth was stretched out, his head and chest reduced to pulp, his remaining hand blown off. What effect would this suicide have on the garrison? Castries decided to conceal it. The chaplains and Captain Le Damany of the medical service dug a grave themselves beneath Piroth's camp bed and hurriedly buried, under a few blessings and a little quicklime, this corpse that was regarded as a thing of shame, before walling up the shelter. They would say that Piroth, like Gaucher, had been the victim of a direct hit. An officer shouldn't commit suicide? When he believes that a fortress has been lost through his fault and life no longer seems possible under such a burden of remorse, suicide is a noble gesture. Piroth refused to blame his mistakes on those who had allowed him to commit them. He paid for them with his life, like a nobleman of old.

A dispatch was sent to Hanoï: "Colonel Piroth died on the field of honor." Navarre forwarded it to Paris, without comment.

At 0530, at dawn, the counterattack was launched with two companies of the 1st BEP, six tanks and the 5th Battalion, Vietnamese Paratroops, which set off halfheartedly. Séguins-Pazzis had to cover nearly three miles of the tangled network of barbed-wire defenses, along a route crossed by two streams; by the time he reached the southern slopes of Gabrielle, it was broad daylight. His troops heard the Viets shout, "Don't shoot, don't shoot, Frenchmen, give yourselves up!" Fifty yards from the tanks, the

Viets machine-gunned the units which tried to link up with the counter-attack. The strong-point dressing station was occupied. The doctor, wounded the day before, had been evacuated, and his place had been taken by an Austrian sergeant of the Legion, a former medical student.

Second Lieutenant Thélot had taken two and a half hours to cover one mile under shellfire. Some Legionnaires were already falling back slowly, supporting one another, with 105's whistling overhead and throwing up clouds of earth as they exploded. A battalion commander went forward, his face worn and haggard. Two tanks gave a roar and headed back toward the central garrison at full speed, their armor plating red with the blood of the men who were hanging onto the turret, their faces a mass of pulp, their legs bare. Thélot gave a drink to some wounded men, then dived into a trench where he could hear the sound of death rattles. Ambulances drove past, invulnerable. The order to return to base was given. One hundred and seventy Algerians had succeeded in escaping. They were directed toward Isabelle. Mecquenem was a prisoner. One of the tall aerials of the command post was broken.

How could Séguins-Pazzis have recaptured Gabrielle, when grazing fire made any progress impossible and when the enemy, thanks to some tall thickets, had been able to advance several hundred yards toward him? The counterattack, which could not be supported from Anne-Marie, seemed doomed to failure before it started, since the mistakes made in its conception and preparation carried the seeds of disaster within them. As in the case of Béatrice, the reinforcements intended for use in counterattacks were given poor cover and used only as stopgaps, an irreparable tactical error. Nobody on the staff had been able to correct it because nobody had imagined the collapse, in a single night, of bastions as solid in appearance as Gabrielle or Béatrice. The French Command had thought only of coming to their assistance, not of recapturing ground where the Viets dug themselves in as soon as they occupied it. Cavalrymen are not born to play with obstacles but to charge straight ahead. Their motto is that of Murat, who leaped into the saddle in front of his squadrons and shouted, "Follow my asshole." Getting out of the camp and its barbed-wire defenses was a difficult problem in itself. The first time Langlais had carried out a practice movement toward Isabelle, at dawn one January day, he had entangled his two battalions in the defenses. The only help Major de Mecquenem could count on was the artillery. And the artillery was weakening.

On the wavelength of the Vietminh radio, a regiment commander was heard asking in French for permission to attack Anne-Marie. "I'll make short work of it!" he said. "A quarter of an hour, all I need is a quarter of an hour. . . . "

Under the ceaseless, harassing fire, the first signs of demoralization appeared on Anne-Marie, where the soldiers of the 3rd Thai Battalion had taken advantage of the darkness and the general excitement to flee into the mountains or to go over to the enemy. Too intelligent to like fighting in the ranks, too versatile not to find means of escaping from necessity when it pressed too hard, and too familiar with the country not to hope that it would provide them with adequate cover, the Thais, who were not all princes or governors, but were nearly all fit to be, found it hard to reconcile themselves to a situation which condemned them to misfortune or death. They bore no resemblance to the thousand wretched men who had fallen back from Laï Chau and were used as slaves for fatigue duty, like the prisoners brought from Hanoï from whom Sergeant Sammarco took a fatigue party every morning. Short in stature, with faces instinct with refinement and courtesy, born for peace, pleasure and the arts, and accustomed to working only under the pressure of need, the troops of the 3rd Battalion were capable of giving excellent service provided they were well disciplined. In certain regions of the Thai country, when a man dies, his brother cultivates only the half of the field he inherits, leaving the other half to the memory of the dead man and to the sweetness of life. The fall of Béatrice, and that of Gabrielle nearby, was too much for them.

On conquered Anne-Marie, where the dead and wounded were collected by the thousand, the Viets made a rush for the food stores, gorged themselves on the army rations and got drunk on *vinogel* and *pastis*. A captured officer asked for a doctor.

"No."

"Why not?" he asked.

"Monsieur, you will learn that on our side we are not in the habit of asking questions."

In Hanoï, where dispatches and telephone calls from Colonel de Castries announced a fresh catastrophe every hour, Cogny's staff followed the disintegration of the entrenched camp in amazement. The most astonishing and frightening thing was that the artillery was not giving as much as it was taking; subjected to a counterbattery and firing wildly, it risked being reduced to total impotence before long. Most of the French observer planes had been destroyed or driven away, and this had robbed the artillery of its eyes; two more Moranes and one Bearcat had just been destroyed on the ground, and, on the rare occasions when a plane was able to fly over the crests, avoiding the Viet antiaircraft fire, the dry mist which had been hanging over the highlands for a week made visibility very poor. Ammunition was being used at such a rate that stocks were running low.

In the command office in the citadel at Hanoï, where Navarre came very rarely, for he worked apart, as in Saigon, in his jealously isolated villa, staff officers looked at each other and said, "We've gambled and lost." In his office, Navarre sat alone, very calm, almost silent, looking at the copy of a dispatch from Castries: "I think we may be split up, and in that case I foresee giving orders to Isabelle to carry on by herself," and Cogny's reply: "You are right to foresee the most disastrous possibilities, but you must think first of standing firm. Am studying eventual withdrawal of part of garrison. Sending you one battalion paras tomorrow."

With bitter satisfaction, Navarre reflected that he had been right, against Cogny, Castries and everybody in the entrenched camp, in not wanting Giap to attack. What he could not forgive himself for was having allowed himself to be duped by them. He did not even use the word "fools." He considered that too weak. "Bunglers" struck him as more suitable. Their appraisal of the enemy had been consistently at fault, either above or below reality. The only mistake that Navarre acknowledged making himself was having paid the slightest attention to their opinions. Incapable of taking an over-all view of a situation, they kept their noses glued to events without ever rising above them. The gunner Cogny had deceived him; the commander of the Dienbienphu artillery had miscalculated; the Air Force had failed to cut the roads, smash the enemy's depots or even spot his gun emplacements. The weather? Atmospheric conditions? Navarre shrugged his shoulders; those arguments would never convince him. The Vietminh had been receiving aid on a massive scale without letup or hindrance since the announcement of the Geneva Conference. Salan had begun it all by sliding the huge banana peel of Dienbienphu under his feet and had lulled him to sleep with his predictions, his deductions and his plan.

Yes, everybody had deceived Navarre, even the Chinese. Without Chinese aid to the Vietminh, Navarre told himself that he could not be beaten by Schoolmaster Giap. He refused to admit that Giap had decided to attack Dienbienphu as far back as December and that the experience of Na San had helped him. Chinese aid and the politicians who had not supported the Commander in Chief's plans—those were the culprits Navarre found to blame for this temporary reverse. He did not say to himself that he had not been expected to be adventurous or to take a gamble, but to show caution and prudence. He smiled disdainfully at the military success little Schoolmaster Giap had wanted to win so that his government could present itself at Geneva with a strong hand; monitoring of the Vietminh radio had revealed this to be the case, and he blamed himself now for not having stressed this point sufficiently to the Pleven commission. But who doesn't need military success? What general doesn't want it? Navarre had not lacked American aid, and thousands of tons of tanks and guns were rusting in warehouses. When Colonel Fleurant, his chief Intelligence officer, came to see him, he said, "Let's have no illusions; they're done for. I hope the Viets aren't going to start again tonight. We shall have to find some other solution."

He probably sent a telephone message to the same effect to M. Dejean, who, suddenly alerted, cabled a warning to his minister about the grim prospect opening up and decided to go to Hanoï.

Why should Navarre have been upset by reverses which he had foreseen when he had outlined the grandiose strategic concept of his campaign? In his opinion, the fact that Giap had hurled himself upon Dienbienphu was a confession of weakness; Giap could not attack anything else before the approaching rains. And what did a local setback matter if Cochin China remained safe from the Vietminh advance and if Central Annam was rid of its vermin? The second phase of "Operation Atlante" was launched that day. It involved thirty-three battalions of the Expeditionary Corps against seventeen Vietminh battalions of which only nine were regular units. Nothing could convince Navarre that the fate of Indochina was being decided at Dienbienphu and that the threat to Central Annam was only a ruse. He would never feel the slightest doubt and never wonder whether he might not have fallen into a trap. In front of men tortured with anxiety, he would congratulate himself on receiving unimportant information about the deserted plateau of the Bolovens, the scene of that "Operation Atlante" which had become the keystone of his strategy.

Who would have dared to suggest to Navarre that he was committing a gigantic error? Who would have dared to give him any advice when advice had brought him where he was? The truth, for Navarre, consisted of listening henceforth to nobody but himself. He was aware that his mortal enemy Giap was at Dienbienphu and that he had taken command of the attacking forces, which suggested that he intended to throw everything he had into that battle, but Navarre concluded that Giap's freedom of action was limited, where as he, Navarre, could deal other blows elsewhere. Joffre did not allow himself to be dazzled by Verdun in 1916, and launched an offensive on the Somme which may have helped Verdun hold out. Navarre refused to give in to the panic which took hold of the staff officers and clung more than ever, in spite of them, to his "Operation Atlante." He would tolerate no contradiction; he would break anybody who questioned his orders. Despite all those who had encouraged Navarre to give battle at Dienbienphu, "Operation Atlante" would take place. So, whereas de Lattre, when everything was breaking up and collapsing, had rushed into battle, taken command of the mobile units himself, shouted at the top of his voice, galvanized his troops and installed his combat post at the very heart of the fighting, Navarre remained in Hanoï and would return a few days later to Saigon.

A note from Cogny to Navarre indicated that it was necessary to foresee the possibility of a reverse at Dienbienphu and the loss of the forces engaged there. It tried to draw conclusions: if the Vietminh exploited its success, within twelve days it could bring one division back into the delta, where that very morning it had just launched an operation along the Hanoï-Haiphong axis, and this would change the balance of forces. Once again Cogny asked for reinforcements.

Cogny sent memos to Navarre, and yet Navarre was right there. To meet, all either of them had to do was go from one floor to the next or open a door, but the two men scarcely spoke to each other any more. They sent each other papers and chiefs of staff. When Navarre sent for Cogny, their conversation never penetrated the solid antipathy dividing them. Defeat settled nothing; each would exercise his wits to place the responsibility for that defeat on the other's shoulders. Navarre was already accusing Cogny of having kept his best troops for the delta, of having bungled his defense plan with forces incapable of counterattack by night, and, as a result of having refused the support he had offered him on March 4, of lacking units fit for battle. At first sight these reproaches seem justified. But when they are subjected to clinical scrutiny, it is apparent that Cogny could not have changed the instrument he had at his disposal. There was not a single battalion in Indochina which was one hundred percent French; even the Legion had "gone yellow." At Dienbienphu, Vietnamese formed half the total force, in which seventeen nationalities were represented. And who had gradually given to a limited operation all the conditions of a challenge to the enemy battle corps? Who had failed to realize that Dienbienphu had outstripped its local significance and assumed the solemn and awe-inspiring character of a merciless match from which a victor and a vanquished were bound to emerge? Who had hesitated to entrust Cogny with the responsibility of conducting the battle as he wished? Who had failed to realize that the fate of the entire Expeditionary Corps was being decided in the basin?

At Dienbienphu, an Air Force Bearcat flown by Sergeant Sahraoui was shot down, and at 1245 a Fleet Air Arm Hellcat flown by Lieutenant Commander Lespinas crashed to the north of Gabrielle. The control tower collapsed like a house of cards under a direct hit and was kept working only by makeshift devices. On the other hand, a helicopter damaged the day before managed to take off. The scale of supplies dropped by parachute was affected by a shortage of the large parachutes necessary for heavy loads. Some of the packages were already falling outside the entrenched camp, on enemy territory. The wounded were piling up in the midst of the garrison with no possibility of getting help to them. In the stores at Hanoï there was a shortage of munitions and canned goods, which Cogny was helpless to prevent, because the stocks of the operational base of Tonkin were the direct responsibility of the Commander in Chief.

In the afternoon, the investment of Dominique by the Viets was begun. Trenches zigzagged down from Béatrice, spread out, split up to allow automatic weapons to be installed, and continued on from Gabrielle toward Anne-Marie. On all sides, picks and shovels were put to work cutting into the ravines and slopes leading to the basin.

What would the next night bring? Colonel de Castries summoned his battalion commanders. Were the Viets capable of keeping up such a costly attack? Victory lends audacity, and Giap, on his side, could take advantage of the darkness and the bad weather to rest his troops, while those of the entrenched camp had no respite. The 6th Battalion, Colonial Paratroops, was going to jump the next day. Some 105-mm. guns had been dropped to replace those which had been destroyed.

At the entrance to the first-aid posts, heaps of sickening dressings were piling up. Equipment lay among hobnailed boots, bush sandals and helmets turned upside down like tortoises on their backs. Some of the wounded dragged themselves as far as the central field hospital, where they imagined that they would find safety. Algerians and Moroccans carried little Vietnamese, their faces twisted with pain, on their shoulders. Coolies and combat troops crowded into the passageways, begging for a place in the stifling catacombs of the surgical unit. They trampled on silk parachutes which had cost a hundred thousand francs each, and used them as sheets, as pillows, as shrouds. Groans came from the bunks crudely fastened together in layers of three by metal tubes. Plasma flowed drop by drop into veins, stubble spread over faces.

Near the ruined X-ray room, their bodies protected by rubber aprons, wearing gloves but not masks, Grauwin and Gindrey opened stomachs, slit thighs to remove shell splinters and bullets or reduce fractures. The medical orderlies smoked so as not to vomit at the nauseating odor of blood. Grauwin had fifty resuscitations to carry out and he had only two liters of blood left. He needed three hundred million units of penicillin and he had fifty million left. The shattered jaws, the blinded eyes, the blown-off legs, the split shoulders, the groans and the telephone calls were almost more than he could bear. Standing in the midst of the debris, this giant of a man could stand it no longer. This was not a battle any more, but a descent into hell. Grauwin, who was a believer, asked God for help. As for the camp, he asked that it beg for a truce.

Some distance away, the morgue pit, where Sergeant Sammarco and his four Legionnaires were still standing guard over Gaucher's coffin, was full to overflowing. Dead men were still being brought there, tied up like parcels in a blanket, with an identity bottle fastened to the neck of each bundle. Sometimes, indeed, there had been no time or opportunity to prepare bodies for burial, and they had simply been laid half-naked on the ground where the shells could still pulverize them. Some of them seemed to be asleep, with one hand on the forehead, while the flies settled greedily on their wounds.

Were these simply the horrors of war or those of disaster? Cogny asked himself this question in anguish. How could he have stuffed these battalions Navarre offered into a camp that was already crowded to suffocation? He knew that the deciding power of Dienbienphu, like that of any fortress, did not lie in defense alone, but in its ability to counterattack. And it was that which was worrying him; Castries was still prostrate from the shock of surprise and seemed to have understood nothing of what Cogny had told him over and over again on March 4. This cavalryman who held in his grip the thunderbolt of his ripostes was paralyzed. He was timidly using his reserves to stop gaps or mend holes, not to strike. In reality, he could not get them together because there were no shelters large enough to contain them and the enemy artillery was making gaps in their ranks, from the positions they occupied—the 8th Assault on the north and the 1st BEP on the west side of the center of Dienbienphu. He had had no time to train them in night fighting, and yet he knew that the Vietminh would attack only under cover of darkness.

Contrary to what has been supposed, there had never been any rehearsals of counterattacks, only exercises for the officers. How could there have been, since the reserve battalions were used during the day on reconnaissance patrols, following which they had to dress their wounds, replace their losses and catch their breath? Séguins-Pazzis had only just managed to reach the southern slopes of the Gabrielle "kidney bean" where the survivors from the garrison had gathered to meet him to escape captivity or death. Astonishingly enough, the aerial photos taken that very morning by a reconnaissance plane showed most of the fortifications of Gabrielle to be intact, whereas those of Béatrice had been smashed by shells, which suggests that the defenders could have held out longer if the artillery of the entrenched camp had given them more help.

On Claudine 5, in his command post in the middle of the rice fields, where his company had built solid shelters and dug trenches, Captain Capeyron had been baffled by the fall of Béatrice. He considered that the essential thing was to sit tight and wait for the reinforcements which would arrive as soon as the weather improved. Where he was, everything had held. He wondered why the paratroops had not put in an appearance and why there was such a gap between Béatrice and the peaks of Dominique. He also wondered how the strong points on Éliane were going to hold out, so close were they to other hills which the enemy could turn into firing points. The answers to all these questions were beyond him. He told himself that he was only a junior officer, and that if he could not understand the situation, it must be crystal-clear to his chiefs. He likewise refused to believe that the French had not at least tried to dislodge the Viets from the conquered positions. No doubts assailed him; the counter-attack would come. It could not fail to come. Around him, nobody asked any questions. Half a mile away, at the end of the landing strip, carcasses of planes were still burning.

Night had scarcely fallen before the thunder of concentrated artillery fire fell upon Dominique. Under the napalm, the mountain looked like a volcano in eruption with burning lava flowing down the sides.

At 2100 hours, M. Dejean reached Hanoï. Navarre, who seemed less gloomy than in the morning, and Cogny explained the situation to him.

At Dienbienphu, the Thais from Anne-Marie had taken advantage of a comparatively calm night to return home en masse, abandoning food, equipment and ammunition as they crossed the enemy lines. Those among them who did not dare leave, fearing the Vietminh more than their guns, took refuge with their leader; one company fell back on Huguette. As it was impossible to hold the strong point any longer, the remaining forces were directed to Isabelle.

Faced with the tragic situation in the hospital, Colonel de Castries, at Grauwin's request and on express instructions from the Commander in Chief, asked for a truce. For fear that the enemy might interpret this request as a confession of weakness, he offered the Vietminh its own wounded prisoners. A message was broadcast several times: "To the Command of the besieging People's Army. We inform you that twenty of your wounded will be carried on stretchers to Ban Ban at 2200 hours tonight. The men carrying them will be unarmed. No activity and no firing will take place in that zone until midnight." On its government radio, the Vietminh reproached the Commander in Chief and Paris with misrepresenting the truce of March 14, but it would come to the rendez-vous and collect its men.

Above his command post, Castries said to the photographer Daniel Camus, "You've come at a fine time, my boy. If they attack again tonight, we're done for."

Camus, who was twenty, was appalled. He told his comrades, but who could believe him? Camus had probably not understood or he had mis-heard a joke in poor taste by Castries. Captain Noël, Castries's chief of Military Intelligence, thought that the Viets had used up their munitions and that the whole business was over. How could the garrison be done for when the 6th Battalion, Colonial Paratroops, was being dropped by forty-two Dakotas in the region of Isabelle at the same time as reinforcements for the 1st BEP and the 8th Assault? The 6th Battalion, Colonial Para-troops, which landed in the midst of mortar shells, meant Bigeard, whose name suddenly made the rounds of Dienbienphu.

With Bigeard present, the garrison lifted its head. His battalion had been dropped over Isabelle at about 1500 hours. Limping, for he had torn a muscle at Séno, he had gone to Isabelle, holding a huge stick in his hand, to ask for a jeep to get to Dienbienphu. This temporary infirmity irritated him. Wearing his cap and escorted by his little staff, he presented himself to Lieutenant Colonel Lalande, who received him wearing his helmet in his shelter. He wanted a jeep, when nobody dared put his nose outside? Bigeard explained that he would avoid the mortar salvos better in a jeep than on foot. Given one, he zigzagged from one company to another and made for the center, where he arrived about 1700 hours and saluted Colonel de Castries.

"Good old Bruno," Castries said to him, "I'm glad to see you."

Bruno was his *nom de guerre*, which he had adopted in August, 1944 when he had parachuted into the Ariège, and which he had kept ever since. At the command post, Bigeard grimaced. It had a gloomy, dismal, stiff atmosphere which he did not like. His meeting with Langlais was chilly; the two officers didn't know each other and, at first glance, didn't like each other. Bigeard got back into his jeep and drove as far as the foot of Éliane 4. The news that he was there traveled fast; some had caught sight of his sharp profile or heard his coarse and insulting remarks. Captain Capeyron and all the junior officers, along with Sergeant Sammarco and all the NCO's, told themselves that things would change now. That night, if the enemy attacked, Bigeard would reply.

The whole of Indochina knew who Bigeard was. They knew his high forehead, his fair crew-cut hair, his bird-of-prey profile, his touchy independence and his rough worker's hands which always bore scratch marks. You could hate him, but you had to respect him. Tense and headstrong under an apparent impassivity, he could not stay put. In his native province, where they say that everybody is sure of himself, he was regarded as a nobleman, whose iron will and soft heart were well known. The nobility of this man who had retained a vulgar way of speaking from his origins consisted of never letting a comrade down.

In any legend, it is difficult to separate fiction from fact and reality from illusion; but legends grow up only around great adventures and great men. In his warlike, animal way, Bigeard was a great man. He sometimes referred to himself in the third person. This was because he recognized clearly and without false modesty who and what he was. Modesty has never been a weapon of conquerors or legendary heroes. To serve him, you had to become a pawn which he moved as he wished and obey him without fear of being trampled underfoot when his frenzied command led him to take short cuts. But, after victory, what a reward his men received!

Botella, who was in command of the 5th Battalion, Vietnamese Paratroops, threw himself into his arms and instantly placed himself under his orders. He made him sit down on a stool made out of a crate, from which Bigeard, after removing his right boot, directed the movements of his companies over the radio. Botella brought him some hot soup and talked sadly about the counterattack on Gabrielle on March 15, when he had had to kick hundreds of his demoralized Vietnamese out of the holes in which they were hiding. In the afternoon, he had gathered his officers together and pointed out those he was keeping. He had asked them to do the same with the NCO's and men in their companies. Then he had told the others, "Get the hell out of here. I never want to see you again."

Impassive under the shells, not revealing whether it was concentration, uneasiness or irony that tensed his long face, Bigeard was in a somber mood; what he had seen astounded him. A fairly wide ravine, covered with rice fields, surrounded each of Éliane's peaks, but the view in the dangerous direction, to the east and northeast, was largely obscured, at fairly short range, by the crests of the hills now known as Mont Chauve and Mont Fictif. The garrison of the entrenched camp had never occupied them, and the Viets were turning them into machine-gun nests. No infantryman who knew his job would ever have agreed to install himself so close to such obstacles without being able to sweep their approaches with his own fire.

Bigeard now understood what had led the French Command to leave the crests unoccupied: it had wanted to draw the enemy closer, in the conviction that, if he dared install himself there, it would smash him with a deluge of shells. In the eyes of General Cogny and Colonel de Castries, they were offering the Viets who ventured there a common grave. Contrary to expectations, the Viets had come and dug themselves in, and the French would have to use up all their ammunition in a single day to drive them away. The same blind faith in the universal virtues of artillery had created the great empty spaces between Béatrice, Gabrielle and the central position, into which the enemy had rushed like a torrent that nobody could stop; contempt for the adversary had led the French Command to prefer theoretical concepts to common sense.

On Éliane 4, everything remained to be done. The Moroccans had left the ground untouched. The 6th Battalion, Colonial Paratroops, began by digging itself in on the west side of the peak overlooking the river and left the eastern slopes to Botella. Fortunately, it was a calm night.

March 17, 1954

Navarre issued an order of the day to the Air Force to stimulate their ardor. But the most determined orders of the day cannot make flying conditions any easier, and can do nothing to change distances, atmospheric circumstances and the characteristics of aircraft.

The American Air Force, the strongest in the world, would never have agreed to commit itself to such an enterprise, with bases incapable of guiding their planes and bringing them down one by one onto the runways. Over the mountainous region between Hanoï and Dienbienphu, which was often obstructed with storms, there was no way to locate one's position. For more than a hundred miles, pilots were reduced to their own guesses, without even radar or a radio beam to direct them. If Navarre was unaware that a whole fleet cannot move like an isolated aircraft, his ignorance was criminal, and if he did know this, then his contempt for the use of the air arm bordered on lunacy. To supply a basin into which pilots only too often had to dive blind, through air space saturated with clouds, in itself called for considerable virtuosity. Yet it does not seem that Navarre's deputy, though he was a flying man himself, ever raised the slightest objection to his chief's grandiose ideas, or that the Chief of the Air Command in Indochina ever thought of rebelling against a mission which his men could not carry out. When anybody spoke up, it was merely to utter a warning. It is thus that the weakness of subordinates and their anxiety to avoid displeasing the great men they serve sometimes lead to irreparable mistakes. What ardor, then, could Navarre hope to stimulate in his Air Force if he did not know that planes, like trains, need pathways in order to move?

That day, the weather over the delta improved, and planes rushed toward Dienbienphu, where the last Morane, which had so far gone unscathed, was now ablaze. Bombs rained down on the new fire points established by the Viets as well as the old positions of Béatrice and Gabrielle, and the black smoke clouds of napalm rose into the sky. In case an aircraft should want to land, the ground staff cleared the airstrip and carried out makeshift repairs to the grids. A helicopter which had been made airworthy took off. Since dawn, Dakotas had been dropping food and ammunition.

With huge red crosses painted on his fuselage, and heralded by repeated messages broadcast on the Vietminh wavelength, a pilot in a medical service plane tried to land, but was forced to fly away by the violence of the mortar fire which greeted him. In the hospital, shells exploded in front of the shelter, in the casualty clearing station and on the huge pile of corpses in the morgue. Scraps of rotting flesh spurted into the air on all sides. Between a couple of salvos, wounded men helped each other climb into the vehicles which had come to fetch them. The Dakota returned and managed to land, but before the cases of plasma it had brought had all been unloaded, the enemy opened fire again. Thirty-two men crowded into the plane, helped by the hostess to clamber inside. Others clung desperately to the tail and, as the plane moved off, were hurled to the ground and stunned by the slipstream of the propellers. Helped by Captain Cornu, who had installed himself beside him at the controls, Lieutenant de Ruffray took off in less than half a mile while a shell exploded among the group of men left on the ground. Too heavy to cross the crests, the plane flew to Muong Saï, unloaded there some of the material it had been unable to leave at Dienbienphu, and took off again for Hanoï; but the most serious casualties had not been evacuated, for only comparatively fit men could have performed the difficult feat of getting on board.

At daybreak, Castries had had what remained of Anne-Marie reoccupied. The northern peaks were lost, and Major Clémençon, who was in command of the battalion of the 2nd Foreign Infantry, on Huguette, took in the southern defenses and spread out to the west as far as Françoise. On Gabrielle, which dominated the axis of the airstrip, the Vietminh had rapidly installed antiaircraft batteries and was filling the positions abandoned by the Thais with 37-mm. guns and heavy machine guns. It was clear that no more planes would be able to land at Dienbienphu or take off from the entrenched camp except at night, and then only at considerable risk. Three days after the beginning of the attack, and contrary to all expectations, Dienbienphu had been deprived of its principal support.

From 1130 to 1210, Cogny flew over the entrenched camp in his Dakota, but shells were straddling the airstrip and his pilot had to give up the idea of landing. Cogny did not feel he should order him down and returned to Hanoï. He turned down a suggestion that he use a plane carrying Red Cross markings, asked General Dechaux to place at his disposal a plane capable of returning to Dienbienphu by night and announced his impending arrival to Castries.

During the afternoon, General Dechaux refused to provide a plane for Cogny, who thought for a moment of going over his head and getting Navarre to issue the order. But the fear of finding himself shut up in Dienbienphu, far from the delta which was his responsibility, persuaded him to give up the idea. Nobody has ever questioned Cogny's courage; he had often been seen in places where generals don't usually go, and he could imagine the reproaches which might be leveled at him later. Yet he ought to find a means of joining the besieged garrison, to restore some of its fighting spirit, rectify some of the mistakes that had been made and shake up Castries, who seemed as sorely tried as his chief of staff. But if, as it was feared, Dienbienphu fell in a few hours, was the enemy to be given an opportunity to capture the commander of the Tonkin forces? That day Cogny faced a problem of conscience which tormented him to the point of tears.

Everybody told him that his place was not at Dienbienphu, and he ended up convincing himself that they were right; thus, by obeying the voice of reason he muffed the finest chance of his career. Why, in fact, didn't he reject advice and discipline and jump by parachute into Dienbienphu together with Colonel de Castries's substitute? What prevented him was the fact that Dienbienphu was not his work, but Navarre's. He would have defended his own work like a fanatic, whereas he hesitated to risk his life for Navarre and give grounds for the belief that he considered himself responsible. Why, then, didn't Navarre jump into a plane, fly over the entrenched camp and give his orders directly to Castries and Langlais as de Lattre would have done? The fate of Dienbienphu had not been decided. Lost through the errors of judgment of one general, Dienbienphu could have been saved through a stroke of genius by another. Cogny could have become the hero and the leader.

March 18, 1954

Breaking away from the formation of Dakotas which had been circling since dawn, Lieutenant Biswang suddenly dived down onto the airstrip, picked up twenty-three wounded and took off under fire, between the shell holes. Behind him Major Darde tried to do the same; he had already landed when the shelling started again, forcing the ambulances to drive away, and he took off empty, straddled by salvos of mortar shells. The doctor accompanying the hostess was seriously wounded, and the plane was struck in twenty-two places. Yet the Dakotas marked with red crosses had only their crews, nurses and tins of plasma on board. The Vietminh was lying when it declared on its radio that the medical service Dakotas were loaded with 105- and 120-mm. shells.

As it happens, the wounded were not the only ones to try to jump into the planes. There were also a military correspondent, the crews of the planes that had been destroyed and the officers Castries had relieved of their posts for incompetence. So far, only the Vietminh was inured to shelling. Under the threat of death, fear paralyzed. Only strong souls held out against panic and refused to show the fear which they felt like the rest. Since March 13, the days at Dienbienphu had been a time of truth.

On Éliane 4, Bigeard met one of his officers going to answer a summons from Langlais, ordered him to go back and made his way painfully toward the combat post, where he arrived white with anger. What was Langlais up to? Didn't he know that Bigeard was in command of the 6th Battalion, Colonial Paratroops? The two officers clashed so violently that Langlais suddenly hit his fist against the prop supporting the roof of his shelter, and cried, "Let's bang our heads against that. We'll soon see which of us has the toughest nut."

Both of them then burst out laughing and shook hands. Thin, gnarled, wiry, their hard faces carved out of stone, with crew-cut hair and pitiless eyes, sons of Mother Courage, like so many who were fighting there, they were subject to the sudden accesses of violence and tenderness of men prepared to die for great causes. Langlais took his new friend Bigeard to the hospital, where Dr. Grauwin injected a strong dose of novocaine in his femoral artery to calm him down.

Sticking it out meant not only vowing to stick it out, but never flinching as well. Sergeant Sammarco, relieved of his guard over Gaucher's coffin, never stopped swearing as he picked up the cases of shells and provisions in the barbed-wire entanglements. Close to the dead whose smell hung over the camp, life had suddenly acquired inestimable value, and, to prevent the corpses accumulating in a morgue which like everything else had been planned on a ludicrously inadequate scale, Castries signed a brief and horrifying notice: "Henceforth those killed in battle will be buried on the spot." The cemeteries on which the packages were raining down no longer had any meaning. The coffins were no longer reserved for officers, and it was out of the question to hope that planes could ever take back to Hanoï dead who no longer had any rank, when the wounded were short of everything and pity was no longer enough to save them. The 105-mm. shells had buried wounded men under the ridiculous shelters of the casualty clearing station. Father Heinrich closed the eyes of the dead and distributed absolutions. Without the silver cross which he wore on his chest, anybody would have taken him for an officer of the Legion, with his low forehead, crew-cut hair and rather heavy face.

Grauwin felt like crying. The terrible sight of broken bodies and blown-off heads filled him with both horror and rage. To reach the shelter where he snatched a few hours' rest, he had to step over piles of amputated limbs. Far from giving in to these grim conditions, he urged his orderlies to fresh efforts, got the engineers to build him the new shelters which the command refused to give him, and asked for blood and penicillin, which planes parachuted to him. With his friend Gindrey, he operated, sawed bones, unwound yards of intestines, stitched chest wounds and got rid of the hundreds of corpses which had overflowed from the morgue and were covering the helicopter landing ground, the roofs of the messes and the dormitories. Trucks carried them away in macabre loads, buzzing with huge purple flies, to graves dug by bulldozers.

Inhumanity and barbarity on the part of the Vietminh? Who respected the laws of war and who broke them? It was easy to remain unmoved when the French fighters machine-gunned the parties of orderlies and porters who were carrying Viet wounded through the bush on bamboo and nylon stretchers to the hospitals in the rear, but one felt sick with horror when Giap's gunners fired on planes bearing Red Cross markings. Giap told me that he never gave any such order; but he did not claim that he had given a counterorder. He was making war. And Langlais himself admits that if he had been given the choice between the arrival of a battalion of reinforcements or the evacuation of the wounded, he would have chosen the reinforcements.

Mindful of the horrors and indignities of war, who would swear that the Viets were wrong to imagine that we were capable of using the international conventions for military ends? General Cogny, to his credit, refused to go on board a medical service plane when the landing strip at Dienbienphu was closed by enemy artillery. That proves that the procedure was conceivable. Dr. Grauwin was forced to carry Legionnaires and arms in his ambulances. If the Viets, whose lookout posts noted every movement inside the entrenched camp, had observed themselves that Major Keller, Colonel de Castries's chief of staff, was relieved from Dienbienphu in a helicopter bearing Red Cross markings and that his substitute arrived in the same way, like Lieutenant Colonel Lemeunier, who volunteered to take Gaucher's place, we might cast doubt on such allegations. It was not they, but people on our side, who made them to me, and the moral integrity of my informers is beyond question; otherwise I would not have taken their testimony into account. The fact remains that the Viets had good reason not to place absolute trust in us, since the first rule of war is to deceive the enemy.

Why should the question of these attacks on medical service planes be avoided? In all wars, there are men of honor and swine on both sides, and it is necessary, in order to save the men of honor, to denounce the swine. Langlais himself admits that the responsibility for the suffering of the wounded lies less with an enemy who refused to show any pity than with a command which failed to organize its medical service or to foresee the difficulties it might encounter.

What remains hidden condemns, and it is in order to justify ourselves that we must tell everything. What did Giap want to do? Close the airstrip in order to stifle the entrenched camp. There was no exception to this rule at Stalingrad either. Far from merely offering no protection, when the Viets hoisted the Red Cross flag themselves, it drew French fire. Professor Ton that Tung, the director of the surgical services of the Vietminh, reminded me, from firsthand experience, that a seriously wounded man the Viets had been unable to evacuate from the hospital at Thien Hoa was thrown into the river by the Kergavérec platoon. I should feel ashamed of the evidence against us only if Dienbienphu had suddenly run short of blameless captains, heroic doctors and poor devils who possessed nothing in this world except human life and honor.

March 19, 1954

On all sides, yard by yard, the enemy's trenches nibbled away at the entrenched camp, passed Dominique 1 on the northwest and Éliane on the south, reached Dominique 2, described a crescent above Isabelle, and invested Huguette and Claudine. Every day, the aerial photos revealed the energy with which this work was being carried out; the enemy knew that victory lay in his shovels and picks. Where did those who wielded them find the resignation of beasts of burden and the strength of heroes which led them to undertake, without any protection to begin with, a battle against the tanks, guns and aircraft of the West? They were told over and over again that if they overthrew the regime supported by the Tays, everything else would follow: the fields plowed and sown so often to enrich great landowners would belong to them; they would get rid of the officials who had exploited them; and their children would be able to go to school without being condemned in advance to poverty, the only legacy which had so far been faithfully handed down from father to son. It was not for nothing that, in his order of the day on the eve of battle, Vo nguyen Giap had reminded his formidable peasants' army that victory would lead to the triumph of agrarian reform. The army of the

Vietminh was an army of peasants determined to conquer their land, and who would hold out for years, if necessary, joined to their earth as to their own flesh, mingled with it in life as in death, one with the roots of the trees, and the mud and excrement of the rice fields. How could the West have gone on stubbornly supporting a feudal regime and corrupt administration without seeing that its hegemony was doomed?

"What a contradiction of our traditions it is that instead of being the liberators of the common people here, lightening their burdens and raising their standard of living, we should, on the contrary, be the bulwark of their oppressors, doubling their power and sharing their profits, which are bound to be all the more considerable as a result!" It was with that accusation, which he repeated to Major Lyautey, who had just arrived in November, 1894, at the headquarters of the occupation forces in Tonkin, that the French representative to the court of Annam tendered his resignation to Governor General de Lanessan, who was determined to support the mandarins against reform. Half a century later, nothing, or scarcely anything, had changed, and the common people gave the name of *bao dai* to the hundred-piastre note needed to obtain the smallest permit. Who had thought of putting an end to all that? A few French officials, who were given scant encouragement by their department, and Uncle Ho, whose victory all the poor longed for so that their girls would no longer have to serve as prostitutes and their boys as house servants.

> Who hit on the idea of the first ricksha?
> The rich foreigner, the rich foreigner.
> Who will hit on the idea of throwing in the water
> The rich foreigner, the rich foreigner?
> The poor Chinaman, the poor Chinaman . . .

The popular son of Shanghai had crossed the frontiers.

To fight at Dienbienphu was to want to tread the ground of one's country without being humiliated by the gendarmes, the policemen or the soldiers of a foreign army. To die at Dienbienphu was to give one's life to that shrewd old cultured peasant and occasional poet who was Uncle Ho, while H.M. Bao Dai went tiger-hunting at Dalat with French generals. Under the roof of the hospital where Dr. Grauwin was amputating legs and opening chests to save men's lives, suffering had the same taste of blood and tears as on the other side, but nobody could prevent the Vietminh guns from firing on Red Cross markings or on the shattered bodies of the soldiers of the Expeditionary Corps. It was a question of winning a merciless battle, and the army which had been crushed for years under

American shells and napalm bombs could not be expected to treat its adversary gently because the fortunes of war had changed sides.

March 22, 1954

In Washington, carrying out the mission with which the French Government had entrusted him, General Ely had met with a friendly reception from Admiral Radford, Chief of Staff of the Combined Services, and from the American generals. Strongly supported by his chief aide, Colonel Brohon, who had gone through the English Staff College, spent four years at the Pentagon on the French delegation to the permanent group, and added to his natural authority an elegant and accurate command of English, General Ely applied himself to the task of dissipating the legend with which General O'Daniel's enthusiasm had endowed the name of Dienbienphu, cautiously hinting that intervention might be necessary to save the garrison. That day, a long telegram from M. Dejean to his minister gave some idea of the gravity of the situation and insisted that priority be given air reinforcements. M. Dejean was simply told that the French Air Force at home had no bombers or turboprop fighters at its disposal. Contrary to M. Bidault's wishes, General Ely asked the Pentagon for nothing, and the results of this supreme cleverness surpassed all hopes. Ready to smash in Tonkin the Communists who had not been crushed in Korea, and drive the Viet vermin out of Dienbienphu, which could one day serve as an advance base against China, Admiral Radford was only waiting for the word.

At the White House, President Eisenhower gave General Ely a warm welcome and instructed Admiral Radford to do everything possible to help Navarre. Radford asked General Ely to postpone his departure for a few days and gave him a written questionnaire to fill in. He would then be in a position to make proposals of concrete aid.

Admiral Radford was a well-built man with a lithe gait. You might have said that he owed a Flemish painter for his bright, delicate complexion, his reddish hair and the perpetually moist gray eyes which tempered the hard mask of his expression. The United States Chief of Staff of the Combined Services was both a sailor and an airman. Versatile, tireless and cold, he had commanded in the Pacific the strongest fleet in the world. He had not been given his post because of his Republican convictions or because he had happened to take Ike to Korea in 1952 and played bridge with him, but because of the strength which emanated from him and the lucidity of his decisions. He was as impressive in intellect as in bearing, a real leader. In his opinion, Southeast Asia was the modern equivalent of the Balkans in the First World War, and, once the Korean War had come to an end, he had taken a passionate interest in the Indochinese conflict. Ely had been struck by the justice and force of his judgments on the conflict and on the commanders in chief of the Expeditionary Corps. "You lost the Indochinese War in 1952," Admiral Radford had said, "when General Salan failed to reoccupy Lao Kay." He had classed General Salan among the timid and fearful, and accused him of having failed to form a Vietnamese army. Radford liked to consider himself the defender of the Western world. To begin with, he lifted the ban imposed by the Pentagon on the use of Packets to drop napalm and gave Navarre full freedom to use the planes provided by American aid however he wished. And, seeing that the President was in agreement, why shouldn't the Viet anthill at Dienbienphu be liquidated?

March 23, 1954

In a letter to Cogny, Colonel de Castries gave an accurate impression of the situation and his position: he was sustaining. What man would have been capable, at the time, of retrieving a position which was compromised to such a degree? Ducournau, perhaps, who, like a boxer in the ring, was always on guard, leaping around his adversary, ready to lash out as he had done at Na San. But it was not Ducournau or Vanuxem or Gilles who was in command at Dienbienphu, but Cavalryman Christian de Castries, shut up in his fortress and entrenched in his command post. He planned no attacks, as he gathered together his firepower and his resources. He submitted. It was as if a spring had broken inside him.

"Then what function did Colonel de Castries perform?" asked a general on the commission of inquiry, upon learning that the organization of the defense and the use of the artillery and the reserves were entrusted to subordinates.

"He transmitted our messages to Hanoï," Langlais replied unhesitatingly, with a touch of humor.

If he had read the memoirs of the Marquis de Feuquières, Langlais could have confined himself to quoting from them the example of M. de Calvo, who was besieged in Maastricht by the Prince of Orange:

This officer, a man of great bravery, who, having served all his life in the cavalry, knew nothing about attacking or defending fortresses, gathered together the principal officers of the garrison, and admitted to them his ignorance of everything concerned with that sort of military operation; he told them to agree among themselves the manner in which the fortress was to be defended and to tell him what had been agreed, begging them to act zealously in the service of the King because his only aim was to hold the fortress; in other words, that he would never surrender it to the enemies of his prince.

Who would dare to condemn M. de Calvo for such noble intentions and so accurate an estimate of himself? Only those who have never known the misfortune of defeat could blame him. I am not one of them. Only those who fought at Dienbienphu are entitled to judge Castries. I am not one of them either. But the post which he occupied, even if he had not wanted it, condemned Castries to act like a hero or resign. Truth compels me to say that he did neither.

What is a hero? A man who displays exceptional qualities in the face of exceptional dangers; tempered steel in battle, gold in the face of corruption. Who can believe that an exception is a habit and that a man can take out a regular subscription to heroism as he can to a periodical? Who can deny that certain heroes crack up like football champions in a poor match? A man can grow tired of behaving like a hero and long to return to the ranks. It may be, therefore, that something cracked in Castries, unknown even to himself, but nobody can prevent him from having been the Castries of old, just as nobody is entitled to reproach, only to pity him for having ceased to be that Castries. After all, he never claimed to be Charles de Foucauld. If he fought, it was not to seek death but to collect rank and honors, those baubles of glory, as Vigny called them, by which soldiers are induced to march and die.

An adventurer rather than a man of method, and more cynical, vain and swashbuckling than was necessary, Castries was not cut out for this particular ordeal. But then, if he was outstripped by events and if he was not capable of defending the entrenched camp, why wasn't he relieved? Nobody dared administer such a rebuke to him, although it was considered. It was rumored briefly that Colonel Sauvagnac, who was in command of the airborne troops in Tonkin, had packed his bags to take his place, and had then unpacked them.

At nightfall, Tourret went to the hospital. Grauwin smiled at him over his operating table, and then felt a twinge of anxiety. Men came to see him when there was something wrong—possibly, he thought, because the hospital, having become the center of all suffering, had taken on the image of Christ crucified. He did not know that it was because he, Grauwin, was the incarnation of pity.

A little shorter than Bigeard, and similarly casual in his dress, Tourret had nothing of the brute about him. In that boldly chiseled mask with the flattened cheekbones, the eyes glowed more sadly than usual, and fresh wrinkles furrowed the brow. Grauwin passed his instruments to his assistant, took off his rubber gloves, led Tourret into the trench and questioned him. Tourret said that he, Tourret, had just been accused by Langlais of having, by his negligence, caused the deaths of some of his men who had been killed by shells, and had been placed under close arrest.

"Just now," said Grauwin, "nobody is in full control of his nerves. What you've just told me doesn't make sense. Don't think about it any more. Come and have a drink."

"Langlais may be right," said Tourret. "If I'm responsible for the death of my men, I can't go on living."

"Come now," said Grauwin, who was thinking of Piroth, "I can't convince you. Would you like to see Father Heinrich?"

"Yes," said Tourret.

Grauwin sent for the chaplain and pushed Tourret into his shelter. He threw a parachute over his table, lit a storm lantern, and put out a prayer book.

"You're right," he said. "I go to confession too when I don't feel sure of myself any more."

And he went out just as Father Heinrich came down into the shelter.

"I waited for Tourret to come out with an anxiety you can imagine," Dr. Grauwin told me later. "But the minute I saw him, I was reassured. He was no longer the same. His face was radiant with joy. He was at peace."

March 24, 1954

Shortly before 1600 hours, among reinforcements for the parachute battalions, Captain Alain Bizard, attached to Captain Botella as second-in-command of the 5th Battalion, Vietnamese Paratroops, dropped at the foot and a little to the south of the Éliane peaks. This big fellow, a jovial, sensitive and cultivated man, was a cavalryman who had just abandoned his branch of the service and the general he had served as aide-de-camp, to join his comrades of the Expeditionary Corps for the third time. Always ready to throw himself into the riskiest adventures, he had chosen Dienbienphu and the paratroops. Botella had immediately asked for him, but bureaucracy was opposed to any officer making a jump who was not a qualified parachutist. In four days at Hanoï, Bizard had made the six jumps which gave him the official blessing.

He reached Éliane 4 and the command post of his battalion just as Captain Koenig's Dakota, hit by antiaircraft fire, caught fire in the air and crashed in a rice field, where it exploded. When he saw his friend Botella, Bizard said to him with a laugh, "Well, here I am. Now we're going to get you out of this shit hole." The chaplain of Isabelle recalled the words of the Gradual of that day: "Have mercy on me, O Lord, for I am weak: heal me, O Lord. All my bones are troubled: and my soul is troubled exceedingly."

In his office in the Pentagon, Admiral Radford put a proposal to General Ely suggesting American air intervention at Dienbienphu. Frank with those he knew, Radford had cold eyes behind his automatic smile of welcome. Although the windows opened on the front of the building and it was daylight, the curtains were drawn and the neon lamps were lit. In spite of the light-gray carpet and the traditional mahogany furniture, the huge room with its dozens of model ships and planes looked like a luxurious operating theater. Here, as in a chemical retort, the chief of the American armed forces weighed world events.

His moist gaze resting on General Ely to judge his reaction, Radford casually made his offer: sixty B-29 bombers, escorted by 150 fighters of the Seventh American Fleet, could crush the Viets at Dienbienphu.

"Beginning when?" asked General Ely, his face barely lighting up.

"I'm going to study the question," replied Radford with the assurance of a man who once he has chosen his path will keep to it whatever the cost.

General Ely went back to the French Embassy, sent a secret cable to the Prime Minister and got ready to return to Paris and her cold, damp spring. In the woods of the Île-de-France the first cuckoos could be heard. General Ely was preoccupied with thoughts that made him look more than ever like the ghost of the Commandant in *Don Giovanni* and gave his complexion the ashen color of impending catastrophe. The B-29's Admiral Radford had just offered him were the official version, discreetly camouflaged, of the dropping on the mountains of Dienbienphu of the A-bomb, which had brought Japan to her knees ten years before. The operation had as yet no name. and General Ely did not know he was returning to Paris with a vulture on his shoulder.

March 25, 1954

In his hole, Second Lieutenant Thélot finished a letter to his brother:

The guns are spitting much less and have withdrawn into the mountains, but the Viets are very close to us in the basin. Now and then I can make out a few through my field glasses. They haven't attacked our strong point yet, but they have come and left leaflets on our barbed-wire defenses. Write to me at S.P. 54,640. Your letters will reach me, for mail is forwarded everywhere without fail; it is dropped to us with our provisions. Reassure our parents. Morale here could not be better.

The *New York Times* published photographs of troops at Dienbienphu across six columns, together with an article on Colonel de Castries, headlined: "War Hero Hailed by Eisenhower . . . De Castries an Aristocrat Who Rose from the Ranks in a Fighting Career."

At nightfall, Bigeard presented himself at the command post where Castries had summoned him. He was not in a good mood and was still using the formidable stick on which he leaned when walking. Before crossing the river, he had swiftly undressed, thrown himself into the water under shellfire and bathed, to set an example for his men. Under his orders they died clean and fresh-shaven. Since he had established himself on Éliane 4, he had forced his troops to wield pick and shovel.

In front of Castries, he clicked his heels and saluted rather curtly, the long peak of his cap pulled down over his nose.

"Bruno, my friend," said Castries, "I want you to go and get the Viet AA to the west."

"When?"

"Tomorrow. Take whatever you need. You've a free hand."

Castries showed him on the map the villages of Ban Ban and Ban Ong Pet, two miles from the command post.

Why deny it? Bigeard was impressed by Castries. This cynical aristocrat descended from a family of French marshals could ask anything of Bigeard, the officer risen from the ranks. Castries had a way of listening or talking, flattering or insulting, which impressed him. Bigeard knew that Castries was not a leader who would set an example and wrest victory from the enemy, but he could not help liking him. Castries's familiarity and friendship for the son of a little railway worker, his self-assurance, haughtiness and elegance, had completely conquered him. Later, in the depths of darkest adversity, he would suppress boos and catcalls and force his comrades to show Castries a respect they no longer felt. Castries could do what he liked; in Bigeard's eyes he remained a prince by divine right, even if he had lost everything which had constituted his legend and his prestige. What appealed to Bigeard was the initiative Castries left him. After all, Bigeard asked for nothing more. To those who surrendered to him part of their authority, Bigeard was devoted unto death.

"Right," said Bigeard. "It will be done. Only two reservations: allow for heavy casualties in the best units and give me more time to prepare the operation."

"We'll see about the casualties. As for time, get to work right away. I'll get them to make you some coffee."

I have seen the command post's coffee mill. It is a machine of unusual size and with a vertical spindle, such as they used to make for army canteens and large communities, and which must have been standard equipment in battalion field kitchens. Its spherical reservoir can hold two pounds of coffee beans. It, too, is on exhibit, together with the iron coffeepot of the GONO staff, in the Viet museum at Dienbienphu.

March 26, 1954

Since March 19, a wave of icy air had produced a sudden deterioration in the weather over the delta, together with a return of drizzle and dry mist in the highlands. That day, the southeast wind improved the weather over the bases in the plain and brought back the damp heat; in the Thai country the clouds broke up toward the end of the morning, but hung around the peaks and produced storms at night. In spite of these difficult conditions, over 750 planes had dropped eleven hundred tons of bombs in the basin and on the crests since the beginning of the battle.

The reconnaissance planes had taken ten thousand photographs. The "firefly" Dakotas buzzed all night above the entrenched camp. Parachutes rained down all day on the roofs of the shelters, the cemeteries and the barbed-wire defenses.

At two o'clock in the morning, Bigeard assembled the officers who were to take part in the operation: Tourret of the 8th Assault, his faithful companion in every fight and especially in the hottest of them all, the retreat from Thu Lé; Thomas, who took Bigeard's place in command of the 6th Battalion, Colonial Paratroops; Guiraud, in reserve with the 1st BEP, with his body all muscle and the long, hard face of a man who expected the worst in order to be able to deal with it; Clémençon, of the 1st Battalion, 2nd Foreign Infantry; Hervouët, the tank commander, who had arrived just before Christmas with both arms in plaster up to the elbow; the Air Force officer Guérin, who, reduced almost to a skeleton by a case of amoebiasis, was lost inside his green dungarees and whom Langlais didn't like; and the gunner Vaillant.

Bigeard defined the mission and explained how he was going to carry it out. During the night, the officers returned to their posts, gave their orders, put their units in a state of alert and then in battle order, and left their positions to go to their starting lines. At dawn, three batteries of 105-mm. guns, two 155-mm. guns and three batteries of 120-mm. guns pounded the targets in turn, while the paratroops went in behind the tanks. Contact was made at 0615. A platoon commander of the 6th Battalion, Colonial Paratroops, Lieutenant Le Vigouroux, leaped onto one of the heavy antiaircraft machine guns which had been turned on the paratroops, shouted into his radio transmitter "Objective reached!" and received a bullet full in the forehead. At 0630, the Air Force appeared with the day, bombing and machine-gunning. The artillery pulverized the enemy counterattacks which tried to cut off the retreat of the units engaged. One by one, the emplacements of 20-mm. guns and 12.7-mm. machine guns were taken, cleared of their gun crews and destroyed with incendiary grenades. At 1500 hours, the order was given for withdrawal, covered by the artillery, the Air Force and a battalion of the Legion, just as a fresh enemy counterattack got under way behind a concentrated barrage of 120-mm. shells. Five 20-mm. guns and twelve 12.7-mm. machine guns had been destroyed. The paratroops had taken two bazookas, fourteen machine guns and a hundred rifles at a cost of twenty dead, including two officers, whom they carried back, and seventy wounded, including five officers. They had taken ten prisoners. Congratulations were showered on Bigeard. On the enemy side, the raid had resulted in 350 dead.

Bigeard entertained no illusions; for such a success not to be ephemeral, the troops who had won it would have to be given time to catch their breaths.

March 29, 1954

In spite of the storm which had been blowing up over the delta since the previous day, the Dakotas took off to drop supplies and munitions into the mud of Dienbienphu. At six thousand feet, the drops were just as poor as at eight thousand. At four thousand, the packages fell inside the entrenched camp, but the antiaircraft batteries hit nearly all the planes. That day, only three of them just managed to limp back to their bases.

Dominique 1 and 2, Éliane 1 and 2 and Huguette 7 were almost completely surrounded by trenches. It was obvious that it was there that the next attack would be made. The Viets were advancing underground and uprooting the barbed-wire entanglements, pushing in front of them rolls of matting stuffed with earth which protected them when a mine exploded. From the crest of Mont Fictif, which had been turned into a fortress proof against all attack, heavy machine guns fired at the Dakotas and bazookas opened fire on anything which moved on Éliane 2, from which it was separated by a ravine.

When the attack was launched, Éliane and Huguette, occupied by the parachutists and the Legion, would hold out. But what about Dominique, whose defense had been entrusted to Algerians? They had been bolstered by the 5th Battalion, Vietnamese Paratroops, but Langlais knew that this was a weak link in the chain. He felt tempted to put Tourret there, with whom he had been reconciled, or Bigeard, but what could be expected of the Algerians? How could they be convinced that it was their duty to get themselves killed for France, which was unwilling to grant them the title of French citizens?

In Paris, where spring had suddenly arrived, the restricted war committee met to study the military and political aspects of the operation now called "Vulture." The direct intervention of the American heavy bombers and their fighter escort would probably provoke retaliation by the Chinese Air Force against the bases of the Expeditionary Corps. Was General Navarre in a position to stand up to it and could the Tonkin bases provide adequate support for the American raids? Colonel Raymond Brohon, General Ely's chief aide, was instructed to go and ask the Commander in Chief for an answer to this question. No record would be kept of this committee meeting, or of those that would follow. Only General Crespin, the secretary of the committee, would be allowed to take notes. No trace of the correspondence concerning American intervention would be left in the files handed on by M. Laniel, in which all that would remain would be copies of telegrams sent in reply to vanished documents. However, the weekly *U.S. News & World Report* would get wind of the affair and divulge it.

Why should the French fear Chinese intervention in reply to American intervention? Materially, whatever may have been alleged, China did not help the Vietminh any more than America helped the Expeditionary Corps. She opened her schools for officers and technicians to the People's Army; she trained the soldiers in her signals and engineering corps and the men who would fly fighters and bombers as soon as she decided to give air bases to the Vietminh; and munitions and antiaircraft batteries crossed the Chinese frontier in whole convoys. But she had no military advisers with powers of decision on the spot, no gunners, no experts. For the past year, she had tipped the scales in favor of the Vietminh with the mere weight of the arms she was delivering.

The statements made by John Foster Dulles and General Navarre about Chinese technicians were inspired simply by their desire to explain away their failures by attributing them to extraneous causes. There may have been a Chinese, General Li Chen Hou, at Giap's headquarters, but there were none at the divisional and regimental command posts, where the nationalist sensitivity of the Central Committee and the People's Army would have made them undesirable. The Vietminh waged its war as it saw fit, and waged it alone. If Navarre was to lose the battle of Dienbienphu, he would lose it to Giap and not because of the Chinese.

Every time I put this question to officers of the North Vietnam Army, indignation transformed every face, "It is inconceivable that we should ever take orders from foreign officers, even Chinese ones. We regard your question as deplorable. Nobody in the People's Army ever prepared baths for the Chinese; nobody ever walked beside their horses." Giap dismissed this allegation as a legend.

Since it was a question of dropping on the solidly entrenched positions of the Vietminh, not, as is still suggested, five hundred tons of bombs, but several A-bombs intended to wipe out the besiegers, it was not unreasonable to fear a violent reaction on the part of China. Mr. Dulles was not unaware of this when, in the voice of an upper-class clergyman, he made a speech at the Overseas Press Club in which he prepared American public opinion for serious risks. "But these risks are far less," he added, "than those that will face us a few years from now if we dare not be resolute today."

Back in Saigon, after attending a farcical ceremony in which Vietnamese officers took an oath of loyalty to Bao Dai, General Navarre wrote a long letter to General Cogny. In the top left-hand corner he added in his own hand: "Personal. Top Secret."

It was to pulverize the giant Cogny. It was as if, sensing approaching defeat, Navarre was unwilling to go under by himself. Even if he could drag only one other man down with him, he wanted that man to be Cogny.

The style of the letter had at least the merit of clarity. Navarre wrote to Cogny: "Do not count on any supplementary aid from me." And he tried at the same time to justify himself. The Vietminh's ability to get Cogny into trouble with relatively small forces, compared with those it could have used if it had carried out its original plan, revealed to Navarre the major role played by Dienbienphu; by pinning down the enemy battalions there Navarre had saved Cogny, if he agreed that his present fears were well founded, from what he called an absolute disaster. In fact, Navarre was oversimplifying with formidable skill, and was forgetting the forces he had already lifted from Tonkin; but above all he was pretending to consider the affair on a numerical level and refusing to take into account the advantages offered on the tactical level by a battle in the delta supported by the air forces on the spot.

Justified and unjustified reproaches, perfidious insinuations, sharp accusations, niggling criticisms such as one might make of an incompetent battalion commander—they were all there. The conventions of military style were used only if they added insult to injury. Navarre suddenly cracked his whip and lashed Cogny with it. But he did this from a distance, after having silently stored up the thunderbolts of an anger which had not exploded in Hanoï.

March 30, 1954

All day long, Dienbienphu had been drenched by torrential rain. At 1830, just as two companies of the 1st BEP were relieving the Moroccans on Éliane 2, a heavy artillery barrage was laid down on the peaks of Éliane and Dominique and Huguette 7, while the batteries of the central garrison and Isabelle were harried. At that hour it is still light at that period of the year.

When, at 1845, the 312th and 316th Divisions launched their attack along six axes, Botella announced almost immediately by radio: "The Moroccans of Éliane 1 are falling back on me." A few moments later, Bigeard called Langlais: "Bruno calling Young Pierre, Bruno calling Young Pierre; the garrison of Dominique 2 is falling back like one man. I can see it running headlong down the hill toward the river." It was the Algerians. Mad with rage, Bigeard looked on helplessly at the debacle.

"My men were calm," he would say later, "and were watching the sight with disgust." The defenses of Éliane 2 had been penetrated. Major Nicolas had not budged, but he had lost contact with Langlais, who wanted the artillery to open fire on his peak; Bigeard asked them to wait. At 2000 hours, Nicolas fell back, submachine gun in hand, to the rear part of the strong point. Dominique 1 had stopped answering. Overwhelmed, the Moroccans were no longer putting up any resistance; the Dang Vo Company alone captured forty-seven of them, but the B-26's caused heavy casualties with their bombing and machine-gunning. Oxen for the slaughterhouse, as Captain Hien called them? Bulls, rather, charging wildly through the darkness, where nineteen of them, that night, planted *banderillas* of napalm on the brows of the hills.

Considering a counterattack by night impossible, Langlais decided to launch it at dawn, with Bigeard and Tourret; then, changing his mind as he remembered Béatrice and Gabrielle, took five companies of the 1st BEP and the 13th Demibrigade from the west face and decided to hurl them, one after another, against Éliane 2. At 2300 hours, the French got to within twenty yards of the Dang Vo Company, which was cut off there under shellfire from Isabelle; three of its men had tried in vain to plant the red flag with the gold star on the peak. Second Lieutenant Thélot was mortally wounded. Like all those telegrams reading "Good health, good luck, love" which comrades sent from Hanoï to the families of soldiers both living and dead, when the letter he had finished on March 25 reached his brother, it would give the impression that he was alive. Two days earlier, his company had relieved some Thais on Dominique 2 in whom Langlais no longer had any confidence.

Langlais's five companies recaptured Éliane 2. When the Legionnaires had set off to take up their starting lines before going into the attack, Bigeard had heard them singing German marching songs which came up to him in the darkness from the floor of the basin. Seven of Captain Hervouët's tanks, in action on Route 41, mowed down the enemy sections going down toward the center. In the zone of Dominique 3, to the east of a dead arm of the river, the 4th Battalion, 4th Colonial Artillery, under the command of Lieutenant Brunbrouck, caught under fire and threatened with encirclement, fired straight at the enemy. In spite of his critical position and one gun out of action, Lieutenant Brunbrouck, who was getting ready to destroy his guns if he was overwhelmed, clung to his 105's and the ground he was defending; he called up fire from the neighboring strong points and from the two 12.7 machine-gun sections which

Langlais had moved from the airstrip so that they could sweep the whole of the south face of Éliane 2 along the left bank of the river.

The dispatches piling up on General Navarre's table in Saigon announced the new disaster. Navarre asked for his plane to be gotten ready to leave for Hanoï. Ripples of this pessimism reached Paris toward the end of the afternoon.

In response to Langlais's demands, Cogny asked Navarre for supplementary resources: 118 Dakotas to drop 295 tons a day. The Air Force had reached its ceiling with 175 tons. "The fate of the battle depends on this," added Cogny. When his operational deputy asked him what reply he should send, Navarre said, "We shall see about that tonight, on the spot."

March 31, 1954

General Navarre reached Hanoï at 1:45 while the Dakotas were dropping reinforcements on the entrenched camp. The doctor of No. 4 dressing station landed sitting astride the hood of a truck.

At the airdrome, Colonel Bastiani presented his chief's apologies; tired out, Cogny had had to go to bed. Navarre went to his command post, where he received the night's reports.

About four in the morning, he sent for Cogny. His aide-de-camp replied that he wasn't allowed to wake him up. With Bastiani, Navarre worked on a fresh series of instructions in which he considered that the gravest eventuality had to be envisaged and the line of action Colonel de Castries was to take clearly laid down. The central garrison and Isabelle were to hold out. The morale of the garrison was to be stimulated by the idea that it was defending the honor of France and Vietnam and holding up the enemy battle corps. All arms and supplies were to be destroyed before they fell into enemy hands. A parachute battalion, which had already been chosen, the 2nd Battalion, 1st Parachute Chasseurs, and a battery of 75-mm. guns were to be the only reinforcements the entrenched camp would receive, unless the prospect of victory became certain.

At dawn, hundreds of Viet corpses lay mingled with those of Legionnaires and paratroopers on the slopes leading down to the river and in the mined ditches bordering the road alongside the river. Lieutenant Brunbrouck thrust his big hands into his pockets and smiled; he was even thinner than usual, but victory lit up his long face. He was twenty-seven.

A platoon from Captain Capeyron's company which had been detailed to relieve the Moroccans of Éliane 2 returned to Claudine 5, its strength reduced to twelve men.

On Huguette 7, Bizard had not budged. The Viets, who had been unable to get close to his position, had been cut to pieces by his machine guns, mortars and grenades, but they had nonetheless succeeded in gaining a foothold in the strong point, and the new trenches they had dug were mixed up with his defense system. As Bizard was refused the reinforcements he had asked for, he altered the disposition of his platoons, and, in order to hold the rest of the strong point better, he mined and evacuated the northern point of the triangle he still occupied.

At seven o'clock in the morning, Navarre sent for Cogny, who arrived at a quarter to eight.

"How do things stand?" asked Navarre.

Cogny described the situation to him as it had been at midnight.

"Then," General Navarre later told me, "I exploded. I bawled him out. And he in return told me to my face what he had been telling others for some time."

Lieutenant Colonel Langlais was slightly hoarse. All night he had been calling his battalion commanders on his microphone. Dédé was Botella; Bruno, Bigeard; Pierrot, Tourret, about whom he still felt a little guilty; and he himself was Young Pierre. Sometimes, to authenticate his orders, he would sing the refrain of the song he used to bellow on holidays:

> Don't fret, Marie, you're pretty,
> Don't fret, Marie, I'll be back. . . .

He summoned Captain Hervouët and his tanks to the rescue: "Young Pierre calling Yvon, get on your Bisons, gallop along the Him Lam road, charge and crush everything that's left!" Highly strung as he was, and subject to sudden fits of anger and bursts of tenderness, he felt relieved. Bigeard's counterattack was about to be launched against Éliane 1 and Tourret's against Dominique 2, and the tanks' guns could already be heard firing in the valley; but the night's fighting cost fifteen hundred men, and the 3rd Battalion, 3rd Foreign, which had been given orders at Isabelle to link up with Éliane, did not succeed, in spite of the support of three tanks, in passing Ban Nong Nhaï, where the 57th Regiment had reestablished barriers. It returned to its lines with fifty wounded and all the tanks damaged; fifteen Legionnaires had disappeared. Langlais asked Hanoï to drop a parachute group as a matter of urgency. Hanoï had replied: "If you hold out against the next big attack, a group of two or three battalions will be sent right away." When he put down the microphone, Séguins-Pazzis pulled him toward his bed, where he collapsed.

"Have a rest," said Séguins-Pazzis. "You've earned it."

That day, between Navarre and Cogny there was open war. The news arriving from the entrenched camp once again confronted the French Command with a tragic reality. The disaster would require culprits. The two men no longer weighed their words. What they had not dared so far to say to each other for reasons of convention and courtesy came out in the open. A crack appeared in the hierarchy.

Navarre had not been to bed, and his complexion stood up to sleepless nights better than Cogny's. If he was affected by the impending catastrophe, it was in his pride; Cogny was affected in his flesh. Navarre was barely known and not liked; if he left, he would only have lost a stake at poker and would go back to the shadows from which he had emerged, back to luxurious rooms and metaphysical speculations. Cogny would never be able to look his men in the face again, for they would blame him for a defeat which he was sure was due to Navarre, to his ignorance of the country, to the advisers with whom he had surrounded himself, to his vain and lofty strategy elaborated in laboratories by fuzzy-minded theoreticians. However large the stake that night had been, the reproaches Navarre heaped on his subordinate for not knowing that Bigeard had been half-buried on Éliane 4 at daybreak, and that on Huguette 7 the ground conquered by the Viets during the night had been completely recaptured, were unjustified. Cogny had made mistakes; he admitted that to himself. He had not scented the dangers posed by an adventure in a region which he did not know so well as the delta; he had deluded himself about the cavalry maneuvers he had planned; he had misjudged Giap's logistic capacities; and above all he had not come out strongly against the Dienbienphu adventure as soon as it had revealed risks out of proportion to its chances of success. Deceived by the successes he had gained near Hanoï, he had not been sufficiently suspicious of the dangers of this new enterprise. Torn between its risks and attractions, he had not been able to decide, even as far as he himself was concerned, what attitude to adopt. Caught up in the game, he had not detected the trap in time and had not demanded a withdrawal from Dienbienphu.

The only mistake of which he felt guilty had been misjudging the enemy artillery, as the others had done, and believing that Colonel de

Castries was the man for the job; his only weakness had been not relieving Castries of his command and not returning to Dienbienphu. As for his refusal on March 4 of the battalions which Navarre had offered him at a time when the Air Force was already cracking under its own efforts, Navarre would only have accused him of incompetence in carrying out his missions if he had accepted. Cogny would have acted quite differently if the responsibility for the conduct of the battle had been laid upon his shoulders.

What separated him sharply from Navarre was that Navarre still counted on "Operation Atlante" to save Dienbienphu, whereas Cogny regarded "Operation Atlante" as a drain which would swallow up everything down to his own reserves. Besides, what decisions had Cogny ever been allowed to take? His views on the need to create diversions in order to prevent the investment of the basin had perhaps been tardy or ineffective, but they were based on the feeling that an attack would be dangerous and that it had to be broken up. However complicated it might seem at first sight, Cogny's thesis did not deserve the contemptuous remarks Navarre made about it. Even now, nothing was lost if a lightning retort were made to Giap. The peaks of Dominique 2 and Éliane would be recaptured if Langlais could throw fresh troops into the battle.

Once again, Navarre replied "no"; he agreed only to contribute one battalion, which would arrive too late, keeping the others for "Operation Atlante," and the ink which flowed from his fountain pen to stimulate Castries's morale remained cold. Nor did Cogny know everything that morning.

Memories have grown confused. Was it at that early morning meeting or at the one the following day that the most violent exchanges between the two generals took place? If Cogny had been bawled out by Navarre as soon as he got up, the incident would have remained in his memory. However tense he was that morning, Navarre did not seem particularly affected by the bad news from the entrenched camp; extremely irritated by a local setback which was still just a comparatively minor incident, he remained set on his plan, in which Dienbienphu occupied only a secondary place. Together, the two generals studied the directive drawn up by Navarre. Cogny suggested an operation based on the delta or on Laos.

"Nothing doing for the delta," replied Navarre. "As for Laos, study the question and bring it up again."

In spite of the storms clinging to the crests and blotting out the valleys, the planes continued to support the entrenched camp. A Dakota was shot down and its crew killed. About 0930, a Helldiver which, to reach Dien-bienphu, had taken the narrow corridor between the Nam Co and the Nam Youm, arrived low over Béatrice, where it was caught in the direct fire of an antiaircraft battery and shot down; its pilot was the little, thin, gentle Lieutenant Andrieux, with a knife-edge profile and bright eyes, who drove the fighters of the *Arromanches* flotilla almost to the breaking point.

About midday, Langlais was awakened by the sound of the bombard-ment. He asked whether there was any news of the planes which were bringing the reinforcements, and which were known as Banjos. Nobody knew anything about them. From all the peaks, the paratroopers watched for the Dakotas which were going to drop their comrades.

"What the hell are they doing in Hanoï?"

Little by little, this cry became an insult. The counterattacks were making slow progress. At 1430 Tourret managed to recapture Dominique 2, where Captain Pichelin was killed, but was then driven back again. On Éliane 1, Bigeard stood fast until darkness. Then Langlais decided to send orders for a withdrawal to Dominique 5 of his paratroopers, who were too exhausted to hold out any longer. Gun by gun, Lieutenant Brunbrouck brought his battery across the river and installed himself on Claudine.

Éliane I and Dominique 1 and 2 had been lost. With Dominique 2, a position of major importance to the defense system had gone under; since the loss of Béatrice, it had barred the northeast passage. Henceforth the Viets could pour freely into the basin, cross the Nam Youm, make frontal attacks on the strong points defending the central position and outflank the last rocky obstacle of Élaine 4. From Dominique 2, which dominated the whole basin, the heart of the entrenched camp was less than a mile away.

At 1900 hours, Langlais left it to Bigeard to decide what to do.

"If you consider that it's impossible to hold the east bank of the river, fall back onto the right."

"As long as I've got one man left alive, I won't abandon Éliane 4," replied Bigeard. "Otherwise Dienbienphu is done for."

In Washington, Senators and members of the House of Representatives put certain questions to Admiral Radford.

"Can the American Air Force save Dienbienphu?"

"It's too late."

"Would a raid lead to the participation of all the U.S. forces, including the infantry?"

"It is possible."

"Do the Chiefs of Staff advise Congress to give the President emergency powers?"

"They haven't considered the possibility."

The leaders of Congress then suggested united action and John Foster Dulles gave his approval. But on a proposal to obtain a Congressional resolution giving the President power to use the Air Force, all the leaders present, to whom nobody dared mention A-bombs, replied with an unequivocal "no." Alarmed by the remarks made by Mr. Dulles and Admiral Radford, they considered that intervention would constitute a positive act of war. President Eisenhower tried to tone down this impression by means of a vague, confused declaration.

From Moscow, M. Alain Savary, tired of waiting for some sign from Ho Chi Minh to open negotiations, set off on the return journey to Paris. M. Savary gathered from the news that his mission had been undertaken too late and that everything was being decided at Dienbienphu.

The underground passages leading to the hospital were packed with a pitiful flock of the Algerians and Morroccans who had stood up so badly to the attack on Éliane and Dominique. They waited prostrate in the mud. Grauwin, told that they were there, came out for a moment.

"Major," said one of them, "you are our father. We have come to serve you; take us on as boys or orderlies. It's all over for us. Up there, there were too many dead. What for? Our wives and children need us at home."

Grauwin gently sent them back to their units. But where were their units? With most of their officers disabled, the North Africans would probably go to the ravaged banks of the river to join the Vietnamese whom Botella had already driven away like frightened rabbits and the disarmed Thais who were hiding in holes from which they emerged at night in search of loot.

Grauwin, who had returned to his instruments after stepping over the bodies being pushed toward the operating table, suddenly heard sobbing. It was Geneviève de Galard who was crying, as she leaned against one wall of the shelter. Stranded for the last three days with her crew, this air nurse, who had had the courage to come back to Dienbienphu, was no longer capable of helping a doctor. The field dressing stations were overflowing with dying and wounded; suffering had become the bread men ate, the dirty water they drank, the stinking air they breathed.

April 1, 1954

Cogny read with amazement the insulting letter which Navarre had sent him on March 29 from Saigon, and which had only just reached him through the official mail. Furious with rage, he spent hours composing several versions of a reply, which he sent off, and then abruptly decided to ask for an appointment, which Navarre granted him for the next day.

What had become of Dienbienphu, where Bigeard was clinging to Éliane, where Grauwin was sheltering his wounded in the mud, and where a bare-headed Langlais was watching for the arrival of the Banjos that were going to drop the two battalions he had asked for? At four in the morning, all hope had been abandoned of recapturing Éliane 2, part of which was left to the Vietminh; at nine, Langlais had launched a fifth counterattack in vain, and the direct fire made it impossible to pick up a large proportion of the packages dropped by parachute. One Dakota was shot down. Relieved by a company of the 1st Battalion, 2nd Foreign Infantry, on Huguette 7, Captain Bizard went down to Huguette 1, where he relieved a Thai company Langlais had had disarmed, for the last Thais holding Françoise had fled and the strong point had fallen without a fight.

And yet, when there were reliable men in command of these Thais, they stood fast. Their 2nd Battalion, which was covering the bridge and the road between Eliane and Dominique, had never faltered because its commander and all the officers and NCO's set them an example. During the night, when the Algerians on Dominique had taken flight, they had not budged. Under the rain which was flooding the basin, they remained stoical. Among their officers, Dienbienphu had transformed a slim, fair-haired hussar, once a model of elegance, into a red-bearded pirate, with a bandage cut out of a parachute around his forehead and one arm in a sling, ready to turn his machine guns on anybody who weakened: Lieutenant Guy de la Malène.

Cogny sent a note to Navarre to argue that the dropping and support of an operation based on Laos was possible if there were eighteen Dakotas and some parachutes available in Laos.

At 1630, Cogny cabled to Colonel de Castries his own version of General Navarre's directive, in which he toned down certain phrases. Castries and Langlais knew that henceforth there was not much they could hope for from Hanoï.

At 1800 hours, the battle formation on Éliane 2, where the tank "Bazeilles" had been destroyed, went across the crest of the peak. During the night the dropping of the 2nd Battalion, 1st Parachute Chasseurs, began. It would last until April 4, for the dropping zone was reduced to the southern part of the airstrip, and the course of the Dakotas, which had to fly very low while avoiding the antiaircraft fire, was extremely narrow. Every night, twelve Banjos barely managed to drop one company.

A B-26, flown by Lieutenant Beglin, failed to return to base. During the night, Huguette 7, overwhelmed by an attack, was swallowed up with the whole of its garrison.

Arriving that day at Saigon, Colonel Brohon left almost immediately for Hanoï in the plane of Commissioner General Dejean, who accompanied him. Time was running out. At 2045, a quarter of an hour after the plane had landed in the rain, Generals Navarre, Bodet and Cogny met at dinner at the Maison de France, with M. Dejean as their host. After the meal, a secret conference took place. As at the meetings of the restricted war committee, there was no secretary and Navarre asked those present not to take notes. No record of the meeting would be drawn up. The conference would not even be mentioned in the memoranda of the aides-de-camp. Colonel Brohon reported on Admiral Radford's proposal and transmitted the questions put by the restricted war committee. Brohon pointed out the dangers presented by the dropping of several A-Bombs, which could not be aimed merely at the enemy's depots, but would have to be placed as close as possible to the center of resistance; however limited the radius of destruction might be, the spread of the thermal blast produced by the geographical position of the basin could present a serious danger for the garrison. Moreover, extreme precision was necessary, and the targets for the bombs would have to be indicated on the ground by colored markers not to be confused with anything else. But the only markers in Indochina were yellow ones, which would be hard to distinguish, at the height the bombers would be flying, from the smoke or mist which often covered the battlefield. Brighter markers would have to be sent from France or dropped by the Americans. Again, how effective would the A-Bomb prove against a deeply entrenched enemy? Was the game of diplomatic complications that would inevitably follow worth the candle? Navarre listened to the opinions of his subordinates and M. Dejean, and postponed his reply till the next day.

After Éliane 4 had suffered a heavy bombardment of 120-mm. shells during the night, Major de Séguins-Pazzis, of Castries's staff, visited the position at dawn. He was taken to the command post, where, taking advantage of a moment's respite, Bigeard was having a drink with his secretary, his adjutant and his radio operators. Realizing that a shell could pierce the roof of his poor shelter, Bigeard had had niches dug out at the bottom of his rat hole, where he could take refuge with his team, like the Viets, when the 105's started raining down. On his way down, Séguins-Pazzis had seen gun emplacements which had collapsed into the mud and corpses half-buried under the debris. Among the haggard faces, Bigeard's, stained with the earth, was impressive for the air of determination it wore in that sinister setting.

"Anybody seeing you so calmly in command of a situation like this," said Séguins-Pazzis, "is bound to think you were born for this sort of thing."

Bigeard smiled. He felt little affection for Séguins-Pazzis. They did not belong to the same race of men. Séguins-Pazzis was not a gang leader like himself, but a traditional officer, an aristocrat to his fingertips, cultured, sensitive, another figure, with his narrow face, his high forehead and his melancholy, from the gallery of El Greco's soldiers.

His compliment carried all the more weight as a result. Séguins-Pazzis made war with elegance and a certain irony. A cavalryman who no longer had much confidence in the effectiveness of cavalry in guerrilla warfare, he had asked to be transferred to the Colonial Infantry and had attended courses in Oriental languages and Moslem affairs. In his opinion, the Indochinese War would not be settled in the field but in men's minds, but he secretly envied Bigeard his simple ideas on the question, just as he admired him for his indomitable spirit.

Bigeard swelled up. The son of the little railway worker of Toul always felt ready to give his life for the praises which fell from the lips of the princes he impressed.

In Hanoï in the morning, a fresh conversation took place at the Maison de France. Sixty B-29's escorted by 150 fighters of the Seventh Fleet could fill the air with the roll of thunder without dropping a thunderbolt. When M. Dejean set off again at 1445 for Saigon, the government's envoy took with him a negative reply from General Navarre. Was this out of fear that the Chinese Air Force might in its turn attack Dienbienphu and the air bases? That is the reason which has been given till now, just as it has always been stated that General Navarre never knew that the B-29's were going to drop A-bombs. A childish lie which does not stand up to examination of the facts; General Navarre, an expert in Intelligence work, could not have failed to know what "Operation Vulture" was to be. Nor was he unaware that the command of such an operation would be bound to be entrusted to someone else, that another general would assume his authority and he would become a subordinate.

The confrontation between Navarre and Cogny took place in the afternoon between 1610 and 1740, in Navarre's office on the ground floor of his villa near the Great Lake. The weather was close and stormy.

"We have written some unpleasant things to each other," said Navarre with affected good fellowship. "Now we must discuss them calmly."

Cogny attacked, raising his voice. He furiously repeated the gist of his reply and told Navarre that he was no longer willing to serve under him, leaving it to him to decide whether he should be relieved of his post immediately. He reminded him that the decision to give battle at Dienbienphu had been the responsibility solely of the Commander in Chief, that the use of makeshift solutions in logistics had always led to disaster, and that he, Cogny, who had never been anything but a subordinate carrying out orders, considered that the fate of GONO probably depended, that very night, on whether reinforcements were or were not sent.

Navarre felt relieved, convinced that Cogny had been betraying him for a long time by criticizing the errors of conception of the current battle to eminent visitors to Tonkin. One day, in Paris, in the presence of General Catroux's wife and some friends, Madame Navarre had taken out of her handbag a letter which had been passed around the drawing rooms and in which her husband had written: "That swine Cogny is betraying me every day." He repeated this to him now.

"If you weren't a four-star general," cried Cogny, "I'd slap you across the face."

Navarre went pale. On the other side of the partition, his secretary heard raised voices, but the two officers were alone. Cogny regained his composure and prepared to withdraw.

"I must ask you to keep this between us," said Navarre.

"I regard that as the first of my duties," replied Cogny, clicking his heels.

April 3, 1954

Taking advantage of the lull, Langlais plunged into what was known as the Métro, that network of saps, trenches and dark corridors in which the garrison moved about to avoid the shells, and where, from March 13 on, nobody had ever seen Castries venture. Possibly, as he told me, because his place was by his telephone. Possibly also because nobody had noticed him when he went out at night. On Castries's place, as on that of Cogny or Navarre, opinions are divided. A leader commands from his command post, that is certain. But he must make certain gestures, and those gestures were not made.

A thin, blue-eyed wolf, with a long, hungry jaw, thin, sharp lips, and big ears which were not pointed as one might expect, Langlais set off by himself, wearing his faded red beret and a pistol at his belt, which was fastened as tight as it would go but was still too big for his waist. A great mind? Langlais had never claimed to be that. He recognized the mistakes he made about men and situations, for he had a great heart. The day before, he had received from his sister a letter bearing the postmark of Malestroit in Morbihan: "The weather is fine. The children are playing at entrenched camps in the garden. I pray heaven to give them as much courage as you have." Tears had suddenly flowed down his face. He naïvely refused to allow people to compliment him and wanted only the friendship which he himself lavished upon the humblest of those he met in the trenches, in front of their holes, in the midst of outspread parachutes, disemboweled tins of rations, abandoned equipment and packages nobody had the heart to open. Men saluted him and he shook hands. He went into the shelters, sat down on the bunks, passed round a bottle of brandy, went back up into the open and leaped from dugout to dugout as far as the forward positions. Bullets ricocheted against banks of earth and whined through the air, and mortar shells exploded. He never batted an eyelid. Devoid of imagination, he thought, "They're going at it hammer and tongs," without reflecting that fate might place him under the next shell. When that nearly happened to him, he brushed down his battle dress with furious gestures, but the timbre of his voice didn't change when he spoke into a microphone and his knees didn't tremble. He had called certain officers cowards. Like Bigeard, he was a man of war and war was his daily bread. He would never think of giving in, because the idea didn't enter his mind. It was different with Bigeard; whatever happened, he never admitted defeat, but he knew that one day he might suffer defeat at the hands of a young challenger.

Langlais therefore was not prepared for the worst. He felt sure of winning, of receiving reinforcements, of recapturing the lost peaks, just as he felt sure of winning, of living, whereas Sergeant Sammarco, since seeing Lieutenant Colonel Gaucher killed, had begun to wonder how all this would end. For a fortnight, detailed to hold certain outposts, he set off with three Thais, chosen at random, and stationed himself for part of the night at a given place on the other side of the barbed-wire defenses, to watch the progress of the enemy's earthworks. When they heard the sound of pickaxes, the Thais told him and Sammarco whispered a warning into his radio transmitter. Then the four men lay flat on the ground to avoid being hit by the shells which fell in front of them. But all the Sergeant Sammarcos who saw Langlais go by felt renewed confidence. They were just going through a bad period; something would happen to alter the situation.

In Hanoï, General Navarre sent General Cogny a reply to his letter of April 1; he took note of Cogny's desire, which coincided with his own personal views, to terminate his tour of duty as soon as the current operation came to an end. Refusing to pursue a futile discussion about the forces Cogny had had at his disposal during the campaign, he declared that the maintenance of the essential positions in the delta remained one of his preoccupations. In the morning, a meeting took place at the citadel between the two generals and the air commander of the Expeditionary Force.

During the night, the last company of reinforcements was dropped along the airstrip, between Huguette and Épervier, in the only dropping zone still available. At 2300 hours, the ground-lighting team had just gotten into position to receive the Banjos when an attack was launched on Huguette. Langlais kept the first planes waiting, but then, preferring the risk of accident to a fall behind enemy lines, decided to make the paratroopers jump into the middle of the entrenched camp. He gave orders to light a drum of gasoline in the river bed a little above the bridge, to act as a beacon, so that the reinforcements, dropped at a low altitude, would fall among the barbed-wire defenses in the hospital zone and on the helicopter landing ground. The prompt intervention of the reserves and the tanks relieved Huguette about midnight.

April 4, 1954

Bréchignac, who was known as 'Brèche," was in command of the 2nd Battalion, 1st Parachute Chasseurs, intended for Épervier; he presented himself in the night, his clothes in rags, at Langlais's command post. Thick-set, with bright eyes and a beaming face, Bréchignac was one of the oldest paras and one of the most accomplished officers in the French Army. Men who spoke of him used to say, "He's a great fellow." He was the rival of Bigeard, who was not particularly fond of him. Unlike Bigeard, he was modest, simple and disinterested. His judgments were clear and sometimes brutal, and he never went back on a decision, but his generosity and his courage were legendary.

The paratroops were not the only ones to jump. Since the situation of the entrenched camp had become known, thousands of volunteers had come forward, sometimes in whole units. Langlais had argued over the radiotelephone for hours with headquarters at Hanoï before they had agreed to drop these volunteers without preliminary training. Anybody could risk one jump in ignorance of what it was like. As for a second jump . . .

For days before their departure, for hours before the chosen evening, the volunteers had been able to gauge the folly of their plan, savor the bitter taste left in their mouths by the proximity of death, and stifle the yawns produced by the contractions of solar plexuses at the sight of the plan of the dropping zone, situated between mines, barbed-wire entanglements and the first enemy trenches. A flight of an hour and a half on the benches inside the Dakotas finished them off. The pilot throttled back, and spiraled down with all lights out toward the darkened basin, jolted now and then by the blast from a salvo of antiaircraft fire. In the framework of the open door appeared fiery gleams and the brief flashes of guns firing and shells exploding. A row of twelve men got up, fastened a snap hook to the cable which would open their first parachute and waited for the order to jump. If they had known, yes, if they had known, they might still have drawn back and nobody would have been entitled to despise them, for what they were doing went beyond human limits. "You count up to three. If you go on falling . . ." With their noses against the backbones of the comrades in front, they groped for the metal handle which could be their salvation, for now it was too late. They would have to plunge into the darkness, telling themselves that if the parachute failed to open, nobody, in the midst of the general misfortune, would retain so much as the memory of such a gratuitous act, which seemed to be swallowed up, in the very eyes of its heroes, in the pit of universal stupidity.

There was a brief moment of panic and despair which was sometimes prolonged by the hesitation of a pilot. After that, most of them no longer remember anything, for it all happened too quickly, and the joy of finding themselves alive, caught in the grappling irons of the barbed-wire entanglements, slapped by the blast from the shells, made them forget the despairing cry which had burst from their lips when they had lost their footing, and the noise and sickening smell of the plane had suddenly given place to the silence and sweetness of the air. How were they to get out of these tangled wires whose claws were tearing their clothes and skin, and which way should they turn to find the promised help? These were secondary questions when they were on their feet, their hearts full of the victory they had won over themselves. The entrenched camp was lost in darkness, but the men ended up, even when they fell on the morgue, in the midst of corpses, by opening the door of a shelter and finding living faces which spoke the same language as themselves and directed them to a regrouping point. Sometimes Langlais would have a surprise visit from a messenger who brought him letters and bottles of muscadet, only to be killed a littler farther on by a mortar shell.

At half-past four, dawn rose upon that Passion Sunday. At five o'clock, the daylight lit up the jagged crests, their blue sides streaked with napalm burns; the bare peaks, the double breasts of Éliane 1 and Éliane 4, which were now known as the "Lollobrigidas"; the plain of gray and yellow clay, bristling with weapons and barbed-wire entanglements, speckled with the thousands of parachutes which nobody picked up any more, swollen with embankments, and dotted with shell holes filled with stagnant rain water. A strange planet inhabited by shadows helmeted in steel or latania, cut in two by a winding river, with a sky humming with planes among which puffs of black smoke appeared only to be blown away by the wind. Near Castries's command post, there still stood a shattered tree trunk whose sap had not dried up, but trickled gently away. As in the Paschal liturgy, the duel between life and death was about to be fought.

That day, a flash of hope passed through the radio aerials when Cogny cabled that the reinforcements sent from France would enable the strength of the garrison to be increased by a battalion. At this news, Langlais gave a howl of joy. But where was the new battalion to be dropped if the advance bastion of Huguette 6 did not hold? At present, a gust of wind was enough to blow the parachutes into the enemy lines. Over Isabelle, it had taken five hours to drop seventy men. During the day, it was worse. A height of ten to twelve thousand feet, which was essential if the planes were to avoid destruction, scattered the packages at random, in spite of every possible sighting system. Without fighter protection, the Packets, which emptied their cargo at one go, like dump trucks, sometimes dropped their six tons miles away. An experiment had been made with containers fixed in the bomb bays of B-26's and dropped almost at ground level; the results had been so poor that the idea had been abandoned. In fine weather, eighteen Dakotas a day succeeded in parachuting their loads, half of which fell behind the Viet lines.

Since March 13, the Expeditionary Corps had been reinforcing the enemy's battle corps by dropping a large part of its supplies on his positions. In the radio broadcast which they made almost every evening, the Viets repeated, "Thank you for the 105's. We shall send them back to you, but with their fuses lit." Molotova trucks and GMC's, porters and sampans, horses and Peugeot bicycles were now being supplemented by planes. When the first Dakotas of the morning arrived, the Viets would laugh and exclaim, "*Tân công trên troi*. Here come the air porters!" This was Navarre's personal contribution, owing to his ignorance of the proper use of airpower, to Chinese aid.

The night of April 4-5, and the day of April 5, 1954

Langlais was getting ready to stretch out on his bunk when the thunder of Giap's 105's descended at 2000 hours on Huguette 6. Clémençon, who was in command of the strong point, called for his reserves. Langlais told him by radio that he was sending him the Clédic Company, of the Bréchignac battalion. Two batteries of the main position belched forth a concentrated barrage.

By 2100 hours, the Viets had gained a foothold in the defenses. At 2130, the Clédic Company, in spite of enemy artillery, succeeded in reaching Huguette 6 and joining the Legionnaires clinging to the strong point, but it rapidly called for help. The new moon had disappeared behind the mountains, and in the darkness the Dakotas were continuing to drop reinforcements in the midst of the barbed-wire entanglements.

Langlais moved up the Bailly Company of the 8th Assault. Tourret asked that it be given tank support.

"How many Bisons in working order?" Langlais asked Hervouët.

"Two."

"Send them off!"

Bailly advanced along the culvert that skirted the airstrip to the east. He came under heavy shellfire before getting near Huguette 6, which he was unable to reach. The Viets had encircled the strong point, barring the way from the south, and fired at the tanks with bazookas. At four in the morning, Langlais called Bigeard, who had followed the whole operation on the radio from his perch on Éliane 4.

"You aren't asleep, are you? I may need you."

Arriving back in Paris on that Sunday evening, Colonel Brohon went to the private house in the rue Puvis-de-Chavannes where General Ely lived, like the shade of a constable of old, in the midst of flags and suits of armor. He was giving him a detailed report on his mission and on the arguments Navarre had used to turn down American intervention when an officer from the Ministry of Defense interrupted the conversation with an urgent message. On second thought, Navarre accepted "Operation Vulture" and wanted it to take place in six to eight days. Why had Navarre changed his mind? How had the Chinese Air Force, which would not fail to retaliate by attacking the air bases of the Expeditionary Corps, suddenly become a negligible factor? Colonel Brohon's features relaxed at the news, and an enigmatic smile passed over the face, as gray and rigid as a death mask, of General Ely, who immediately summoned a meeting of the restricted war committee at Matignon.

The atmosphere was stormy. In the late afternoon, the Prime Minister and M. Pleven had been surrounded by demonstrators at the Ceremony of the Flame at the Arc de Triomphe. Alerted by the news from Dienbienphu, the Association of Indochina Veterans had called upon its members to boo the ministers. Trapped by the crowd for ten minutes, M. Pleven, like M. Laniel, had had difficulty in getting back to his car.

Colonel Brohon was invited to speak, and repeated what he knew of Dienbienphu and what General Navarre had said to him. Some members of the government tried to convince themselves that the situation was not so very tragic and asked questions in the hope that Brohon would sustain their illusions. As one witness put it, the replies fell like the blade of a guillotine, and Crèvecoeur's idea of saving Dienbienphu with the battalions from Laos was also demolished. General Fay triumphed, and Ely assumed a grief-stricken expression.

The restricted war committee now agreed that the only hope of saving Dienbienphu lay in "Operation Vulture," provided, to quote the words used by General Navarre in his telegram, it was prompt and massive.

There was not much time. It was decided to send for the United States Ambassador in Paris for consultation. Somebody suggested that this would be difficult on a Sunday and at that time of night, for it was nearly midnight. In less than three minutes, Mr. Douglas Dillon answered the telephone. He was coming. The meeting was suspended. In front of the Foreign Ministry, M. Laniel asked the ambassador to ask the American Government to launch "Operation Vulture.".

Mr. Dillon promised to get in touch with his government immediately. However, he suggested that, contrary to what had been thought at first, the President of the United States might be obliged to consult Congress. Thanks to the difference in time, it might be possible to obtain a reply the next day. Two aircraft carriers of the Seventh Fleet, which were equipped with A-bombs, were cruising in the Gulf of Tonkin. At the same moment, the admiral in command of this squadron and his staff were flying over the entrenched camp of Dienbienphu in the darkness. The buzzing of the Dakotas which were dropping flares and napalm bombs prevented Langlais from hearing the thunder of the jets, on board which the American officers were already reconnoitering the route and the target.

Six guns of the batteries supporting the operation on Huguette 6 were destroyed. They were replaced with 120-mm. mortars. Bigeard came down from Éliane 4 and drove in a jeep with Langlais to Huguette 3, where they found Clémençon. In front of maps and aerial photos, Bigeard composed his scenario and dictated his orders to his secretary, who typed them out on the spot, calling for air support at daybreak and taking command of the whole operation. He ordered the forces on Huguette 6 to hold fast, and the Bailly Company of the 8th Assault not to allow itself to be ejected from the ditch where it was.

Bright-eyed, drinking the coffee served by a Legionnaire, and determined to win this round, he sent Lieutenant Le Page into action at six o'clock with the leading company, which reached the Bailly Company, passed it, carried along with it the units which had been brought to a halt and recaptured all the lost ground. The enemy took evasive action and withdrew, pounded by the artillery and the mortars. Twenty-one very young Viet soldiers put their hands up and surrendered. Heaps of corpses lay in the barbed-wire entanglements. The planes flew in and finished off the job. Langlais admitted that he had never seen so many dead before. Of the four battalions of the 308th and 312th Divisions which had been attacked, one had been wiped out. There remained forty Legionnaires of the company holding Huguette 6, and twenty men of the Clédic Company; most of the officers involved in the operation had been killed or wounded. The company of the Bigeard battalion which had led the counterattack merged with the Bailly Company, which had been reduced to a shadow of its former self. The dead were hurriedly buried in the trenches.

This was a victory which Castries had failed to win on Béatrice and Gabrielle and which a mere battalion commander had just obtained with modest resources. It was an expensive victory, but it proved that success at Dienbienphu depended on the quality of the commanders as much as it did on the tactical situation. However mad it may have seemed, the organization of the defense system was perhaps not entirely stupid. With determined men with quick reactions and strong nerves, it might have proved Giap's undoing. Even now, all was perhaps not lost. The trouble with Dienbienphu was that Navarre had accumulated all the risks of defeat by accepting battle in a basin two hundred miles from Hanoï and at a moment when the enemy's strategy, having reached its highest pitch of perfection, bore within itself the cause of the disaster. Choosing the worst time and place for a battle, Navarre had not even been able to pick a winning side. It was as if he had surrounded himself with nothing but losers.

In Washington, darkness had just fallen over the Capitol when John Foster Dulles, at the State Department, received the coded cables from his ambassador in Paris. The question no longer struck him as quite so simple since he had made his speech at the Overseas Press Club to prepare public opinion for coming events and then gathered together the leaders of Congress to explain to them the situation in Indochina and Admiral Radford's intentions. The firm rebuff he had suffered compelled him to abstain from any initiative and to take refuge in what one Senator had just called, for want of a better term, united action by the free nations. The French Ambassador in Washington had probably not had time to inform his government of this development when Mr. Douglas Dillon was summoned by the restricted war committee in Paris at midnight.

The defense of Laos for which General Navarre had assumed responsibility without receiving express orders to do so, and the mistakes committed in an attempt to maintain it, might now involve a heavy risk to all mankind. Night had not finished unfolding its darkness over the planet, but at Dienbienphu the two exhausted adversaries had returned to their corners. A glorious sun beat down on men's necks and on the ground where the corpses of the night and the morning were beginning to decompose.

April 6, 1954

The restricted war committee, meeting once again in Paris, was taken aback by the telegram which Mr. Dulles had just sent his ambassador in Paris. The mountain had given birth to a mouse: the only action that could take place in Indochina would have to bring together, in addition to the three great Western powers, Australia, New Zealand, Thailand and the Philippines. The resounding proposals made by Admiral Radford, ready to destroy anybody who did not think as he did, to exterminate the Communists whom he had fought in Korea, and to undertake an atomic crusade against China by forcing the State Department's hand, had come up against Congress's fears and been bogged down in international procedure. President Eisenhower rapidly resigned himself to burying the whole thing under a jumble of opinions.

London was consulted and asked for additional information. It was already practically certain that if, by any chance, air intervention took place, A-bombs would not be used. Nobody would dare to take an irrevocable step before the Geneva Conference, which was due to open on May 8, and in any case, a large majority of prudent men would always prefer seeing their exports increased to saving lunatics. Great Britain had freely relinquished her Indian Empire. Why should she risk a war to support the fools who were hanging on in the Far East? If diplomacy could serve any useful purpose, it was going to be fully employed to cage the vulture which Admiral Radford had placed on General Ely's delicate shoulder.

Did Navarre for his part raise hopes that outside intervention was going to save Dienbienphu? Nothing induced him to do so. He decided, in any case, to launch within about ten days a supporting operation with four of Crèvecoeur's battalions from Laos and three parachute battalions dropped close to Dienbienphu—Cogny's satellite, in fact, but without the mobility it had been hoped to give it and launched only in the final extremity.

For a long time, Navarre had been thinking of artificial rain as a decisive solution. An officer who was an expert in scientific matters had come from Paris with some sacks of charcoal impregnated with silver iodide. By parachute he had dropped some little baskets which he had set on fire, and the air currents had spread the smoke inside the huge supercooling clouds. In some places, hailstones had fallen as a result.

Navarre had dreamed of using this method to make the roads used by the enemy convoys unserviceable and thus stop Giap's munitions supplies. In spite of some disappointing experiments, he refused to be discouraged. But it is not easy to improvise control of the clouds and the winds, and here again technique was defeated by ants possessed of souls and a faith.

The only hope of saving Dienbienphu, as Navarre now knew, lay in atom bombs dropped by the B-29's of the United States Air Force flying due east from Clark Field in the Philippines, winged horses drawing behind them the brilliance and the power of the sun. When they appeared, the sky would suddenly turn to fire and reduce to ashes the soldiers no classical weapon could defeat. Navarre's stars would stay sewn to his epaulets, but Langlais would see others fall on the mountains, and how far would these rebound? How would the world accept this extension of the reign of Hiroshima? What hatred would be reaped by the nation which had burnt to death one hundred thousand men and women on the soil of their ancestors in order to rectify the error of judgment of one general? Was that what occurred to Navarre when he had first refused the B-29's, or was he just clinging to the post of Commander in Chief which he would have lost if he had accepted them?

He returned to Saigon, where he would be able to follow the development of the political situation better than in Hanoï.

April 8, 1954

The French Ambassador in Washington conveyed to Mr. Dulles his government's disappointment.

"Since no direct and probably decisive help had been planned for Dienbienphu," said M. Bonnet, "there was no point in hurriedly forming a coalition which, in any case, would come about after the battle and might, in the eyes of the French public, compromise the chances of concluding an acceptable agreement at Geneva."

"It is inconceivable," replied Mr. Dulles, "seeing that the United States is not directly engaged in the conflict, and without any fresh open provocation, that the United States should take the initiative in such a warlike act, which would need the previous permission of Congress."

"In that case," replied M. Bonnet, with a diplomatic gentleness more terrible than anger, "I must express to Your Excellency regret that the possibility was considered and that the hopes dashed today were ever raised."

April 9, 1954

Storms had broken out all night, mingling their thunder with that of the shelling. Gun Crew Commander Hoang da Hung's battery shot down a Helldiver of Flotilla 3F, flown by a big, phlegmatic sailor of twenty-four, Sublieutenant Laugier, the son of an Orléans solicitor. As he was baling out, his parachute, opening too soon, caught in the tail and he crashed with his plane near Claudine 5. A platoon of the 3rd Company of the 1st Battalion, 13th Demibrigade, rushed to help him, with Captain Capeyron at its head, and brought back his shattered body. Sublieutenant Laugier was one of the last of the dead to be buried in a coffin.

All day long, under the straw roofs of surgical block No. 1 in the mountains about seven miles northeast of Dienbienphu, on the other side of the blue crest of Phou Fa, Professor Ton that Tung operated on men with head wounds.

On March 27, at the medical school installed in the forests of Tuyen Quang, where he was training about a hundred young surgeons, Professor Tung had received a rather grubby piece of paper bearing the all-powerful signature of Vo nguyen Giap which ordered him to join the Tran Dinh army immediately as the Commander in Chief's medical adviser. A Molotova ambulance took three nights to reach Giap's headquarters, over roads on which the vehicles skidded on the muddy slopes; in spite of napalm and bombing raids, nobody felt in any danger. "It was simple," he told me later. "We were all drunk with victory." A fellow student of Giap's at the University of Hanoï, Professor Tung had a big jovial face, bubbling over with intelligence.

The health situation of the People's Army was serious. Six assistant doctors could not manage to give first aid to seven hundred wounded who were evacuated by convoys of porters toward the hospitals in the rear, after wounds had been dressed and broken limbs put in plaster. The most serious problem was the countless swarms of yellow flies which laid their eggs in all the wounds, which were teeming with maggots. Professor Tung experimented with all the pharmaceutical products at his disposal, except for ether, which was contraindicated.

It was also necessary to salvage the slightly wounded men so that they could be sent back into battle, with their wounds closed and cicatrized, even if only temporarily. Finally, the head wounds caused by trench warfare and the absence of steel helmets were many and serious. Professor Tung operated on them himself. He had learned how to remove foreign bodies by suction and then close the skull again, and he had passed on his technique to a few young surgeons in one week. As he had no electrocoagulators, he touched the blood vessels with a white-hot platinum wire. However, there remained a scourge against which nobody could do anything, and that was the wind from Laos. When it blew, it dried throats to the point of producing nosebleed and a tightness which spread to the chest and the heart.

That day, at the operating table where he had been standing since morning, his face hidden behind his gauze mask, his forehead streaming with sweat, Professor Tung tried to breathe calmly and remain impassive under the fierce bites of the flies and ticks attacking his ankles. The storm had begun again about midday and was hiding the mountains under clouds which protected them from the planes. As during the night, it was sometimes difficult to distinguish between the sound of thunder and that of shelling. Professor Tung spoke little, and in moments of impatience expressed himself in French. His desire to adapt the Vietnamese language to the precision of the surgeon's art had led him, since joining the insurrection, to try to create a scientific vocabulary, but the foreign words which occasionally came automatically to his lips caused him no embarrassment. He had conceived the ambition of beating France in this field too, since an expeditionary corps had taken the place of the professors and the culture to which she owed the prestige that she still enjoyed in men's minds. Like his friend Giap, Tung remembered the lessons of that French Revolution which was still spreading the virus of liberty across the world, and of which at times they both felt themselves to be the sons with greater justification than the generals of its army and the representatives of its government.

April 10, 1954

About midnight, dropped with the first company of the 2nd BEP, under Lisenfeld's command, Corporal Antoine Hoinant, a Belgian by birth, who had come from "Operation Atlante" equipped with what he called "morale," found himself on Claudine, with the Legionnaires of the 13th Demibrigade. He considered himself lucky, for many of his comrades had fallen in the river, in the barbed-wire entanglements or on top of field guns. For his first jump by night, he had been spoilt; the plane had been straddled by tracer bullets, and when the door of the Dakota had been opened, his platoon leader, Lieutenant Pétré, had said, "They're firing straight at us." His company, which was composed almost entirely of Vietnamese, had regrouped as best it could and had taken up position with the 8th Assault, along the river, at Épervier. What struck Corporal Hoinant, who was a calm, level-headed fellow of twenty-eight, was the total lack of organization of the position where he found himself. "The trenches were often dug only to knee level," he told me later. "There were no shelters, no blockhouses, nothing."

For the past two days, Bigeard had been trying to bluff the Viets. On the radio, a huge number of imaginary units was given directions, baffling the enemy listening posts, and the term "battalion" was applied to the ghosts of companies.

Before dawn, the men of the four companies of the 6th Battalion, Colonial Paratroops, waited, their hearts pounding wildly, for the twenty 105-mm. guns and the twelve 120-mm. mortars to open the fire which would support the minutely orchestrated action. At six o'clock, within ten minutes eighteen hundred shells fell on Éliane 1, while the heights were blinded by smoke bombs and Mont Fictif and Mont Chauve neutralized by the forty 81-mm. mortars of the main position, by the small-arms fire of the 1st BEP, the 8th Assault and the 5th Battalion, Vietnamese Para-troops, and by the section machine guns. The tanks pounded Éliane 1 with direct fire. Thirty seconds later, under the trajectories of the machine guns, the first waves of the Trapp Company hurled themselves at the west slope and hung on there in spite of the Vietminh batteries which laid down a terrifying barrage between the two crests. A second company, that of Lieutenant Le Page, was engaged with a team of flame-throwers whose flashes could be seen from a distance. Waiting on Éliane 10, at the foot of the peaks, the Bréchignac battalion was ready to intervene. In the earphones of the radio receivers, the rasping voice of Bigeard, who was directing the operation with eight radio sets around him from his observa-tion post on Éliane 4, announced that the Viets were falling back. At 1400 hours, Le Page signaled to Bigeard: "Objective reached."

Lieutenant Le Page was happy. Éliane had been completely conquered —later on, he would say "possessed." He would admit that in the morning he thought of her, as of all the strong points whose romantic names covered the valley and the hills, with the sudden desire a man feels for a lovely girl seen in the street or on the terrace of a café. For Lily, whom the Legion had installed near her, men may well have fought with knives in a brothel.

Blood was flowing everywhere. In the heat which the mist intensified, there floated a smell of petroleum, burnt flesh and corpses with their wounds covered with green flies. Bursts of automatic fire cracked like whips. Bullets scratched the ground, raising tiny clouds of dust. Carefully aimed, the 120-mm. mortar shells reduced everything to pulp. Under their battle order, the bodies of the living ran with sweat. Before calling Langlais to tell him, "Bruno calling young Pierre, mission accomplished," Bigeard waited for the companies to adjust their firing plan in front of them, and piled up thousands of grenades on the position to stop up the dangerous gaps. "I'm beginning to consider a counterattack a privileged mission," Lieutenant Le Page thought as he greeted the companies of the 2nd Battalion, 1st Parachute Chasseurs, which came to relieve him on the huge, gaping cemetery which Éliane 1 had become; the operation had cost the paratroops a hundred men and the Viets five times as many. The Vietminh regiment commander responsible for Éliane 1 (Peak D3 to the enemy) was reduced to the ranks as a disciplinary measure.

H.M. Bao Dai left for France, where he hoped to prove that he was the incarnation of his country's strength. One might laugh were it not for the fact that political comedy leads to conflict and death. Only the Commissioner General of France and the Emperor's government and staff felt or pretended to feel any respect for Bao Dai. Since the announcement of the Geneva Conference, the Vietnamese Army had started breaking up. Mobilization notices were not enforced. The only young men to be called to the colors were those who couldn't escape or students who, certain of becoming officers, hoped to obtain lucrative posts. Out of 94,000 individual mobilization orders issued in a single year, under threat of court-martial for evaders, a little over 5,400 were obeyed. To fill the gaps, raids were made in the rice belt and in the towns. Hemmed in by gendarmes, the recruits were taken in trucks to training camps. Soldiers and officers didn't always speak the same language and didn't come from the same social strata. In the month of April, 1954, alone, the Vietnamese Army would admit to 3,848 deserters. The percentage of men posted missing in battle was five times that of the dead and wounded, whereas in the Expeditionary Corps, in spite of the fact that it included 63,000 Vietnamese, it was only 10 percent. Six months after the formation of the light battalions, a quarter of their strength had gone. For whose sake should the troops of the Vietnamese Army get themselves killed?

A brilliant officer when he was in the French Air Force, Lieutenant Colonel Nguyen van Hinh, whom his father, M. Nguyen van Tam, then

Prime Minister, had appointed Chief of Staff of the Vietnamese Army, had covered himself with stars and honors and had embarked on a way of life worthy of his exalted position. The Vietnamese generals drove around in American cars and gave cocktail parties without suspecting that the fate of their country was being decided. Their hatred for Communism was governed by the advantages which capitalism offered them: medals, women, money.

One of the few Vietnamese officers who knew why they were fighting was Colonel Leroy, the son of a woman of the rice belt and a peasant of Beauce who had come out to the Far East as a soldier. As a child, he had taken buffaloes out to graze. The head of the little Catholic Kingdom of Bentré situated to the south of Saigon between two branches of the Mekong, on which he took guests boating to the strains of an orchestra, he held religious fetes with pagan luxury, quoted Pascal and Montesquieu, and had his troops' swords marked with a cross. A sworn enemy of M. Tam, he tried to establish an honest administration, denouncing the provincial governors who committed embezzlement, the officials who used the public labor force to build them houses, the landlords who got the militia to cultivate their land, the officers who robbed the state, and the administration which misappropriated millions of piastres intended to pay the troops or increased the number of ration-card holders to falsify catering estimates. The only minister who did not transfer funds from his department to his bank account admitted to a French general, "I'm fed up with being honest."

Apart from the French high commissioners who supported his government and wanted to convince themselves that all was well, who indeed would dare to imagine that anybody could get himself killed for H.M. Bao Dai? What soldier in this army could be expected to fight to enrich the big landlords and the provincial governors, and what sacrifices could be demanded from sergeants who, on account of their birth, had become colonels in eighteen months? And why should the best of them, if they had no capital to put away in Europe, compromise themselves by serving the Tays when they doubted whether the Tays were going to win? When Cogny wrote that serious signs of weakness had been discovered in the thirty Vietnamese battalions in Tonkin, he was employing a euphemism; he meant that men were mutinying, deserting their posts or refusing to fight when the Expeditionary Corps was sometimes faced by bands of guerrillas aged thirteen to eighteen who fought until they were killed. For a time, there was a rumor that the French were simply going to clear the delta plain and move its population below the 16th Parallel.

Since de Lattre's death, what kind of Vietnamese honor could still be found in the ranks of H.M. Bao Dai's army, trained by the French and paid by the Americans? What fatigue and pain would men endure for the sake of what country? Who was the incarnation of this people oppressed for centuries by its mandarins and its invaders and consumed by the hunger for justice? H.M. Bao Dai or Uncle Ho, Vo nguyen Giap or General Hinh? On his arrival in Paris, M. Bao Dai had the impudence to declare that the crowd which had just gathered around him showed that the hour of unanimity was approaching. It was certainly approaching. But not for him.

April 11, 1954

During the night, furious counterattacks had been launched against Éliane 1. At daybreak, Langlais went as usual to tour the two companies of the 1st Parachute Chasseurs, which had stood firm. With his body-guard, he stepped over the enemy corpses which nobody had had time to bury. A dying man looked at him imploringly, his open chest swollen with bloody blisters. He could not be moved, and in the casualty clearing stations the surgeons were no longer able to save everybody. Now, when Grauwin had thirty men with stomach wounds to operate on, he picked ten and, with morphine injections, helped the others to die. Some of them, knowing his affection for the commander of the 8th Assault, would cling to his legs, saying, "Don't let me down. I belong to Tourret's battalion. . . ."

Langlais, who knew all about that, turned away. He climbed up the hill, where a load of 120-mm. shells, in one-ton packages, which nobody had picked up, had been left for weeks with its giant parachutes torn and dirty. Éliane 1, where the men lived in holes with the sides falling in, was nothing but a huge chaos of mud and debris. Langlais silently shook hands. Smoke was rising into the hot, still air from an ammunition dump which had just finished burning. Somber, almost ashamed of the comfort which still existed in the central zone of the command post, Langlais knew that his men could not hold out much longer under the shellfire which bludgeoned will power before it reduced bodies to pulp.

As there were no trenches between the different peaks of Huguette, a complete operation was required every time food and water had to be taken to them. Langlais consequently decided to abandon Huguette 6 in order to concentrate his forces more closely. Did he think that he could ever recapture what he no longer had the power to hold? With Huguette 6 lost, parachute drops were going to become even riskier; the men who fell in the river and the barbed-wire entanglements would be able to extricate themselves, but the supplies would be lost.

In the morning of this Palm Sunday, Father Guidon, the chaplain of Isabelle, picked a few leaves from the bushes and went to celebrate his Mass at the artillery command post. In the afternoon, he waited for Pastor Tissot, the only Protestant chaplain, who had joined the entrenched camp by parachute. "The boys," the pastor often said, "tend to forget that Sunday is the Lord's Day. We have to remind them." Together they visited the wounded.

Isabelle was under heavy shellfire. From the little room where two Legionnaires had offered him a refuge to force him to leave the hole in which he lived under a few inches of earth and bamboo, Father Guidon was looking at the shells falling on the neighboring shelters and thinking that his friend was not going to come, when he heard footsteps. The gentle face followed by the long, slightly bowed figure of the pastor appeared in the doorway.

"Shall we go?"

"No, you come down here," said Father Guidon. "At least you'll be safe from the shells. You've had enough of those already."

And the two men sat down on the camp bed and sang Bach chorales while the ground was shaken by explosions.

"Let us praise the Lord. . . ."

The phlegmatic pastor, who suffered slightly from faulty articulation, and the stern-faced missionary had the same gaze full of faith.

"Shall we go?" repeated the pastor.

"Let's wait a little," replied Father Guidon, stroking the long black beard streaked with white hairs which covered his thin cheeks.

"But what about our pastoral duty?"

"I admire you," said Father Guidon, who had changed his commando beret for a helmet. "Shellfire doesn't seem to have any effect on you."

"Whatever may happen," replied Pastor Tissot, "the Lord is always with us. What is the point in worrying about anything?"

Father Guidon thought that there was no great hurry, but he went out behind the pastor. "Need I add that we walked fairly fast?" Father Guidon said to me later. "They were giving it to us hot and strong! We reached the passage leading to the main infirmary and the pastor was going inside when, with a deafening noise, I was hurled to the ground and the breath was knocked out of me. I said to myself, 'That's funny, it doesn't hurt to die; you just don't see any more.' When I found that I wasn't dead, I threw myself into the arms of the medical orderlies who had come to meet me. I was choking. They gave me an injection, and laid me out on the billiard table where Lieutenant Résillot looked me over. Among the orderlies there was a Negro, a former prisoner of the Viets who spoke a little Vietnamese, and when the prisoners sometimes complained about the food, he used to say to them, 'Did Ho Chi Minh give you chicken every day?' "

In the late afternoon, concentrated artillery fire was directed on Éliane 1, where Langlais sent the dwindling reserves of the 6th Battalion, Colonial Paratroops. The men climbing toward the bald crest of the peak, which was crackling with sparks and shrouded in smoke, knew what was waiting for them, but the officers gave them no time to think and led them on. The first waves mowed down the Viets who had followed close behind their barrage, and, jumping from hole to hole, they succeeded in recapturing the position. When a company of the 1st BEP relieved them, Lieutenant de Fromont had been killed and one platoon of the 6th Battalion, Colonial Paratroops, had been reduced to seven men, of whom only three would remain by the time they stopped in a minefield and screamed into the darkness for somebody to come get them. The internal radio of the counterattacking battalions vibrated with curses, cries of hope and calls for help.

April 12, 1954

At dawn, all available units had to be thrown in to recapture once again, one by one, the lost emplacements. The corpses piled up on the sinister peak of Éliane 1, which had been pounded over and over again by the artillery and where the debris of guns and equipment mingled with the red clay. Bréchignac's battalion was still hanging on, in trenches half-filled in on top of hurriedly buried bodies. The smell there was not that of the perfume with which Mary anointed Christ's feet at Bethany, the day the feast of the resurrection of Lazarus was celebrated, but that of the dead man in his grave and of excrement. The reinforcements that arrived by parachute every night could no longer make up for the losses. The new surgical unit dropped during the night was inadequate. Bigeard had left his shelter on Éliane 4 to share Langlais's command post, where he took over command of improvised operations.

It was generally agreed that Castries had lost his grip and had abandoned the business of directing the defense operations to these two officers; he no longer presided over the daily meetings at which the situation was studied and the future line of action decided. In fact, the weight of the battle lay on the shoulders of a lieutenant colonel who had received no staff training, and Cogny's only role now was that of director of the administrative areas. In his shelter, where he took his meals alone, Castries had at least the merit of remaining calm, settling quarrels and allaying anger caused by Langlais's temper and sharp tongue. One day, Langlais had said offensively to Lieutenant Colonel Voineau, "So we don't salute any more, do we?" And had thrown his glass of whisky in his face.

"Do you want to fight?" Voineau had asked, going white at the insult. Castries had intervened.

But the junior officers and the sergeants had seen him driving about in a jeep with his secretary too often in the past not to imagine that he was lying low with her in his command post. As for him, he had lived too much with Moroccans not to think that a leader must avoid all fraternization.

April 14, 1954

The false news of the launching of "Operation Condor" spread through the entrenched camp like a flash, and every face instinctively turned toward the west. The garrison imagined battalions advancing by forced marches across the bush toward the entrenched camp and receiving at the right moment the support of paratroops dropped in the neighborhood of the basin. They saw the whole situation reversed and the Viets, caught in a pincer movement, fleeing into the mountains. But a reconnaissance patrol sent out in the direction of Laos did not even reach the villages a mile from the outer defenses.

A dispatch from Castries, clearly inspired by Langlais, summed up the situation in a gloomy, prophetic phrase: "The fate of GONO will be decided before May 10." It also included this bitter comment: ". . . whatever the regulations about parachute training." For in Hanoï they were still talking about the unorthodox and dangerous conditions of the first jump made by volunteers.

As if to back up this forecast, Langlais and Bigeard listed the forces they had left: on the western perimeter, the remains of three battalions of the Legion—814 men; one Moroccan battalion of two companies on the southwest; the parachute battalions on the other perimeters—about 2,500 men. The rest no longer counted.

At that date, it should therefore be noted that the garrison of Dienbienphu had little more than three thousand men in a condition to fight. On March 12, 1954, on the eve of the battle, there had been nearly eleven thousand. Since March 13, four battalions had been dropped by parachute. There had not been twelve thousand dead or wounded. Where were the others? When making his inventory of the garrison, Langlais insisted on counting only men, not shadows. He omitted those on Isabelle, who were isolated and encircled, and all those who had no reason to risk their skins—in other words, the vast majority of the so-called "French Union" units. The officers, noncommissioned officers and men, whether Europeans or Vietnamese, who were still holding out had a reason for not giving in which the others lacked. However flimsy that reason might seem to those who did not belong to the great suffering body of the army, it retained its value and was called military honor and loyalty to a flag. Here again, the quality of a leader was capable of saving what had been given up for lost.

The positions of the opposing forces, which were no longer even separated by barbed-wire entanglements, had become charnel houses; the adversaries were dug in thirty yards apart, ready to leap at each other's throats. At that distance, they could call out to one another. One day the Viets had shouted, "We're bringing you some wounded," and fixed a rendezvous. In the end, the exchange did not take place. Another time, an envoy had advanced with a white flag close to a strong point and said, "We have two of your wounded. Come and get them." Setting off with an orderly and a Hungarian sergeant of the Legion with a splendid waxed mustache, the stretcher-bearers, caught in machine-gun fire from a neighboring unit, had come back with only one wounded man and the sergeant killed.

On Huguette 6, where he was now installed, Bizard, the cavalry captain turned parachutist, had lost nothing of his good humor. Like his friend Botella, who was in command of his own battalion, he was waiting with magnificent naïveté for the event that would bring victory. For two weeks, the only sleep the captains and lieutenants had been able to obtain had been while sitting in their holes, when a lull happened to fall, like a bird which still dared to approach the sinister valley. At night, they kept their earphones on and the radio switched on to the wavelength that would alert them. The dead, who were piled up when there was time, and over which a few yards of trench were sometimes filled in, were rotting everywhere, and their stench invaded the shelters, mingled with the other smell, even more atrocious, or vomit.

When the routine enemy barrage opened up in the evening, every company lost three or four more men. They took advantage of the darkness to pick up packages in the vicinity, dig a few trenches and send out fatigue parties who brought back, when they could, a few jerry cans from the water purification plant. With the return of the morning light, fresh hope was kindled; there was no longer any need to fear attack. In the dressing stations and first-aid posts, the doctors despaired of destroying the swarms of maggots. In their nightmares, they saw their foul processions climbing the walls, covering the beds and stretchers, and storming the wounds of their patients, whose prostration already resembled death. Cresyl and quicklime in the shelters were not sufficient; the corpses should have been buried deep in the earth, the approaches to the trenches disinfected, and the flood of mud in which the flies laid their grubs on excrement, urine and human refuse halted. The glory of Dienbienphu celebrated by the newspapers of the free world was that of fighting on the bloodiest dunghill in Asia, in the name of the West and for the love of the pretty girls who had given their names to the peaks. One final scourge, which the garrison was spared for some mysterious reason, was missing: the mosquitoes had fled.

As on the previous days, at about 2200 hours, the loudspeakers in the French lines howled appeals in Vietnamese toward the Viets: "Oh, enemy brothers, we feel sorry for you. Your infantrymen are already nearly all dead. Only you are left, and your turn will come. Why don't you return to Hanoï with us by air?" The machine guns and the mortars replied. Captain Hien, former chief of staff of the 57th Regiment, who recorded this in his notebook, heard these words twice: "You have had enough. Give yourselves up. Your lives will be easier."

"Even if our lives had been ten times harder," he told me later, "we wouldn't have given ourselves up. Why not? We knew at that time, since our victory on Him Lam, that we would win. And even if we had been told that we were all going to die, we would have accepted that. I, too, have been afraid of death, but when hatred filled us, nothing could stand in our way."

April 15, 1954

For some time, there had been a lot of talk of promoting Castries. A real hero ought to be a general, and President Eisenhower himself had expressed surprise to General Ely that Dienbienphu should be under the command of a mere colonel. Madame de Castries bestirred herself. Rumors of these claims were already widespread since Captain Hien had mentioned them in his notebook on the evening of March 30 in the basin of Dienbienphu. Among the Viets, any divisional or regimental commander who suffered the slightest reverse was relieved of his command without so much as a warning, and one of the questions which the French actually discussed, with disaster staring them in the face, was whether or not to give a general's stars to a luckless commander. It is true that the person of the commander of GONO was bound up with the legend which the drama had created. The names of certain officers of the entrenched camp were beginning to become famous, and the idea of a number of exceptional promotions, announced in the midst of the battle, seemed a worthy reward for their merit. How could the government forget the camp commander without repudiating him? Once again, the whole garrison had to be rewarded in his person. Moreover, Castries had the functions of a lieutenant general; it was because he had been considered worthy of carrying them out that he had been chosen and appointed. Gilles, at Na San, had been made a brigadier in his molehill; Castries had to be promoted in his turn. In a series of telegrams, Navarre demanded these stars as a boost for the garrison's morale. He got them.

At a meeting of the Cabinet, M. Marc Jacquet insisted that Colonel de Castries should not be made a brigadier. "If he gets out, we'll see," he said. "There's no hurry." That was also the opinion of the Secretary of State for War, M. Pierre de Chevigné, who was afraid that the entrenched camp was doomed. "The victory of the Viets will be less striking," he said, "if they capture only a colonel." Other members of the government pressed for Castries to be given his stars. "It will put new life into him," they maintained, as if battles were won with stars.

Shells were raining down over the whole of the entrenched camp; recoilless guns installed on the lost peaks picked out any men who still tried to collect packages dropped by parachute.

The valley of Dienbienphu, in which certain visitors in December, 1953, had discovered the atmosphere of a delightful picnic, had become a valley of tears and death. Suffering was everywhere, but hope did not abandon the officers who met at the end of every afternoon in the dugout where Langlais and Bigeard summed up the situation. It was, indeed, this hope which helped them to bear certain little local defeats of a temporary nature, since the Godard column was on the way and the American bombers were getting ready to take off from Manila. Among those who were watching the garrison's death agony from afar, who could have had the courage to reduce that hope to its true proportions? Who could have dared to persuade Langlais, Bigeard, Captain Capeyron or Sergeant Sammarco and all the others that they could no longer count on a reversal of the situation and that "Operation Condor" had not yet been launched?

The great topic of the day was the radiotelephone conversation in which Cogny had announced to Castries that he was a brigadier general, that Langlais, Lalande and Bigeard were promoted to the next higher rank, that a few officers were listed for special promotion and that the garrison and its commander were awarded a mention in dispatches.

Castries gave his shoulder straps to Langlais, who blackened the red in them with India ink; Langlais passed his on to Bigeard. As for the stars for the new brigadier, since, according to Madame de Castries, it was impossible to find any in Hanoï, Cogny offered those he had worn before he had taken command of the Tonkin forces.

"I'm sending you some stars and something to celebrate them with," said Cogny. "The whole world has its eyes fixed upon you. Fifty-two journalists from all over the world are in Hanoï to follow what you are doing."

All the packages which fell inside the entrenched camps were ransacked. Nothing was found. According to Madame de Castries, the stars arrived, brought to her husband by a parachutist who jumped that evening. According to Castries, they were forged on the spot in a Legion workshop. The Vietminh radio, however, announced that they had fallen, together with the bottles of brandy and the boxes of Legions of Honor, Military Medals and *Croix de guerre*, in their lines. The toasts were drunk in *vinogel*.

April 18, 1954

In the night, fearing that the code might have been broken, Major Clémençon had used English to tell Captain Bizard that Huguette 6 was going to be evacuated. That day, Bizard was twenty-nine years old, and that Easter dawn was the hour at which the women coming to embalm

Christ's body found the tomb empty; so many reasons to remember what happened. The counterattack failed to reach its objective. At eight o'clock, Bigeard decided not to throw any more units into action and announced that he was calling off the operation. Bizard replied that he was going to get through under his own steam. To do this, he had to withdraw through all the trenches separating him from his support units and cross the whole airstrip under the fire of the Viet machine guns. Of the two hundred men who tried to reach the other Huguette strong points, eighty got through.

In all Christendom, in Hanoï Cathedral as in the churches of Europe, the first hallelujahs were being sung. At Dienbienphu, where the men went to confession and communion in little groups, Chaplain Trinquand, who was celebrating Mass in a shelter near the hospital, uttered that cry of liturgical joy with a heart steeped in sadness; it was not victory that was approaching, but death. The surgeons had been operating since five in the morning. In the fog, which was gradually breaking up, a violent artillery and mortar barrage suddenly fell on the central position; the earth rained down on the wounded and on the altar. A salvo of 105's landed on Captain Capeyron, who was taking his battalion commander a file of proposals for mentions in dispatches; the Legionnaire accompanying him had one arm blown off, and a Moroccan who happened to be standing nearby was killed. Capeyron had only a shell splinter in the chin and a slight scalp wound. As he went into the infirmary, he was torn between happiness at having been spared and the feeling that the time was coming when Claudine would suffer the fate of Huguette 6. But then where would he fall back to? It would be the end.

Captain Bizard received reinforcements taken from the disbanded companies of the 5th Battalion, Vietnamese Paratroops, and from the 8th Assault and went to rest for a few hours on Éliane 4. The strong point Opéra was created to break the waves of the attacks between Huguette 1 and Épervier. It was not given a woman's name like the others, but that of the Métro station from which tourists emerged to go to the Café de la Paix, among the prostitutes from the Madeleine, sitting with their *café crème*. The news from Dienbienphu was spread over five columns on the front page of the newspapers, but the Easter holidays had turned Paris into a city whose sole preoccupation was the approaching pleasures of summer.

Langlais went to confess his sins to Father Heinrich and told him, "We are heading for disaster."

"We must accept that in expiation of our sins," the priest replied.

"Oh, no!" exclaimed Langlais. "I don't want that sort of consolation from you. Tell me that I'm wrong, that there's still some hope. Perform a miracle if need be."

A miracle would have been the launching of "Operation Vulture," as Navarre hoped it would be. He had come to Hanoï to spend a couple of days with General Partridge, commander of the U.S. Air Force in Southeast Asia. But, that morning, the British ambassador in Washington telephoned John Foster Dulles at his home to inform him that his government would not be taking part in the conference arranged for April 20 on Southeast Asia. The Secretary of State was extremely angry.

April 23, 1954

Unable to hold out any longer, Huguette 1 had fallen during the night. Two companies which had gone to its help had been practically wiped out. At seven o'clock, General de Castries sent for Langlais and Bigeard. Huguette 1 had to be recaptured; otherwise nothing more could be dropped by parachute. Bigeard was to mount the operation.

Bigeard grimaced. All the battalions, reduced to a quarter of their strength, were worn out; only one was still on its feet, with a strength of nearly four hundred men, but it was holding the Éliane strong points, on the other side of the river; that was the 2nd BEP. Even if the attack succeeded, that battalion would be broken up and the entrenched camp would no longer possess the smallest reserves. For all these reasons, Bigeard did not want to risk his last forces and considered this counterattack dangerous and futile. Langlais backed him up. The hundred or so men who were dropped every day were barely sufficient to make up for half the losses. Often sent into action as soon as they arrived, most of them were dead by the time dawn broke. What would happen when the 2nd BEP was wiped out? Who was going to take its place on the left bank? General de Castries insisted; the counterattack would take place. Bigeard, for all that he hated useless losses and sterile efforts, gave way. Castries remained one of the rare leaders who impressed him.

Units of the 1st Parachute Chasseurs, of the 6th Battalion, Colonial Paratroops, and of the Legionnaires from Claudine took the place on Éliane of the 2nd BEP, which had to take up position by 1330 on its starting lines: one light infantry company in the north trench of Huguette 2, two companies in the culvert along the airstrip, opposite Huguette 1, and one reserve company farther down, opposite Épervier. The attack had to be launched on the dot, as soon as the artillery barrage was lifted, a matter of routine for trained troops. Command of the operation was naturally entrusted to the battalion commander of the 2nd BEP, Major Lisenfeld. At 1345, twelve fighters and a B-26 swooped down to deal with any resistance which might hold up progress. "It's in the bag," declared Bigeard, who pretended to feel no anxiety and withdrew.

Lieutenant Klotz of Flight 11F, who had dived very low in his Hellcat over Huguette 1, thought that he had been hit at ground level just as he was flattening out. In fact, his plane had been seen to catch fire before he dropped his bomb. His first reaction was to gain altitude and head south to try to land on the Isabelle airstrip, but then, remembering that one of his comrades who had tried the same maneuver had exploded in flight before touching the ground, he decided to abandon his plane as quickly as possible. Convinced that his parachute was not opening, he was trying to pull it out himself when the wind caught it and he dislocated his shoulder.

Watched by his fellow pilot, Petty Officer Goizet, he fell in the rice fields a quarter of a mile south of Éliane 2. From the bullets whistling about his ears and tearing up the ground a few feet away, he suddenly realized in terror that he was being shot at. Like any pilot, he was unprepared for this ordeal; his job consisted of braving other dangers. Pressing himself to the ground, he told himself that he had to try to reach the stream separating him from Éliane 2 and take shelter in it. From Éliane, Captain Capeyron's company, which had already gone to the help of Sublieutenant Laugier on April 9, and Petty Officer Goizet in his Hellcat, opened fire on the gun crews on Mont Chauve in order to outstrip the Viet squad which was trying to capture him. Lieutenant Klotz suddenly saw, about a hundred yards away, a huge Legionnaire running toward him. "You're not going to stay here," Klotz said to himself, "while a fellow risks his life for you." He rushed to meet him and made it. The Legionnaire, who had just been wounded in the cheek and was bleeding, tucked him under his arm and carried him off.

"Take that thing off," said the Legionnaire, pointing to the bright yellow life jacket which sailors wear under their parachute harness.

Lieutenant Klotz got rid of it, and once again allowed himself to be carried in rushes as far as the Éliane strong point, where he was given first aid.

The 2nd BEP had not been able to leave its starting lines at the prescribed hour; it had not been in position on account of an overtight calculation of the time needed to bring it from Éliane and mistakes made on the way. Four B-26's and the artillery took over from the fighters and pounded Huguette 1, where there were only about a dozen Viets left, dazed by the bombs and shells and incapable of holding out much longer, while smoke screens masked the heights to the east. When, thirty minutes late, the companies went in, the enemy machine guns, back in action, brought under their fire the landing strip they had to cross. A single section managed to reach a bomb crater, near the carcass of the Curtiss of the Blue Eagle Company which had been burnt out on March 13.

At 1500 hours, Castries sent for Bigeard, who had not slept for several nights and had collapsed onto his bunk.

"I have the impression that the attack is hanging fire," he told him. "Go and see."

Bigeard drove in a jeep under shellfire to Huguette 2, where the command post of the operation was installed.

"It must be going all right," Lisenfeld told him. "I'm not getting any news from my units."

Bigeard quickly noticed that the radio receivers were out of order. He shouted, shook everybody up with bursts of insults, called the company commanders who were pinned down by the enemy's fire and sized up the situation: all the Viet weapons, which had returned to Huguette 1, were mowing down the units which ventured onto the airstrip. When an operation was a failure, Bigeard didn't insist. He played to win, like the Viets. If he lost, he pulled out. He used the B-26's and the artillery to blind the batteries and ordered a rapid withdrawal. Of the company to which Corporal Hoinant belonged, sixty men remained and he himself was made a platoon leader. The company sergeant major to the company commander, Lieutenant Guérin, who had both legs almost blown off by a shell, fired a bullet into his head, so that nobody else would risk his life trying to get him back. The company lay down in the culvert until evening, when the 8th Assault relieved it. What astonished the Viets that day was the timidity of the five tanks which had not fired at them at close range.

A hundred and fifty yards from the Isabelle positions, the chief of staff of the 57th Regiment tried some *vinogel*. "With a little sugar it wasn't bad," he told me later. Giap had given orders to move the trenches as close as possible, in order to pick up the bulk of the supplies dropped by parachute. To the west of Isabelle, Captain Hien noted that the trenches had been dug to a depth of only six feet and asked the company commander to have them dug eighteen inches deeper. Some soldiers offered him a handkerchief cut out of parachute silk and decorated with fine embroidery. Somewhere else, he was given some French coffee to drink which had been heated in a little smokeless stove.

At nightfall, for it was impossible to leave Éliane 2 during the day, Lieutenant Klotz was taken to the hospital, where Grauwin anesthetized him before setting his shoulder. "That must have been preferential treatment," said Klotz. "Putting me to sleep for such a little thing." Grauwin opened his last bottle of champagne in his honor, and took him to see Langlais. At Dienbienphu, everybody loved sailors. They fought to help the garrison of the entrenched camp without counting the risks; they went into nose dives over pockets of resistance, whereas the Air Force respected the safety regulations. One of the flight commanders, Lieutenant Andrieux, had been shot down on March 31. The other, Gérard de Castelbajac, was known for his taste for holidays and his pink complexion, fair hair and blue eyes, which had earned him the nickname of "Bébé Cadum." Everybody liked this Gascon cavalryman who had joined the Navy, with his rapier and his plumed hat. By the end of the campaign, his flight crew, which always backed him up to the hilt, would have lost six pilots out of fifteen.

A few days before, Klotz had suggested dropping a package on Dienbienphu containing three bottles of whisky for Castries, Langlais and Bigeard, together with a note signed by all the members of Flight 11F. To do that, it would be necessary to fly low over the command post without any valid tactical reason; Castelbajac had hesitated for twenty-four hours, and then decided that it was worth it. The kindness had been appreciated and had increased everyone's affection for sailors. Klotz was made much of. Castries behaved as coldly as ever when he welcomed him, but Major de Séguins-Pazzis took him on his staff and made him responsible for liaison with the air command post.

Coming into contact with Langlais and Bigeard, whose prestige was growing day by day throughout the Expeditionary Corps, Lieutenant Klotz, who had thought that Dienbienphu was done for, changed his mind. Because, luckier than Sublieutenant Laugier, shot down in the same circumstances on April 9, he had escaped death? Or because the Legionnaires had saved him from the Viets? The contagion of these men filled him with tremendous hope. He thought most of all of Lieutenant Lespinas, who had been shot down on March 15, and whose death had deeply affected him at the time. A close friendship had linked him with that thin, highly strung young man, always ready for love and war, and whose respect he had wanted to earn. No, nothing was decided. At Dienbienphu the actors in the play imagined that they could still win. Klotz had only one regret: that he had not brought his pipes and a stock of English tobacco with him. He felt invulnerable. He told himself that if life had any meaning, it should be possible to wrest victory from the enemy's hands.

In Paris, where he had stopped on his way to Geneva, Mr. John Foster Dulles met M. Georges Bidault, who told him that if "Operation Vulture" was not launched before long, the entrenched camp would go under; a succession of fresh catastrophes was likely to follow. All could still be saved if the United States Government decided to throw in the B-29's from Manila. At a dinner given that evening at the Quai d'Orsay, Mr. Dulles took Mr. Eden to one side to inform him of the plan for "Operation Vulture," whose salient features General Ely's Staff had communicated to the British Staff. Thoroughly alarmed, Mr. Eden got Mr. Dulles to promise that nothing would be done without the agreement of Mr. Winston Churchill's government.

April 24, 1954

Cogny received the reply to his telegram of the previous day in which he had conjured up the shade of Marshal de Lattre in order to crush Navarre. Navarre told him curtly that the situation had nothing in common with that of 1951 and that he was keeping the government informed of events as seen from a better vantage point than his own. The decision to drop a supplementary battalion, like the decision to launch "Operation Condor," would follow.

Cogny insisted and called for the formation of a large mobile force in Tonkin. At 2220, Navarre sent him another coded telegram from Saigon, in which he asked him four questions about Dienbienphu's capacity for resistance.

Was "Operation Condor" worth launching? That was the problem which Navarre, waiting for "Operation Vulture," could not manage to solve. The objections which Cogny's satellite had raised at the time seemed to have lost their force. On April 16, Cogny had not concealed the fact that the effectiveness of "Operation Condor" remained doubtful; at least a fortnight would be necessary for the Laos group to approach

Dienbienphu, and, even supported by two or three battalions dropped by parachute to the south of the basin, Crèvecoeur would not be strong enough to force the blockade. But at least he could hamstring the Viets and distract them for a while from attack on the entrenched camp. On the other hand, if the operation failed, what General Navarre regarded as a mere tactical reverse risked turning into a disaster of strategic proportions. After all, if Dienbienphu fell, as it seemed it must, Navarre thought that all he would have lost would be thirteen battalions and four artillery batteries—not even a tenth of his pawns; but if, under catastrophic conditions, he attempted a salvage operation, that operation could lead to a huge disaster. Cogny knew that as well as he did, but he was ready once again, without the slightest pity for Navarre, to risk everything in order to relieve Dienbienphu.

Ever since the beginning, Navarre had claimed responsibility for Dienbienphu. When success had seemed assured, Cogny had loudly proclaimed the magnitude of the expected victory; with defeat threatening, Cogny gave the impression of trying his best to hurl the Commander in Chief into the abyss and of leaving a sinking ship. Like everybody else, he had hoped for a fight without forming an accurate estimate of the enemy's resources. A gunner by training and experience, he had not worried about the enemy batteries. Paradoxically, Cogny, who knew how cunning the Viets could be, had not been sufficiently mistrustful. He had been infected by the contagion of overconfidence like the rest. The differences of opinion between the two generals crowned everything. One cannot help thinking that a century earlier the defeat of Balaclava had been due to the discord between two generals of the Franco-British Expeditionary Corps in the Crimea, Lord Lucan and Lord Cardigan, who preferred to see their army suffer a disaster rather than speak to each other, in the secret hope that one of them would die with the cavalry brigade which they allowed to go to its death. "They were no longer capable of understanding each other," writes Cecil Woodham-Smith, the historian of that hatred. It is true, however, that Cogny could do nothing without the agreement of Navarre, who refused him everything.

In Paris, in a letter intended to appease the French Government's resentment, Mr. Dulles expressed the opinion that a massive air attack would probably make no difference to the fate of Dienbienphu, but declared that if the entrenched camp fell, its fall would make no difference to the military position of the West in Indochina or to the military aid which the U.S.A. was ready to give. M. Laniel and M. Bidault thought that they discerned in this note a sincere regret on the part of the United States Government at being unable to help France because the military situation seemed hopeless. M. Bidault replied that, however black it might appear, the situation could still be completely reversed, if a dispatch from General Navarre was to be believed, and if use was made of the information which a military expert had brought back from the battlefield itself: there was a unique opportunity to destroy the whole of the enemy battle corps if "Operation Vulture" was launched in the next few hours. This telegram echoed the cry of Shakespeare's Richard III at the Battle of Bosworth: "A horse, a horse! My kingdom for a horse!" To save Navarre's kingdom, there was nothing left but aircraft, to the misuse of which he owed his defeat, and little baskets of activated charcoal which were dropped into the clouds in an attempt to produce a deluge over the Viets. The Foreign Minister's letter was nonetheless ambiguous. The military expert whose name was not revealed was none other than General Ely; he had been to Dienbienphu on February 19, but he had not just returned, as was suggested. Contrary to what M. Bidault impudently declared, no new factor had arisen which could modify General Ely's opinion. The heavy mystery with which the Quai d'Orsay's style enshrouded itself was nothing but diplomatic mendacity.

At one stroke all the chances of air intervention were revived. What a *coup de théâtre* it would be if the fortunes of arms were to change sides! This hope was reborn that Saturday afternoon, at a time when in the embassies only idle ushers usually answer the telephone, but the imminent opening of the Geneva Conference had led to unusual activity in the foreign ministries of the Western powers. Urgent coded messages jammed the Atlantic cables in the darkness which gradually covered Europe and crept toward America, while the sun was preparing to rise from behind the mountains over a valley which stank of death and defeat. Nobody had the strength to bury the corpses any more. They were pushed out of the trenches into shell craters, where they rotted. To advance across open ground, the Viet soldiers covered their faces with gauze masks which protected them from the smells and poisonous fumes, and the besieged garrison looked toward the southwest where Crèvecoeur's battalions were expected to appear.

In Paris, if M. Bidault walked beneath the gilded ceilings of the Quai d'Orsay toward the tall windows overlooking the Seine, it must have been toward the northwest that he gazed in search of a last gleam of the long twilight in the sky. Salvation could come only from London where, alarmed by the proportions the affair was assuming and preceded by a warning telegram, Mr. Anthony Eden had hurriedly returned. M. Bidault felt no doubts. Since 1951, between the "We must" of General de Lattre and the "We cannot" of the Army Chief of Staff, he had chosen the "We must." If Navarre considered himself the paladin of the Western world, M. Bidault had decided to be its crusader. He would not hesitate either to cut off heads or to press buttons in order to bring about the victory of his political religion and annihilate the infidels.

April 25, 1954

An extraordinary meeting of the British Cabinet came to an end after agreeing that there should be no Allied action unless the Geneva Conference failed. Mr. Anthony Eden attributed little importance to the French military expert's opinion that there was still some hope for Dienbienphu. But the whole situation changed when the French Ambassador informed Mr. Eden of Washington's new plan which Congress was reported to be ready to approve: the American Government, having received an SOS from France, no longer excluded the possibility of intervention. On the contrary, it had never been closer to entering the conflict, and the A-bombs were to be dropped on April 28 by its naval aircraft, on condition that Great Britain raised no objection. Mr. Eden called another meeting of the Cabinet at four o'clock in the afternoon, to decide on the British attitude. The British Chiefs of Staff gave their support to the policy of nonintervention. Regarding an adventure whose consequences would have been incalculable, it was condolences and regrets that Mr. Eden offered M. René Massigli, the French Ambassador, who had spent the day going backward and forward between the French Embassy and the Foreign Office. Mr. Eden even refused to cooperate in issuing a common statement.

For Navarre and Cogny, the only question that arose was to know how long Dienbienphu could be kept on the edge of the precipice pending the arrival of the squadron of B-29's. Even without A-bombs, the tornado of fire and steel dropped by sixty or eighty heavy bombers in several waves would churn up the ground like a gigantic plow, especially if the bombs exploded beneath the surface, to get at the men and weapons underground. Admittedly the Vietminh artillery would probably not be affected under its rocks, but the infantry would be pulverized by whole battalions, the lost ground could be recaptured and massive reinforcements from

Hanoï dropped by parachute would have no difficulty in regaining possession of the principal defense positions.

General Caldera, bomber chief of the Far East Air Force, had completed his reconnaissance mission and took leave of his hosts before returning to Manila. He told M. Maurice Dejean that the operation was possible in all weathers without it being necessary to install radio guidance aids in rebel territory. Besides, French officers would serve as guides on board the leading aircraft in the American formations. In three nights, eighty bombers whose range allowed them to make the return journey with an ample margin could break the enemy's grip on Dienbienphu and shatter Tuan Giao's depots.

Strangely enough, General Caldera seemed less sure of himself in the presence of General Lauzin. Was this due to forgetfulness regarding events ten years old? The former air commander of the Expeditionary Corps noted particularly the difficulties the raid presented for that massive fleet of aircraft, which must avoid any error of navigation and aim, and he got the impression that the raid would not take place, for the Americans wanted to check their aim by three transmitters, with which it was impossible to provide them. Until the end of the month, nights would be dark, and it was not until about May 10 that they could count on the moon; it would be easy to light up the battlefield and mark the targets, unless the Viets, getting wind of the raid, lit fires in the mountains, or if the storms that would start gathering toward the end of the day with the return of the warm, moist winds reduced visibility to zero. Here again, the Americans would not agree to the French Air Force marking their targets; they trusted only themselves.

Cogny wired his reply to Navarre's questions: how long did he think Dienbienphu could hold out, and was it worth launching "Operation Condor"? He considered that the entrenched camp could hold out for another two or three weeks, except in the event of a general attack. As for "Operation Condor," it was limited but useful, and ought to be launched without delay.

In the afternoon, Admiral Radford brought Mr. Winston Churchill a personal message from President Eisenhower. Had Mr. Churchill telephoned President Eisenhower to say, "This must be stopped"? In any case, it was too late; the chips had been down since morning, and Mr. Eden left for Geneva.

The Chief of Air Staff at Saigon, leaving for Manila with final instructions concerning "Operation Vulture," would make the journey in vain. To get into the air the squadron of B-29's, each loaded with eight tons of bombs intended to reduce Giap's divisions to pulp, would take seventy-two hours, but the signal for the launching of the operation would never be given. The British Prime Minister was already composing in his mind the noble speech of compassion which he would deliver to M. Laniel, while reminding him of the dark days of Tobruk. England did not want to spoil the prospects which had been opened up for her markets by her recognition, back in 1950, of the Chinese Communist regime.

That day, the whole Dienbienphu airstrip was lost. Three Viet regiments had fought for nearly a month to take three strong points, each held by about a hundred men. Langlais had made the enemy pay dearly for this victory.

⊣5⊢ The Twilight of the Gods

What is the use of an army of two hundred thousand men of which only one hundred thousand will really fight, while the other hundred thousand will hide in countless ways? Let us have only a hundred thousand, but men we can count on.

—Ardant du Picq

D.B.P., whose initials are known only to a few initiates, because they set off determined and came back on foot, D.B.P., on the threshold of this paper, ought to plunge me into sadness and harden my soul, which is a little bitter at the moment. But my soul is twisted and tied in knots; my parched heart is only airsick. . . .

—Captain Jacques Allaire
Béret Rouge, May, 1962

April 26, 1954

Suddenly, while in Hanoï the rain and the cold alternated with close, dull weather, at Dienbienphu summer arrived.

Navarre replied at considerable length to Cogny. He began: "If I understand you correctly . . ." and it is easy to imagine the gesture of irritation which he was unable to suppress when he read the fifth paragraph in Cogny's last dispatch. It is true that once again Cogny's meaning was shrouded in obscurity. To understand it, it was necessary to read the involved text several times in order to get at the hidden implications.

What exactly was the meaning of the "opposite view" which Cogny mentioned? What was the precise sense of the sentence, "I absolutely reject the simple hypothesis of the increased moral value of sacrifice," when the question put to him possessed a tragic clarity: "Are you in favor of reinforcing Dienbienphu?"

To this question, Cogny, who had just reached the age of fifty, replied as usual by neither "yes" nor "no." He hedged. He side-stepped. He made distractions. He was asked to give a straight answer, and he talked about the moral value of sacrifice. Yet there was nothing ambiguous about the situation. Several times a day, he heard Castries's voice, spoke to him, received radio messages from the entrenched camp. He knew how things stood. Nobody was more conversant with the situation than he. Should they go on dropping battalions or not? If he believed that all was lost and that the men who were still throwing themselves into the barbed-wire entanglements risked dying for nothing, if he was sure that they ought to stop this bloodletting and keep the remaining forces to defend the delta, nothing would have been simpler than to say so.

Thus one might suppose, though without being certain, that he was refusing to send fresh units to their death; but at the end of that paragraph he referred to the continuation of resistance and called for decisions to save Dienbienphu. Navarre, who was at least consistent even in error, had good reason to begin his reply with the words, "If I understand you correctly . . ."

Here, Cogny seems to have fallen into a trap in suggesting that all would be saved if his advice were taken. He knew that without the intervention of the B-29's, in which he still seemed to believe but which was becoming increasingly problematical, all was lost and that it was honor alone that had to be preserved. Who could have been taken in by those quibbles of his? Who could have failed to distinguish behind the complicated phrases a desire to detach himself from the fate of the vanquished? The profession of arms will always reject sophistries and ambiguities, because they are not of the same nature as its vocation; Navarre's had been broken against the reality of forces in which he had not believed; Cogny's would fare no better in the light of the questions put to him. That day, Navarre's thought had the rigor and the rectitude of a sword:

If I understand you correctly, you consider reinforcement of Dienbienphu justified only if continued resistance assures a favorable outcome. I do not share this point of view and consider that military honor as well as hope, even without the assurance of a favorable outcome, justifies additional sacrifice. Now a favorable outcome can be hoped for as a result of the Geneva Conference, which may produce either a cease-fire or American intervention in case of failure. Am therefore determined to prolong resistance of Dienbienphu as long as possible.

The rest of the long dispatch was of secondary importance, and one wonders why Navarre took so long to reach this sincere tone and this clear vision. It was to him that the garrison of Dienbienphu owed the greater part of its misfortunes, and in any case it was a bit late to think about safeguarding honor. But in the time of trial General Navarre suddenly raised himself to an exemplary dignity. Above all, he possessed the singular merit of accepting his responsibilities and imposing his will. If only he had been quicker to combine with that merit the clear-sightedness, common sense and determination which would have spared the Expeditionary Corps such a humiliating reverse, and Vietnam an independence which would not have been a repudiation of France!

This time, the chips were down. The Foreign Ministers of France, Great Britain, the United States and the U.S.S.R., the delegates of North Korea and the Associated States, and the Prime Minister of the Chinese Republic installed themselves in the depths of the Geneva parks in villas built for the holidays of heads of state or for comfortable, antiseptic and rarely illegitimate amours. It was no use for M. Laniel to send his ambassador in London to make a final plea to the noble cigar-smoker. It was too late for anybody to try to break the spell cast, in spite of the damp spring, by the swans on the banks of Lake Léman. Raised voices were frowned upon. The noise of the bombing and shelling at Dienbienphu did not reach Geneva even through the coded telegrams and the cables of the special correspondents of the international press. You had to be Sergeant Sammarco, Corporal Hoinant or Captain Capeyron, who, with the same naïveté which had led them to hope for an easy victory, now called themselves "poor bastards," deceived by the country they served and the army that employed them, to go on believing that Crèvecoeur's battalions were going to achieve a breakthrough or that the rains were going to bring the Molotova trucks to a halt.

Inside the French Government, a minister went to see M. Laniel.

"We are behaving contemptibly," he said. "We must show the garrison of Dienbienphu that we are with them. I ask your permission to leave for Hanoï and to jump by parachute in order to share Castries's fate."

"You're mad," replied the Prime Minister. "I have no desire for the Vietminh to take a member of the government prisoner."

This madman, who had a gift for the gestures of which so many reasonable men are so sparing, was a flying man who had remained young in heart despite his age. Rich in wealth and wit, loving women, luxury and danger like a lord of the Renaissance, laughing at the strong and ever ready to help the weak, hating hypocrisy and convention, he was one of the last gentlemen of the century, always prepared to perform sublime acts with a touch of humor. Bravado? Certainly not. He would have jumped at Dienbienphu as he had fought in Spain against the Condor Legion. He was General Édouard Corniglion-Molinier. Alas, what was he doing in that ship of state whose figurehead was an ox?

April 27, 1954

The night's storms had not broken up and had accumulated such a mass of clouds over the mountains and the basin that no plane could get through. Twenty Dakotas returned to base without dropping their loads. Colonel Lalande tried to get a little elbowroom on Isabelle; all his patrols were waylaid and returned with dead and wounded.

Cogny answered the Commander in Chief's restatement of the situation with a lengthy telegram clarifying his point of view. In his opinion, although military honor was dearer to him than anything else, the object to be achieved could not be simply the moral value of sacrifice; any reinforcements dropped on Dienbienphu at present would only weaken the vital position of the delta in the general collapse that would follow the fall of the entrenched camp. Cogny therefore thought that the negotiation of a cease-fire was preferable, and he asked for his previous dispatches to be brought to M. Dejean's notice.

Navarre launched "Operation Condor." It would take a week, if all went well, for Crèvecoeur to reach the crests overlooking the basin. Why had Navarre waited so long when Cogny had wired Castries on April 14 that the operation had been decided on, and when Sergeant Sammarco had not stopped looking toward the west ever since? Because he had placed greater reliance on American intervention, which he now knew would not take place.

In London, after Colonel de Brébisson had managed, without really convincing them, to get a few British military experts to reconsider their judgments, the French Ambassador, M. René Massigli, asked in the name of M. Laniel for an interview with Mr. Winston Churchill. To the ambassador's dismay, Mr. Winston Churchill cut short the conversation by declaring that he wanted to hear nothing more about the military side of the question.

April 28, 1954

At Geneva the conference on Indochina could not begin before the discussions on Korea, where hostilities had come to an end nine months earlier. Touchiness, questions of precedence and pricks to self-esteem would delay its opening until May 10. H.M. Bao Dai, who had returned two days before to his princely residence on the Côte d'Azur, added his personal obstruction in an attempt to save his mansion and his tiger hunts at Dalat, like his cut of the takings in the gambling houses and brothels at Cholon. The rest of his possessions had been safe for a long time. Having lost his game of poker, M. Bidault had failed to understand that an act of humility on his part would save the lives of a few hundred men who had not begrudged giving their blood for their country or what it represented. The equivalent of three annual classes of officers had been killed in two years in a war which the French Government knew it could not win, which it had refused to stop in time and which was going to swallow up the whole French Empire.

At Dienbienphu, storms were still bursting over the basin and the garrison was wading about in slimy mud. The fighters and bombers could give no support to the entrenched camp, and twenty-two Dakotas returned to base with their loads. Colonel Nicot warned the GOC Air Command that the strain on the air crews of his transport planes was so great that he was not sure of being able to drop the two parachute battalions and supply the units in "Operation Condor," which he considered a practical impossibility in any case. However, the Crèvecoeur column took the Muong Khoua outpost, captured in the February raid of the 308th Division. Ten Dakota crews were taken from the transport units to fly the Packets which the Flying Tigers refused to take up.

Eight men succeeded in landing on Isabelle during the night. If this weather continued, the garrison's resistance would have to be calculated not in weeks but in days.

Seven miles away, on their way to Surgical Unit No. 5, Professor Tung and his little escort sat down for a moment in a hamlet which had been given the napalm treatment and of which only a few burnt beans remained. All the inhabitants had disappeared. Only two little black pigs and a goat were wandering through the ruins. Professor Tung was exhausted; for two nights, without stopping, he had been operating on head wounds. He kept going only by repeating to himself what Uncle Ho had said to him recently: "We must win." Professor Tung knew that the Americans were threatening to intervene with heavy bombers. He looked at the wasteland around him, thought about the problems he had not solved, and yet said to himself, "It will be fine here, later on. . . ."

At the wheel of his GMC loaded with 105-mm. shells, driver Tha gritted his teeth. The mud came up over the hubs, and it was impossible to move without engaging the two live axles in ruts which the wheels refused to leave, as if they were deep rails. To repair tire covers torn by the sharp ridges of the road surface, a bolt would be inserted into the hole and a nut screwed on. The day before, on a hairpin bend in the Fa Dinh Pass which had just been attacked by planes, the truck in front had broken down, next to the crater of a delayed-action bomb which looked as if it would explode any moment, for the mountain was shaken every now and then by explosions. It was impossible to back up or to pass, and the Molotova in front skidded on the slope as soon as it tried to give the truck a tow. Finally, by pumping air through the tubes, the feed circuit of the carburetor had been restored. When the bomb exploded, the convoy had just moved away. A little grimace appeared on Tha's childlike face at the thought, but sweat trickled down his back.

In Paris, where the press was giving more and more space to the news from Dienbienphu, spring had arrived. The chestnut trees were in flower. The poplars raised their shafts of trembling foliage above the quays, and these pictures filled the minds of the men fighting in the mud for a country which seemed to have abandoned them. If the headlines or the articles in the papers that reached them proved to them that emotion and shock were gradually taking hold of public opinion, they could not forget that it was the nation's lack of interest that had brought them into this hole. In front of them, another nation was helping its army to victory.

That day, a declaration was published recognizing the complete independence and full sovereignty of Bao Dai's Vietnam. It was the work of the Vice Premier, who was responsible for Indochinese affairs, the lively little old man who for fifteen years had foreseen every disaster without being able to avoid any of them, and without ever ruling himself.

April 29, 1954

"The French will soon be unable to hold out any longer under the monsoon. When they are forced to leave their flooded trenches and casemates, victory will be ours." This extract from an order of the day which Giap had no desire to keep secret was widely broadcast by the official Vietminh radio. Where were the hopes which Navarre had placed in the approach of the rains—as if only the Viets could be adversely affected by them—which he had tried to bring on earlier than usual by artificial means? Did he blame the technicians once again for having failed in their task? The storms broke over the garrison of the entrenched camp as yet another calamity. Only a few planes succeeded, that day, in venturing into the turbulent mass of cumulo-nimbus clouds to drop sixty Legionnaires over Isabelle, in the darkness between the walls of the mountains.

Navarre and Cogny continued to send each other denunciatory telegrams. Navarre sourly observed to his subordinate that the offensives considered in order to cut the Vietminh's lines of communication had not been suggested by Cogny, but were outlined in his own orders, and that if they had not been undertaken, it was because Cogny himself had admitted they would serve no useful purpose. On his side, Cogny pointed out that the Commander in Chief had made no decision regarding the replacement of the American pilots of the Packets, when the entrenched camp, whose stocks of small arms were almost exhausted, had received no supplies for the last forty-eight hours.

That evening, Langlais had invited to dinner in the command post mess the air nurse whom the world press was beginning to call the angel of Dienbienphu. When she arrived, General de Castries said to her, "Geneviève, I've got something for you."

He took out of a drawer a cross of Chevalier of the Legion of Honor lent by a parachutist officer and pinned it on Mademoiselle de Galard's breast with a *Croix de guerre* which Langlais had found in the bottom of a canteen.

April 30, 1954

The mammoth correspondence between Navarre and Cogny continued to jam the mails and radio transmitters. How many secretaries were employed typing out the acidities and futile arguments which occupied the two men, separated by several hundred miles and an undying hatred?

Navarre held Cogny responsible for everything that went wrong. Cogny blamed Navarre for all past reverses. An exasperated Navarre would soon conclude his messages with a formula which put a stop to recriminations: "Received your dispatch to which there will be no reply. Position entirely unchanged." It was left to Cogny, too late, to juggle his resources so as to replenish the stocks of food and munitions; it was left to him to decide, too late, on the choice of transport planes and the methods to be used. Navarre remained above all that. One wonders whether the feelings they entertained for each other might not have gone, without their knowing it, as far as putting the rival's downfall before the garrison's safety, as in the case of Lord Lucan and Lord Cardigan, whose officers said of them, "Pity the man who gets caught between those two scissor blades."

May 2, 1954

The heat was so oppressive that more storms broke out and swamped the basin. Already, it was difficult to move about; mud invaded all the shelters and the hospital. With telluric impurities infecting their wounds, a fresh calamity overtook the wounded of both armies, whom the stretcher-bearers had difficulty carrying to the first-aid posts, but those on one side were plunged into utter misery while the joy of victory helped the others bear their pain and diminished their fear of death. As for Langlais and Bigeard, why shouldn't they have found a supreme hope at the bottom of that abyss? If the rains continued like this, the Viets would no longer be able to use their trenches. They would have to advance into the open, and then the French machine guns and artillery would mow them down. Victory would go to whichever of the two adversaries refused to give in.

The Commander in Chief saw the situation in a different light. His control over General de Castries was practically nonexistent, and in any case subject to intermediaries and difficult liaison. He knew now that the garrison was living its last hours and that its final hope lay in Geneva.

Coming to Hanoï without even announcing his arrival to Cogny, Navarre considered that it was impossible to go on fighting at Dienbienphu. Since the government did not want any surrender and Navarre refused to leave the garrison to die, he called for a study of "Operation Albatross," a variant of "Condor" and an offshoot of "Xenophon": an attempt to break out toward Laos, leaving the wounded with their medical officers.

During the night, which was comparatively clear, the 1st Battalion,

Colonial Paratroops, which had arrived from France a few days before, began raining down among the defenders.

"What the hell have they sent us here for?" its commander, Captain de Bazins, innocently asked. "Everybody knows it's all over. Don't expect too much from us; my men are tired."

"Shut your trap," said Bigeard.

"Tired?" exclaimed Langlais, "And what about us? We don't want you to give us any advice, but simply to fight beside us."

To the north, along the axis which the planes usually followed, on the first heights of what had previously been Anne-Marie, the Viets had installed a powerful searchlight which pinpointed the Dakotas with its brilliant ray and enabled the antiaircraft batteries to take better aim.

May 3, 1954

The power of illusion and example is remarkable. At Dienbienphu, which was in its death throes, nobody, except Castries, who spoke to Cogny every day, and his new chief of staff, Lieutenant Colonel de Séguins-Pazzis, could believe that the end was near. However horrible the reality might be, nobody among those who were fighting imagined that the Expeditionary Corps could ever drink the dregs of humiliation. There was not a single truck left in working order, and the last jeep of Bigeard and Langlais, riddled with holes, lay in a shell crater with its wheels in the air. In the hospital and the dressing stations, those who could were asked to return to the fight. The lame, the one-eyed, the one-armed stood up.

"No, not all of you," said Grauwin. "Not all of you."

"If our pals are going to die, we might as well die with them."

They went back into the mud of the strong points, to join men who no longer had the time to shave and whose eyes were red with lack of sleep. A brigade of shadows and of humble knights who had fallen from the sky with their squires and their soldiers, mercenaries faithful to the end because they felt that their fate was bound up with that of their masters, who had gradually become their friends in the great melancholy community which is the army. Among the volunteers of all ranks who had asked to jump over Dienbienphu when nothing forced them to, you would expect to find Legionnaires. But why Vietnamese and North Africans, whose affection for France and certain Frenchmen, stronger than all the propaganda to which they were subjected, had thrust them into the misery of a war which was not their war and might carry them to the very depths of suffering and destitution? Why orderlies, secretaries and soldiers who had come to the end of their tour of duty and were on the point of returning to Europe with a little nest egg and the prospect of strolls along river banks with pretty girls? Why did those innocent foot-sloggers throw themselves into the darkness where the blue shaft of the searchlight now roved in its search for them? Not from selfish motives, for love of glory or gain. They had no careers to further. They were following the example of young officers who could not go on living with the thought that their comrades were dying. Was it Heaven that looked after them? Grauwin, who attended the injured after every jump, had noted the infinitesimal number of accidents that army of volunteers suffered: two broken thighs, two broken legs, six sprains. No more than with professionals. Langlais, who embraced them when they presented themselves to him and pinned a parachutist's badge on their chests, had been right when he had opposed headquarters in Hanoï and argued against giving them any training.

None of those who decided to jump into the darkness through the door of a Dakota had any illusions about the fate awaiting him; all of them knew they were falling into the antechamber of death. Paris was fawning over the Russian ballet company which had just arrived to give a series of performances, and the papers reported that a great many cocktail parties were being given at Geneva. The men at Dienbienphu were rather surprised that anybody should be mad enough to join them, and if they had been capable of crying, it would have brought tears to their eyes, as it does to ours.

"Did you realize, in Hanoï, what it was like here?"

"Yes, we had some idea. Had to do it for the fellows."

It was different for professional soldiers who were dropped in groups, because it was their time. Captain de Bazins, who had gotten himself bawled out the day before by a bad-tempered Bigeard, and who had one thigh smashed by a shell that very morning, was a professional soldier. There are even more striking cases. General Navarre's aide-de-camp, Captain Pouget, another cavalryman, jumped with the 1st Battalion, Colonial Paratroops. When they saw his great carcass and his good-natured country-squire face, with his forehead half-covered by tousled hair, everybody burst out laughing. What, had he left his exalted post of lickspittle? Wasn't he advising his big chief any more? Did he by any chance imagine that he was going to find glory here instead of shit? Well drilled in the principles of the hierarchical system and the military virtues, and brought up to respect the traditions of Saint-Cyr and martial glory, this strapping young fellow was heavyhearted when he landed in the barbed-wire entanglements. From beneath his thick black eyebrows he looked at the disaster and said nothing. The injustice of this welcome did not surprise him, but he was too devoted to the man he had been serving not to take onto his own shoulders the cross which fate had just offered his chief. If he was here it was out of a sense of dignity and also because his chief could not come. Without knowing it, Navarre was taking up position in the mud of Éliane 4, in the person of his aide-de-camp Jean Pouget, who laughed a little bitterly under the sarcastic gibes of his comrades. Another cavalryman, like Castries, Séguins-Pazzis, Bigeard and Lieutenant de la Malène, he set out to show that cavalrymen, even when they are deplorably lacking in genius, know how to behave.

Everything was sacrificed to the supreme purpose of fighting men, which is to break bread with comrades whose fatigue and danger you share, and whom you attach to yourself by such bonds forever. If only the adversaries wading about in the yellow clay, their shoulders covered with waterproof sheets to protect them against the rain, had abandoned their ideologies! Castries told his wife on the radiotelephone, "Don't worry. I've been a prisoner of war before. I'll manage. . . ." Langlais and Bigeard said nothing. In Hanoï there were comrades who would go on sending telegrams to their families for them for a while, until . . .

As for Giap, he would go on to the end. The stupidity of our fathers and our fathers' fathers had turned him and the men of the Vietminh into rebels to begin with and Communists later, and they had so many injustices, so many prisons and so many dead to avenge that they would not stop—and we would do the same in their place, provided we had the blood of free men flowing through our veins. But Professor Tung and Grauwin—they, I feel sure, would have agreed between themselves to call a halt, to bury their dead, to care for their wounded, and to make the living understand that there is no more stupid way of settling scores than on a battlefield.

Like Grauwin, Tung was fighting against the gangrene which muddy shell splinters produced in wounds, against the swarms of yellow flies which sucked the corpses and sought out the living to lay their horrible eggs on them, against the humid heat of the storms, against the water that flooded all the dressing stations and dormitories. Grauwin appealed to God for help. But where was God, on that field of death from which pity had fled? In Mademoiselle de Galard's smile? In the Blessed Sacrament which the chaplains carried on them all the time, ready to give to the dying?

May 4, 1954

The last private telegram which Hanoï transmitted to Dienbienphu informed Captain Désiré of the birth of a daughter who bore the name of the strong point where he had been when his Thais had deserted: Anne-Marie.

At two in the morning, the attack was resumed on Huguette 4, which was swallowed up, while Éliane was harried all night. A counterattack launched at six o'clock and blocked by infantry fire was bogged down in the mud. At Isabelle, Colonel Lalande launched an attack toward the west. Two officers and Pastor Tissot were wounded. A B-26 was shot down over the Vietminh zone. Although most of the packages dropped by the transport planes were no longer picked up, supplies went on being parachuted to the entrenched camp in order to deceive the enemy as to the garrison's real capacity to continue the fight.

A long telegram from Cogny instructed Castries to study "Operation Albatross." Langlais summoned the superior officers of the camp to General de Castries's shelter: Lemeunier, Bigeard, Vadot and Séguins-Pazzis. Langlais had few illusions about the Crèvecoeur column under Godard's command, not because he did not feel a lively respect for his chief, but because his battalions were composed of North Africans, unsuited for jungle warfare, and of Laotians, incapable of facing up to the Vietminh. On the other hand, Langlais would have gladly put his trust in the mountain commandos, if any had existed in the retreat zone, and in Cogny's satellite. Colonel Trinquier, thanks to a fund in the form of bars of silver, had just recruited fifteen hundred Meos and was beginning to come upcountry with them from the Plain of Jarres toward Muong Son, about sixty miles south of Dienbienphu as the crow flies.

To try to break the grip of the enemy divisions, it was decided to form three columns—the paratroops with Langlais and Bigeard, the Legionnaires with Lemeunier and Vadot, Isabelle with Lalande—along three routes which were drawn by lot: the first by way of Ban Kéo Lom, which fell to Langlais, the second along the valley of the Nam Noua and the last along the Nam Ou. Albatross? The name of this bird of the austral seas meant nothing under the circumstances. At Dienbienphu this operation was called "Operation Bloodletting," to show how few illusions the garrison entertained; it would cost nine men out of every ten.

Near the command post, in a heap of papers which the mud was gradually covering up, Sergeant Sammarco found an old issue of *Caravelle*, which he looked through out of curiosity. Under the photographs of M. Pleven and H.M. Bao Dai, he read with bitter melancholy the statements made by the Minister for the Armed Forces on his arrival at Orly after his tour of inspection in Indochina. Sergeant Sammarco believed everything his leaders told him, but he smiled at these stereotyped phrases which encouraged an attitude of reasonable optimism toward the future. He did not not know that the art of ruling, like diplomacy, is the art of compromising and, often enough, of lying, but he was beginning to have his suspicions. Would the Crèvecoeur column arrive in time? Was the Geneva Conference going to open? "If they knew," Sammarco said to himself, "that none of the men wounded on Huguette two days before could be brought back to the field dressing station . . ." Yes, if the diplomats who had just unpacked their suitcases in the splendid houses in the Geneva suburbs could have seen that valley where the living no longer had the strength to bury the dead, the little caviar sandwiches would have stuck in their gullets and they would have made haste to reach an agreement.

On the neighboring heights, Professor Tung, weakened by dysentery, had just discovered that a quinacrine solution drove the flies away and killed the grubs. But the gangrene remained, as it did for Grauwin, his major preoccupation. With the rain pouring down outside, he opened wounds, dressed edemas produced by the mud and amputated limbs to save bodies. "Even in this deluge we'll stick it out," he was told by the men who were brought to him, and who, thinking that he was capable of performing miracles, asked him to send them back into battle. From time to time, even during the night, the sound of shelling shook the sky.

Professor Tung may have reflected that none of this fitted in with the idea most people have of great events. A victory is something you imagine in the glory of the morning sunshine. This victory in the rain, with a stomach shot to hell, was not quite what he had expected. He came close to thinking, like Grauwin, that the victories which men win over other men are just so many defeats unless some common enemy is destroyed. If, one day, the two sides succeeded in going beyond their respective humiliations, Dienbienphu might take on another dimension. But who would realize that? It would be a long time before a country like France, even if she was the mother of all revolutions, would admit that it was possible to rebel against what she claimed to be and no longer was.

The paratroops of the 1st Battalion, Colonial Paratroops, who had jumped a few hours before at Dienbienphu, advanced in single file through the passages or ran across the open ground to relieve the Legionnaires on Éliane 2. A shell killed the captain detailed to meet them. One platoon installed itself at the very spot where the Viets were digging a tunnel to destroy the position. All night, in the lulls between the bombardments, Sergeant Chabrier listened for the small comforting noise of the underground work; every silence put him on his guard; every resumption of the sound of pickaxes reassured him. When dawn broke, Sergeant Chabrier wrote these words in his notebook: "I was glad to hear the sound of digging and to see the daylight. . . ."

May 5, 1954

It had rained all night.

The Pouget company relieved the Edmé company to which Sergeant Chabrier belonged. Moving away for a moment, Sergeant Chabrier heard the obsessive sound of the pickaxes near the carcass of the tank "Bazeilles," whose machine gun was still intact, and which I found again nine years later in a little corrugated-iron shed, on show at the very spot where it was moored, near the grave of the two soldiers who had blown it up on April 1. The weather had effaced its name, but you could still read the number of its registration plate—IC 94151—and that of its steel turret— C or G 76004. Captain Capeyron had seen it there, like all those who came onto Éliane 2, and the name "Bazeilles," which evoked the idea of a merciless battle of old, had made him think, "That's probably what lies in store for us."

From the command post of the 13th Demibrigade where he had gone, under a hail of shells, to get some batteries for his battalion's radio sets, Sergeant Kubiak brought back the news, which was spreading through the camp like wildfire, that Crèvecoeur was only thirty miles from Dienbienphu.

Rediscovering more warfare, the Viets were trying to blow up the underground passages which enabled the defenders of Éliane 2 to reach the crest without being exposed to shellfire. Working ceaselessly in small teams, with compasses to guide them, they were burrowing forward like moles. That day, Captain Pouget tried to reach the entrance to the sap, but his sortie was halted at the barbed-wire entanglements; the only man who succeeded in crossing them, Sergeant Clinel, was killed. The Viets destroyed the machine-gun positions with artillery fire and pounded them into the mud, and then tried to take them with a grenade attack. A few nights before, a member of a suicide squad, with a plastic bomb at his waist, had almost reached one of the blockhouses.

The aerial photographs taken the day before, in spite of the bad weather, showed that the last open space between the main position and Isabelle was cut up by three successive lines of trenches. For Professor Tung visiting the wounded on the mountain slopes fifty yards from his surgical block represented an almost insoluble problem, but the flies had fled in the face of the quinacrine solution. "Here iron and steel melt. Only men survive." Professor Tung remembered these words which he had read in an account of the Battle of Stalingrad and repeated them to himself all day long.

May 6, 1954

When "Operation Xenophon" had been under consideration, Cogny had described it as an undertaking subject to tremendous risks and requiring, if it was to succeed, large rescue forces and strong air support. How could the three little columns of "Operation Albatross" succeed in crossing trenches stuffed with automatic weapons, where the enemy had disposed his reserves in depth and prepared them to go into action in all directions. None of the officers Langlais had gathered together at ten o'clock would have entertained the slightest illusions on that score if they had not known that human nature was capable of miracles. That morning's miracle came from the sky: it was a fine day and the return of the planes was already something of a victory.

The chief of Military Intelligence reported on the enemy's losses, and Langlais told his team once again, "We must hang on. We must force a draw. On the other side they're just as exhausted as we are." Bigeard decided on the counterattacks which were to relieve the threatened strong points, and artillery officer Vaillant made a note of the support he was required to provide. There were two days' rations left, and the last company of the 1st Battalion, Colonial Paratroops, was due to jump from 2300 hours on. Just as the meeting was coming to an end, a dispatch from Hanoï announced that a general attack would probably be launched during the night, for the last round.

Captain Hervouët asked Grauwin to take the plaster off his two broken forearms so that he could take part in the final engagements in the turret of his tank.

As they were obliged to fly very low over the pocket handkerchief which remained for parachute drops, two Packets were hit by antiaircraft fire. The first managed to return to base; the other crashed and exploded seventy-five miles southeast of Dienbienphu, at Muong Het. Its pilot, one of the most famous of the Flying Tigers, Earl MacGodern, nicknamed MacGoon and "Earthquake," because of his voice and his bulk, had already had his plane riddled with bullets three times.

Langlais and Bigeard set off through the chaos to inspect the eastern defenses. The men they met were nothing but shadows racked by hunger, fatigue and wounds. Behind the automatic weapons there were men with one eye, one arm, one leg. A bottle of brandy which Langlais had received from Hanoï was passed around the men in the cave on Éliane 4 where Major Bréchignac had established his command post. The great reconciliation was sealed. The wolves of the same pack no longer bared their teeth when they saw one another. At Agincourt, too, the French knights had insulted one another and ridiculed one another's breastplates, courage and lance pennants. All petty disputes and rivalries gave way before the threatened danger. Joined indistinguishably in the same ordeal, paratroopers and Legionnaires, red, blue or green berets, fought without envying one another any more.

At 1500 hours, the order to attack that evening was given to the Vietminh regiments and aroused extraordinary enthusiasm. From the lines of the Expeditionary Corps the men being harangued by the political commissars could be seen through field glasses throwing their helmets into the air and dancing. They could almost be heard singing. Most of them were children between eighteen and twenty, like trooper Tran ngoc Duoï, a young man with a thin, laughing face who could scarcely read and write. Detailed to take Peak C2 (Éliane 4), which the Viets called "the Saddle" on account of its shape, his regiment was due to leave its positions at 1800 hours to occupy its starting lines fifteen minutes later; the mile or more separating the two positions would therefore have to be covered almost at a run by way of the main trench leading to Peak D3 (formerly Dominique 5).

Suddenly, toward the end of the afternoon, the Vietminh harrying fire was intensified. The last shelters and blockhouses which had stood up to the rains caved in. Hurriedly returning to their maps and radio sets,

Langlais and Bigeard waited for the attack. Their plans were soon made: Bréchignac was holding the last heights in the east with the remains of a few battalions and two companies of the 1st Battalion, Colonial Paratroops, Thomas the left bank, Tourret the centre, Guiraud, Clémençon and Coutant the west and the south, with Charnod of the Air Force. The artillery would intervene only to help the heights; the battalions' mortars would look after the rest. At 1730, a terrifying artillery barrage was laid down on the whole entrenched camp.

In Saigon, M. Maurice Dejean, returning from Hanoï where he had spent a couple of days, declared that the military situation was neither more nor less unfavorable than six months or a year before, and that the delta was well in hand. In Paris, headlines about the entrenched camp covered the front pages of the papers, but people questioned on the streets were still not quite sure where Dienbienphu was or what was happening there. It was not the nation that was fighting there, but a corps of professional soldiers. The weather had turned cold again. The whole of France was shivering in the rain and a large depression was approaching from the west.

The night of May 6-7, 1954

At Isabelle, all the 105-mm. guns but one had been destroyed. On Éliane, where a terrible storm of shells had just broken, Major Botella heard Langlais calling Bréchignac on the radio.

"Young Pierre calling Brèche, Young Pierre calling Brèche, who is that deluge meant for?"

"Brèche calling Young Pierre; it's for Éliane 2."

The shelling moved to Éliane 3, then to Éliane 4, while the guns on former Éliane 1 and Mont Fictif opened fire. Langlais sent three tanks still capable of movement over to the left bank, at the foot of the peaks.

At 1815, hard on the heels of their last salvo, the Viets, wearing gauze masks, hurled themselves against Éliane 2. Using radio communication between its companies and battalion command posts for the first time, the 98th Regiment was in position in front of the peaks of Éliane 4.

Botella replied with his mortars and his recoilless guns. The Viets got as far as his command post but were driven back by Vietnamese troops, who, when they had good officers and NCO's, fought as fiercely as their brothers on the other side, just as North Koreans and South Koreans had fought one another. One of their officers, Captain Phan van Phu, saw his company reduced to thirty men.

At 2100 hours, signals orderly Tran ngoc Duoï of the People's Army went into action with his unit. In the white light of the flares which had taken the place of the moon in its first quarter, he could make out the movements of the counterattacks. In spite of shell splinters in his head and right leg, he refused to allow himself to be evacuated, sheltered a wounded platoon commander and went on carrying out his orders with a limp. When a dynamiter was killed, he took his charge, placed it, lighted it and went back to his mission. The Viet troops were cut to pieces by the mortars, but the following waves covered them and went on.

On Éliane 2, which was held by two companies of the 1st Battalion, Parachute Chasseurs, under Captain Pouget, a Viet jumped in front of Sergeant Chabrier, pointed an automatic pistol at him and shouted, "Give yourself up. You're done for—" then fell back dead. At 2300 hours a great silence suddenly descended on the position, and Pouget said to himself, "Perhaps they're going to let us have a bit of peace?" But then, like the spray of a huge black wave breaking almost noiselessly against a jetty, the earth was hurled high into the air by the thousands of pounds of explosive in the Viet mine, and fell with a thunderous din on the roofs of the shelters and into the trenches. The crater which opened under the defenders' feet and buried them still exists. The vegetation has not returned to it, but the rains fill it in a little every season.

The shock troops, who had been waiting for the signal of the explosion to go into action, felt the earth rumble and hurled themselves screaming at the shattered position. Section Leader Dang phi Thuong, under the orders of the commander of No. 7 Platoon of the 3rd Company of the 98th Regiment, advanced rapidly through the hail of bullets from automatic weapons toward the smashed blockhouses, but found his way barred by the fire from Sergeant Chabrier's platoon, which mowed the attackers down and toppled them into the muddy crater which the mine had opened. "What a sight for sore eyes!" cried one of the machine gunners. But the weapons ended up by jamming, the stocks of ammunition by running out, and the swarm of Viets overran the position. The 12.7-mm. machine gun on the tank "Bazeilles" was the last to fall silent.

At midnight, the five Dakotas which were to drop the last company of reinforcements asked, in the interests of their safety, that no more flares be sent up. Langlais and Bigeard hesitated. Even if it was dark, how could the pilots make out the tiny dropping zone in the midst of all the fires of the battle? Wouldn't the Viets take advantage of the darkness to resume the attack? Near the door of the Dakota, the pockets of his battle dress stuffed with whisky for General de Castries and brandy for Langlais, and worried in case he should break his bottles when he landed, Captain Faussurier waited for the green lamp to light up. Finally Bigeard queried Lieutenant Le Page on the radio.

"The flares must come first," Le Page replied unhesitatingly.

Langlais ordered the planes to turn back, and the men of the 1st Battalion, Parachute Chasseurs, returned to Hanoï, sick at heart. In the shelter of the camp headquarters where Geneviève de Galard was sleeping, sheltered under a table, on a mattress of parachutes, Bigeard felt a certain comfort at the thought that the sacrifice of that company had been avoided; a hundred men could no longer alter the course of events. Calls for help were jamming the lines to the artillery and the radio links with the strong points. As for the enemy radio receivers, they resounded with shouts of victory.

With one of his radio operators killed and the other hit by a bullet in the stomach, Pouget had stopped answering calls from the main position. He had been given up for dead and no more calls had been sent out to him. At four in the morning, he operated his transmitter himself and got through to Major Vadot.

"I've reoccupied all of Éliane 2, but I've only thirty-five men left. If we're to hold out, you've got to send me the reinforcements you promised. Otherwise it'll all be over."

"Where do you expect me to find them?" Vadot answered calmly. "Be reasonable. You know the situation as well as I do. Not another man, not another shell, my friend. You're a para. You're there to get yourself killed."

On the wavelength of the Éliane command network the Viets played the record of the "Song of the Partisans," and now and then their waiting voices took up the refrain:

> Friend, can you hear the black flight of the crows
> In the plain? . . .

"The swine," muttered Pouget, "the swine."

At Éliane, Botella had fifty mortar shells left and a few cases of grenades. The loudspeakers of Bigeard's radio receivers vibrated: "Dédé calling Bruno, the ammunition's running out."

"Brèche calling Bruno, we're nearly finished."

On all the hills, the strong points changed hands several times within a few hours. The enemy hurled himself at any breach he made, then fell back in disorder. Dead and wounded dropped to the ground. On the west face, Claudine 5 was overrun, near a tank which could not fire any more.

Sitting out in the open near his radio set, Pouget watched the 120-mm. mortar shells pounding Éliane 4 where Botella was holding out. The ground was cracking open. Pouget saw some Viets running along the crest of Éliane 4, lit up by the flares dropped by the planes. Down below, Dienbienphu was burning and fireworks were spurting from the shell stores. Now and then a few stars appeared through the clouds which filled the darkness.

At 0410, before his eyes, along the whole front of Éliane 2, the Viets stood up without firing. Pouget heard them shouting: "Di di, di di! Forward, forward!"

The survivors of Éliane 2 had one machine-gun charger and one grenade left. Pouget ordered the sole remaining lieutenant and those men who could still walk to return to the main position, and, falling back from one hole to the next, found himself reunited with them at the foot of the peak, in a trench full of corpses which they piled up to protect themselves.

Another shrieking tidal wave surged from the ground and broke over the 5th Battalion, Vietnamese Paratroops, covering Captain Phu; but a handful of Legionnaires and paratroops counterattacked again, recaptured some lost trenches, pushed aside the dead and dying to place their machine guns in position, and brought their fire to bear on the shadows in the flat helmets. Officers who were not yet twenty became company commanders or died when, like Second Lieutenant Phung, they called for mortar fire to be directed on them. Of the 6th Battalion, Colonial Paratroops, twenty men remained alive around Major Thomas. Sergeants gathered survivors together and rushed into the attack. Who would be victor or vanquished when this night came to an end? To help the men hanging onto the last peaks, Langlais withdrew some platoons from battalions in the center and threw them into the action among the burning eastern peaks. Everywhere men stumbled over shattered bodies. In the light of the flares which the wind carried toward the mountains, faces ran with sweat and with thick black ink. On Éliane 2, where since four in the morning nobody had answered Bréchignac's calls, the groaning of the wounded filled the dawn. Behind the eastern crests, the sky was turning golden.

May 7, 1954

On Éliane 10, at the foot of the peaks, day was breaking. The enemy was advancing everywhere, searching the shelters. Besieged in a block-house, Lieutenant Le Page managed to escape with a couple of men. The miracle was that Éliane 4 was still alive, that Bréchignac and Botella were still in command, calling for help. But what help could they be given? Lemeunier went into Langlais's shelter; he had gathered together a few Legionnaires and was ready to fight his way to the west.

"Not to the west," said Langlais. "To Éliane 4 where they're still hold-ing out."

Langlais emerged from his shelter into the brutal light of summer. In the sky, Dakotas were dropping supplies. In all the trenches leading to the hospital, pitiful files of men trampled on corpses gradually being buried by the mud. Wounded men nobody could attend to any more were left where they lay. Turned loose by the Viets, who had told them, "Go back to your people and tell them we are coming," some battalion medi-cal officers got through to Grauwin with the half-naked cripples who had returned to the fight a few days before.

On the other side of the river and the shattered ammunition dump swarmed the hundreds of men who had taken refuge weeks before in holes in the river banks in order to avoid the fighting, and whom Langlais compared to the crabs on tropical coasts. Dregs of humanity, deserters— Langlais could not find words sufficiently contemptuous for them. He could have mown them down with machine-gun fire or crushed them with a few 105-mm. salvos, but he turned away in disgust. Like Bigeard now, he was beyond all that. Like Béatrice, Gabrielle, Anne-Marie, Huguette and Dominique, Éliane had a new lover. . . .

Under the bursts of automatic-pistol fire, Pouget had felt the corpses he was sheltering behind tremble. A grenade exploded near his helmet, stun-ning him. As in a nightmare, he heard a little nasal voice saying, "You are a prisoner of the Democratic People's Army of Vietnam. You are wounded. We shall take care of you. Can you walk?"

He looked up at his victor in the gauze mask.

"And my comrades?"

"We shall attend to them. Their wounds will be dressed. The medical orderlies are coming."

Pouget got laboriously to his feet. It was all over for him. He was stripped to the waist, with no weapons or marks of rank, hairy and haggard. Somebody helped him to walk. His radio operator leaned on his shoulder.

> Friend, can you hear the muffled cry of the country
> Being loaded with chains?

He was no longer strong enough even to hum the tune the Viets had been broadcasting all night. Defeated, he refused to resign himself. At the end of the suffering and humiliation that awaited him and were already escorting him, he knew that he was going to find the great explanation and salvation.

Suddenly the artillery in the east opened fire again and the shells started falling once more. Long, deep, whistling notes pierced the general din. Hope suddenly mingled with amazement. Captain Capeyron, Sergeant Sammarco, Corporal Hoinant and a great many others, surprised to see the first salvos fall between the positions, turned toward the west. Voices cried, "It's Crèvecoeur!" Faces revealed a joy which did not yet dare express itself freely, but which would burst forth a torrent ready to turn against the course of fate and carry everything with it. Yes, it must be the Crèvecoeur column, which the radiotelegraphers had been claiming to be in touch with for days and which they had said was approaching, which was swooping down from the mountains into the valley with an apocalyptic din. Men did not know whether to shriek or weep for joy. They were already hoisting themselves out of their holes when the range lengthened, reached the command posts and crushed the innocents getting ready to meet their saviors. They were expecting Crèvecoeur, but what they heard was the thunder of Stalin's organs.

Three men dressed in mud, haggard, their faces black with stubble and smoke, staggered up and collapsed on the ground. Bigeard bent over one of them and took his hand. Was he crying? It no longer mattered at this moment when everything had been surpassed, when the grandeur of the ordeal made them giddy, when words were no use except to those witnessing from afar the death agony of Dienbienphu. Bigeard, who had never been known to utter a cry of commiseration, simply said over and over again, "Poor Le Page . . ."

He was weeping for a whole body of knights massacred in vain because a general had flung his army into the enemy's trap, giving in to the bluster of those who had urged him to throw himself into the wolf's jaws. Among those who would be cited among the dead and the prisoners, how many names represented the flower of that army, sacrificed turn and turn about, for centuries past, for great causes and solemn idiocies! Bigeard had a vague suspicion that the disaster taking place had achieved nothing but a crucifixion, of which countless former high commissioners, secretaries of state or prime ministers were already washing their hands with affected delicacy. Obsessed by the idea of the coolie's pole on his shoulder, he could not yet imagine what was waiting for him. Who could tell? The diplomats were gathered together at Geneva; everything might be arranged at the last moment. He did not know that the men by whose fault battles are lost are not those whom they kill. Without suspecting it, it was himself that Bigeard discovered beneath the masks of clay and blood drying on his lieutenants' faces.

"Stop shelling. . . ." Bréchignac had just asked Bigeard to spare Éliane 4 a bombardment that would kill off the wounded when he received a report from Botella that any further resistance was impossible. Botella then called Bigeard.

"Dédé calling Bruno, Dédé calling Bruno . . ."

It was the same metallic voice which used to announce, "Objective reached." Bigeard pressed the transmitter switch.

"Bruno here."

"Dédé calling Bruno. It's all over. They're at the command post. Good-bye. Tell Young Pierre that we liked him."

A click. A curter voice: "I'm blowing up the radio. Hip hip hooray . . ."

It was nine o'clock. On the heights surrounding Éliane 4, in the rice fields in the ravines, swarmed a host of little armed men, dressed in coarse green cloth, with sandals cut out of tires on their feet, helmets of interlaced bamboo decorated with the ruby of a red star on their heads, and gauze masks over their faces, who came running out of their hiding places in the forests and mountains. They reached the crests of Éliane in a huge roar which was carried along in waves by gusts of wind as they arrived on the summits. Spreading out over the sides and ridges of the Élianes, they uttered shouts of triumph and raised their weapons in a victorious gesture at sight of the yellow curves of the river and the plowed fields of the entrenched camp. On the double crest of Éliane 4, they could be seen jumping over the ruined trenches, crossing the tangled barbed-wire defenses, and stepping over piles of corpses lying on top of one another in the macabre reconciliation of death, or stretched out on their backs, their arms open, their faces eaten by flies, their mouths still full of a last groan, men fallen from their crosses, nailed to the pulverized ground among the wretched wooden supports of the shelters, or swimming in the slimy mud.

In the face of this swarm of human insects sprung up from all sides, the artillery of the entrenched camp, nearly out of ammunition and gun crews, remained silent. It had three hundred 105-mm. shells left and ten 120-mm. Fighters dived out of the sky, dropped bombs, fired their machine guns and spread disorder for a moment, but the swarm gradually resumed its advance when the planes disappeared after the ten minutes at their disposal. Botella decided to stay at his command post, but ordered Second Lieutenant Makowiak to rejoin the main position with a few uninjured men and a few wounded who could still walk. Soon afterward, the Viets surrounded him and took him into their lines. Section Commander Dang phi Thuong, second-in-command of Platoon No. 7 of the 98th Regiment, returning the action to give Élaine the *coup de grâce*, saw him go by, surrounded by guards, bare-headed and balding, on his way to the first regrouping center where he would find Bréchignac and Pouget, mute with misery. At Opéra, Bizard was holding out and getting ready to launch a counterattack against the Élianes, but Langlais incorporated him into the defense system of the main position.

Capeyron, who was searching near Éliane 2 for some men from his company who had gone up there during the night, was hit by some grenade splinters which slashed his left wrist and groin like a razor.

At ten o'clock, from his office in the citadel at Hanoï, Cogny called Castries. The storms moving over the whole region crackled in the receivers. The conversation, which might be the last contact with the entrenched camp, was recorded in the radio room.

"Good morning, my friend," said Cogny. "What resources have you got left?"

Castries's voice was clear, slow, deliberate; a little shrill, as it always was on the telephone. Now and then, he searched for a word, corrected himself, repeated himself. Cogny punctuated his remarks with muffled words of acquiescence.

"The 6th Battalion, Colonial Paratroops, the 2nd Battalion, 1st Parachute Chasseurs, and what was left of the Algerian Rifles."

"Yes."

"In any case, there's nothing to be done but write the whole bunch off."

"Yes."

"Right . . . At the moment, that's what's left, but greatly reduced of course, because we took, we drew on everything there was on the western perimeter in an attempt to hold out in the east. . . ."

"Yes."

"What's left is about two companies from the two BEP's put together . . ."

"Yes."

". . . three companies of Moroccan Rifles, but which are no use at all, you realize, no use at all, which are completely demoralized . . ."

"Yes."

". . . two companies of the 8th Assault . . .

"Yes."

". . . three companies of BT2's, but that's only to be expected because it's always that way, it's the Moroccan Rifles and the BT2's that have the most men left because they don't fight."

"Of course."

"Right, and out of the 1st Battalion, out of the 1st Battalion, Foreign Infantry, there're about two companies left, and about two companies of the 1st Battalion, 13th Demibrigade. It's . . . they are companies of seventy or eighty men."

"Yes. I see."

"Well, there you are. . . . We're defending every foot of ground."

"Yes."

"We're defending every foot of ground, and I consider that the most we can do. . . ."

Static suddenly interrupted the transmission.

"Hello, hello," Cogny repeated.

"Hello, can you hear me, General?"

". . . that the most you can do?"

". . . is to halt the enemy on the Nam Youm. Right?"

"Yes."

"And even then we would have to hold the bank, because otherwise we wouldn't have any water."

"Yes, of course."

"Right, So, well, that's what I suggest we try, I'll try to bring that off, ah, I've just taken, I've just seen Langlais, we're in agreement about that. And then, damn it all, I'll try, I'll try, conditions permitting, to get as many men as possible out toward the south."

"Good. That'll be by night, I suppose?"

"What's that?"

"By night?"

"Yes, General, by night of course."

"Of course. Yes."

"And I . . . I need your permission to do that."

"All right, fellow."

"You give me permission?"

"I give you permission."

"Anyway, I'll hold out, I'll try to hold out here as long as possible, with what is left."

Castries paused for a while, then intimated that he had nothing more to say.

"General?"

"Yes, all right."

"That's it. . . ."

"From the ammunition point of view, have you . . . is there anything to be recovered?" Cogny asked very quickly.

"Ammunition. That's more serious, we haven't any."

"There isn't anything that . . ."

"We don't have any, you see. There are still a few 105-mm. shells, but . . ."

A sentence in the transcript is undecipherable. Castries may have referred to 155-mm. shells, for all those guns were unserviceable.

". . . they aren't any use here."

"Yes."

". . . for the moment. And as for the 120-mm., the 120-mm. shells . . ."

"Yes."

"I still have, I must still have, between 100 and 150."

"Yes."

"Which are all over the place, you see."

"Yes, of course." Cogny repeated.

"Which are all over the place. We can't . . . it's practically impossible to collect them. Obviously the more you send, the better, eh?"

"Yes."

"So we'll hold out, we'll hold out as long as possible."

"I think the best thing," said Cogny, talking fast, "would be for the Air Force to put in a big effort today to bring the Viets to a halt."

"Yes, General. The Air Force must keep up its support, eh? Nonstop, nonstop. Yes, and about the Viets, I'll put you in the picture as to how they stand."

"Yes."

"In the east the Viets have thrown in everything they've still got."

"Yes."

"Including two regiments of the 308th Division."

"Really? Yes."

"You see? On the western perimeter at the moment there isn't anything, there can't be anything but the 36th Regiment."

"The 36th, yes, I think so too."

"Just the 36th Regiment, eh? The 102nd Regiment . . ."

Suddenly he was cut off.

"Hello, hello," Cogny repeated in a panting voice while the technicians tried to re-establish contact.

"Can you hear me?" Castries continued.

"The 102nd Regiment, you were saying?"

"Yes, General."

"The 102nd Regiment?"

"Just that they've been thrown in on the eastern perimeter . . ."

"Yes."

". . . the 102nd Regiment and the 88th Regiment."

"That's it."

"You see? Plus what . . . plus what remained of the 312th . . ."

"That's it. Yes."

". . . and now the 316th."

"Yes."

"You see?"

"They've thrown everything in on the eastern perimeter," said Cogny.

"But you see, as I foresaw, the 308th, as I think I've already mentioned, escapes me, you see, as usual."

"Yes, that's it. . . . Good, well, what about the withdrawal to the south?" asked Cogny. "How do you envisage it? Toward Isabelle or a scattered movement?"

"Well, General, in any case, in any case they'll have to pass south of Isabelle, won't they?"

"Yes, that's right."

"But I'll give orders, I'll give orders to Isabelle, too, to try, to try to pull out, if they can."

"Yes. Right. Well, keep me in the picture so that we can give you the maximum air support for that operation."

"Why, of course, General."

"There you are, my friend."

"And then, why, damn it all, I'll keep here, well, the units that don't want to go on it . . ."

"That's it, yes."

". . . the, how shall I put it, the wounded of course, but a lot of them are already in the enemy's hands, because there were some in the strong points, Éliane 4 and because . . . and Éliane 10."

"Yes, of course."

"You see? And I'll keep all that under my command."

"Yes, fellow."

"There you are."

"Good-bye, fellow."

"I may telephone you again before . . . before the end."

"There now, good-bye, Castries, old fellow."

"Good-bye, General."

"Good-bye, fellow."

Castries put down the receiver. Two hundred miles away, Cogny did not look at the officers standing silently around him. Sweat was running down his forehead. Hanoï lay crushed under the heat of the storm which refused to break.

At midday, Bigeard went to see General de Castries.

"It's all over," he told him. "If you agree, I'll get out of here at nightfall with my men. But we've got to make the Viets think that we're still holding out, and to do that the artillery, mortars and automatic weapons have got to keep on firing. Leave a good man here—Trancart, for instance."

"No," replied Castries. "I won't give that job to anybody. I'll stay, Bruno, old fellow. Don't worry; we'll keep on firing all night. At daybreak we'll cut our losses."

At 1300 hours, Captain Capeyron took up position on Junon with fifty-four Legionnaires. Sergeant Sammarco, at whose feet a 75-mm. shell had landed without exploding, said to a pal, "If we get out of this alive, we'll get blind drunk for a fortnight." In readiness for the sortie, Sergeant Kubiak emptied the flasks of rum in the "Pacific" ration crates into his water bottle. Langlais, Bigeard and their staff officers had some hot soup. Together they studied the situation and summoned the battalion commanders who were going to take part in "Operation Bloodletting." Tourret, Guiraud and Clémençon were unanimous in the opinion that it was impossible. However slim the chances of success, for they were completely cut off, they would have to make the attempt, but the Viets occupied the whole of the left bank, except for the bridge which they were trying to capture, and, like broken-down horses on the point of collapse, paratroopers and Legionnaires were at the end of their tether. One of the two boxers had been knocked out.

At 1530, accompanied by Bigeard, Lemeunier and Vadot, Langlais went to see General de Castries. He did not know that a telegram sent from Dienbienphu at 1400 hours had fixed the cessation of hostilities for seven the next morning. At Isabelle, where there were still two thousand shells left for a solitary 105-mm. gun, Colonel Lalande had permission to attempt a sortie. Castries was free to decide Langlais's fate and that of the remaining officers and men. He said to Bigeard, "You're going to pay dearly for all this, Bruno. You ought to try to make a break for it with a few men."

Who could possibly pull off that sortie? Perfectly calm and self-assured, Castries agreed that within five miles all of them would be overcome by exhaustion. Castries dismissed the officers and remained alone with Langlais. Exactly what they said to each other has been forgotten. Between the remarks exchanged with Bigeard, or by radio with Cogny, everything has become confused. Besides, what can they add to what was? Even monks end up, under the influence of communal life, hating one another.

These two men so different in character and methods no longer had any grounds for dispute. Who bore the responsibility for the fall of Dienbienphu? Neither of the two. Outstripped by events, Castries had failed to react at the right moment, but he had not wanted this post for which he was completely unsuited. He had not deceived anybody; others had been mistaken about him. He had been honest enough to warn Navarre, "If it's a second Na San that you want, pick somebody else. I don't feel cut out for that." And he had lacked the necessary humility to see that he ought to be replaced. Cynical and frivolous as he was, was it his fault also that he didn't like Langlais and Langlais didn't like him? Was Langlais, also to blame if, preoccupied with the patrols he had been ordered to organize every day, he had been unable to rehearse the counterattacks intended to recapture outposts which nobody expected to fall? To imagine that he should have demanded the necessary time and resources from Castries and Gaucher is to be wise after the event. It is necessary to go back in time, to breathe the atmosphere of optimism which reigned among the garrison, to hear the roar of Piroth's artillery when it fired its salvos into the mountains at the slightest alert. Who had had any premonition, at the time, of the disaster which had just occurred? As for his animosity toward Castries, that was only skin-deep. Langlais had made offensive remarks on several occasions about Castries's reluctance to leave his shelter, but if everybody paid homage to Langlais's spirit, who hadn't quarreled with him and suffered from his anger and bad temper?

"It's all over," said Castries. "We mustn't leave anything intact."

A brief access of emotion suddenly misted over Castries's eyes and froze Langlais's icy features. When Langlais saluted, Castries stepped forward with his hand outstretched, and Langlais, without saying a word, threw himself into his arms.

About 1600 hours, in the course of a radiotelephone conversation, Lieutenant Colonel de Séguins-Pazzis offered Colonel Lalande the choice between a pitched battle and an attempted sortie toward the south. Lalande was given no indication that the main position would not hold out until the following morning. He chose a sortie at nightfall, issued the orders prepared for that purpose, and sent out reconnaissance patrols toward the south, along both banks of the Nam Youm, to gauge the resistance the enemy was likely to offer. Since the direction of the sortie had been altered from the southwest to due south, there were no maps or guides available. Moreover, only one track seemed to be practicable, by way of Muong Nha, Ban Ta Mot and Ban Pha Nang, and Lalande had to change his plan.

On returning to his command post, Langlais gave orders for the destruction of all weapons, optical and signals equipment. Bigeard remained aloof from all this. The news spread at once that surrender was imminent. Sergeant Sammarco had the barrels of rifles and machine guns thrust into the ground for the last cartridges to be fired. With incendiary grenades they soldered the breeches of the 105-mm. guns or melted the mortars and the bazookas. The ammunition was thrown into the river. The engines of the tanks which were still in working order were raced without any oil. The chaplains gathered together their chalices and holy oils. Grauwin buried a few bottles of penicillin with markers to indicate their position.

The fighting began again and the Viet battalions gradually advanced toward the center, surrounding paratroop units which fell immediately. There was no longer any question of fighting. Already, on the left bank, white rags were being waved among the Moroccans and the river-bank population. Dressed in green, with motley scraps of parachute material in their helmets and their duck trousers rolled up to the knees, the Viets appeared from all sides, in a silent, overwhelming flood. The river was crossed at 1700 hours. Hearing his battalion commander utter an oath, Sergeant Kubiak turned toward Castries's command post over which a huge white flag was waving. It suddenly occurred to Captain Capeyron that he ought to burn the 3rd Company's flag. Bending over the fire which his Legionnaires had hurriedly lit, he had just seen the last letters of the word "Loyalty" embroidered on the silk eaten up by the flames when the Viets arrived. A Viet officer gave the order: "Hands up!"

Capeyron did not obey. Some Viets came up and kicked him in the buttocks. Some Legionnaires broke ranks to intervene. Pale with humiliation, Capeyron restrained them.

"Don't move. It's too late."

In all the trenches on Éliane, the Viets began piling up the corpses from both sides and covering them with earth. On the summit of Éliane 2, they erected a sort of bamboo cenotaph, thirty feet high, which they decorated with white silk parachutes.

Algerians and Moroccans who had remained in hiding for days and nights on end came out into the open, waving rags and, naturally choosing the word which in all the armies of the world has always meant the end of fighting and the fraternization of former enemies, shouted, "Comrades!"

Company Commander Tho, entrusted with the task of establishing a clearing station, found the prisoners unusually docile; most of them stretched themselves as if they had been lying down for a long time and did breathing exercises. They were sent to the rear in groups of ten or so, without guards, simply being shown the way to the first collecting center. The head of the surgical block at Him Lam, Dr. Nguyen duong Quang, a pupil of Professor Tung, had tents made of parachute material put up to shelter the wounded, and started for the hospital.

"Here they come." These were the words you heard everywhere. In his shelter, Langlais hurriedly burnt his letters, his private notebook, the photographs of the woman he loved and even his red beret. He kissed Geneviève de Galard and gave her a message for his mother while his staff officers destroyed the command archives and the typewriters. He put on his old bush hat, which made him look like a melancholy sailor in a sou'wester. Why had he burnt his red beret when Bigeard had kept his? It was because he was afraid the Viets would use it as a trophy; unconsciously, he also wanted to spare what he held dearest in the way of military uniform the humiliation of defeat. Born for action, he suddenly found himself deprived of everything and at a loss as to what to do, whereas Bigeard, without decorations or marks of rank, but with his red beret pulled down over his head, was already preparing his escape; he rolled a nylon map of the highlands round his ankle and thought of hiding in a hole, under a pile of parachutes. Why shouldn't he succeed in escaping?

Little by little, the camp started swarming with activity, while clouds of smoke rose into the air and the ground shook with the explosions of material being blown up. Demoralized by the savagery of the fighting and by the bombardment which had gone on without stopping since the evening of May 1, thousands of haggard men, who had been drinking the yellow river water out of buckets since the purification plant had been destroyed, regained hope of surviving. Spontaneously, as if they had been slaves all their lives, they formed up in columns, knotted little squares of white material to the ends of sticks, and allowed themselves to be driven toward the northeast along the sides of Route 41 beneath the contemptuous gaze of the Legionnaires and the paratroopers. These were not the pictures of the disaster which would be taken a few days later by cameramen rushed to the spot to reconstruct, with docile North Africans disguised as paratroopers, the scenes the Vietminh had dreamed of. How many were there, at that moment, who preferred captivity to insolence? Ten thousand? And are we entitled to think that Dienbienphu would never have fallen if they had fought like the other two thousand who were preparing to force a way out?

The guns destroyed, the sandbags ripped open, the shelters in ruins, the burned-out trucks lying in puddles of yellow water—everything showed that the defeat was complete. Dirty parachutes covered the hills and the valley, hung on the river banks, clung to the parapets of the bridge and the barbed-wire entanglements like torn spiders' webs. There could no longer be any doubt about it: all was lost. Some, like Sergeant Sammarco, said to themselves, "It wasn't worth the trouble of killing so many people." Most remained silent. Corporal Hoinant, who had never seen anybody but his chief, Major Guiraud, could not understand anything any more. He had been told that it was essential to hold out until the Geneva Conference was over, and now they had just given in. As for hoping, he had abandoned all hope since he had been deceived with the assurance, repeated every day, that Crèvecoeur was on the way.

"Come out with your hands up. . . ."

If the fortunes of war had gone the other way, Hoinant and Sammarco considered that the victory of the paratroops and the Legion would have been more harshly imposed on the defeated side. Neither of them had witnessed the humiliation inflicted on Captain Capeyron and, through him, on all the vanquished. They noted the correct behavior and lack of hatred of the Viets, who said to them, "The war is over." Perhaps. Commandos jumped down into the trenches, holding their noses because the smell was so atrocious, and ransacked the command posts in search of documents. Others, in token of their joy, threw grenades into the river, where they exploded with a muffled noise. Grauwin inspected the uniforms of his medical orderlies and distributed armlets on which red crosses had been painted with Mercurochrome.

"Whatever you do," Grauwin told his team, "don't leave my side."

In Hanoï, where he had heard Castries outline the situation to him once again, Cogny had the signal switched to the floor below, to General Bodet, whom Navarre had left on the spot to represent him and who wanted to bid Castries the official farewell, worthy of the Commander in Chief and his brilliant deputy.

Bastiani, Cogny's chief of staff, intervened.

"Wait a minute," he said to Cogny. "You didn't mention the question of the white flag."

Catapulted out of his seat by a terrible premonition, Cogny rushed downstairs and burst into Bodet's office just as Navarre's deputy, in his shrill little voice, was saying to Castries, "Good-bye, my friend. And all the very best. You've put up a good fight."

Cogny pushed him to one side and snatched the receiver from his hand. Navarre had never conceived the possibility that the white flag might be hoisted. In his directive of April 1, he had declared that under no circumstances was the idea of capitulation to be considered.

"Hello, hello, Castries? . . . Hello, Castries?"

"General?"

"Look, man, naturally you've got to call it quits. But one thing certain is that everything you've done so far is superb. You mustn't spoil it all now by hoisting the white flag. You're overwhelmed, but there must be no surrender, no white flag."

Did Castries suddenly realize the extent of his blunder? Probably nobody will ever know, and General de Castries and Séguins-Pazzis will take their secret to the grave. What is striking about the recording of this conversation—and the copies I have heard have been cut at precisely this point—is Castries's embarrassment after Cogny's injunction and the argument he uses to justify himself. To justify himself for what if not for having hoisted the white flag?

"Ah! Very good, General," Castries replied after a pause, in a heartbroken voice. "It was just that I wanted to protect the wounded."

"Yes, I know. Then protect them as best you can, letting your [. . .] act on their own [. . .]. What you've done is too fine to be spoilt like that. You understand, don't you?"

"Very good, General."

"Well, good-bye, fellow, see you soon."

There was no "*Vive la France!*" as the commander of the entrenched camp was reported saying. Radio operator Mélien, who was putting the signal through from an office near Castries's, concluded for the benefit of his opposite number in Hanoï, "The Viets are a few yards away. We're going to blow up the transmitter. So long, fellow."

The white flag which Sergeant Kubiak had seen flying over Castries's command post while Bigeard and Langlais were getting ready in their shelters to receive the Viets was hurriedly taken down.

Cogny informed Madame de Castries of the fall of Dienbienphu and asked her to keep the news secret. In Cogny's anteroom Mr. Hedberg, a journalist on the *Expressen*, was waiting.

There was the sound of feet running over the roof of the shelter. When Platoon Commander Chu ta Thé's squad reached the superstructure of Castries's command post at a gallop, did it unfold and wave the red flag with the gold star that day, or was the scene reconstructed later? On the French side, nobody knows. The only flag that Sergeant Kubiak saw flying over Castries's command post was the white one. He stated this in writing, and the official periodical of the Foreign Legion published his story in its issue of April, 1963, without anyone protesting.

When the Viets entered the command post and pushed aside the door curtain, Castries was waiting for them standing, unarmed, his sleeves rolled up. He had changed his shirt and trousers and, as usual, was wearing his medal ribbons. The parachutist Sergeant Passerat de Silans, who belonged to Langlais's signals section, maintains that at the sight of the submachine guns aimed at him Castries cried, "Don't shoot me." This doesn't sound like Castries, who may have said, in an attempt to change the squad's threatening attitude, "You damn fools, you aren't going to shoot, are you?"

Grauwin glanced toward the sap and caught sight of Castries, pale under his red forage cap, a cigarette between his lips, dazzled by the sunlight. He was promptly driven away in a jeep to be questioned by the Viet Military Intelligence. Did Grauwin also see, as he would subsequently write, Langlais, with his frozen, unseeing face, and Bigeard, his head bent under his beret, swept away in a crowd of prisoners? Langlais and Bigeard had come out together, without putting their hands up, but at a different time from Castries, whom they would not see again for ten days. Grauwin, his heart pounding, went down to the hospital. A Viet soldier, his legs covered with mud, his belt hung with grenades, appeared and gestured toward the sap.

"Outside!"

In the operating theater, where Lieutenant Gindrey of the medical service was bending over a torn body, men lay groaning on stretchers, waiting their turn. Followed by Geneviève de Galard and his medical orderlies, Grauwin came out onto the terreplein, where some wounded men, who had just been put down near some rotting corpses, watched him go by like salvation disappearing from sight.

In the vicinity of the command post, the Viets called for Langlais, who went toward them.

"That's me."

He was surrounded and Bigeard followed him, walking among his staff. The Viets also shouted, "Bigeard! . . . Where is Bigeard?"

His hands thrust deep into his pockets, Bigeard went on walking in the long column, anonymous and walled up in a silence from which he would not emerge for days, ready to seize the slightest opportunity to escape. They could look for the wolf Bigeard themselves. He carried nothing on him, not a single packet of cigarettes or tin of rations, while some prisoners were bent under suitcases stuffed with food. His faithful orderly, knowing what he was like, had taken a carton of Lucky Strikes for him from Castries's command post. No doubt Bigeard knew that he was down on the canvas, but he was already getting to his feet. The fight wasn't over. Nothing was over as long as life went on flowing through his veins. This business was not simply an affair between the West and the rebels, the Expeditionary Corps and the People's Army; it was a scrap between the Viets and himself. How had these little men, the youngest of whom looked like boys of fifteen and who had always avoided battle for fear of meeting their match, managed to win? How were fresh humiliations to be avoided in the future? What lessons were to be learned from this affair and from this army of ants which had fought on empty bellies but with their heads full of the ideas and the hope with which they had been crammed? These were the questions which haunted him. He, too, had heard the "Song of the Partisans" all night on the Viet wavelength. He felt sick at heart.

For the moment, shutting out everything around him, his shoulders hunched so as not to irritate anybody, he watched through half-closed eyes for any relaxation of the guards' supervision so he could escape into the mountains with a few companions, as Second Lieutenant Makowiak would do, reaching an outpost in Laos. From the generosity of the People's Army, Bigeard expected nothing. Defeated, he would suffer the lot of the defeated, without ever accepting it. "Poor bastards." He kept repeating this insult to punish himself and the simpletons who had thought they were bound to win because their camp was stuffed with artillery and heavy machine guns and received supplies every day by air from Hanoï. Perhaps he remembered that at Agincourt, too, the French had despised the enemy and had prepared for battle with the same arrogant self-assurance. But above all else, there must be no tears such as he had seen on the faces of some of his comrades. Victory over the ants of the totalitarian regimes was won in other ways; as for the victory parade, led by a band through the streets of a capital, which some officers had vaguely dreamed of, once the Viets had been laid out in the barbed-wire entanglements, Bigeard laughed at the idea. Here it was, the victory planned by the staffs of the Expeditionary Corps and approved by the government. He did not know that in a few weeks the prisoners would be gathered together and made to march all day long, with bowed heads, in columns of eight, a procession of shame escorted by little men armed with automatic pistols, in front of the cameras of the Communist world; but when he was asked to take part in the reconstruction of the capture of the command post, he would reply, "I'd rather die." And the Viets would not insist.

If the Viets were calling for Bigeard everywhere, it was because they wanted to see at close quarters the wolf finally in captivity with the sheep. How could they recognize him with nothing to distinguish him from the men plodding like a procession of caterpillars toward the northeastern heights?

Under a sky suddenly empty of planes, the little group of doctors crossed the bridge. The last packages of the seventy tons which twenty-eight Dakotas had dropped during the morning were spread out; 105-mm. shells, food supplies, small arms, pharmaceutical products, canned milk, everything henceforth belonged to the victor. On the other bank the medical team was stopped and Grauwin was ordered to return to care for the wounded. Dr. Nguyen duong Quang had just inspected the hospital, which he had found far better equipped than his own; he had noted that the Vietminh soldiers were treated on an equal footing with the French. Touched by Grauwin's sadness, he had some coffee brought to him.

At 1755 a dispatch from Cogny asked Colonel Lalande at Isabelle to tell him his plans for the coming night. Lalande was still unaware that the main position had fallen. He learned it only at 1830 from the decoding of a message and the sudden opening of a bombardment which blew up his ammunition dumps, cut his telephone wires and set fire to his dressing station. After which the Vietminh radio told him on his own wavelength, "It is useless to go on fighting. The rest of the garrison are prisoners. Give yourselves up."

About 2000 hours, guided by the Thais who had not yet dared to desert and wanted to disappear into the country, the 12th Company of the 3rd Foreign tried to escape along the right bank, following the curves of the river. Radio contact was poor and it was difficult to follow its progress. From the firing which broke out, it was possible to locate more or less accurately the points where it had met Viet resistance. A little later, the 11th Company set off between the track and the left bank. About 2100 hours, silence seemed to indicate that it had succeeded. One by one, in the total darkness, all the units followed, laboriously extricating themselves from the barbed-wire entanglements and the muddy trenches. The noise of fighting came from the south, where the 57th Regiment was barring the way with one battalion on each side of the Nam Youm. At 2300 hours, Captain Hien, who with a third battalion was blocking the junction of the Nam Youm and the Nam Noua, where Route 41 met the track from Laos, was ordered to return. An attack created disorder among the bulk of the units, cut them off, split them up and overwhelmed them. Soldiers of the People's Army and the Expeditionary Corps mingled with one another. Voices shouted, "Don't shoot. You will be well treated." Colonel Lalande then decided to try to hold out on the spot and ordered his units to return to Isabelle, where utter confusion reigned.

In Paris, it was nearly five o'clock. M. Joseph Laniel, the Prime Minister, mounted the tribune of the National Assembly to announce, in a voice which he tried to keep steady, the fall of Dienbienphu. All the deputies, except those on the Communist benches, rose to their feet. The stupor of defeat suddenly weighed upon the city, where the papers were publishing dispatches which had arrived out of order, mutilated by the Saigon censorship. A special edition of *France-Soir* carried a banner headline spread over eight columns: "DIENBIENPHU HAS FALLEN." *Le Monde* announced that the plane of Bao Dai, who had been accused for some days of delaying the evacuation of the wounded by his stay on the Côte d'Azur, had narrowly escaped an accident. The weather was fine that Friday afternoon, and the chestnut trees in the Bois de Boulogne and along the quays were in flower. The theaters and movie houses would be open that evening as usual.

About one o'clock in the morning of May 8, a small group of French-speaking Viets waving a white flag advanced toward the command post of Isabelle. "Let us pass," they told the soldiers who stopped them. "We want to see your commander, Colonel Lalande." Colonel Lalande agreed to see these envoys, who told him, "All further resistance is useless. Don't be stubborn." Lalande then gave orders for a cease-fire.

For Bigeard and Langlais the darkness was falling, whereas it seemed to Captain Hien as if a long night had come to an end. Everywhere the news of the victory spread like wildfire from village to village. Professor Tung, on his way toward the hospitals in the rear, had learned it at 2000 hours. Already people were shouting, "It's all right. We know." The entrenched camp looked like a huge flea market where the victors were dividing their booty of bars of soap, flashlights and canned foods. Lights were shining in the basin, where there was no longer any fear of air raids which would kill as many French as Viets. Yet planes continued to fly over the region, ready to drop flares or bombs on the poor stars in the valley.

General Navarre's former aide-de-camp was marching with ten thousand prisoners toward the Tonkin camps. The Viets had tied his hands behind his back because he had refused to answer their questions. Throughout the world, where Waterloo had created less of a sensation, the fall of Dienbienphu had caused utter amazement. It was one of the greatest defeats ever suffered by the West, heralding the collapse of the colonial empires and the end of a republic. The thunder of the event rumbles on.

Requiem for
the Battle of Dienbienphu

Shall we go send them dinners and fresh suits,
And give their fasting horses provender,
And after fight with them?

—SHAKESPEARE
Henry V, Act IV

It is the spirit which wins battles and will always win them, just as it has won them in all periods of the world's history. The spiritual and moral qualities of war have not changed since those days. Mechanical devices, precision weapons, all the thunderbolts invented by man and his sciences will never get the better of that thing, so despised at the moment, called the human spirit.

—BARBEY D'AUREVILLY

In war, a great disaster always indicates a great culprit.

—NAPOLEON

When it happened, and although I had prophesied it, the disaster of Dienbienphu appalled me. The injustice and the tragedy which had overtaken some of my comrades stirred me, and I felt a desire not to avenge them but to render them an honor which, for the time being, they thought they had lost.

Then, two years ago, for no apparent reason, the drama of Dienbienphu took me once again by the throat, and I spent a night following the

288

river which had bubbled its way across the battlefield in the midst of the fires. I remembered that ten months before, during the Algerian war, a similar sign had been given to me to which I had paid no attention. All the threats of a conflict between the army and the nation were rooted in that still aching wound which had to be reopened in order to extract the cause of the disease: that ambiguity about the nature of the causes to be defended, as well as about the morality of the means, which our military leaders had not denounced.

There were reasons why Dienbienphu was a victory for the less well equipped of the two armies. At the bottom of everything was faith or the lack of faith, the will of a people or its decline. In the words of a trivial but very common expression, money, women and power were the three ruling motives in Indochina at that time. Clever ones made a fortune; the soldiers killed or were killed. The corruption of conscience, the misuse of whatever French chivalry still remained, the cowardice of government leaders in the face of a truth which they refused to see because it would have called for virtues they did not practice—everything predisposed the country for one of the greatest abominations of the century.

To Be Ashamed or Not?

Why should we be ashamed to pronounce the name of Dienbienphu? If a general was defeated at Dienbienphu, it was doubtless because he was lacking in genius. Perhaps also because politicians don't have the same concept of honor as generals. Finally, it can be said of France that she showed the most complete indifference toward her army, and that this crime of omission is known as "failure to assist persons in danger." Punishable by law in the case of ordinary citizens, it leads, when the whole nation is guilty, to that resignation from which a people never recovers, and which it pays for, sooner or later, with its own death.

When, a century earlier, the disaster suffered by the Crimean Expeditionary Corps shook England, the British Government, like the French Government after Dienbienphu, would have been only too glad to hush up the affair if public opinion had not been moved by the articles of Sir William Howard Russell, the first war correspondent. The government was defeated, but no disciplinary action was taken against the two men responsible for the massacre of the Light Brigade or against the quartermaster general. A whitewashing commission made it possible for the accused to clear themselves. If it had not been for the indignation of

Florence Nightingale, who had devoted herself to the care of the wounded and threatened to publish her personal notes, the whole affair would have ended there. But Florence Nightingale, who became the idol of the public and the terror of Parliament, whipped up the anger of town and country, and the British people demanded information and sanctions. It did not obtain all it asked for. A few months later, the Indian Mutiny diverted attention to the dangers the Empire was facing in the Far East, just as the rebellion in Algeria made the French forget Dienbienphu.

If the British people is in the habit of wanting to know the causes of its defeats, why shouldn't the French people have the courage to look fearlessly at one of the biggest strategic blunders in its history?

RESPONSIBILITY OF THE FRENCH PEOPLE

If the men defeated at Dienbienphu were put on trial in the name of the French people, of what would they be accused? Of having misjudged a situation and an enemy. But who had appointed General Navarre to the post he occupied? Who had laid down the mission which his predecessors and he had to carry out, if not the successive governments of the Fourth Republic? Why had those governments placed no check on the generals? In reality, the conduct of the Dienbienphu enterprise was characterized as much by the incompetence of the High Command as by the monstrous indifference of a nation. Can it be said in that nation's defense that it thought the war was being fought in peacetime by mercenaries in order to preserve some rubber plantations, cotton fields, Christian communities or schools? In the long run, hundreds of thousands of men wearing French uniform lived out there the dull or exciting life of an army, contracted diseases, received wounds and in some cases were killed, simply to serve, in the last resort, the most stupid imperialism in the world, which disguised its refusal to lose its dividends and its markets as a crusade against Communism. Our ardent militarists ought to have brought to an end by negotiation this war which it was impossible to win. Nobody imagined that France's presidents and premiers would involve their country in an ordeal on this scale. The trouble was that once the ordeal became obvious, no one dared condemn it. Ministers claimed they were defending the West—M. Pleven with the self-righteousness of an honest man, M. Bidault by means of the atomic deflagration of "Operation Vulture." There were few villains, but rather fools or fanatics, weaklings or schemers, all united in that ignorance, peculiar to governing circles, of those whom they govern. What charge can be laid against them except that of having remained in office and having allowed the bill for their mistakes and their cowardice to be paid with the blood of others? As for the generals, nobody can doubt their devotion to their country's service. Blind, deaf and less intelligent than it is said to be the French people is the first culprit. It has never given anything which has not been snatched from it.

DEAD PASSIONS

My luggage had not been in my room overlooking the courtyard of the Hôtel Métropole in Hanoï more than ten minutes before I felt stifled. And yet, nine years after Dienbienphu, I found myself where I had wanted to be in order to obtain a better understanding of our defeat. However well prepared I was to take it, the shock of my return was greater than I had expected. You imagine yourself immune to dead passions, but the shadow of a face is enough to revive them in full force.

For me, the Hôtel Métropole was not this sinister waiting room where Soviet overseers dozed in armchairs beneath the gaze of an undernourished porter, but the meeting place of the flower of French chivalry. The same revolving door which was pushed by dull functionaries turned in those days for officers and their batmen, the Amazons who served in the army, journalists from all over the world and local adventurers. Stirred up by the fans on the ceiling, a din of mingled shouting and singing filled the foyer and overflowed into the restaurant where people called gaily to one another. You could recognize the grenades and kepis of the Foreign Legion, the shoulder straps of the Air Force, the gilt anchor of the naval officers from Haiphong, the bush uniform of the parachutists, the red tabs of the gunners, the five-pointed star of the Moroccans.

Now and then, in the midst of their court, you caught sight of de Lattre's former "marshals" who had come to spend an evening on the town before setting off again at dawn for their provinces: Vanuxem's disquieting face, Gilles's furrowed brow, Clément's sharp nose as he tossed down one whisky after another, Castries's cynical mouth, Blankaert's monocle. Outside, their windshields let down on their hoods, jeeps roared away or unloaded new arrivals in front of this luxury caravanserai whose noisy atmosphere, since even the chaplains were there, inevitably recalled that of the command posts of the Frankish Kingdom of Jerusalem. The smell of horses was replaced by that of exhausts, the swords and pikes by the submachine guns of the bodyguards. It was here that dealings in current securities were conducted, and here that Bigeard's aquiline profile under his red beret could be seen advancing like a new glory among the hollow-cheeked masks of the men preparing to return to Europe. On the upper floors, where visits were exchanged from room to room, the sound of showers and the whirring of fans mingled with the general hubbub. When, suddenly, the thunder of artillery shook the sky, nobody broke off his conversation; like the roar of the fighters flying over the city or the noise of the convoys whistling in the avenues, gunfire occasionally disturbed the peace of Hanoï. On the shores of the Little Lake, Legionnaires pressed against the violet tunics of the prostitutes.

I went out. Ten years later, in this country where the generations are driven along by a galloping birth rate, all that remained of a defeated regime was a few words of an inscription engraved in the curb of a pavement, at a crossroads: "STANDING FORBIDDEN." Policemen silently controlled the crossing of bicycles and pedestrians by means of traffic lights. The cafés of old had become propaganda rooms, the luxury shops sold saucepans, the glitter of the women's tunics had been transformed into the uniform ugliness of the national garment. Nobody could take me for anything but a Russian. I hailed a ricksha and got into it.

"The French Delegation."

The man looked at me dully, and called a crony, then some passers-by.

"France, France. Maison de France."

SHADES OF MY COMRADES, WHERE ARE YOU?

All I could think of doing was to repeat that name, as in the old days, and nobody understood me. A crowd gathered which a policeman dispersed with a slight gesture. To him too I said, "France." He did not seem to hear or even see me; he drove away a swarm of flies without so much as a glance at the living corpse which had attracted them. This horrible comparison did not occur to me immediately, but it forced itself upon me when, back at the necropolis of the hotel, nobody at the reception desk would condescend to guess what I meant.

I was lost among men who no longer understood me, buried under a mass of ruins and forgetfulness which might have been piled up by the centuries. Gone were my Viet-killing colonels, the military bands, the convoys of GMC's loaded with dust-grimy men, the professors, the street names, the taverns where the cool beer flowed freely, the beautiful Eurasians with the slit dresses; gone were the men who had died for H.M. Bao Dai and the portly high commissioners with the little linen hats. Shades of so many comrades eaten up by the prickly heat at times when storms refused to break and when ten soldiers a day died of heat, handsome, blue-eyed, conquering captains with few words and pure hearts, where were you? Where were they fighting, all the Legionnaires, Moroccans, Algerians and paratroopers whom the ambulances used to bring back to the sound of wailing sirens, their chests opened by mines, their bellies riddled by machine-gun bullets or grenades, pissing blood through all their veins, the very memory of whose memory had disappeared? As a French journalist, a *bao phap*, received on an equal footing with the Bulgars or the Serbo-Croats, I was condemned to a program of visits to cooperative farms and industrial workshops, to the menus of communal restaurants where Russians drank glass after glass of vodka and ate chicken with their fingers, because a battle had been lost two hundred miles away, around an administrative center whose name had set the teletypes of the whole world clattering.

All that remained of a half-century of French occupation was some straight avenues lined with trees and colonial villas, some museums, some schools, some stadiums and institutes, a government palace and a stucco cathedral. Hardly anybody remembered who had built them.

The Victors and the Vanquished

On my first evening in Hanoï, I felt buried alive among the dead of Dienbienphu and I did not sleep. Sometimes, dozing off, I thought I could hear the laughter of old, the happy din of men returning from a night on the town. I turned on my bedside lamp; I listened. The city was asleep, with every door closed, full of law-abiding men joylessly fathering children on women worn out by the struggle for food, all of them thin, with amoebas eating up their bowels and livers, haunted by the obsession of obeying the Party rules, and due to be summoned from their bunks before dawn by the whistles of the physical education monitors. They were not so poor as they had been, since the war no longer laid waste their fields, and they were exalted, though not far removed from poverty, by the pride of having defeated a well-fed Western army equipped with tanks and planes. As for the regime they had chosen, the only one that had been able to rid them of the injustice and the peculation which we had supported with the mandarins, what right had I, one of the vanquished, to condemn them? To understand the reasons for our defeat, to go beyond it and cast upon the actors in that tragedy the light which, at the very least, would reveal some of the truth, I had first of all to practice a virtue which was not given to our generals: humility.

THE KEYS OF HISTORY

There are no easy, final explanations for military defeats any more than there are for lovers' separations; it is necessary to uncover long successions of misunderstandings and disappointments which gradually lead a couple to hate each other or a general to make a mistake. True, it is difficult to write history when one is the contemporary of those who have made it, when one has been their comrade in arms and has eaten and drunk at the same table with them. But the historian who, to retrace the drama of Dienbienphu, has nothing but records half a century old will not be better equipped than I was, for documents do not yield their secrets any more easily than men. It will not be possible for him to register, like a photographic film or a magnetic tape, the pictures, expressions or voices of the actors in their parts. Did they themselves know, when I saw them, why they had been victorious or defeated? Some attributed the defeat to the stupidity or lack of experience of a commander in chief and his advisers, some to a system, others to political decisions beyond their understanding, and some, finally, to the courage and intelligence of their adversary.

Nothing is so simple or so absolute as that. Everything hangs together; every word, every attitude and every deed influences those that follow, overlapping and intermingling. After a certain moment, it was no longer possible to save Dienbienphu, whereas at an earlier date a sensible decision would have averted the disaster, or the relief of an inadequate commander might, in spite of all the mistakes that had been committed, still have led to victory.

Was Dienbienphu a battle lost in advance? I don't believe so. Even under the circumstances in which it was begun, a few intelligent men could have overcome distances, obstacles and adversity, and wrested victory from an enemy whose resources were not unlimited. These men existed; they were not used, or they were used too late, without the means to show what they were capable of. Even when fate seems to govern them, events do not lead men blindly when men refuse to submit to them. Several times I thought I had reached the heart of the problem. In fact, I needed a whole bunch of keys and a few picklocks to advance from one door to the next, from one dead end to another, retracing my steps only to lose my way again, and finally finding a secret chamber without being sure that it was the only one. One of these keys was my journey to Dienbienphu.

A historian sitting in a library or dipping into chests stuffed with archives can bring the Battle of Waterloo to life. Accounts of the fighting and descriptions of the setting and the characters exist. Day by day and hour by hour, he can fix the positions of the different armies on maps. Yet nothing can take the place of the impression which the historian, provided he has some imagination, obtains for himself from a confrontation with the battlefield. Familiarity with the layout of a landscape gradually diminishes the shock which the initial contact produced, just as one stops hearing the trains which shake the house where one lives. It seemed to me essential to go to Dienbienphu, but it is easier to find traces of a battle on the ground than in men's souls.

It was therefore not without some trepidation, after my first night in Hanoï, that I set off to the west in a little Soviet command car whose driver switched off the ignition to save gas every time a slope made it possible to drive without using the engine. An officer on General Vo nguyen Giap's staff accompanied me, as well as the interpreter.

The first evening, we stopped at the cooperative farm of Moc Chau. The beds had been prepared in a dormitory where the evening meal, which we shared with the farm managers, was served. I was examined with a curiosity mingled with uneasiness. We talked about the war. In 1952, I had, for the first time, declined the honor of bearing arms when I realized, after a few weeks' travel across Indochina, that we were serving an unjust cause or that, if we were determined to throw ourselves into a just crusade, we were fighting it without the ardor and disinterestedness which such a crusade required. Perhaps it was necessary to fight in Indochina to keep some strategic bases. But against a whole people which spurned us because we had robbed it of its land and its sovereignty? In that case, so much the worse for the strategic bases of the West! I could fight for the West only if I was not at the same time supporting the sordid combination of interests which soiled its cause, for fighting involves the risk of death and a man dies only for what he loves.

THE PEOPLE OF FAITH

Upset at seeing me eat so little, they asked me what I liked, and I could not tell them since they could not give it to me. Besides, I was not hungry for the foods I had left behind in Europe, but for what I could learn from their lips of that faith, capable of moving mountains, which we had contemptuously dismissed as fanaticism, in which our military leaders had refused to believe, and which had broken our battalions, our tanks and our planes. My companions were all simple folk who respected the army and conveyed to me the fear which our Expeditionary Corps had aroused in them. They all belonged to that common people, undoubtedly one of the most sorely tried and worthiest on earth, whose hordes we had met or passed ever since we had left the suburbs of Hanoï, to that endless, swarming world of small tradesmen and peasants, of men and women bowed under the yoke or bent over the plow. That morning, I had seen them cutting rice, one handful at a time, with sickles, in the fields where it had been flattened by storms, binding it in tiny sheaves so as not to lose the smallest grain, or already planting it out blade by blade, harrowing and rolling the mud behind buffaloes which sank into it up to the belly, their huge horns looking like crescent moons. What had those thin men and those women withered after their first child still to fear from me?

That harassed, hurried, agitated people resembling human ants, moving huge loads, overwhelmed by the climate, forced to draw its subsistence from its poor valleys and mountains, pounding every clod of earth with a hammer or irrigating its rice fields bucket by bucket, fertilizing every inch of ground even in the courtyards of its houses in order to grow vegetables on it, condemned to work to appease its hunger to the point of seeing no hope of rest except in death, was the same people that had been victorious at Dienbienphu, after traveling on foot, as it traveled now, for hundreds of miles, living on boiled rice and dried fish.

That evening, in the little town where we stopped, the engine of the generator had broken down and everything seemed to have gone back half a century. In the light of oil lamps we talked about what had separated us and about what could join us together. I was questioned about France and Europe, and I was asked why the heirs of the Revolution of 1789 should have opposed a movement inspired by the ideas it had launched.

We drank bitter tea and my companions scarcely dared to dip their lips in the cups I had poured a little brandy into. Who could possibly believe that they had been sent into battle drunk with spirits when the only drink which made them merry was the small beer in which they toasted one another on feast days? The only intoxication which gave them the courage to run shrieking toward machine guns and barbed-wire defenses was the idea of the freedom they were winning and the honor conferred upon them by their status as Uncle Ho's soldiers. In vain I would try to sleep, giving a groan now and then, and asking myself why I was so far from home, among foreigners who had defeated us, resting near a captain who was paid less than a French miner and who was also wondering about the reasons for my journey.

After another stop at Son La, where the peace of the night was shattered by the din and the explosions of an exercise in street fighting, we arrived, covered with dust and shaken by the bad roads, at Dienbienphu. I had recognized from afar the jagged outline of its mountains, and, thinking that the winding Route 41 overlooked the basin for some distance, I half-expected a heart-rending shock, followed by another night peopled with nightmares and full of the thunder of shells and shouting. In reality, the vegetation obscured the view, and the road, from which we startled a turtledove, slipped between the hills. From the wide space which abruptly followed the winding gorges we had been driving through for hours, I suddenly realized that I had arrived. These herds returning to the stable to the sound of their bells, this valley filled with the glory of light, these grassy peaks, these peasants who, their day's work done, were mingling with soldiers outside the straw huts of a village—this was the setting in which the West had suffered one of the greatest disasters in its history. The workings of the human mind are very strange. I felt nothing of what I had expected; an odd serenity, of which I was almost ashamed, came over me. I had reached my objective, and when, in the golden light of the setting sun, exactly nine years after the beginning of the operation, I looked down from the guest house at the setting where three of General Gilles's paratroops battalions had been dropped on both sides of the river, it seemed to me that all mystery had fled.

THE BATTLEFIELD

A high, thick fleece of umbelliferous bushes with white or blue flowers covered the ground of the peaks and the valley where the fiercest fighting had taken place. To reach the main defense positions, you had to follow paths from which you dared not stray without running the risk of blowing yourself up on a mine, but children ventured across the still visible traces of the trenches to bring home rolls of barbed wire, which are now used as fences.

Military buildings have taken over the site of the village, which has been partially rebuilt to the south on both sides of the road, now bearing the number 42. When a truck goes by, the dust it raises settles on the shops and straw houses along the roadway crowded with little black pigs, hens and ducks which you take care not to scare away. That is where people gather at dawn on Sunday morning for the market. The young

Thai women, who have set off the day before from all the neighboring hamlets, shelter their lovely faces and their hair under cone-shaped hats made of strips of plaited bamboo which have been decorated and varnished. Dressed in black satin skirts and colored blouses with embroidered fastenings, with their bunches of keys attached to their belts by silver chains, they help the matrons selling betel bark, leaves and branches, cottonseed, rattan buds, dried fish packed into little nets, fruit from their orchards, confectionery and pieces of cane sugar, cages of poultry and birds, pigs tied by their trotters and wickerwork. At this fair you can also find tobacco leaves, bunches of pods like slices of orange with star-shaped hearts, scraps of parachute material and silk parachute cords, soldiers' water bottles and jerry cans dating back to the battle.

Loaded with necklaces of old coins and with their ears torn by the weight of their earrings, the Xa women who live halfway up the slopes, or the Meo women who have come down from their mountain homes, barter pineapples and vegetables for peppers or seeds, while dark-skinned men, with wrinkled faces under their turbans, and chests barred by crossbelts, offer for sale monkeys caught in traps or pigs they have raised.

At nine o'clock the crowd disperses and sets off on the journey back to the hamlets. The next day, life begins again. The women pound the rice, the men go to the fields, and the children, sitting on the backs of the buffaloes, take the herds to graze. As soon as the teams of harvesters have finished their work, Chinese tractors with five plowshares from a state farm plow up the clay mingled with bones. In the rice fields, the traces of their tracks have replaced those of Captain Hervouët's tanks; half-buried under the vegetation, their shattered carcasses filled with earth rust in the vicinity of the command post, on one of the peaks of Éliane and among the corpses on Isabelle, where corn grows on the former gun emplacements.

On the hills where no fighting took place, thousands of acres of coffee bushes have been planted, and the jungle is being cleared along the Nam Noua. In the hamlets, 105-mm. and 75-mm. shell cases line the pavements, and water is boiled in old army mess tins. The grids from the airstrip are used as hearths in front of the houses. In the morning, at this season of the year, the clouds collide with the crests and the sky rests like a lid on the sides of the basin. The cocks can be heard crowing far away. "Never fight on a terrain which looks like a tortoise turned upside down. Never camp there for long." General Navarre did not know this principle from a classical Chinese military manual.

Already the signs of the battle are no longer as clear as they had been. The violence of the storms is gradually filling up the trench furrows; the vegetation is cicatrizing the wounds of the earth; suckers are springing from the stumps of shattered trees. Traces of the chaos on Béatrice and Éliane can still be seen: rents in the earth which have not closed and the scorches of explosions. You can pick up bits of metal, pieces of corrugated iron jagged by rust, shell and cartridge cases, just as you could at Verdun fifteen years after the First World War. The earth still seems red with the blood which had flowed, and a microscope would probably reveal that human organic remains are mingled in it, merged at last in the fraternity of enemies reconciled in death. Then you imagine the landscape as the battle had shaped it, a sinister plowed field, glistening with rain, bristling with aircraft carcasses and destroyed tanks, with propeller blades and barbed-wire entanglements poking out of the mud, strewn with packages still attached to the parachutes scattered about in the tens of thousands, with corpses nobody had time to bury and with haggard living men.

THE GRAVES

In this vast collection of debris, a single cemetery of five hundred Vietminh soldiers, dominated by a façade in the shape of a pagoda in front of which four national heroes are buried, has been laid out a little way from the road, at the foot of the peaks of Éliane, which still bear the marks of fire and steel. Five hundred bodies identified after the last of the fighting, and laid to rest among the flowering trees, on top of the ten thousand dead of the People's Army? What a sinister joke! There are two steles: one raised on Béatrice to the glory of Pham dinh Giot, who threw himself on the embrasure of a blockhouse and stopped it up with his chest to allow an assault wave to advance, and the other, a more imposing one, on Éliane 2, in front of a tree trunk riddled with shell splinters, which stubbornly continues to put forth branches whose white, large-petaled flowers open in the spring. It is a *cay hoa ban*, a symbol of chaste and innocent love, rooted in the fidelity of Tristan and Isolde, as it is understood in Vietnam.

That is all that is reserved for the dead of that vast slaughter. Of the former French cemeteries of Isabelle and Claudine, now covered by corn or bush, of the soldiers shoveled at random into trenches, pounded into the earth by shells, buried under water or found after the fall of the entrenched camp, nothing remains but a mausoleum on a scale befitting the victory or the disaster: the basin of Dienbienphu, molded of human flesh and rising to the crests which surround it with their ramparts. Everywhere I went, I asked where the graves of our soldiers were. Nobody answered me. For them, I had brought from France a rose which the journey had withered. I crushed it between my fingers near the winnowers who, with the gestures of holy dancers and great blows of their fans, were separating the straw from the grain of the new harvest, and I let its dust scatter like seed toward the sky, the fields and the memory of the two thousand soldiers, two colonels and one hundred other officers of the Expeditionary Corps who had become dust in that dust.

Toward the end of my stay, learning that the authorities were going to organize a reception in my honor on the eve of my departure, I asked my interpreter to tell the captain accompanying me that I considered it improper for me to attend such a reception because I thought it insulting to my country that the memory of its dead should have been obliterated. I added that, though I did not know what the reaction to this information would be in my country, where there was no lack of cemeteries of former enemies, I could not, as a former French officer, forgive this insult to my army. I also added that this would make no difference to any feelings I might have for the Vietnamese people and its army or to the events I was studying, but that the victor, in a battle such as that one had been, was under an obligation to respect the vanquished. Glory should perhaps go to one side, but paradise was not reserved for the victorious. There should be pity for all the victims of human folly. In order to be able to accept the invitation extended to me, I asked that at least a stone should be erected to the memory of the French soldiers who had died at Dienbienphu.

What would we have done with the Vietminh corpses if we had been the victors? That was the question the captain asked me immediately, and I refused to reply. I knew perfectly well. We would have shoveled them into a huge common grave, like dogs, and General de Castries would certainly never have thought of ordering a parade to pay them the honor they deserved. But in any case I could not refrain from protesting at this insult to my countrymen. Not only did I consider it regrettable, but I said that it was ignoble, for a victor honors himself in paying honor to the vanquished.

Two days later, the major in command of the garrison attended the showing of an extremely boring propaganda film with me. Afterward he indicated that he would like to speak to me. I joined him in the assembly room in the guest house where teacups placed upside down were always ready for some austere rite of welcome. The captain who acted as our guide at Dienbienphu had joined the one who had accompanied me from Hanoï. As it was nearly ten o'clock in the evening and the generator would soon be switched off for the night, an oil lamp had been lit on the long table in the middle of the room. This time we remained standing.

The major had a face like marble, sad and cold. Short and motionless, he spoke in a soft voice, weighing his words. The preliminary remarks, broken up by the translations, were lengthy and solemn, as the customs of the country require. The major began by recalling that I had said, in the course of a previous meeting, that if the soldiers of the Vietminh could bear a grudge against the living who had fought them, not only should they show no rancor against the dead, but on the contrary should show pity for them since the cause which had killed them was, in their eyes, unjust.

"It is not our fault," said the major, "if the bodies of the French soldiers have not been gathered together and honored. The prisoners told us that the cemeteries were mined so that if we tried to exhume them in order to count them we should fall victims to our curiosity. We therefore avoided looking for your cemeteries or even approaching them."

Absolutely motionless, making not the slightest gesture with his hands, gazing fixedly at the interpreter, who occasionally stumbled and stammered with emotion, the major spoke with impressive self-assurance, only glancing up at me for a split second while what he had said was being translated. Like the other officers, he understood French well enough to be able to correct the translator now and then, but found it difficult to speak.

"We showed respect for your dead as often as we could," the major continued, "without your doing the same on your side. I remember myself having given honorable burial to soldiers of your country. When we attacked an outpost and then withdrew, without managing to remove all our dead, we used to find their bodies booby-trapped when we came to get them the following night, or else gone without trace. We thought of your idea of raising a stone to the memory of the French soldiers, but what would that stone or cross mean if there was nobody beneath it? In any case, we shall try to satisfy you and show you that we nurse no rancor and no desire for vengeance."

With these words he fell silent. I had listened to him intently, standing head and shoulders above all four of them, impressed by the gravity of the conversation.

"I do not know what prisoners gave you information of that sort, but I am inclined to consider it false," I replied. "The officers who could have given you the most reliable information on that point were the doctors who remained on the spot for some time after the battle. I doubt whether they could have told you that, just as I doubt whether the French Command, which had other preoccupations at the time, could have carried out such a plan. In any case, I will look into it. Even if what you say is true, for that war was so horrible that nothing can be ruled out, I beg you to overcome any resentment you may have felt and to raise a memorial, however modest it may be, to the dead French soldiers. True, you are entitled to consider the cause they served a bad one, but you also have a duty to think of their mothers. For a mother, there are no good or bad causes, only dead sons. What I am asking you to do, I am asking on behalf of all the mothers in the world."

At my last word, the electric light, which had grown dimmer, went out, and our shadows started dancing in the poor, trembling light of the oil lamp. One of the captains bent down and turned up the wick. I then saw the pale face of the interpreter as he translated my last sentence, his eyes wide-open, as if he were filled with anguish.

The major raised his head and, scarcely opening his mouth, replied in a voice so low I could hardly hear it, "You ask us for that on behalf of all the mothers in the world. You ought to have thought sometimes of ours; they would have suffered less. But your suggestion will be considered; it will be passed on to General Giap, and I hope that the decision he takes will answer your wishes. That will prove that we know how to make allowances for the misfortunes which your government imposed on the French people and that we want nothing but your friendship."

I held out my hand to him and we parted. Followed by his captain, the major went down the staircase from the guest house to the road. Dim shadows, they plunged into the starry night, and for a long time I saw the light color of their calico uniforms moving toward the valley until they gradually vanished. The other captain and the interpreter also went away, leaving me the lamp, by whose light I took a few notes before getting under the mosquito net of my bed. It seemed to me that the earth must be weighing a little more lightly on the dead of Dienbienphu, as the sky did on me.

A few days later, I did not need to raise the matter with Giap. It was he who said to me first, "As regards the French dead of Dienbienphu, it shall be as you wish. Their bodies, if we find any, will be gathered together and a monument put up to commemorate them."

Dr. Grauwin, whom I saw again on my way through Phnom Penh, assured me that the booby-trapped cemeteries of the entrenched camp were just a legend. I believed him gladly. For the sake of Dienbienphu.

THE DEFEATED GENERAL

It is not on the peaks that you feel ashamed, but in the valley. On the metal handrail of the bridge, built by French engineers, a pilgrim had chalked two lines by the Vietnamese poet To Hun, who played a considerable part in his country's resistance.

> *Muong Thanh, Hong Cum, Him Lam,*
> *Hoa ban taï trang, vuon cam taï vang. . . .*

Muong Thanh, Hong Cum, Him Lam,* spring is breaking out again everywhere, the orange trees are loading themselves with flowers. . . .

There are kitchen gardens on the banks which much blood has fertilized, near the gray water with the greenish tints in which tens of thousands of men bathed and drank to quench the thirst aroused by the wind from Laos. A path leads from the river to the former site of the central command post, where the steel arches which supported the superstructure are going rusty. A board fastened to a pole bears this inscription, which I got the interpreter to translate for me: "Here, on May 7, 1954, the People's Army captured the defeated General de Castries and all his staff." Why was the ignominious term "defeated" added? If Castries's desk chair with its green arms streaked with damp is exhibited in Hanoï, his square iron table, one of the radios and the wide typewriter on which orders and rosters were typed have been left in this museum. Here more than anywhere else, you feel crushed by that host of men, small in stature but great in courage, who hoisted their guns onto the highest crests, shot down our planes and smashed our battalions.

Nearby are some tanks with their armor holed and their tracks half-embedded in the soil; the turrets, which still turn on their bearings, bear the deep scars of the shots which pierced them and burnt the steel as if it were flesh. On one of them you can still read a name: "Ettlingen." Huge wasps nest inside the mouths of their 75-mm. guns. They look like warships which have run aground on a beach covered with wreckage, scattered shells, broken trucks, aircraft propellers sticking out of the ground like swords and shattered guns in the midst of piles of shell cases.

A mute, solitary representative of the vanquished in the midst of my attentive victors, I inspected the whole battlefield like that. I took notes

---

* The Thai names for the sites of Dienbienphu, Isabelle and Béatrice.

sitting on the edge of the ditch, now almost entirely filled in, where Castries played bridge with his officers to while away the long waits between attacks. The thick vegetation which has covered the trenches, the barbed-wire entanglements and the mines prevented me from reaching the hospital where Grauwin and his surgeons opened bellies, reduced fractures and amputated legs for two months, and the morgue where hundreds of corpses waited for the grave dug by a bulldozer. For me, all this was desolation. For my companions, it was victory. They did not feel the sun which beat down upon my neck, and they breathed in delightedly the sugary smell of the harvest which made me feel sick.

Whose fault was this defeat?

WHOSE FAULT?

First of all, it was the fault of the quality of the men opposing us. Cruel ants, good pupils and clever imitators? Perhaps. There is nothing to distinguish their generals from their private soldiers except the star they wear on their collars. Their uniform is cut out of the same wretched material, they wear the same boots, their cork helmets are identical and their colonels go on foot like privates. They live on the rice they carry on them, on the tubers they pull out of the forest earth, on the fish they catch and on the water of the mountain streams. No beautiful secretaries, no prepackaged rations, no cars or fluttering pennants, no rams with ribbons tied to their horns led in front of military bands. But victory, damn it, victory! I presume to say to the leaders of the armies entrusted with the task of guarding the West: "If, one day, you have to defend yourselves against them, don't rely on your strategic principles and your missiles any more than Navarre did on his artillery. On the day the Chinese atom bombs, which you will never have seen placed in position, are more powerful and better aimed than yours, you will get a shock." As we did. Those thin warriors who shed tears over flowers before going to get themselves killed make my blood run cold.

Next, the fault lay with the mediocrity of our leaders, who hoped to repeat the unfinished experiment of Na San at twice the distance from their bases. With the frivolity which led them to take the enemy for a fool; with the jealousy that divided them; with the weakness of an army whose leaders are always chosen by seniority. With their self-satisfaction; their ignorance of the enemy; their overcomplacent opinion of their own troops and resources. The word for this is presumptuousness. O generals of the Republic who died on the field of battle at the age of twenty-nine!

O grotesque old men with worn cheeks who spat out your catarrh at dawn and rose laboriously from table after dinners with high commissioners!

To command in Indochina meant possessing luxurious villas, cars and women, entertaining and intriguing. War was accompanied by a circus of officers, tents, refrigerators, staffs and organizations designed to enable these staffs to move about, sit down, eat and sleep in comfort. How many divisional, brigade and regimental commanders knew how to suffer with their men, lead the same life they did, and move about on foot, as invisible, silent and formidable as the enemy who surrounded them? How many a battalion commander of the Foreign Legion got a coolie to follow him into action, carrying a cask of wine to warm his guts? In spite of the tons of bombs dropped on the Viet lines of communication, the road by which the People's Army received its munitions was never cut, and it was not Chinese aid which defeated General Navarre, but Peugeot bicycles, with loads of four or five hundred pounds, pushed along by men who never ate their fill and who slept on nylon sheets spread on the ground. General Navarre was not defeated by the enemy's resources, but by his intelligence and his will to win.

The naïveté of military leaders is frightening. How can Navarre have forgotten that it was he who decided, on December 3, 1953, to everyone's astonishment, to give battle at Dienbienphu? How can he attribute the disaster to an unanticipated move on the part of Giap, who launched his offensive eight months earlier than expected? What obliged Navarre to base his reasoning on the hypothesis that the enemy would never make any change in his methods and resources, and that Giap would not be impertinent enough to upset the plans of a general who had been through the Center for Advanced Military Studies? What forced him to install himself in that entrenched camp where even the latrines were not sheltered? What excuse can he have for continuing to think that he succeeded in preventing the enemy's divisions from pouring into Laos when a single one of them swept away the seals he had affixed on the road to Luang Prabang?

It is easy to understand why Navarre should not admit having committed errors of judgment. They are so flagrant that there is no need for him to make public confession of them; it was not the announcement of the Geneva Conference which made Giap decide to attack Dienbienphu, but the general mobilization order which he issued on December 6, 1953. To pretend that the consequences of a disaster would depend on the way

France took it is also far too easy. Navarre was the only person, along with Colonel Berteil, his strategic adviser, to remain completely blind. Nobody asked him to take risks which, in his own plan, he himself had undertaken to avoid. Nobody placed him under an obligation to defend Laos. Everybody warned him of the vulnerability of the Expeditionary Corps, whose unity was destroyed by the seventeen nationalities of the soldiers composing it. Whom could he possibly convince that a serious blow could still be dealt the Vietminh, when "Operation Atlante" had wasted his reserves and Dienbienphu was sinking under the terrified gaze of the West? Who could still place any trust in his optimism and send him the resources he asked for in order to intensify a war he had not known how to fight?

Of all this Navarre was unaware or pretended to be unaware. In his eyes, one battalion was as good as another. He played with the right ideas and the wrong pawns. Starting from reasonable principles, he did nothing but make mistakes. Wanting an open battle, he allowed himself to be shut in; refusing a general engagement with the bulk of the enemy's forces, he provoked just that, without realizing that he was staking the fate of the whole war on a single throw of the dice; a specialist in Intelligence work, he consistently doubted the information he possessed; confronted with his defeat, he denied its importance and attributed his setback to external causes and not to his own mistakes; finally, incapable of leading men, he misused those he had. But who picked him out of all the generals available? A Prime Minister and a President of the Republic. Who ever repudiated him? An Air Force colonel and his direct subordinate, Cogny. In government circles, nobody dared. Inside the Expeditionary Corps, nobody told the truth to anybody else. Navarre humiliated Cogny, Cogny took his revenge on Navarre; Castries lied to the press, M. Dejean to the ministers, and the ministers to the Assembly and their Prime Minister. Blood flowed and the French people remained silent.

At Agincourt there was the same presumptuous attitude; the English would be crushed if they dared to appear, and it was suggested that they should be sent turkeys to feed them and horses with which to fight. In the hour of truth, the corpses of the French cavalry, who had refused to enlist shopkeepers, were piled up six feet high in places. At least, on that occasion, the French Army had an excuse: its King was mad. In 1954, Navarre, questioning Grauwin on his return from captivity, suddenly exclaimed in irritation, "I have been betrayed by everybody!" Cogny, on the other hand, wept. So did Salan, who had engendered Dienbienphu.

Wipe the Slate Clean and Start Again

Who has not tried to wipe the slate clean? The officers who returned from captivity were hidden away, and their protests were stifled before they could alert public opinion. It was hinted that, having passed through the hands of the Viets, they had come home contaminated. They were indeed contaminated: they were ashamed of having survived. Some of them still ask themselves whether they were not responsible for the fall of Dienbienphu because they did not hold out one more night. Above all, they had seen how a war is won and what qualities they could demand in their leaders. Neither Bigeard nor Bréchignac was questioned by a commission of inquiry which accused nobody.

Lions led by asses? Let us say rather, to be respectful, lions led by other lions whose manes were moth-eaten and who felt the need to telephone Mother every day to reassure her. If many of the best battalion commanders, junior officers and sergeants who fought at Dienbienphu are now in prison for having risen at a given moment against the state, the reason is to be found in Dienbienphu, in the distrust they contracted there for the quality of their leaders and in the indifference of the nation which allowed them to fight for causes it did not support. One gesture, at least, might have comforted them; none was made. Navarre did not even fly over Dienbienphu where his former aide-de-camp was fighting in the mud.

It has been said that Navarre was greatly changed after the defeat. After the Crimean disaster, Lord Raglan, who was in command of the Expeditionary Corps, died of grief during the terrible winter which completed the ruin of his army. It has been hinted that Navarre thought of committing suicide. There have been rumors that some officers sent him a revolver in a case. He is still alive, convinced that in 1954 he suffered a tactical reverse and won a strategic success. If he had any doubts on the subject, Berteil, his evil spirit, would be there to dispel them. And Castries's first words, on his return from captivity, were to ask if his wife hadn't made too many faux pas. He, too, who had called the Viets cowards, did not die of grief; the legend had turned him into the hero of Dienbienphu, and if he had hoisted the white flag over his command post for a moment, that was probably "to protect the wounded."

In our day, provided the popular magazines turn it into glory, military shame can be swallowed without much trouble and doesn't prevent a fellow from riding every morning in the Bois; and when a man like the artillery commander of the entrenched camp commits suicide because his errors of judgment have brought about a disaster, his body is hidden away and his act of despair is attributed to a nervous breakdown. Colonel Piroth may have been a simple man, but he had a truer concept of military honor than Navarre and Castries. He knew that he was responsible. It is not duplicating machines that a military leader's decision sets in motion, but killing machines.

I said all this to myself at Dienbienphu last December, a few days before an amoebiasis turned me for some time into a limp rag. Every evening, just as the sun was disappearing while wreaths of blue smoke from fires lit in the rice fields rose toward the crests, an army of crows, which had set off at dawn in the opposite direction toward the cornfields of the state farm, crossed the basin. For a long time their cawing echoed among the hills close to the house where I was staying, and in the forests over which they circled before swooping down. Their rear guard sometimes settled after night had fallen. Did they look back nostalgically to the courage which had fattened them up, nine years earlier? Did they hope, as they flew over the valley, that the men below would start killing one another again? Their cawing and the beating of their wings seared the dusk and filled me with profound melancholy. And although I know that one must not confuse the cawing of crows with cries for justice, it seemed to me that something of the spirit of the dead lived again in those flocks of mournful birds.

A defeat can be swallowed, except by those whom it has destroyed, and it can be explained. A people is entitled, in any case, to demand an explanation of it. But to go so far as to pride oneself on it . . . To go so far as to give the name of Dienbienphu to a class at Saint-Cyr . . . Why not Agincourt, Waterloo or Sedan? Why not Dunkirk? Or else the name of Piroth? The sole glory of Dienbienphu belongs to the victors and to a few of the vanquished such as Bréchignac, Bigeard, Langlais, Botella, Tourret and a great many captains and lieutenants who had never known that the white flag, unseen by them, had been hoisted over their heads. But it is of General Navarre and M. Pleven that one thinks when one hears that sinister name. That is no reason for being proud.

The Seed of Eternity

To flee the Far East, one has merely to step aboard the Boeings of Air France. Without leaving the night which covers the globe, you cross the continent where men work just to avoid dying of hunger and to extract a few grains of rice from the earth. At dawn you reach Europe, where other men can drink water without spewing up their guts. It had been a fine idea I had had to write this book, which had taken me from North Vietnam to the capital of Laos, where, at the thought of dying in that kingdom of filth and prostitution, I struggled to hold out and return home to escape from the amoebas and from Dienbienphu which were eating me up. At Phnom Penh, where I recounted my journey in a weak, toneless voice, Grauwin stuffed me with medicines and opium pills and dragged me to the airport. I was haunted by the faces of the prisoners on their return from captivity, living skeletons with burning eyes, lost in their clothes. Without even having fired a single shot, without having experienced anything of their ordeals, I was coming home with a scrap of parachute material from "Operation Castor" and a small bag of yellow clay mixed with a little scrap iron.

Telling the truth is never easy—still less the truth in which you find yourself moving shovelfuls of shame and stupidity, courage and cowardice. In spite of the fact that when I started gathering material for this book I knew how the tragedy ended, I thought I was going to tell the story of a battle. I would have preferred a victory or an honorable defeat, but it was a disaster which unfolded before me, patiently marinated and stewed by the staffs of the Expeditionary Corps and served up with great effect.

To begin with, I had hoped at least to take some few liberties with the facts and the characters and, without deforming them, shape them to my liking, as I would have liked them to be or as I had imagined them at first. Respect for the truth and the fact that, even though everybody thinks they are dead, the principal characters are still alive, forced me to respect in every detail the story of the tragedy. I had to content myself with deeds that were performed and words that were spoken; sometimes more reliable testimonies obliged me to correct grandiose images. Navarre, for example, did not, as he had told me at first, fly over Dienbienphu during the night of May 6-7, 1954, or shed tears above the entrenched camp in its death agony; he left Hanoï for Saigon on May 5 at 11:15 and did not order his pilot to alter course. Yet it had a certain dignity, that picture of a general weeping for his dead warriors. On August 26, 1346, on the evening of the Battle of Crécy, Philip VI had at least uttered this grief-stricken appeal to the guards of the Château de Broye: "Open to the unfortunate King of France. . . ."

It is easy to understand why those who returned with honor from

Dienbienphu still bear the scars of failure, incompetence and defeat. They were deceived, like cuckolded husbands. They ought to have known that they were not loved, or at least guessed that the mercenaries under their command were no match for men who were fighting for their country, and that bitterness would be the fruit of their useless efforts.

Useless? I stopped believing in that word a long time ago. In the order of human qualities, everything goes to show that characters, like destinies, are founded on defeats as much as if not more than on victories. A man is only a sum of his attitudes, and success, even if it is posthumous, is always there in the end when he has managed to overcome obstacles.

Victory is intoxicating only if it avenges adversity. There are no useless sacrifices except in parliamentary speeches. The rest is suffering, blood and death, which carry their seed into eternity.

Dramatis Personae of the Battle of Dienbienphu

ANDRIEUX, LIEUTENANT COMMANDER JEAN DOMINIQUE. Born Sepetember 19, 1924, was in command of Flight 3F on the aircraft carrier *Arromanches*, and was shot down over Dienbienphu on March 31, 1954.

AURIOL, VINCENT. President of the Republic until January 16, 1954, at the age of 69. Would have spared the country and its army this ordeal if he could have done so. His Greek professor at Toulouse was General Navarre's father.

BERTEIL, COLONEL LOUIS. Unfortunately for General Navarre, was his operational second-in-command and an adviser to whom he listened far too readily. Muddle-headed and self-satisfied, he was accused in 1954 of having boasted of being the putative father of Dienbienphu. In staff circles the initials of Dienbienphu (DBP) signified *"Du Berteil Pur,"* or "Pure Berteil." On the retired list with the rank of brigadier general. Has written *De Clausewitz à la guerre froide.*

BIDAULT, GEORGES. 55 years old,* Foreign Minister. In 1945, after scamping a speech to the Constituent Assembly, he asked General de Gaulle in an aside, "I didn't talk too much nonsense, did I?" The reply was: "You didn't have time." During the battle of Dienbienphu, M. Bidault had plenty of time.

BIGEARD, LIEUTENANT COLONEL MARCEL MAURICE. Born February 14, 1916 at Toul, the son of a railway worker. Before 1939, he was just a minor clerk in a branch of the Société Générale de Toul. A sergeant major in a fortress regiment, he owed the discovery of his vocation to a major of the British Army who parachuted him into France in 1944, with the fictitious rank of major, as leader of the Ariège maquis.

Bigeard scarcely ever left Indochina after going there with Leclerc in October, 1945. In command of an isolated company, he lived in the Thai country, training battalions to fight and live like the enemy whose methods he analyzed and copied. Politeness is not his forte. Born to command, unable to pretend or to compromise, jealous of everything he possesses, he dislikes obeying orders, and as he lashes out if the orders he is given strike him as idiotic, his superiors find him troublesome; but, thrust into the midst of danger on his own, he always demands everything from himself and others.

* Asterisks throughout refer to ages at the time of Dienbienphu.

311

He is a winner. He has made Calonne's dictum his own: "If it's possible, it's done; if it's impossible, it will be done."

At 37, he had the innocence and the toughness of a fanatic. His gentleness hides a furious impatience; his masklike face can suddenly light up in anger and rage, his blue eyes take on the sombre brilliance of steel. Eight years of almost uninterrupted fighting have given him a mystical view of the army, of his comrades, of death. In a sort of flirtation with danger, he never carries any arms on him in combat, and constantly tells his men, with the familiar parachutist *tutoiement* which lacks only the word "Brother" to become religious: "Learn to look death in the face. You are born to die. You're going where men go to die." His men love him, many of his companions find him unbearable, the enemy fears him, and the government never knows how to use him.

BODET, GENERAL PIERRE. Born in 1902 at La Rochelle. A product of Saint-Cyr. In command of the Air Force in Indochina from 1947 to 1950. Chief of Planning and Operations in Central Europe in 1953, he accompanied General Navarre to the Far East as Deputy Commander in Chief. Kept a couple of monkeys in his official villa. Promoted to four-star rank on April 1, 1954, it was he who would say to General de Castries, at 1700 hours on the following May 7, at the moment Dienbienphu fell, "All the very best." On the retired list.

BORDIER, CAPTAIN. Leader of the Thai partisans, son-in-law of Governor Deo van Long and a famous pig breeder. Went off to obtain dental treatment two days before the expected battle. Not been seen since.

BOTELLA, MAJOR ANDRÉ. Born November 20, 1913 at Blida in Algeria. Parachutist. Promoted to rank of major on April 21, 1954 at Dienbienphu, where he was in command of the 5th Battalion, Vietnamese Paratroops, he was one of those who went on fighting as long as they had any strength and ammunition left. Sentenced after the *putsch* of 1961 to one year's imprisonment with suspended execution of sentence, and struck off the Army List.

BRÉCHIGNAC, MAJOR JEAN. Born September 29, 1914. A product of Saint-Cyr. In command of the 2nd Battalion, 1st Parachute Chasseurs, at Dienbienphu. One of the great figures of Indochina, Bigeard's emulator, and one of the most accomplished officers of this period. Sentenced after the *putsch* of 1961 to two years' imprisonment with suspended execution of sentence and struck off the Army List.

BROHON, COLONEL RAYMOND. Born September 7, 1911 at Blendecques in the Pas-de-Calais. A product of Saint-Cyr. Fought in the RAF, and went through the Center of Advanced Military Studies. Was chosen to act as the government's secret envoy to General Navarre in April, 1954, in connection with "Operation Vulture," probably because he was familiar with the Pentagon and because he possessed an exceptional quality: great civic courage equal to his physical courage. Slim, elegant, cold, slightly ironic, as cultivated as a professor of philosophy who is also the commander of a squadron of supersonic aircraft, capable of unbending but not of deviating from the strictest logic, he cut to ribbons, on his return from Hanoï, the illusions of the restricted war committee. Left the services at his own request, in 1960, at the age of 49, with the rank of general of the Air Force.

CABANIER, REAR ADMIRAL GEORGES-ÉTIENNE. Born November 21, 1906 at Grenade in the Haute-Garonne, former submarine commander during the war, assistant secretary general to the Ministry of National Defense, he acted as the government's secret envoy to General Navarre in November, 1953. Very much the sea dog and unswervingly loyal to the régime, he is also a born diplomat by reason of his courtesy. Now Naval Chief of Staff.

CASTELBAJAC, LIEUTENANT COMMANDER GÉRARD DE. Born September 15, 1923. In command of Flight 11F on the aircraft carrier *Arromanches* during the battle of Dienbienphu. One of the great figures of the Fleet Air Arm. Now a corvette commander.

CASTRIES, GENERAL CHRISTIAN MARIE FERDINAND DE LA CROIX DE. Born August 11, 1902 in Paris, did not reach the rank of captain until the age of 38. The slowness of this progress was not due simply to the cavalry. Castries, who had enlisted as a private without going through Saint-Cyr, had a stormy career. For want of horses, he fell back on planes; he held a civil pilot's licence. In 1940 he held out for three days against a German battalion reinforced by tanks and Stukas. Taken prisoner in 1941, he escaped after three attempts and in 1944 landed at Saint-Raphaël with the First Army; later on, Karlsruhe would be taken thanks to a bold maneuver which he directed under Navarre's orders. Placed on the retired list after Dienbienphu, he has put on weight and goes riding in the Bois every morning.

COGNY, MAJOR GENERAL RENÉ. Born April 25, 1904 at Saint-Valéry-en-Caux in the Seine-Maritime, a fishing port and seaside resort, he is, like Navarre, a Norman by birth. His grandfathers were agricultural laborers, his father a police sergeant and then a customs clerk at Yvetot. Young Cogny went to the *lycée* with a scholarship. Determined as he was, there was no stopping him; when he left the Military Academy, he was an artillery officer, held a diploma in political science and was a doctor of law. Captain Cogny of the Third Army, taken prisoner in the Vosges, escaped from Stalag XIIIA in 1941, was promoted to the rank of major in 1942, and entered the Resistance. Arrested in 1943, he spent six months in Fresnes, and was deported to Buchenwald and then to Dora, which he left in 1945. After working for the Minister of the Armed Forces, he was seconded to the staff of General de Lattre de Tassigny, who liked neither half-wits nor fools and took him with him to Indochina. His rise really began there. On the death of the marshal, whom he served and admired far beyond ordinary bounds, he took command of the 2nd Tonkin Infantry Division, at Haï Duong, at the height of the infiltration of the delta, where he spent his days hunting the Viets and his nights giving artillery support to his hard-pressed outposts. Installed in the midst of his batteries, he sometimes emerged to direct a large-scale operation, cleaning up a few hundred square miles of territory and pounding fortified villages to smithereens after evacuating the civilian population. His major preoccupation was holding the delta. Cogny had become the man of the rice fields and the master of the mobile groups when Navarre chose him to succeed General de Linarès as commander of the armed forces in Tonin. Now a lieutenant general and Commander in Chief in Central Africa.

CORNIGLION-MOLINIER, GENERAL ÉDOUARD. 55 years old,* Minister of State, former pilot, a man of wit and a *condottiere.* He was the only member of the government who asked permission to jump over Dienbienphu "to make some gesture." He would have made the jump if permission had been granted, out of a love of adventure and a sense of honor. Died in 1963.

COTY, RENÉ. Elected President of the Republic on December 23, 1953, at the age of 71, paid with his tears for the trust he placed in his ministers and generals. He took five years to collapse with the Fourth Republic after the fall of Dienbienphu. The President of the Fifth Republic made a speech over his grave.

DECHAUX, BRIGADIER JEAN. Born in 1903. A product of the Military Academy. In command of the Northern Tactical Air Group in Indochina which was entrusted with the task of supporting the Dienbienphu campaign. Tough with others. On the retired list.

DEJEAN, MAURICE. French Ambassador, appointed at the age of 54, thanks to M. Paul Reynaud, Commissioner General in Indochina. Gave dinners, tried to discover the Commander in Chief's plans and cabled bad news to his minister. After the disaster, sent General Salan a whisky bill which he considered it was not up to him to pay. Now French Ambassador in Moscow.

DONG, PHAM VAN. The leader of the Vietminh delegation at Geneva. Born In 1906, the son of a mandarin at the court at Hué, he started taking an interest in politics as a student. After a stay in Canton, he was arrested in 1930 and imprisoned at Poulo-Condor where he spent six years. An excellent public speaker, he became Minister of Finance in 1945, a delegate at the Fontainebleau Conference in 1946, then Secretary of State for the National Economy, and finally Vice President of the North Vietnam Government in 1949. As far back as 1950, he was named by the Indochinese Communist Party as Ho Chi Minh's successor. M. Pham van Dong's charm, intelligence and determination make him one of the strongest and most attractive personalities in Southeast Asia.

ELY, LIEUTENANT GENERAL PAUL HENRI ROMUALD. Born at Salonika December 17, 1897, Chief of Staff of the Armed Forces, President of the Committee of Chiefs of Staff, and, as a result, adviser to the Minister of the Armed Forces, M. René Pleven, he never dared to repudiate anybody. Promoted to general and given the task of liquidating the Indochinese War, he waits, in the shadow of flags and suits of armor, to be recalled to the high office which he cannot get over having lost.

FRIANG, BRIGITTE. Born in Paris, former deportee at Ravensbruck and Zwodau, in 1953 she was a journalist on the magazine *Indochine Sud-Est Asiatique.* Qualified as a parachutist in Indochina, she made six operational jumps. She was worshiped for her good nature and respected for the courage and nobility of her life.

GALARD-TERRAUBE, Geneviève de. A great deal has been written about her, through none of her doing. An air nurse, she belonged to the team in the northern zone, under the command of Yvonne Cozanet and had as her companions six other young women who shared the missions to Dienbienphu: Michèle Lesueur, Aimée Calvel, Christine de Lestrade, Paule Bernard, Brigitte de Kergolay and Élisabeth Gras.

On March 26, 1954, Geneviève de Galard was in the Dakota which had barely landed before it was forced to take off again under mortar fire without having taken the wounded on board. She therefore considered that that mission did not count and insisted on going on the flight the following day. Yvonne Cozanet accepted her claim. On the twenty-seventh she was unable to leave Dienbienphu and remained there to the end.

GAUCHER, Lieutenant Colonel Jules. Born September 13, 1905. A product of Saint-Cyr. In Indochina since 1940, he was in command of the Legion battalions in the main position at Dienbienphu, and was killed in his shelter on March 13, 1954.

GIAP, General Vo nguyen. Born September 1, 1910 at An Xa, in the province of Quang Binh in Central Annam. In 1934 he became a bachelor of Philosophy at Hanoï, where he took a degree in law on October 14, 1938.

Nothing seemed to mark him out as a future strategist. Endowed with a very strong character, he refused a scholarship to study for a doctorate in Paris, and devoted himself to social questions. An ardent revolutionary, he was watched by the police and served a term of imprisonment. Then he earned his living teaching history in a private school, married the daughter of Dan taï Maï, the dean of the faculty of letters, and contributed to the newspaper *Le Peuple*. It was then that he met Pham van Dong and left for China to go through a course of military training. His wife, who remained in Indochina, was arrested and sentenced to hard labor; she died in prison.

He is said to have told General Leclerc, "I have been to a military academy—that of the bush and the guerrilla war against the Japanese." Now Minister of Defense of North Vietnam.

GILLES, Brigadier Jean. Born October 14, 1904. A product of Saint-Cyr. Won his brigadier's stars at Na San. Led the paratroops who jumped at Dienbienphu on November 20 and 21, 1953. Died in 1961.

GRAUWIN, Major Paul. Was the incarnation of charity. Has written *I Was a Doctor at Dienbienphu*. (New York, The John Day Company, 1955) Having returned to civilian life, he continues to practice his art and his love for his fellow men at Phnom Penh in Cambodia.

GUIRAUD, Major Maurice. Born June 8, 1915. A product of Saint-Cyr. Was in command of the 1st Battalion, Foreign Paratroops (1st BEP). Retired with the rank of lieutenant colonel.

HINH, General Nguyen van. Born September 20, 1915 at Thang Tam in South Vietnam, was a lieutenant colonel in the French Air Force when his father, M. Nguyen van Tam, Bao Dai's Prime Minister, appointed him Chief of Staff of the Vietnamese Army. A Marauder pilot during the Second

World War, a mathematician and a very good technician, he then forgot his European training and covered himself with stars. The Emperor's favorite, devoted to his master, hunting tigers and the pleasures of life, knowing that blood and gold flow freely in war, and possessed of unbounded ambition, he played a subtle and risky political game. When Bao Dai fell from power, he fled to Cambodia to escape from M. Ngo dinh Diem. Nimbly rejoining the French services as a colonel, he quickly forgot this Asian episode and in 1963 donned the uniform of an Air Force brigadier.

HO CHI MINH. He has often changed his name. Born as Nguyen van Cung on May 10, 1890 at Kim Lien, in the province of Nghé An, he subsequently called himself Nguyen tat Than, Nguyen aï Quoc, and finally Ho Chi Minh. After a brief schooling at Hué College, the young man traveled the world plying every sort of trade, as steward, gardener, street cleaner, bottle washer. He worked in Marseille, New York, London and Paris. In this last city he belonged to societies for Socialist youth and contributed a few articles to *L'Humanité* and *Le Populaire*. In 1921 he wrote *Le Procès de la colonisation française*. In 1923 he was in Moscow, in 1925 at Canton, in 1930 at Hong Kong. Hunted by the French for his revolutionary activities and arrested by the English, he escaped only to be imprisoned a little later by the Chinese. Fifteen months in prison produced 112 poems. In 1944 he returned to Indochina and took to the bush. After the Japanese occupation came something like an alliance with the French, a stay in Paris as a distinguished visitor, and then the break—"the remorse of his life," he is said to have told Jacques Duclos.

Uncle Ho has remained a bachelor in order to serve his country better. David Schoenbrun quotes him as saying, "It was not in Moscow that I learned what revolution was, but in Paris, in the capital of Liberty, Equality and Fraternity." And Father Delissalde reports that, according to Ho Chi Long, "he reads the Bible once a year and regards Christ as the first Communist leader."

JACQUET, Marc. 40 years old,* Deputy for the Seine-et-Marne and Mayor of Barbizon, Secretary of State for relations with the Associated States. Smoked his pipe and played a walk-on part with a certain cunning. Lost his briefcase at the Karachi stop before Dienbienphu; the Fifth Republic rewarded him for this with a ministerial portfolio.

LANGLAIS, Colonel Pierre Charles Albert Marie. Born December 2, 1909 at Pontivy in Morbihan, a bad-tempered, Breton-speaking Breton. A product of Saint-Cyr and a former member of the Sahara Camel Corps, he set off for Indochina with the rank of major after the Second World War. In 1953 his third tour of duty ended with Dienbienphu and captivity. One of the most striking figures in the battle, Colonel Langlais displayed admirable courage and determination. Now a brigadier. Has written an account of his experiences at Dienbienphu.

LANIEL, Joseph. Prime Minister at the age of 64. An honest weaver and a man who stood loyally by his friends. Never understood anything about politics, Indochina and Dienbienphu and went bravely to the slaughterhouse. At Matignon he was known as "poor Joseph." François Mauriac has immortalized him with the nickname "Oxhead."

LAUZIN, MAJOR GENERAL HENRI EMMANUEL CHARLES. 51 years old,* took General Chassin's place in June, 1953 as commander of the Air Force in Indochina. During the Dienbienphu campaign he tried rather too gently to correct the errors Navarre was making in the use of the Air Force, authorized his crews to take exceptional risks, and offered Colonel de Castries a balloon to try to spot the enemy's batteries. On the retired list.

LEMEUNIER, LIEUTENANT COLONEL MAURICE. Born February 2, 1906. A product of Saint-Maixent and a traditional Legionnaire officer, he volunteered to take the place of Lieutenant Colonel Gaucher, killed on March 13, 1954, at the head of the 13th Demibrigade, and became one of the personalities of Dienbienphu.

LETOURNEAU, JEAN. Born September 18, 1907, Deputy for the Sarthe, had been the minister in charge of relations with the Associated States and French High Commissioner in Indochina for three years when General Navarre arrived. As High Commissioner he took orders from himself as minister. Sailed a skillfull course between the reefs. Survived.

LONG, HIS EXCELLENCY DEO VAN. Governor of the Thai country, descendant of the Black Flags, had become a powerful feudal ruler in his fief, always selling himself to the highest bidder and yielding to the strongest power. Representing the Vietnamese authorities in the Thai country and treated as a prince by the occupying authorities, he now lives in retirement in France.

NAVARRE, GENERAL HENRI. Born July 31, 1898, at Villefranche de Rouergue in Aveyron, to a mother related to the Murat family and the Lebaudy sugar firm, and a father who was a brilliant Greek scholar and Dean of the Faculty of Letters at Toulouse and had Vincent Auriol as a pupil.

Young Navarre prepared for Saint-Cyr and, because everyone went riding on his grandparents' estate, the cavalry. At the age of 18, in 1916, he enlisted in the infantry to go to Saint-Cyr, finished the war in the dragoons, learned German during the Occupation, followed a course of advanced German studies, went to the Middle East, entered the Staff College at the age of 28, and took part in the Riff campaign. Head of the German section on the Army Staff in 1939, head of General Weygand's Intelligence section in French Africa in 1940, then head of the Intelligence and counter-espionage service in Occupied France, secretary to General Koenig in 1945, in 1946 secretary general to the Commander in Chief in Germany where the French High Commissioner was René Mayer, he was a brigadier at the age of 47. In 1948 he was in command of the division at Constantine, where the same René Mayer was Deputy Mayor. In 1950 he returned to Germany to take command of the 5th Armored Division in which he had served in 1944 as colonel commanding the 3rd Moroccan Spahis, with Major de Castries under his orders. His troops had captured Karlsruhe 24 hours ahead of de Lattre, who had never forgiven him.

Navarre had scarcely been appointed before he set to work gathering information. He went to see General Valluy and asked him whom he would have taken with him if he had been chosen. "As my deputy," replied Valluy, "a flying man, General Bodet, and as my chief of staff, Gambiez." Navarre sent for them immediately, and as his aide-de-camp picked Captain Pouget, whom he already knew.

Many ministers were very favorably impressed by General Navarre's personality. He was judged to be very intelligent and clear-sighted. It was admitted that he had never undertaken to win the Indochinese War and that he had only counted on restoring the situation. Later on, the same ministers would say to him, "We were influenced by qualities which we like to find in civilians. In fact, those are qualities which it is always dangerous for military men to possess." Now in retirement in the brick industry.

NICOT, COLONEL JEAN LOUIS NOËL. Born in 1911 in Paris. A product of Saint-Cyr, an enthusiastic and accomplished flying man, with a brilliant war record and a Staff College certificate, he volunteered to serve in Indochina and took command of military air transport from August, 1953 to the end of the war. He had the singular courage to draw the Commander in Chief's attention to the risks involved in the choice of Dienbienphu and, while always demanding the utmost from himself and his crews, to protest on several occasions at the fantastic conditions under which they were employed. He is now in prison at Tulle for having helped General Challe fly to Algiers in a military aircraft.

PIROTH, COLONEL CHARLES. Born August 14, 1906, was in command of the artillery in the entrenched camp of Dienbienphu. Overwhelmed by the consequences of errors for which he recognized he was responsible, he committed suicide during the night of March 14-15, 1954, preferring death to defeat and dishonor.

PLEVEN, RENÉ. Minister of the Armed Forces, 52 years old,* went to visit Dienbienphu in February, 1954 with full powers and came back on March 1 after decorating General Navarre with the star of Grand Officer of the Legion of Honor. Has declared that he was unaware that certain generals disapproved of Dienbienphu and has washed his hands of the blood of the just.

REVOL, COLONEL JACQUES LOUIS. 44 years old,* nicknamed "Nimbus," General Navarre's cautious and cunning secretary. Now a brigadier.

REYNAUD, PAUL. Vice Premier in charge of Indochinese affairs at the age of 75. Convinced of the need to negotiate, he did not do so in order to avoid repudiating his friend Laniel. A proud gentleman with an incisive mind, more or less betrayed by M. Jacquet, he did not resign so as not to embarrass the government.

SALAN, LIEUTENANT GENERAL RAOUL. Born at Roquecourbe in Tarn June 10, 1899. A product of Saint-Cyr, in command of the French forces in Indochina after 1945. Badly treated by de Lattre, he obtained his revenge on succeeding him. Nicknamed "the Chinaman" on account of his cunning, his broad impassive face and a few habits contracted in the Far East, he begot the child of misfortune which Navarre conceived, but could have saved it in time. When Navarre fell, his first words on taking the plane to

Saigon with General Ely were to order champagne. Has several times contributed articles to *L'Express* signed with three stars. Has more than one trick up his sleeve and is not necessarily doomed to end his days where he is now: in prison at Tulle.

SEGUINS-PAZZIS, LIEUTENANT COLONEL HUBERT DE. Born December 16, 1913 at Orléans. A fine horseman and a brilliant and cultivated officer, he asked to be transferred to the Colonial Infantry in order to serve in Indochina, where he became General de Castries's last chief of staff. As he cannot lie and does not want to harm his fellow officers, he never talks about Dienbienphu. As a colonel, he took part in the Évian negotiations.

TOURRET, MAJOR PIERRE. Born December 30, 1919 in Paris. A product of Saint-Cyr and a disciple and companion of Bigeard's, he was in command of the 8th Battalion, Assault Paratroops, at Dienbienphu. With his delicate, scrupulous character, his warm heart and his indomitable spirit, Major Tourret was one of the pillars of the entrenched camp. Now a lieutenant colonel.

VADOT, MAJOR MICHEL. Born September 4, 1912 at Dijon. A product of Saint-Cyr, and chief of staff to Lieutenant Colonel Gaucher and then to Lieutenant Colonel Langlais, he was the traditional Legionnaire officer par excellence. He was a credit to the Legion and in the worst conditions displayed the most admirable *sang-froid* and good humor. Now a colonel and a Foreign Legion Inspector.

Bibliography

I. BOOKS

AINLEY, HENRY, *In Order to Die*, London, Burke, 1955.

ANDRÉ, VALÉRIE, *Ici, ventilateur*, Paris, Calmann-Lévy, 1954.

AMOUROUX, HENRI, *Croix sur l'Indochine*, Paris, Domat, 1955.

Année politique, L', 1953, Paris, P.U.F., 1954; *1954*, Paris, P.U.F., 1955.

ANONYMOUS, *The Battle of Vien Tiane*, Bangkok, Charlermnit Press, 1961.

——, *Dateline . . . Saigon, Our Quiet War in Indochina*, Washington, Mutual Security Agency, n.d.

——, *Les premiers jours de notre combat, récits de la résistance vietnamienne*, foreign language edition, Hanoï, 1958.

——, *Règlement d'infanterie du Viet Nam, Le bataillon et la compagnie d'infanterie dans l'attaque d'une position fortifiée*, Paris, Bureau de l'état-major des F.T.N.V., 1954.

——, *Ten Years of Fighting and Building of the Vietnamese People's Army*, Hanoï, 1955.

——, *The Vietnamese Working Class in the Long and Hard War of Resistance*, Hanoï, 1955.

ASSOCIATION D'ÉTUDES ET D'INFORMATIONS POLITIQUES INTERNATIONALES, *La trahison communiste. Pour comprendre les événements d'Indochine*, Paris, 1954.

BARALE, JEAN, *La IVe République et la guerre*, Aix-en-Provence, La Pensée universitaire, 1961.

BARJOT, ADMIRAL PIERRE, *Histoire de la guerre aéronavale*, Paris, Flammarion, 1961.

BAUER, HANS E., *Verkaufte Jahre*, Gütersloh, C. Bertelsmann Verlag, 1957.

BLEUZE, PIERRE, *Les leçons de Caïn*, Paris, P. de Méyère, 1961.

BODARD, MAG, *L'Indochine, c'est aussi comme ça*, Paris, Gallimard, 1954.

BONHEUR, GASTON, *Veillée d'armes sur un champ de bataille*, Paris, Les Imprimeries Réunies, 1955.

BONNET, COLONEL GABRIEL, *Les guerres insurrectionnelles et révolutionnaires de l'antiquité à nos jours*, Paris, Payot, 1958.

BORNERT, LUCIEN, *Les rescapés de l'enfer,* 2 vol., Paris, Nouvelles Presses Mondiales.

BOURDENS, HENRI, *Camionneur des nuées,* Paris, France-Empire, 1957.

BOYER DE LA TOUR, GÉNÉRAL PIERRE, *Le martyre de l'armée française—de l'Indochine à l'Algérie,* Paris, Les Presses du Mail, 1963.

BROSSARD, COMMANDANT MAURICE RAYMOND DE, *Les ailes de Neptune,* Paris, France-Empire, 1959.

BRUGE, ROGER, *Un sergent para,* Paris, France-Empire, 1959.

BRUZON, E.; CARTON, P.; and ROMER, A., *Le climat de l'Indochine, aperçu général et régime des vents,* Saigon, Imprimerie d'Extrême-Orient, Saigon, n.d.

BURCHETT, WILFRED G., *North of the 17th Parallel,* Hanoï, Le Fleuve Rouge, 1955.

BURDICK, EUGENE, and LEDERER, WILLIAM J., *The Ugly American,* New York, Norton, 1958.

BUTTINGER, JOSEPH, *The Smaller Dragon: A Political History of Viet Nam,* New York, F. A. Praeger, 1958.

CARTON, P., *Le climat de l'Indochine et les typhons de la mer de Chine,* Hanoï, Imprimerie d'Extrême-Orient, 1947.

CASTELBAJAC, BERTRAND DE, *Saut O.P.S.,* Paris, La Table Ronde, 1959.

CATROUX, GÉNÉRAL, *Deux actes du drame indochinois. Hanoï, Dien Bien Phu,* Paris, Plon, 1959.

CHASSIN, GÉNÉRAL L. M., *La conquête de la Chine par Mao Tsé Tung,* Paris, Payot, 1952.

———, *Aviation-Indochine,* Paris, Amiot-Dumont, 1954.

CHAUMONT-GUITRY, GUY DE, *Lettres d'Indochine,* Paris, Alsatia, 1951.

COEDES, GEORGES, *Les peuples de la péninsule indochinoise,* Paris, Firmin Didot, 1962.

COLE, ALLAN B., *Conflicts in Indochina and International Repercussions: A Documentary History 1945-1955,* New York, Cornell University Press, 1956.

COURTADE, PIERRE, *La rivière Noire,* Paris, Éditeurs Français Réunis, 1953.

DANNAU, JEAN-PIERRE, *Guerre morte,* Saigon, Société Asiatique d'Éditions, 1954.

———, *Indochine profonde,* Saigon, Société Asiatique d'Éditions, 1955.

DELISSALDE, R. FRANCIS, *J'étais aumônier en Indochine,* Préface de W. d'Ormesson, Nice, Chez l'auteur, Hôpital Pasteur, 1958.

DELMAS, CLAUDE, *La guerre révolutionnaire,* Paris, Que sais-je?—P.U.F., 1959.

DELPEY, ROGER, *Soldats de la boue: Vol. 1, La bataille de Cochinchine; Vol. 2, La bataille du Tonkin; Vol. 3, Glas et toscin; Vol. 4, Parias de la gloire; Vol. 5, S.O.S. Tonkin;* Givors, A. Martel, 1950-1961.

DEMARIAUX, JEAN-CLAUDE, *Les secrets des îles Poulo-Condor,* Paris, Peyronnet, 1956.

DESPUECH, JACQUES, *Le trafic des piastres,* Paris, Les Deux Rives, 1953.

——, *Missions inutiles à Saigon,* Paris, La Table Ronde, 1955.

DEVILLERS, PHILIPPE, *Histoire du Viet Nam, 1940-1952,* Paris, Le Seuil, 1952.

DEVILLERS, PHILIPPE, and LACOUTURE, JEAN, *La fin d'une guerre, Indochine 1954,* Paris, Le Seuil, 1960.

Dictionnaire diplomatique, Vol. VI, Paris, Académie Diplomatique Internationale, 1957.

DINFREVILLE, JACQUES, *L'opération Indochine,* Paris, Les Éditions Internationales, 1953.

EDEN, SIR ANTHONY, *Full Circle,* Boston, Houghton Mifflin, 1960.

EXCIDEUIL, HENRY D', *Rizières sanglantes,* Paris, Peyronnet, 1954.

Forces aériennes françaises, Special number: *Indochine,* Paris, 1953.

FALL, BERNARD B., *Le Viet Minh. La république démocratique du Viet Nam 1945-1960,* Paris, Armand Colin, 1960.

——, *Street Without Joy,* Harrisburg, Pa., Stackpole, 1963.

FELIXINE, LUCIEN, *L'Indochine livrée aux bourreaux,* Paris, Nouvelles Éditions Latines, 1959.

FRÉDÉRIC-DUPONT, *Comment la France a-t-elle perdu l'Indochine,* Paris, Imprimerie Chantenay, 1955.

——, *Mission de la France en Asie,* Paris, France-Empire, 1956.

FRIANG, BRIGITTE, *Les fleurs du ciel,* Paris, Robert Laffont, 1955.

GADEA, JOSÉ, *La Légion en avant,* Paris, Le Scorpion, 1961.

GAUBRY, JULIETTE, *Tricornes et bérets,* Paris, P. Horay, 1954.

GEOFFRE, FRANÇOIS DE, *Inconnu à bord,* Paris, Martel, 1954.

GIAP, GÉNÉRAL VONGUYEN, *L'armée populaire de libération du Viet Nam,* 1952.

——, *Dien Bien Phu,* Hanoï, foreign language edition, 1959.

——, *Guerre du peuple, armée du peuple,* Hanoï, 1961.

GOËLDIEUX, CLAUDE, *Quinze mois prisonnier chez les Viets 1950-1952,* Paris, Julliard, 1953.

GRAHAM, LIEUTENANT COLONEL ANDREW, *Interval in Indochina,* Preface by Sir Hubert Graves, London, St. Martin's Press, 1956.

GRAS, CHEF DE BATAILLON Y., *Deux revers du C.E.F. en Indochine—Cao Bang et Dien Bien Phu,* Paris, École supérieure de guerre, 1961.

GRAUWIN, MÉDECIN-COMMANDANT PAUL, *J'étais médecin à Dien Bien Phu,* Paris, France-Empire, 1956.

——, *Seulement médecin,* Paris, France-Empire, 1956.

GUILLAIN, ROBERT, *La fin des illusions. Notes d'Indochine, février-juillet 1954,* Paris, Centre d'Études de Politique Étrangère, 1954.

GUILLOT, MAURICE, *La grande occasion,* Paris, Nouvelles Éditions Debresse, 1959; reissued by Les Presses de la Cité, 1963, as *Les Juteux.*

GUILLMET, BERNARD, *Le temps en Indochine, à l'usage des navigateurs aériens,* Paris, Haut-Commissariat de France en Indochine, n.d.

HALLE, GÜNTER, *Légion étrangère: Tatsachenbericht nach Erlebnissen und Dokumenten von Rückkerhrern aus Viet-Nam*, East Berlin, Verlag Volk und Welt, 1952.

HAMMER, ELLEN J., *The Struggle for Indochina*, Preface by Rupert Emerson, Stanford, University Press, 1954.

HEYMARD, JEAN, *Vérité sur l'Indochine*, Paris, Nouvelles Éditions Debresse, 1962.

Ho CHI MINH, *Carnets de prison*, Paris, Seghers, 1963.

HORA, COMMANDANT CHARLES, *Mon tour du monde en 80 barouds*, Paris, La Pensée Moderne, 1962.

HOUGRON, JEAN, *La nuit indochinoise:* Vol. 1, *Tu récolteras la tempête;* Vol 2, *Rage blanche;* Vol. 3, *Soleil au ventre;* Vol. 4, *Mort en fraude;* Vol. 5, *Les Asiates;* Paris, Domat, 1950 and 1954.

HUARD, MÉDECIN GÉNÉRAL PIERRE ALPHONSE, *L'extrême Asie et le corps humain*, Saigon, S.I.L.I., 1948.

——, *Les chemins du raisonnement et de la logique en Extrême-Orient*, Saigon, I.D.E.O., 1949.

——, *Sciences et technique de l'Eurasie*, Saigon, Le Van Tan, 1950.

HUARD, MÉDECIN GÉNÉRAL PIERRE ALPHONSE, and DURAND, MAURICE, *Connaissance du Viet Nam*, Hanoï, École française d'Extrême-Orient, 1954.

ISOART, PAUL, *Le phénomène national vietnamien*, Paris, Librairie générale de droit et de jurisprudence, 1961.

JAUNEAUD, JEAN HENRI, *De Verdun à Dien Bien Phu*, Paris, Éditions du Scorpion, 1959.

JEANDEL, ABBÉ PAUL, *Soutane noire, béret rouge*, Présentation du Général Gilles, Paris, La Pensée Moderne, 1957.

JENSON, FRITZ, *Erlebtes Viet Nam*, Berlin, Dietz Verlag, 1955.

JOHN, COLIN, *Nothing to Lose*, London, Cassel, 1955.

JUBELIN, CONTRE-AMIRAL ANDRÉ, *Pilotes d'hélicoptères*, Paris, France-Empire, 1957.

KLIMASZEWSKI, TADEUS, *Ucieklem z Legii cudzoziemskiej*, Warsaw, Czytelnik, 1954.

KLUGE, THEODOR, *Die Völker und Sprachen des Indo-China-sischen Raumes*, Berlin, 1953.

LACOUTURE, JEAN, *Cinq hommes et la France*, Paris, Le Seuil, 1961.

LACOUTURE, JEAN, and DEVILLERS, PHILIPPE, *La fin d'une guerre, Indochine 1954*, Paris, Le Seuil, 1960.

LA GORCE, PAUL-MARIE DE, *La République et son armée*, Paris, Fayard, 1963.

LANGLAIS, COLONEL PIERRE, *Dien Bien Phu*, Paris, France-Empire, 1963.

LANIEL, JOSEPH, *Discours prononcé à l'Assemblée nationale le 6 janvier 1954*, Paris, Imprimerie Nationale, 1954.

——, *Le drame indochinois, de Dien Bien Phu au pari de Genève,* Paris, Plon, 1957.

LARTEGUY, JEAN, *Les Centurions,* Paris, Presses de la Cité, 1960.

——, *Le mal jaune,* Paris, Presses de la Cité, 1963.

LAURENT, ARTHUR, *La banque de l'Indochine et la piastre,* Paris, Les Deux Rives, 1954.

LE BRUN-KERIS, GEORGES, *Indochine, Tunisia, Maroc,* Limoges, Les Presses Rapides, 1954.

LEDERER, WILLIAM J., *A Nation of Sheep,* New York, Norton, 1961.

LE GUEN, LIEUTENANT JACQUES, *Jacques Le Guen, mort pour la France. Extraits de lettres,* Paris, Imprimerie P. Mersh, 1956.

LEROY, COLONEL JEAN, *Un homme dans la rizière,* Préface de Graham Greene, Avant-propos de Jean Lartéguy, Paris, Éditions de Paris, 1955.

LE SAGE, ROGER, *Go!* Préface du Général Massu, Paris, France-Empire, 1958.

——, *Tout vient du ciel,* Paris, La Pensée Moderne, 1958.

LE THANH KHOI, *Viet Nam. Histoire et civilisation,* Paris, Éditions de Minuit, 1955.

LYAUTEY, PIERRE, and BARRÈS, CLAUDE, *Un héros révolté: Claude Barrès,* Paris, Julliard, 1959.

MALOIRE, ALBERT, *Femmes dans la guerre,* Paris, Louvois, 1957.

MALOIRE, ALBERT; CAVET, CHRISTIANE; and ISAIA, J. F., *Flashes dans la bataille,* Paris, Louvois, 1957.

MANSFIELD, MIKE, *Indochina. Report of Senator M. Mansfield on a Study Mission to the Associated States of Indochina,* Eighty-third Congress, 1953.

MARCHAND,GÉNÉRAL JEAN, *Dans la jungle Moï,* Paris, Peyronnet, 1951.

——, *Le drame indochinois,* Paris, Peyronnet, 1954.

——, *L'Indochine en guerre,* Paris, Les Presses Modernes, 1954.

MASSON, A., *Histoire du Viet Nam,* Paris, Que sais-je? P.U.F. 1960.

MERCIER, ANDRÉ-FRANÇOIS, *Faut-il abandonner l'Indochine?,* Préface du Maréchal Juin, Paris, France-Empire, 1953.

MITTERAND, FRANÇOIS, *Aux frontières de l'Union française. Indochine, Tunisie,* Préface de Pierre Mendès-France, Paris, Julliard, 1954.

MONTEIL, VINCENT, *Les officiers,* Paris, Le Seuil, 1955.

MORDAL, JACQUES, *Marine Indochine,* Paris, Amiot-Dumont, 1953.

MUS, PAUL, *Viet Nam. Sociologie d'une guerre,* Paris, Le Seuil, 1952.

——, *Le Viet Nam chez lui,* Paris, Centre d'études de Politique étrangère, 1946.

——, *Le destin de l'Union française,* Paris, Le Seuil, 1954.

NARDELLA, BRUNO, and LEONELLI, CHARLES, *Douze ans de légion,* Paris, Le Scorpion, 1960.

NAVARRE, GÉNÉRAL HENRI, *Agonie de l'Indochine,* 1st ed., Paris, Plon, 1956; 2nd ed. (with passages suppressed and a reply to M. Laniel's book), Paris, Plon, 1958.

NEWMAN, BERNARD, *Report on Indochina,* London, Robert Hale, 1953.

NGO VAN CHIEU, *Journal d'un combattant du Viet Minh,* Paris, Le Seuil, 1955.

NGUYEN AÏ QUOC (HO CHI MINH), *Le procès de la colonisation française,* Paris, Librairie du Travail, 1921.

NGUYEN DAC KHÉ, *De la co-souveraineté à la souveraineté vietnamienne,* 1953.

NGUYEN HUU CHAU, *Les reflets de nos jours,* Paris, Julliard, 1954.

NGUYEN QUOC DINH, *La question du statut de l'État associé d'après la constitution de 1946,* Paris, Librairie générale de droit et de jurisprudence, 1952.

NGUYEN THAI BINH, *Viet Nam. The Problem and a Solution,* Paris, Parti démocrate du Viet Nam, 1962.

NGUYEN TIEN LANG, *Les chemins de la révolte,* Paris, Amiot-Dumont, 1953.

NGUYEN VAN HUYEN, *La civilisation annamite,* Paris, Direction de l'Instruction Publique de l'Indochine, 1944.

NGUYEN VAN TAM, *Viet Nam en marche,* Hanoï, 1955.

NIESSEL, GÉNÉRAL ALBERT, *Un symbole, l'insigne des forces armées en Indochine,* 1952.

PAGNIEZ, YVONNE, *Naissance d'une nation. Choses vues au Viet Nam,* Paris, La Palatine, 1954.

——, *Le Viet Minh et la guerre psychologique,* Paris, La Colombe, 1955.

——, *Français d'Indochine,* Paris, Flammarion, 1953.

——, *Ailes françaises au combat,* Paris, La Palatine, 1957.

PALU, MARIE-THÉRÈSE, *Convoyeuses de l'air,* Paris, Éditions du Siamois, 1957.

PERCHERON, MAURICE, *Contes et légendes d'Indochine,* Paris, François Nathan, 1955.

PHAM QUYNH, *Essais franco-annamites,* Hué, Bui Huy Tin, 1937.

——, *Nouveaux essais franco-annamites,* Hué, Bui Huy Tin, 1938.

PHAM VAN DONG and VO NGUYEN GIAP, *American Imperialism's Intervention in Viet Nam,* Hanoï, 1955.

PHAN QUANG DAN, *Volonté vietnamienne. Le parti républicain; ses buts, son programme,* Switzerland, Dornach, Éditions Thiêt Thuc, 1951.

PHAN THONG THAO, *La cause vietnamienne. Viet Nam struggle,* Parti nationaliste vietnamien, Parti Daï-Viet, n.d.

PIREY, PHILIPPE DE, *Opération gachis,* Paris, La Table Ronde, 1953.

REDIER, ANTOINE, *Debout les vivants! Nos morts d'Indochine et de Corée nous parlent,* Paris, Nouvelles Éditions Latines, 1954.

RENALD, JEAN, *L'enfer de Dien Bien Phu. Récit d'un correspondant de guerre,* Paris, Flammarion, 1955.

REVERS, GÉNÉRAL GEORGES MARIE-JOSEPH, *Documents publiés par le général Revers relatifs à son rôle dans l'affaire des généraux,* n.d., c. 1950.

RIDGWAY, GENERAL MATTHEW B., *No Place for Complacency,* New York, American Council of NATO, 1953.

RIESON, RENÉ, *Mission spéciale en forêt Moï,* Paris, France-Empire, 1955.

——, *Le silence du ciel,* Préface d'Odette Rousseau, Paris, La Pensée Moderne, 1956.

RIFFAUD, MADELEINE, *Les baguettes de jade,* Paris, Éditeurs Français Réunis, 1953.
ROLAND, PIERRE, *Contre-guérilla,* Paris, Louvois, 1956.
ROY, JULES, *La bataille dans la rizière,* Paris, Gallimard, 1953.
——, *Le fleuve rouge,* 1957.
——, *Les belles croisades,* 1959.

SABATIER, GÉNÉRAL, *Le destin de l'Indochine,* Paris, Plon, 1952.
SAINTENY, JEAN, *Histoire d'une paix manquée,* Paris, Amiot-Dumont, 1953.
SAINT-JULIEN, A. DE, *Loin,* Paris, Nouvelles Presses Mondiales, 1955.
SAINT-LAMAIN, JEAN, *L'école des zéros,* Paris, Éditions du Scorpion, 1962.
SASORITH, KATAY D., *Le Laos,* Paris, Berger-Levrault, 1953.
SCHOENBRUN, DAVID, *As France Goes,* New York, Harper, 1957.
SCHUTZE, GÜNTER, *Der schmutzige Krieg. Frankreichs Kolonialpolitik in Indochina,* Munich, Janus Bücher, 1959.
SHEN YU DAI, *Peking, Moscow and the Communist Parties of Colonial Asia,* Cambridge, Massachusetts Institute of Technology, 1954.
SIMON, PIERRE HENRI, *Portrait d'un officier,* Paris, Le Seuil, 1958.
STALINE, JOSEPH, *Le marxisme et la question nationale et coloniale,* Paris, Éditions sociales, 1950.
SWIGGETT, HOWARD, *March or Die,* New York, Putnam, 1953.

TANHAM, GEORGE K., *Communist Revolutionary Warfare: The Viet Minh in Indochina,* New York, Praeger, 1961.
TAURIAC, MICHEL, *Ni fleur ni couronne,* Paris, Les Anciens d'Indochine, 1951.
——, *Le Trou,* Paris, La Table Ronde, 1955.
TOURNOUX, JEAN-RAYMOND, *Secrets d'État,* Paris, Plon, 1960.
TRAN DO, *Récits sur Dien Bien Phu,* Hanoï, foreign language edition, 1962.
TRINQUIER, ROGER, *La guerre moderne,* Paris, La Table Ronde, 1961.
TROPET, PIERRE, *Guet-Apens,* Paris, René Lacoste, 1956.
TRUONG CHINH, *The Democratic Republic of Viet Nam Is Seven Years Old,* Viet Nam Central Information Party, 1952.
——, *Rapport à la première conférence nationale du Viet Minh de 1953,* Hanoï, foreign language edition, 1955.

VEYRENC, LYLIANE, *Opératrice de cinéma en Indochine,* Paris, Debresse, 1955.
VUCCINE, H. J., *Dien Bien Phu,* Luchon, 1956.

WILBER, EDWIN L., *Silver Wings,* New York, Appleton, 1948.

II. PRINCIPAL ARTICLES

1952

Indochine—Sud-Est Asiatique
    July, No. 8:   "La panoplie Viet Minh"
    October, No. 11:   "Capitaines et Maréchaux" by Jules Roy
                                    "La Presse Viet Minh"

December, No. 13:   "Psychologie du combattant Viet Minh"
Paris-Match
  July 5, No. 173:   Article by Graham Greene
  July 12, No. 174:   Article by Graham Greene

1953

Caravelle
  June 28:   "Lettre du général Navarre à tous"
  September 20:   "Lettre du général Navarre à tous"
L'Express
  May 23, No. 2:   "Les pages censurées du rapport sur l'Indo-
                          chine"

  July 11, No. 9:   "Albert Sarraut lance un appel à Ho Chi
                          Minh"

  October 24, No. 23: ⎫
  October 31, No. 24: ⎬   "La vérité sur l'adversaire en Indochine"
  November 7, No. 25: ⎭

  December 19, No. 31:   "La paix trahie en Indochine"
Expressen
  November 28:   Interview with Ho Chi Minh by Svante
                          Löfgren

Forces Aériennes Françaises
  December: Supplement to No. 87, "Indochine 1953"
Indochine—Sud-Est Asiatique
  January, No. 14:   "Les étrangers chez le Viet Minh"
                          "Un ancien capitaine autrichien est devenu
                            le fils adoptif de Ho Chi Minh"
  June, No. 19:   "L'économie Viet Minh"
Le Monde
  March 11-15:   "Le Viet Nam à l'épreuve" by Jean La-
                          couture

  April 30:   "Pour quoi nous combattons" by J.-J. Servan-
                          Schreiber

  May 21:   "Il faut savoir sortir d'une guerre" by Max
                          Arnaud

  July 29:   References to an article in *Life* criticizing
                          French action in Indo-China

  August 7:   General Navarre's press conference at Hanoï
  September 30:   "Faut-il prendre cet argent?" by J.-J. Servan-
                          Schreiber

  October 2:   "De durs combats en perspective dans le
                          delta tonkinois" by Max Arnaud
  October 27:   "Une question sur l'Indochine" by J.-J. Ser-
                          van-Schreiber

| December 1: | Commentaries on Ho Chi Minh's interview |
| December 15: | "La croisade et le policier" by J.-J. Servan-Schreiber |

Life Magazine
| December: | "Bold French Get the Jam" (photographs by Howard Sochurek) |

France-Observateur
| July 30: | "En un combat douteux" by Roger Stéphane |
Paris-Match
| May 2, No. 216: | Article by Jules Roy |
Politique Étrangère
| July-August: | "Contre feu vietnamien" by Jean Lacouture |
Revue du Génie Militaire
| May: | "La bataille de Na San" by Commandant A. Casso |

Temps Modernes
| August-September: | Special number on Vietnam |

1954

Allgemeine Schweizerische Militarische Zeitschrift
| September: | "La guerre d'Indochine. La 8ᵉ campagne annuelle et la bataille de Dien Bien Phu" by J. Pergent |

L'Aurore
| June 12-16: | "Mon mari le général" by the Comtesse Jacqueline de Castries |

Aussenpolitik
| July: | "Die Kriegsleben von Dien Bien Phu" by F. von Senger |

Berichte und Information
| June 14: | "Gefallen in Dien Bien Phu" |
Bohemia
May 16:	"Factores geograficos del desastre de Dien Bien Phu" by Salvador Massip
May 23:	"Tumbas españoles en Dien Bien Phu" by Francisco Pares
July 4:	"La caida de Dien Bien Phu vista por Geneviève de Galard" by Bernard Ullmann

Caravelle
| March 29: | "Retour de Dien Bien Phu" by X.M.N. |
| June 7: | "Lettre du général Navarre à tous" |
Combattant d'Indochine
| March 21: | Article by E. J. Masenello |
Economist
| March 21: | "After Dien Bien Phu" |

Esprit
  May: "La République, son armée, sa politique"; "Indochine, premier front" by J. M. Domenach and Philippe Devillers

  July: "Force et faiblesse de Pierre Mendès France"; "Dien Bien Phu en images" by J. M. Domenach and G. V.

  November: "Journal d'une fin de guerre" by François Sarrazin
                                  "Sud Viet Nam et responsabilité français" by Léon Vandermeersch

L'Express
  January 27:   M. Jacquet's ideas on Indochina
  March 6:   "Ma mission auprès du Viet Minh" by Buu Hoi
  May 2:   "Je n'ai pas envie de m'attendrir" by Jules Roy

Le Figaro
  April 23:   "Journée d'épreuves" by Max Olivier
  May 6:   Report by General Gilles
Forces Aériennes Françaises
  July, No. 94:   "L'Armée de l'Air en Indochine"
  December, No. 99:   "L'Armée de l'Air"
France-Soir

                                    Reports by Lucien Bodard

Frig . . . Écho
  October-November: "Frigéco rend hommage au héros de Dien Bien Phu," with a photograph of Madame de Castries lovingly bent over a refrigerator, under the general's pennant.

Gegenwart
  May 22:   "Die Schlacht der 56 Tages—Dien Bien Phu" by R.H.

Hinh Auh Viet Nam
  December: Account of the Battle of Dienbienphu
Hommes et Mondes
  April, No. 93:   "Comment conclure la guerre d'Indochine" by Jacques Chastenet

L'Humanité-Dimanche
  April 11:   "Le cours du sang versé en Indochine monte à la bourse de New York"

Indochine—Sud-Est Asiatique
  April, No. 28:   "Vingt-quatre heures de Dien Bien Phu" by Henri Amouroux
  June, No. 30:   "La voix de Dien Bien Phu" by Robert Aeschelmann

July, No. 31:   Report on the press camp at Hanoï
August-September, No. 32:   "Mort d'une guerre" by Bruno Rajan

L'Information
May 4:   "L'ex-général nazi Falken-Hauser: les Fran-
                                       çais rééditent à Dien Bien Phu les erreurs
                                       d'Hitler à Stalingrad"

Manchester Guardian
June 6:   "Britain's Rejection of U.S. Intervention
                                       Plan"

Le Monde
February 14-16:   "Week-end à Dien Bien Phu" by Robert
                                       Guillain
March 18:   "Quatre coups de main du Viet Minh" by
                                       Robert Guillain
March 19:   "L'aide chinoise au Viet Minh" by Robert
                                       Guillain
April 4-6:   "Péril sur le Tonkin" by Robert Guillain
April 14:   "Dans l'attente d'un troisième assaut" by
                                       Max Clos
April 22:   "Pratiquement privée de secours aérien, la
                                       défense de Dien Bien Phu se resserre sur
                                       quelques kilomètres carrés" by Charles
                                       Favrel
April 28:   "N'y a-t-il plus personne?" by J.-J. Servan-
                                       Schreiber
April 29:   "Sauver l'armée française" by Robert Guil-
                                       lain
May 2 and 3:   "Dien Bien Phu. Qui? Pourquoi? Com-
                                       ment?" by Robert Guillain
May 4:   "Les erreurs et les malheurs de Dien Bien
                                       Phu" by Robert Guillain
May 6:   "Les pluies de la mousson transforment
                                       Dien Bien Phu en un lac de boue" by
                                       Max Clos
May 8:   "Dien Bien Phu a bouleversé l'équilibre des
                                       forces en notre faveur, assure le chef
                                       d'état-major de l'armée vietnamienne"
May 12:   A Communist communiqué on the fall of
                                       Dienbienphu
May 30-31:   "Échec de l'armée vietnamienne" by Robert
                                       Guillain
June 5:   "Hanoï en juin" by Max Clos
June 11:   "L'Indochine au secret" by Robert Guillain
July 1:   "Comment les Américains n'interviennent
                                       pas en Indochine"
                                       "Chronologie d'une crise"

August 3-4:   "La stratégie révolutionnaire du Viet Minh"
September 18:   Interview with General de Castries
La Nef
  Cahier No. 7:   "Asie du Sud-Est: Indépendance et dés-
                                    illusion" by Tibor Mende

New York *Herald Tribune*
  April 29:   Article by David Lawrence
  April 30:   Article by Walter Lippmann
New York Times
  February 28:   "Life and Death on Hill 135" by Tillman
                                    Durdin
  March 25:   "War Hero Hailed by Eisenhower" (Gen-
                                    eral de Castries)

La Nouvelle Critique
  March: "Le vrai visage de la résistance vietnam-
                                    ienne" by Nguyen van Ba

L'Observateur d'Aujourd'hui
  December 24-31   "Ma *mission* auprès du Viet Minh" by Paul
                                    Mus

Paris-Match
  Reports
  March 20, No. 260
  March 27, No. 261
  April 10, No. 263:   "Sur le rail du delta on se bat aussi pour
                                    Dien Bien Phu"
  April 17, No. 264:   Article by Charles Favrel
  April 24, No. 265
  May 8, No. 267:   "Les aviateurs à Navarre: Vous demandiez
                                    l'impossible"

  May 15, No. 268
  May 22, No. 269
  June 5, No. 271:   Press conference by Geneviève de Galard
  June 12, No. 272
  September 18, No. 286
Paris-Presse—L'Intransigeant
  March 19:   "The last page"
Perspectives
  June 12:   "Les erreurs militaires de la campagne
                                    d'Indochine"

Politique Étrangère
  July-September: "L'Amérique et l'Indochine du débarque-
                                    ment japonais de 1940 à Dien Bien Phu"

La Presse
  September 14:   "L'amour à Dien Bien Phu"
Le Revue de Défense Nationale
  April: "Images de guerre—Dien Bien Phu" by Ad-
                                    ministrative Officer Silvestri

June:	"Paris, Washington et Londres devant le drame indochinois" by J. Vernant
July:	"Réflexions sur Dien Bien Phu" by Camille Rougeron

La Revue des Deux Mondes
July 1:	"Lettre du Tonkin et de la Cochinchine" by Maurice Bedel
November 1:	"Scènes de guerre au Tonkin" by Bernard Beuchot
December 1:	"Ailes françaises en Indochine" by Yvonne Pagniez

Revue Maritime
June:	"Les porte-avions en Indochine"

Revue de Paris
August:	"La leçon de Dien Bien Phu" by Louis Koeltz

Semaine du Monde
September 10:	Report

Temps Modernes
May:	"Le rendez-vous de Dien Bien Phu" by T.M.
June:	"Comportement politique des institutions catholiques au Viet Nam" by Jean R. Clementin
July:	"De huit ans d'occasions manquées à la conférence de Genève" by Jean Rous

U.S. Naval Institute Proceedings
July:	"The Meaning of Dien Bien Phu" by Maurice Dejean

U.S. News & World Report
May 7:	"What Comes after Dien Bien Phu?"

Wiking Ruf
June:	"Deutsche Jugend in Dien Bien Phu" by Hermann Schild

1955

Army Combat Forces Journal
June:	"The Bloody Lessons of Indochina" by Major Lamar McFadden Prosser

Forces Aériennes Françaises
January, No. 100:	"Les hélicoptères en Indochine"
March, No. 102:	"Opérations en Indochine" by General Lauzin
October, No. 108:	"A.L.O.A. en Indochine" by Lieutenant Colonel Luthereau
December, No. 110:	"Formation des pilotes vietnamiens"

France-Soir
December 25-30:   "Les deux Viet Nam ont un an" by Lucien Bodard

Historia
June: "L'évasion d'un officier" (Makowiak) by L. Bornert

Jours de France
June 20:   "Le Général Navarre Parle"
The Reporter
January 27:   "The Enigma of Ho Chi Minh" by Robert Shaplen

Revue d'Action Populaire
September-October: "Deux ans de captivité chez le Viet Minh" by Paul Jeandel

Revue de Défense Nationale
December: "Quelques aspects stratégiques de la guerre d'Indochine" by Admiral Castex

Revue des Deux Mondes
February 1:   "Coup d'œil sur l'Extrême-Orient" by Paul Mousset
August 15:   "Le Général de Lattre au Tonkin" by B. Usureau

Revue de Paris
January: "Le destin du Viet Nam" by George Manue
Temps Modernes
January-February: "Pierre Mendès France ou les ambiguïtés" by Marcel Peju

Tropiques
February: "Dien Bien Phu—La dernière nuit" by Colonel Langlais

1956

France-Dimanche
May 10:   "C'était le P.C. de Castries"
Military Review
October: "Indochina, the Last Year of the War: Communist Organization and Tactics" by Bernard Fall
December: "The Navarre Plan" by Bernard Fall
Paris-Match
May 12:   "La leçon de Dien Bien Phu" by Jean Farran
Politique Étrangère
April: "Corée et Indochine" by Bernard Fall
July: Study of the Indochinese Union

Revue de Défense Nationale
March: "Les données de la Défense de l'Indochine"
                                by General Navarre (reply to an article
                                by Admiral Castex)

Revue des Deux Mondes
January: 1-15:   "Tableau de l'Union française—Indochine"
                                by Georges Manue

Revue Historique de l'Armée
No. 3:   "Le matériel dans la bataille de Dien Bien
                                Phu" by Léonard

Revue Maritime
December: "Souvenirs de Nam Dinh" by Louis Julien-
                                Binard

Revue de Paris
February: "Saigon et le nouveau Viet Nam" by Pierre
                                Monchenin

                            1957

Esprit
June: "Les deux Viet Nam" by Tibor Mende
Forces Aériennes Françaises
April, No. 125:   "Le renseignement aérien en Indochine" by
                                Commandant Jarry

Perspectives
March 9:   "A propos *d'Agonie de l'Indochine*"
Revue des Deux Mondes
June 15:   "A travers l'Asie rouge—Le Vietnam du
                                Nord" by Claude Dulong

Revue Militaire d'Information
March-April: "La   guerre   révolutionnaire"   (special
                                number)

                            1959

Journal of the Royal United Services Institutions
February: "The French Army and la guerre révolution-
                                naire" by Peter Paret

                            1960

South East Asia Treaty Organization
                                "Communist Subversion in the S.E.A.T.O.
                                Area" by Bernard Fall

                            1962

Aux Carrefours de l'Histoire
November: "Pourquoi Dien Bien Phu?" by Bernard Fall

Béret Rouge
   April-May, No. 39:   Special number on Dien Bien Phu
Képi Blanc
   August-December: "Opération Castor . . . Verdun 1954" by
                            Sergeant Kubiak

Marine Corps Gazette
   January: "Guerrilla Warfare" (special number)

                            1963

Le Figaro Littéraire
   May 4:   "Voici la vérité sur Dien Bien Phu" by
                            Colonel Pierre Langlais

Képi Blanc
   January-May: "Opération Castor . . . Verdun 1954" by
                            Sergeant Kubiak

Sunday Times
   March 3:   Article by Graham Greene

Index

ABOUT THE AUTHOR

Jules Roy, born in Algeria in 1907, was an officer in the French army, then the air force, from 1927 to 1953. As bomber commander in the R.A.F. he received the Distinguished Flying Cross for thirty-seven missions over Germany. In 1953 he resigned from the army in Indochina "in order not to participate in a war which he considered unjust and idiotic."

He has written three plays, several essays on flying, among them an appreciation of Antoine de St. Exupery, and has been a reporter for the Paris weekly, *l'Express*. Two of his novels, *The Navigator* (1955) and *The Unfaithful Wife* (1956), have been published in the United States. His book, *The War in Algeria* (1960), was described by *The New Yorker* as "the most moving condemnation to date of the war and the most authoritative explanation of its cause," and by the *New York Times* as "lucid, precise and courageous. Roy's great merits are objectivity, impartiality and a righteous anger."

In order to write *The Battle of Dienbienphu,* Roy spent many months in North and South Vietnam and spoke with all the principal actors. The book was a huge best-seller in France, with more than 200,000 copies in print. The author spent the fall of 1964 traveling throughout China and is currently at work on a book about the Chinese Communist Revolution.